Jefferson Himself

The Personal Narrative of a
Many-Sided American

A Drawing by Benjamin Henry Latrobe

Jefferson Himself

The Personal Narrative
of a Many-Sided American

Edited by BERNARD MAYO

The University Press of Virginia
Charlottesville

*First printing for the
University Press of Virginia 1970*

Tenth printing 1998

STANDARD BOOK NUMBER: 0-8139-0310-6
LIBRARY OF CONGRESS CATALOG CARD NUMBER: 70-87871

Printed in the United States of America

TO
Hamilton Basso

PREFACE

IN THIS STORY of Thomas Jefferson, told in his own words, I have tried to present an intimate and rounded portrait of a great and many-sided American. The materials for it have been his voluminous writings, especially his thousands of letters written (as he said) 'in the warmth and freshness of fact and feeling' and forming 'the only full and genuine journal' of his life. These have been woven into a narrative account of the man, of his private and public life, his varied interests and achievements. But it is more than a personal history of our greatest democrat. Filled with his 'reflections on the things which have been passing,' it is an eyewitness account of the birth and first half-century of the American nation, written by Jefferson himself.

Wherever the reader dips into this book he will find that Jefferson, whether speaking of politics, religion, economics, science, or education, is concerned with one great objective: the freedom and happiness of man. The author of the Declaration of Independence not only gave immortal literary form to the rights of man, but throughout his long career he waged war on many fronts to give them reality. His was a militant democracy, and he was well aware that future generations must continue the unending struggle to translate democratic faith into democratic practice. To our own generation he speaks with especial force and eloquence. To Americans and all peoples who fight that tyranny against which he swore eternal hostility, Thomas Jefferson is an ever-living and ever-inspiring champion of man's inalienable rights.

BERNARD MAYO

CHARLOTTESVILLE, VIRGINIA
October 5, 1942

CONTENTS

stitution interpreted; farmers vs. stockjobbers — A wave of financial speculation — Bursting of the paper bubble — Fattening on the follies of the Old World — Spain must give us free use of the Mississippi — Will France aid us in obtaining Spanish New Orleans? — Justice from Britain if we remain neutral — Northwestern Indians, and the British — Southwestern Indians, and the Spaniards — Conquest and commerce — Washington should serve a second term — I tremble at the threat of disunion

ILLUSTRATIONS

CHAPTER I

Education of a Virginian

LIKE many another American, Thomas Jefferson was fond of
saying that a family coat of arms may be purchased as cheaply
as any other coat, and there is a touch of New World insouciance
in his remark that his mother's Randolph family traced its pedigree
far back in England and Scotland, 'to which let everyone ascribe
the faith and merit he chooses.' Kinship with the distinguished
Randolphs of Virginia insured to him a high social position. But
in the account of his ancestry which opens this chapter he preferred to write about his self-educated and enterprising father,
Peter Jefferson.

His father was an early settler in the foothills of the Blue Ridge
Mountains. Out of wilderness lands he had created several tobacco
plantations, the most important of which was Shadwell, where
Thomas was born on April 13 (April 2, old style), 1743. He had
served his pioneer community as a surveyor, magistrate, sheriff,
colonel of militia, and member of the colonial House of Burgesses
from the county of Albemarle. When he died, his son Thomas was
fourteen, old enough to have received the impress of the sturdy
qualities which had made his father a leader in the Virginia
upcountry.

Young Jefferson was a keen-minded and attractive boy of
seventeen, tall, freckled, with blue-gray eyes and reddish hair,
when he entered the College of William and Mary at Williamsburg,
the colonial capital. There he came under the influence of three
remarkable men, each of whom in his fashion contributed greatly
to the boy's education. By good fortune, as he modestly says, he

became intimately acquainted with Professor William Small, who
gave him a lifelong interest in mathematics and science; with
George Wythe, the scholarly lawyer and teacher of the liberal
ideas which inspired the Revolutionary generation of Virginians;
and with Francis Fauquier, the able and popular governor of the
colony, a fellow of the Royal Society in London who wrote on
economic and scientific subjects, a musician, wit, and polished
man of the world.

In the little metropolis of Williamsburg young Jefferson played
his fiddle at Fauquier's concerts in the Governor's Palace. At the
Capitol he heard eloquent and rebellious speeches by Patrick
Henry, of whom he gives a sharp and vivid picture. Like other
fashionable young men he danced and flirted, frequented the Coffee
House and taverns, the playhouse and traveling exhibitions, and
spent vacation days at Tidewater plantations, horse-racing, fox-
hunting, and enjoying 'the revelries of the neighborhood and
season.'

His reminiscences are pointed up by letters written at the time
to his fellow students. Especially revealing are those to John Page,
of Rosewell plantation on York River. In them he describes his
misadventures on Christmas Day of 1762, the rats that ate his
jemmy-worked silk garters and new minuets, and the leaky roof
that spoiled his watch-paper picture of Rebecca Burwell; his
repugnance at times for musty books and his longing to make the
grand tour of Europe; his lover's sighs and apprehensions, his proposing to Rebecca at a dance in the Apollo Room of the Raleigh
Tavern at Williamsburg, and his disappointment in love. Instead
of the grand tour he made a tour as far north as New York, and he
consoled himself by thinking of the comforts of a bachelor who was
'an inhabitant, and a young inhabitant too, of Williamsburg.'

After two years at William and Mary he spent five years as a
student in the law office of George Wythe, his beloved mentor
and foster father. Wythe profoundly influenced his development.
He was a great teacher, and he well deserved the grateful tribute
Jefferson pays to his character, his learning, and his devotion to
'liberty and the equal and natural rights of man.'

Under Wythe's guidance he read widely and deeply, following
the general program of studies which he outlined at the time to his

friend Bernard Moore. He steeped himself in the Greek and Latin classics, and filled his commonplace notebook with quotations from the political philosophers and legal historians, the great poets and prose writers. He read French and Italian, studied German, wrote an informed and revolutionizing essay on the Anglo-Saxon language, and with zest applied himself to the natural sciences, which were so useful in everyday life and 'so peculiarly engaging and delightful.' The young Virginian developed an amazing capacity for hard and sustained labor, sensibly balanced by exercise and recreation. His mind became disciplined, skeptical and critical, concerned with the practical application of scientific principles and social theories.

In 1767 at the age of twenty-four he was admitted to the bar, and in the years preceding the Revolution he built up a very successful practice which averaged about three thousand dollars a year. He rode the circuit of county courts, and deepened his understanding of human nature by handling the usual run-of-mine cases. From the beginning he appeared in important and profitable cases before the General Court in Williamsburg, the highest court in the colony. In 1767 he had a total of 154 cases, 68 of them in the General Court. Two years later he had as many as 405, 198 of them in the high court at Williamsburg. He was a hard-working young lawyer. Yet the items in his account books for these three years show that he found time to play on his new violin and to attend shooting matches, concerts, puppet shows, and the theatre at Williamsburg, where the Virginia Company of Comedians in the spring of 1768 delighted him with a repertory ranging from *The Beggar's Opera* to *The Constant Couple or a Trip to Jubilee.*

Meanwhile he increased his landholdings to five thousand acres, double the amount he had inherited from his father, and from his farms he drew an income of about two thousand dollars a year. At Shadwell he managed the affairs of his home plantation, collected a library, and began the building of a new house just across the Rivanna River from his birthplace. It was on the summit of a mountain which he called Monticello, the Italian for 'little mountain.' The fire which destroyed Shadwell in 1770 caused him to hasten work on the new dwelling. Moreover, he was looking forward to the day when he would bring his bride to Monticello, to the beautiful blue hills of Albemarle where his home lands had been staked out thirty years before by Peter Jefferson.

My father, Peter Jefferson

The tradition in my father's family was that their ancestor came to this country from Wales, and from near the mountain of Snowden, ... but the first particular information I have of any ancestor was of my grandfather, who lived at the place in Chesterfield called Ozborne's, and owned the lands afterwards the glebe of the parish. He had three sons: Thomas, who died young; Field, who settled on the waters of Roanoke and left numerous descendants; and Peter, my father, who settled on the lands I still own, called Shadwell, adjoining my present residence.

He was born February 29, 1707–8, and intermarried 1739 with Jane Randolph, of the age of nineteen, daughter of Isham Randolph, one of the seven sons of that name and family settled at Dungeoness in Goochland. They trace their pedigree far back in England and Scotland, to which let everyone ascribe the faith and merit he chooses.

My father's education had been quite neglected, but being of a strong mind, sound judgment, and eager after information, he read much and improved himself, insomuch that he was chosen with Joshua Fry, professor of mathematics in William and Mary College, to continue the boundary line between Virginia and North Carolina which had been begun by Colonel Byrd; and was afterwards employed with the same Mr. Fry to make the first map of Virginia which had ever been made, that of Captain Smith being merely a conjectural sketch. They possessed excellent materials for so much of the country as is below the Blue Ridge, little being then known beyond that ridge. He was the third or fourth settler, about the year 1737, of the part of the country in which I live. He died August 17th, 1757, leaving my mother a widow, who lived till 1776, with six daughters and two sons, myself the elder. To my younger brother he left his estate on James River, called Snowden after the supposed birthplace of the family; to myself the lands on which I was born and live.

He placed me at the English school at five years of age and at the Latin at nine, where I continued until his death. My teacher, Mr. Douglas, a clergyman from Scotland, with the rudiments of the Latin and Greek languages taught me the French; and on the death of my father I went to the Reverend Mr. Maury, a correct classical scholar, with whom I continued two years; and then, to wit, in the spring of 1760, went to William and Mary College, where I continued two years.

The learned Dr. Small; the gay and polished Fauquier

It was my great good fortune, and what probably fixed the destinies of my life, that Dr. William Small of Scotland was then professor of mathematics, a man profound in most of the useful branches of science, with a happy talent of communication, correct and gentlemanly manners, and an enlarged and liberal mind. He, most happily for me, became soon attached to me and made me his daily companion when not engaged in the school, and from his conversation I got my first views of the expansion of science and of the system of things in which we are placed. Fortunately the philosophical chair became vacant soon after my arrival at college and he was appointed to fill it *per interim*, and he was the first who ever gave in that college regular lectures in ethics, rhetoric, and belles lettres.

He returned to Europe in 1762, having previously filled up the measure of his goodness to me by procuring for me from his most intimate friend, George Wythe, a reception as a student of law under his direction, and introduced me to the acquaintance and familiar table of Governor Fauquier, the ablest man who had ever filled that office. With him and at his table Dr. Small and Mr. Wythe, his *amici omnium horarum*, and myself formed a *partie quarrée*, and to the habitual conversations on these occasions I owed much instruction.[1]

Attic wit and chamber music

At these dinners I have heard more good sense, more rational and philosophical conversations, than in all my life besides. They were truly Attic societies. The Governor was musical also, and a good performer, and associated me with two or three other amateurs in his weekly concerts.[2]

Mr. Wythe continued to be my faithful and beloved mentor in youth and my most affectionate friend through life. In 1767 he led me into the practice of the law at the bar of the General Court, at which I continued until the Revolution shut up the courts of justice.[3] A close intimacy with him during . . . forty-odd years, the most important of his life, enables me to state its leading facts. . . . Little as I am able to contribute to the just reputation of this excellent man, it is the act of my life most gratifying to my heart. . . .

My beloved mentor and foster father

George Wythe . . . inherited from his father a fortune sufficient for independence and ease. He had not the benefit of a regular education in the schools but acquired a good one of himself, and without assistance, insomuch as to become the best Latin and Greek scholar in the state. . . . He also acquired by his own reading a good knowledge of mathematics and of natural and moral philosophy. He engaged in the study of the law . . . and . . . became . . . the first at the bar, taking into consideration his superior learning, correct elocution, and logical style of reasoning, for in pleading he never indulged himself with a useless or declamatory thought or word. . . .

He was early elected to the House of Representatives, then called the House of Burgesses. . . . In August, 1775, he was appointed a member of Congress and in 1776 signed the Declaration of Independence, of which he had in debate been an eminent supporter. . . . In 1777 he was chosen Speaker of the House of Delegates, being of distinguished learning in parliamentary law and proceedings, and towards the end of the same year he was appointed one of the three Chancellors. . . . On a subsequent change of the form of that court he was appointed sole Chancellor, in which office he continued to act until his death, which happened in June, 1806. . . .

A teacher devoted to the rights of man

No man ever left behind him a character more venerated than George Wythe. His virtue was of the purest tint, his integrity inflexible, and his justice exact; of warm patriotism and, devoted as he was to liberty and the natural and equal rights of man, he might truly be called the Cato of his country, without the avarice of the Roman, for a more disinterested person never lived.

Temperance and regularity in all his habits gave him general good health, and his unaffected modesty and suavity of manners endeared him to everyone. He was of easy elocution, his language chaste, methodical in the arrangement of his matter, learned and logical in the use of it, and of great urbanity in debate; not quick of apprehension but, with a little time, profound in penetration and sound in conclusion. In his philosophy he was firm, and neither troubling, nor perhaps trusting, anyone with his religious creed, he left the world to the conclusion that that religion must be good which could produce a life of such exemplary virtue. . . . Such was George Wythe, the honor of his own and the model of future times.[4]

Youthful temptations

When I recollect that at fourteen years of age the whole care and direction of myself was thrown on myself entirely, without a relation or friend qualified to advise or guide me, and recollect the various sorts of bad company with which I associated from time to time, I am astonished I did not turn off with some of them and become as worthless to society as they were. I had the good fortune to become acquainted very early with some characters of very high standing, and to feel the incessant wish that I could ever become what they were. Under temptations and difficulties I would ask myself what would Dr. Small, Mr. Wythe, Peyton Randolph do in this situation? What course in it will insure me their approbation? I am certain that this mode of deciding on my conduct tended more to correctness than any reasoning powers I possessed. . . .

From the circumstances of my position I was often thrown into the society of horse racers, card players, fox hunters, scientific and professional men, and of dignified men; and many a time have I asked myself in the enthusiastic moment of the death of a fox, the victory of a favorite horse, the issue of a question eloquently argued at the bar or in the great council of the nation, well, which of these kinds of reputations should I prefer? That of a horse jockey? a fox hunter? an orator? or the honest advocate of my country's rights?[5]

Patrick Henry

In 1759–60 . . . I first became acquainted with him. We met at
Nathan Dandridge's, in Hanover, about the Christmas of that
winter, and passed perhaps a fortnight together at the revelries of
the neighborhood and season. His manners had something of the
coarseness of the society he had frequented; his passion was fid-
dling, dancing, and pleasantry. He excelled in the last and it attached everyone to him. The occasion perhaps as much as his idle
disposition prevented his engaging in any conversation which
might give the measure either of his mind or information. Opportunity was not wanting, because Mr. John Campbell was there, who
had married Mrs. Spotswood, the sister of Colonel Dandridge. He
was a man of science and often introduced conversations on scientific subjects. Mr. Henry had a little before broken up his store, or
rather it had broken him up, and within three months after, he
came to Williamsburg for his license and told me, I think, he had
read law not more than six weeks.[6]

Mr. Henry began his career with very little property. He acted,
as I have understood, as barkeeper in the tavern at Hanover Court
House for some time. He married very young, . . . got credit for
some little store of merchandise, but very soon failed. From this he
turned his views to the law, for the acquisition of practice of which,
however, he was too lazy. Whenever the courts were closed for the
winter session, he would make up a party of poor hunters of his
neighborhood, would go off with them to the piney woods of Flu-
vanna and pass weeks in hunting deer, of which he was passionately
fond, sleeping under a tent, before a fire, wearing the same shirt the
whole time, and covering all the dirt of his dress with a hunting-
shirt.

A jury lawyer, but he spoke as Homer wrote

He never undertook to draw pleadings if he could avoid it or to
manage that part of a cause and very unwillingly engaged, but as
an assistant, to speak in the cause. And the fee was an indispensable
preliminary, observing to the applicant that he kept no accounts,
never putting pen to paper, which was true. His powers over a
jury were so irresistible that he received great fees for his services. . . .

After about ten years' practice in the country courts he came to the General Court, where, however, being totally unqualified for anything but mere jury causes, he devoted himself to these, and chiefly to the criminal business.[7]

When the famous Resolutions of 1765 against the Stamp Act were proposed I was yet a student of law in Williamsburg. I attended the debate, however, at the door of the lobby of the House of Burgesses, and heard the splendid display [in the 'Treason Speech'] of Mr. Henry's talents as a popular orator. They were great indeed; such as I have never heard from any other man. He appeared to me to speak as Homer wrote.[8]

At nineteen, plagued by the Devil

This very day [Christmas, 1762, at Fairfield plantation], to others the day of greatest mirth and jollity, sees me overwhelmed with more and greater misfortunes than have befallen a descendant of Adam for these thousand years past, I am sure; and perhaps, after excepting Job, since the creation of the world. . . . You must know, dear Page [John Page of Rosewell, a college friend], that I am now in a house surrounded with enemies who take counsel together against my soul; and when I lay me down to rest they say among themselves, come let us destroy him. I am sure if there is such a thing as a Devil in this world, he must have been here last night and have had some hand in contriving what happened to me.

Do you think the cursed rats (at his instigation, I suppose) did not eat up my pocket-book, which was in my pocket within a foot of my head? And not contented with plenty for the present, they carried away my jemmy-worked silk garters and half a dozen new minuets I had just got, to serve, I suppose, as provision for the winter. But of this I should not have accused the Devil (because you know rats will be rats, and hunger, without the addition of his instigations, might have urged them to do this), if something worse, and from a different quarter, had not happened.

The Devil and Rebecca Burwell's picture

You know it rained last night, or if you do not know it, I am sure I do. When I went to bed I laid my watch in the usual place, and going to take her up after I arose this morning, I found her in the same place, it's true, but *Quantum mutatus ab illo!* all afloat in water, let in at a leak in the roof of the house, and as silent and still as the rats that had eat my pocket-book. Now you know if chance had had anything to do in this matter, there were a thousand other spots where it might have chanced to leak as well as this one, which was perpendicularly over my watch. But I'll tell you, it's my opinion that the Devil came and bored a hole over it on purpose.

Well, as I was saying, my poor watch had lost her speech. I should not have cared much for this, but something worse attended it; the subtle particles of the water with which the case was filled had, by their penetration, so overcome the cohesion of the particles of the paper of which my dear picture and watch-paper were composed that, in attempting to take them out to dry them, good God! *Mens horret referre!* My cursed fingers gave them such a rent as I fear I never shall get over. This, cried I, was the last stroke Satan had in reserve for me; he knew I cared not for anything else he could do to me, and was determined to try his last most fatal expedient. . . .

However, whatever misfortunes may attend the picture or lover, my hearty prayers shall be that all the health and happiness which Heaven can send may be the portion of the original, and that so much goodness may ever meet with what may be most agreeable in this world, as I am sure it must be in the next. And now, although the picture be defaced, there is so lively an image of her imprinted in my mind that I shall think of her too often, I fear, for my peace of mind; and too often, I am sure, to get through old Coke this winter; for God knows I have not seen him since I packed him up in my trunk in Williamsburg.

That dull old scoundrel, Lord Coke

Well, Page, I do wish the Devil had old Coke, for I am sure I never was so tired of an old dull scoundrel in my life. What! are there so few inquietudes tacked to this momentary life of ours that we must need be loading ourselves with a thousand more? Or, as brother Job says (who, by-the-bye, I think began to whine a little under his afflictions), 'Are not my days few? Cease then, that I may take comfort a little before I go whence I shall not return, even to the land of darkness, and the shadow of death.'

But the old fellows say we must read to gain knowledge, and gain knowledge to make us happy and admired. *Mere jargon!* Is there any such thing as happiness in this world? No. And as for admiration, I am sure the man who powders most, perfumes most, embroiders most, and talks most nonsense, is most admired. Though, to be candid, there are some who have too much good sense to esteem such monkey-like animals as these, in whose formation, as the saying is, the tailors and barbers go halves with God Almighty; and since these are the only persons whose esteem is worth a wish, I do not know but that, upon the whole, the advice of these old fellows may be worth following. . . .

The young ladies; especially Rebecca

If there is any news stirring in town or country, such as deaths, courtships, or marriages, in the circle of my acquaintance, let me know it. Remember me affectionately to all the young ladies of my acquaintance, particularly the Miss Burwells, and Miss Potters, and tell them that though that heavy earthly part of me, my body, is absent, the better half of me, my soul, is ever with them, and that my best wishes shall ever attend them. Tell Miss Alice Corbin that I verily believe the rats knew I was to win a pair of garters from her, or they never would have been so cruel as to carry mine away. This very consideration makes me so sure of the bet that I shall ask everybody I see from that part of the world what pretty gentleman is making his addresses to her.

I would fain ask the favor of Miss Becca Burwell to give me another watch-paper of her own cutting, which I should esteem much more, though it were a plain round one, than the nicest in the world cut by other hands; however, I am afraid she would think this presumption, after my suffering the other to get spoiled. If you think you can excuse me to her for this, I should be glad if you would ask her.[9]

Travel might ease love's torments

How did Nancy look at you [Page] when you danced with her at Southall's? Have you any glimmering of hope? How does R. B. do? Had I better stay here [at Shadwell] and do nothing, or go down and do less? or, in other words, had I better stay here while I am here, or go down that I may have the pleasure of sailing up the river again in a full-rigged flat? Inclination tells me to go, receive my sentence, and be no longer in suspense; but reason says, if you go, and your attempt proves unsuccessful, you will be ten times more wretched than ever. . . . I have some thoughts of going to Petersburg, if the actors go there in May. If I do, I do not know but I may keep on to Williamsburg, as the birth night will be near. . . .

Have you an inclination to travel, Page? because if you have, I shall be glad of your company. For you must know that as soon as the Rebecca (the name I intend to give the vessel above mentioned) is completely finished, I intend to hoist sail and away. I shall visit particularly England, Holland, France, Spain, Italy (where I would buy me a good fiddle), and Egypt, and return through the British provinces to the northward home. This, to be sure, would take us two or three years, and if we should not both be cured of love in that time, I think the Devil would be in it.[10]

The grand tour first: will Rebecca wait?

The rival you mentioned I know not whether to think formidable or not, as there has been so great an opening for him during my absence. I say *has been*, because I expect there is one no longer. Since you have undertaken to act as my attorney, you advise me to go immediately and lay siege *in form*. You certainly did not think, at the time you wrote this, of that paragraph in my letter wherein I mentioned to you my resolution of going to Britain. . . . If I am to succeed, the sooner I know it, the less uneasiness I shall have to go through. If I am to meet with a disappointment, the sooner I know it, the more of life I shall have to wear it off; and if I do meet with one, I hope in God, and verily believe, it will be the last. . . .

This is a subject worth your talking over with her; and I wish you would, and would transmit to me your whole confab at length. I should be scared to death at making her so unreasonable a proposal as that of waiting until I return from Britain, unless she could first be prepared for it. I am afraid it will make my chance of succeeding considerably worse. But the event at last must be this, that if she consents, I shall be happy; if she does not, I must *endeavor* to be as much so as possible. . . .

Philosophizing, but not for our gay acquaintance

The most fortunate of us, in our journey through life, frequently meet with calamities and misfortunes which may greatly afflict us, and to fortify our minds against the attacks of these calamities and misfortunes should be one of the principal studies and endeavors of our lives. The only method of doing this is to assume a perfect resignation to the Divine Will, to consider that whatever does happen, must happen; and that, by our uneasiness, we cannot prevent the blow before it does fall, but we may add to its force after it has fallen. . . . Such, dear Page, will be the language of the man who considers his situation in this life, and such should be the language of every man who would wish to render that situation as easy as the nature of it will admit. Few things will disturb him at all; nothing will disturb him much.

If this letter was to fall into the hands of some of our gay acquaintance, your correspondent and his solemn notions would probably be the subjects of a great deal of mirth and raillery, but to you, I think, I can venture to send it.[11]

A pole chair, a pair of keen horses, and Rebecca

I will now endeavor to forget my present sufferings and think of what is more agreeable. . . . Last Saturday I left Ned Carter's where I had been happy in other good company, but particularly that of Miss Jenny Taliaferro; and though I can view the beauties of this world with the most philosophical indifference, I could not but be sensible of the justice of the character you [William Fleming, a fellow student] had given me of her. She is in my opinion a great resemblance of Nancy Wilton, but prettier. I was vastly pleased with her playing on the spinette and singing, but could not help calling to mind those sublime verses of the Cumberland genius

> Oh! I was charmed to see
> Orpheus' music all in thee.

When you see Patsy Dandridge, tell her 'God bless her.' I do not like the ups and downs of a country life; today you are frolicking with a fine girl and tomorrow you are moping by yourself. Thank God! I shall shortly be where my happiness will be less interrupted.

I shall salute all the girls below in your name, particularly Sukey Potter.

Dear Will, I have thought of the cleverest plan of life that can be imagined. You exchange lands for Edgehill, or I mine for Fairfields, you marry Sukey Potter, I marry Rebecca Burwell, join and get a pole chair and a pair of keen horses, practise the law in the same courts, and drive about to all the dances in the country together. How do you like it? [12]

Disappointed in love

In the most melancholy fit that ever any poor soul was, I sit down to write to you [John Page]. Last night, as merry as agreeable company and dancing with Belinda [that is, Rebecca] in the Apollo [Room of the Raleigh Tavern] could make me, I never could have thought the succeeding sun would have seen me so wretched as I now am! I was prepared to say a great deal; I had dressed up, in my own mind, such thoughts as occurred to me, in as moving a language as I knew how, and expected to have performed in a tolerably creditable manner. But, good God! When I had an opportunity of venting them, a few broken sentences, uttered in great disorder, and interrupted with pauses of uncommon length, were the too visible marks of my strange confusion!

The whole confab I will tell you, word for word, if I can, when I see you, which God send may be soon. . . . The court is now at hand, which I must attend constantly, so that unless you come to town, there is little probability of my meeting with you anywhere else. For God's sake come. [13]

Marriage? — No, thank ye!

With regard to the scheme I proposed to you [Will Fleming] some time since, I am sorry to tell you it is totally frustrated by Miss R. B.'s marriage with Jacquelin Ambler, which the people here tell me they daily expect; I say the people here tell me so, for (can you believe it?) I have been so abominably indolent as not to have seen her since October, wherefore I cannot affirm that I knew it from herself, though am as well satisfied it is true as if she had told me. Well, the Lord bless her, I say! but Sukey Potter is still left for you. . . .

You say you are determined to be married as soon as possible, and advise me to do the same. No, thank ye; I will consider of it first. Many and great are the comforts of a single state, and neither of the reasons you urge can have any influence with an inhabitant, and a young inhabitant too, of Williamsburg.[14]

Rustications, and love squeezes

Affairs at William and Mary are in the greatest confusion. Walker, M'Clurg, and Wat Jones are expelled *pro tempore*, or, as Horrox softens it, rusticated for a month. Lewis Burwell, Warner Lewis, and one Thompson have fled to escape flagellation.[15]

My letter of January 19 [1764] may have been opened.... We must fall on some scheme of communicating our thoughts to each other which shall be totally unintelligible to everyone but ourselves. I will send you [Page] some of these days Shelton's Tachygraphical Alphabet, and directions. Jack Walker is engaged to Betsey Moore, and desired all his brethren might be made acquainted with his happiness.... I have sent my horses up the country, so that it is out of my power to take even an airing on horseback at any time.[16]

This letter will be conveyed to you by the assistance of our friend Warner Lewis. Poor fellow! never did I see one more sincerely captivated in my life. He walked to the Indian camp with her yesterday, by which means he had an opportunity of giving her two or three love squeezes by the hand; and, like a true arcadian swain, has been so enraptured ever since that he is company for no one.[17]

Misadventures on a pleasure tour to New York

Surely never did small hero experience greater misadventures than I did on the first two or three days of my travelling. Twice did my horse run away with me, and greatly endanger the breaking my neck on the first day. On the second I drove two hours through as copious a rain as ever I have seen, without meeting with a single house to which I could repair for shelter. On the third, in going through Pamunkey, being unacquainted with the ford I passed through water so deep as to run over the cushion as I sat on it, and, to add to the danger, at that instant one wheel mounted a rock which I am confident was as high as the axle, and rendered it neces-

sary for me to exercise all my skill in the doctrine of gravity in order
to prevent the center of gravity from being left unsupported, the
consequence of which would, according to Bob Carter's opinion,
have been the corruition of myself, chair and all into the water....
I confess that on this occasion I was seized with a violent hydro-
phobia....

The situation of this place [Annapolis] is extremely beautiful, and
very commodious for trade.... The houses are in general better
than those in Williamsburg, but the gardens more indifferent.... I
would give you an account of the rejoicings here on the repeal of
the Stamp Act, but this you will probably see in print before my
letter can reach you. I shall proceed tomorrow to Philadelphia,
where I shall make the stay necessary for inoculation [against
smallpox], thence going on to New York I shall return by water to
Williamsburg about the middle of July [1766].[18]

Bold in the pursuit of knowledge

When I was a student of the law [under George Wythe, 1762–
1767]..., after getting through Coke Littleton, whose matter cannot be abridged, I was in the habit of abridging and common-
placing what I read meriting it, and of sometimes mixing my own
reflections on the subject.... They were written at a time of life
when I was bold in the pursuit of knowledge, never fearing to follow
truth and reason to whatever results they led, and bearding every
authority which stood in their way.[19]

I was led to set a due value on the study of the Northern languages, and especially of our Anglo-Saxon, while I was a student of
the law, by being obliged to recur to that source for explanation of
a multitude of law terms.... Some ideas occurred for facilitating
the study by simplifying its grammar, by reducing the infinite di-
versities of its unfixed orthography to single and settled forms, in-
dicating at the same time the pronunciation of the word by its correspondence with the characters and powers of the English alphabet.[20]

If we may throw aside the learned difficulties which mask its real
character, liberate it from these foreign shackles, ... endeavors to

give it the complicated structure of the Greek and Latin languages
. . ., and proceed to apply ourselves to it with little more preparation
than to Piers Ploughman, Douglas, or Chaucer, then I am persuaded its acquisition will require little time or labor, and will
richly repay us by the intimate insight it will give us into the genuine
structure, powers, and meanings of the language we now read and
speak. We shall then read Shakespeare and Milton with a superior
degree of intelligence and delight, heightened by the new and delicate shades of meaning developed to us by a knowledge of the
original sense of the same words. This rejection of the learned
labors of our Angle-Saxon doctors may be considered, perhaps, as a
rebellion against science. My hope, however, is that it may prove a
revolution.[21]

A stiff program of studies

Before you [Bernard Moore, a fellow student] enter on the study
of law a sufficient groundwork must be laid. For this purpose an
acquaintance with the Latin and French languages is absolutely
necessary. . . . Mathematics and natural philosophy are so useful
in the most familiar occurrences of life, and are so peculiarly engaging and delightful, as would induce everyone to wish an acquaintance with them. Besides this, the faculties of the mind, like the
members of the body, are strengthened and improved by exercise.
Mathematical reasonings and deductions are therefore a fine preparation for investigating the abstruse speculations of the law. . . .
This foundation being laid, you may enter regularly on the study
of the law, taking with it such of its kindred sciences as will contribute to eminence in its attainment. . . .

Till eight o'clock in the morning employ yourself in . . . agriculture . . . chemistry . . . anatomy . . . zoology . . . botany . . . ethics
and natural religion . . . religion sectarian . . . natural law. . . .
From eight to twelve read law. . . . In reading the Reporters enter
in a common-place book every case of value, condensed into the
narrowest compass possible. . . . This operation is doubly useful,
insomuch as it obliges the student to seek out the pith of the case
and habituates him to a condensation of thought, and to an acquisition of the most valuable of all talents, that of never using two words
where one will do. It fixes the case too, more indelibly in the mind.

From twelve to one read politics. . . . In the afternoon read history. . . . From dark to bedtime: belles lettres, criticism, rhetoric, oratory. . . . Read the best of the poets . . . but among these Shakespeare must be singled out by one who wishes to learn the full powers of the English language. . . . Criticize the style of any book whatsoever, committing the criticism to writing. Translate into the different styles, to wit, the elevated, the middling, and the familiar. . . . Undertake at first short compositions . . . paying great attention to the elegance and correctness of your language. Read the orations of Demosthenes and Cicero; analyze these orations, and . . . read good samples also of English eloquence. . . . Exercise yourself afterwards in preparing orations on feigned cases.[22]

But health is worth more than learning

Exercise and recreation . . . are as necessary as reading; I will say rather more necessary, because health is worth more than learning.[23] A strong body makes the mind strong. As to the species of exercise, I advise the gun. While this gives a moderate exercise to the body, it gives boldness, enterprise, and independence to the mind. Games played with the ball, and others of that nature, are too violent for the body, and stamp no character on the mind. Let your gun, therefore, be the constant companion of your walks. Never think of taking a book with you. The object of walking is to relax the mind. You should therefore not permit yourself even to think while you walk; but divert yourself by the objects surrounding you.

Walking is the best possible exercise. Habituate yourself to walk very far. The Europeans value themselves on having subdued the horse to the uses of man; but I doubt whether we have not lost more than we have gained by the use of this animal. No one has occasioned so much the degeneracy of the human body. . . . I would advise you to take your exercise in the afternoon; not because it is the best time for exercise . . . but because it is the best time to spare from your studies.[24]

A convivial, as well as studious, young lawyer

1768: — April 5, paid at [Williamsburg] Coffee House 7½ [pence]. Paid Colonel Henry half subscription money for map, 15/

[shillings]. April 11, paid for seeing an elk 7½. April 18, paid at play house 5/. April 27, paid for play tickets 22/6. April 29, paid at play house 10/. April 30, paid at Concert 5/.

May 2, paid at play house 5/. May 5, paid at a Concert 5/. May 6, paid at play house 5/. May 7, gave Jupiter [his body servant] to pay Bramer for candles 4/, Mayer for bread 7½, Burdet for candles 2/6. May 25, paid Dr. Pasteur for violin £5. May 30, paid for play tickets 15/. Paid Cary Wilkerson for books 26/. Paid at play house for punch 3/9.

June 1, paid T. Skinner for pineapples and oranges 12/6. June 17, paid Bailis for pomatum 1/3. June 18, gave in charity 20/. June 20, paid at Concert for tickets 20/. August 20, paid at Read's for whiskey 6/. Won at shooting 1/6. September 4, paid at Hornsby's for fiddlestrings 3/. September 13, paid at Hornsby's for fiddlestrings 2/3.

Puppet shows, tygers, horse races, and books

1769: — April 11, paid for seeing a hog weighing more than 1,050 pounds 1/. April 14, paid for seeing a puppet show 7/6. April 17, paid towards publishing a poem I never saw nor ever wish to see 2/6. Paid at Singleton's for punch 1/6. Paid for two tickets at puppet show 5/. April 26, paid for ticket to puppet show 2/6.

May 5, paid Pelham for playing on organ [in Bruton Parish Church] 2/6. Paid sexton 1/3. Paid at Charlton's for arrack 5/. May 30, gave M. Maury to pay for books in England . . . £7–10. June 20, paid women at Staunton for singing 3d 3/4. June 21, lost at pitchers with T. Bowyer 7d½. June 23, paid at Bowyer's for punch 2/. Paid T. Bowyer for entertainment £1–19. Lost with Mr. Madison at pitchers 7d½. June 27, gave in charity 20/.

August 11, paid at race at Charlottesville 5/9. September 21, gave a woman to buy cakes 5/. September 30, lost shooting at Moon's muster 2/6. Paid at Moon's muster for brandy 12/6. October 17, paid Craig for mending microscope and perspective glass 2/6. October 23, paid legerdemain man 2/6. Paid at play house for punch 1/6. October 24, gave an Indian 3d 3/4. October 27, paid for seeing a tyger 1/3.[25]

The burning of Shadwell in 1770

My late loss may perhaps have reached you [John Page] by this time; I mean the loss of my mother's house by fire, and in it of every paper I had in the world, and almost every book. On a reasonable estimate I calculate the *cost* of the books burned to have been £200 sterling. Would to God it had been the money, *then* had it never cost me a sigh!

To make the loss more sensible, it fell principally on my books of Common Law, of which I have but one left, at that time lent out. Of papers too of every kind I am utterly destitute. All of these, whether public or private, of business or of amusement, have perished in the flames. I had made some progress in preparing for the succeeding General Court; and having, as was my custom, thrown my thoughts into the form of notes, I troubled my head no more with them. These are gone, and like the baseless fabric of a vision, leave not a trace behind. . . .

If this conflagration, by which I am burned out of a home, had come before I had advanced so far in preparing another, I do not know but I might have cherished some treasonable thoughts of leaving these my native hills; indeed I should be much happier were I nearer to Rosewell and Severn hills — however, the gods, I fancy, were apprehensive that if we were placed together, we should pull down the moon, or play some such devilish prank with their works.

Once again love's advocate

I reflect often with pleasure on the philosophical evenings I passed at Rosewell on my last visits there. I was always fond of philosophy, even in its drier forms; but from a ruby lip it comes with charms irresistible. Such a feast of sentiment must exhilarate and lengthen life, at least as much as the feast of the sensualist shortens it — in a word, I prize it so highly that, if you will at any time collect the same *Belle Assemblée*, on giving me three days previous notice I shall certainly repair to my place as a member of it. Should it not happen before I come down, I will carry Sally Nicholas in the green chair to Newquarter, where your periagua (how the —— should I spell that word?) will meet us. . . .

I expect [William Fontaine, a mutual friend] will follow the good old rule of driving one passion out by letting another in. *Clavum clavo pangere* was your advice to me on a similar occasion. I hope you will watch his immersion as narrowly as if he were one of Jupiter's satellites; and give me immediate notice, that I may prepare a dish of advice. I do not mean ... to advise him against it. On the contrary, I am become an advocate for the passion.[26]

CHAPTER II

Young Squire of Monticello

L ATE in 1770 Jefferson removed to Monticello, setting up bachelor's quarters in a one-room brick cottage until the main house became habitable. He soon had every reason to push forward ambitious plans for his new mountain-top plantation. For the young lady who occupied the principal place in all schemes for the future, the musical young lady for whom that summer during his courtship he ordered a forte-piano from London, had consented to be his wife. She was Martha Wayles Skelton, a slender, auburn-haired, and much-courted widow of twenty-three, who lived on her father's plantation not far from Williamsburg. Following the marriage festivities on New Year's Day of 1772, the young couple journeyed upcountry more than a hundred miles through January snows to Monticello, and there in the little brick cottage spent their honeymoon and the first winter of their married life. The next ten years, as Jefferson tells us, were years of unchequered domestic happiness.

In spite of the interruptions of law and politics and war, his private life during these ten years was that of a many-sided young squire, a cultured Virginia gentleman who was an architect, scientific farmer, and literary essayist, an amateur astronomer and a pioneer scholar in meteorology and natural history. The house of classic simplicity and proportions which he designed and built was the first of many architectural creations that profoundly influenced the whole course of American architecture. It was a two-story brick pavilion with wings, entered front and back by columned porticoes, connected with its service buildings by hidden passageways; a house which commanded a magnificent view of the Blue Ridge Mountains to the west, the hamlet of Charlottesville in the valley immediately below, and on the east a stretch of red-clay farmlands which Jefferson called his sea view. Here at his beloved Monticello, with his wife and children, his farms and his books, he spent the happiest years of his life in 'philosophic evenings and rural days.'

On his mountaintop Jefferson built roundabout walks and terraced gardens, planted domestic and imported trees and seeds, and kept minute records to see whether foreign specimens could be adapted to the American soil and climate, often comparing notes with Philip Mazzei, an Italian gentleman whom he had induced to start a vineyard in the neighborhood. He trained and directed his slaves in the many farming and building operations of a large plantation which was a little community in itself, with its house and field servants, its waving green fields and orchards and pastures, its horses and cattle and poultry, its gristmill and sawmill and workshops. A bold and skillful horseman, he daily mounted one of his Virginia thoroughbreds and rode over his adjoining farms, conferred with his overseers about the tobacco which he sent down the Rivanna River to warehouses on the James for shipment to England, and often stopped at his deer park, where the tame deer eagerly ran up to eat corn out of his hand.

In his library, surrounded by the books which later became the nucleus of the Library of Congress, he read fiction as well as 'the learned lumber' of law and history and science, sketched on his drafting board, and carried on his correspondence with scholars and statesmen. He wrote frequently not only to political colleagues with whom during these years he was creating an American nation, but to scientists such as David Rittenhouse, the Philadelphia astronomer, to whom he reported his observations on the great eclipse of 1778. He was fond of saying that Nature had intended him for the tranquil pursuits of science, rather than a public career, for science was his supreme delight. At the same time, as he tells us, music was the favorite passion of his soul, and one of his dreams was to have his own orchestra at Monticello.

When the Chevalier de Chastellux, an accomplished Parisian and scholarly member of the French Academy, visited Jefferson in the spring of 1782, he was impressed by the classic symmetry and elegant taste of Monticello. He was even more impressed and charmed by Mr. Jefferson, 'the first American who has consulted the fine arts to know how he should shelter himself from the weather.' Chastellux described his host as a tall man not yet forty, with gentle manners, warm heart, and animated mind; a little reserved at first, he noted, but very soon 'we were as intimate as if we had passed our whole lives together.' On one memorable evening they drank punch and read the poems of Ossian far into the night. Not only poetry but science, politics, and the arts were the topics of 'a conversation always varied and interesting . . ., for no object had escaped Mr. Jefferson; and it seemed as if from his youth he had placed his mind, as he had done his house, on an elevated situation, from which he might contemplate the universe.'

Ever since his student days Jefferson had made notes and sketches of the thousand and one things that interested him. From these memoranda he wrote in 1781 his *Notes on Virginia*, a book which gave him a high literary and scholarly reputation at home and abroad. In it he discussed the elegant and useful art of architecture, described Harpers Ferry and the Natural Bridge (of which he became the owner in 1774), revealed his agrarian philosophy and love of farming, and lashed out at the slavery system. He described the contents of an Indian mound on the Rivanna, reported on the whimsical shapes assumed by a neighboring mountain, and made use of weather observations patiently recorded at Monticello, where, as he once said, he could look down into Nature's workshop and see clouds and hail and snow and rain fabricated at his feet.

His intense Americanism as well as his knowledge of natural history is shown in his successful refutation of the Count de Buffon, then the world's outstanding naturalist, who had asserted that the animals of the New World were fewer and smaller in size than those of Europe, and that there was something in the American environment which caused both animals and aborigines to degenerate. Jefferson compiled long lists of species to prove his point, and later in Paris he was to give Buffon visual proof in the shape of horns and hides of American animals. In Paris, too, Jefferson was to meet the Abbé de Raynal (and with his six feet two of American flesh and bone he was to tower over the little French scholar), who had applied this theory of New World degeneracy to American whites. In refuting Raynal, Jefferson wrote his eloquent passage on the genius of America.

In September of 1782 Jefferson was dealt a crushing blow by the death of his wife. A state of dreadful suspense had been closed by catastrophe, as he finally managed to write Chastellux, in a letter which contained one of the very few references to his wife to be found in his writings. None of the letters which he and Martha exchanged were allowed to remain even for his children to read. In later years his oldest child described Jefferson's inconsolable grief. Upon the death of his wife he fainted, and the family feared he would never revive. For three weeks he kept to his room, pacing the floor almost incessantly night and day, and when he finally left the house it was to go on long and lonely horseback rides.

It was his daughter Martha who later described this 'first month of desolation.' She and her sister Mary were the only two of Jefferson's six children to survive infancy. Soon after his wife's death he placed Martha in a school at Philadelphia, and began a series of letters to her, followed by others to Mary, which reveal his deeply affectionate nature. Henceforth these two motherless daughters were to be his source of happiness: Martha, who resembled him, and Mary, who grew up to look very much like the Martha Skelton whom he had courted in the happy year of 1771.

A piano for the future Mrs. Jefferson

I have lately removed to the mountain from which this is dated [Monticello, February 20, 1771]. . . . I have here but one room, which, like the cobbler's, serves me for parlor, for kitchen and hall. I may add, for bedchamber and study, too. My friends sometimes take a temperate dinner with me and then retire to look for beds elsewhere. I have hope, however, of getting more elbow room this summer.[1]

I must alter one article in the invoice [wrote Jefferson in June of 1771 to his business agent in London]. I wrote therein for a clavichord. I have since seen a forte-piano and am charmed with it. Send me this instrument then instead of the clavichord: let the case be of fine mahogany, solid, not veneered, the compass from double G to F in alt, a plenty of spare strings; and the workmanship of the whole very handsome and worthy the acceptance of a lady for whom I intend it. I must add also ½ dozen pair of India cotton stockings for myself @ 10/ sterling per pair, ½ dozen pair best white silk ditto; and a large umbrella with brass ribs, covered with green silk and neatly finished.

By this change of the clavichord into a forte-piano and addition of the other things, I shall be brought in debt to you, to discharge which I will ship you of the first tobacco I get to the warehouse in the fall. I expect by that time, and also from year to year afterwards, I must send you an invoice, with tobacco, somewhat enlarged, as I have it in prospect to become more regularly a paterfamilias. . . . I shall conclude with one petition: that you send me the articles . . . as soon as you receive this, and particularly the forte-piano, for which I shall be very impatient.[2]

Offer prayers for me [he wrote a friend in August of 1771] at that shrine to which though absent I pray continual devotions. In every scheme of happiness she is placed in the foreground of the picture, as the principal figure. Take that away, and it is no picture for me.[3]

Marriage: ten years of unchequered happiness

On the 1st of January, 1772, I was married to Martha Skelton, widow of Bathurst Skelton, and daughter of John Wayles; then twenty-three years old. Mr. Wayles was a lawyer of much practice, to which he was introduced more by his great industry, punctuality, and practical readiness, than by eminence in the science of his profession. He was a most agreeable companion, full of pleasantry and good humor, and welcomed in every society. He acquired a handsome fortune, and died in May, 1773, leaving three daughters; the portion which came on that event to Mrs. Jefferson, after the debts should be paid, which were very considerable, was about equal to my own patrimony [actually it was equal to his property of five thousand acres and about fifty slaves], and consequently doubled the ease of our circumstances.[4]

1772: — January 1, gave Revd. W. Coutts £5. Borrowed of Mr. Coutts 20/. January 2, gave Revd. Mr. Davies marriage fee £5. January 3, gave a fiddler 10/.[5]

[My wife was] the cherished companion of my life, in whose affections, unabated on both sides, I ... lived ... ten years in unchequered happiness.[6]

Happily gardening and building at Monticello

1772: — January 26, The deepest snow we have ever seen. In Albemarle it was about three feet deep. March 30, Sowed a patch of later peas. July 15, Cucumbers came to table. Planted out celery. Sowed a patch of peas for the fall. Planted snap beans. July 31, Had Irish potatoes from the garden. Julius Shard fills the two-wheeled barrow in 3 minutes, and carries it 30 yards in 1½ minutes more. Now this is four loads of the common barrow with one wheel. . . . September 1, To enclose the top of mountain, the garden, and fruitery, will take 1,450 yards of paling. October 8, Gathered two plum-peaches at Monticello. November 12, In making the Roundabout walk, 3 hands would make 80 yards in a day in the old field, but in the woods where they had stumps to clear, not more than forty, and sometimes 25 yards.

1773: — Mrs. Wythe puts one-tenth very rich superfine Malmsey to a dry Madeira, and makes a fine wine. March 12, Sowed a patch of early peas, and another of marrowfats. March 31, Grafted five French chestnuts into two stocks of common chestnuts. April 1, Both patches of peas up. Set out strawberries. May 22, First patch of peas come to table. Note, this spring is remarkably forward. . . .

1774: — March 15, Sowed the following seeds, and distinguished them by sticking numbered sticks in the beds: Aglio di Terracina, Garlic. No. 15, Radicchio di Pistoia. Succory or Wild Endive. 26, Cipolle blanche di Tuckahoe. The Spanion onion of Millar. . . . 46, Cochlearia di Pisa (scurvy grass or perhaps horse-radish). . . . March 23, Sowed the following seeds. . . . 48, Cavolo broccolo Francese di Pisa. Broccoli. . . . 72, Siberian wheat. March 29, Peach trees at Monticello in general bloom.

March 31, Laid off ground to be levelled for a future garden. The upper side is 44 feet below the upper edge of the Roundabout and parallel thereto. It is 668 feet long, 80 feet wide, and at each end forms a triangle, rectangular and isosceles, of which the legs are 80 feet and the hypotenuse 113 feet. Planted the following trees, seeds, etc. Twenty-four apple trees. Nineteen cherry trees—from

the mountain plains.... Cherries of different kinds from Italy....
About 1,500 olive stones.... Lamponi. Raspberries (the seeds) in
3 rows.

April 5, Planted thirty vines just below where the negro garden
wall will run, towards the westermost end. Eight of them at the
westermost end of the row were Spanish Raisins.... And at the
eastermost end were six native vines of Monticello. They were
planted by some Tuscan Vignerons, who came over with Mr.
[Philip] Mazzei....

April 11, In making a stone wall in my garden, I find by an accurate calculation that 7½ cubical feet may be done in a day by
one hand, who brings his own stone into place and does everything.

May 4, The Blue Ridge of mountains covered with snow. May
5, A frost which destroyed almost everything.... May 14, Cherries
ripe. May 16, First dish of peas from earliest patch. July 23,
Cucumbers from our garden. July 31, Watermelons from our
patch.[7]

On books: a defense of fiction

August 4, 1773. My library:... in all 1,256 volumes. Note,
this does not include volumes of music, nor my books in Williamsburg. For library: [669 volumes to be purchased at] £218–19.[8]

I sat down with a design of [making] a catalogue of books to the
amount of about fifty pounds sterling, but could by no means satisfy
myself with any partial choice I could make.... A view of the
second column in this catalogue would I suppose extort a smile
from the face of gravity. Peace to its wisdom! Let me not awaken
it. A little attention however to the nature of the human mind
evinces that the entertainments of fiction are useful as well as
pleasant....

But wherein is its utility? asks the reverend sage, big with the
notion that nothing can be useful but the learned lumber of Greek
and Roman reading with which his head is stored. I answer, everything is useful which contributes to fix in the principles and practices of virtue. When any original act of charity or of gratitude, for
instance, is presented either to our sight or imagination, we are
deeply impressed with its beauty and feel a strong desire in ourselves of doing charitable and grateful acts also. On the contrary,

when we see or read of any atrocious deed we are disgusted with its deformity, and conceive an abhorrence of vice. . . .

Sterne's Sentimental Journey

I appeal to every reader of feeling and sentiment whether the fictitious murder of Duncan by Macbeth in Shakespeare does not excite in him as great a horror of villainy as the real one of Henry IV by Ravaillac as related by Davila? And whether the fidelity of Nelson and generosity of Blandford in Marmontel do not dilate his breast and elevate his sentiments as much as any similar incident which real history can furnish? Does he not in fact feel himself a better man while reading them, and privately covenant to copy the fair example? We neither know nor care whether Laurence Sterne really went to France, whether he was there accosted by the Franciscan, at first rebuked him unkindly, and then gave him a peace offering; or whether the whole be not fiction. In either case we equally are sorrowful at the rebuke, and secretly resolve *we* will never do so; we are pleased with the subsequent atonement, and view with emulation a soul candidly acknowledging its fault and making a just reparation.

Considering history as a moral exercise, her lessons would be too infrequent if confined to real life. Of those recorded by historians few incidents have been attended with such circumstances as to excite in any high degree this sympathetic emotion of virtue. We are, therefore, wisely framed to be as warmly interested for a fictitious as for a real personage. The field of imagination is thus laid open to our use and lessons may be formed to illustrate and carry home to the heart every moral rule of life. Thus a lively and lasting sense of filial duty is more effectually impressed on the mind of a son or daughter by reading King Lear than by all the dry volumes of ethics and divinity that ever were written. This is my idea of well written romance, of tragedy, comedy, and epic poetry.[9]

The glow of one warm thought

I think the Greeks and Romans have left us the present models which exist of fine composition, whether we examine them as works of reason or of style and fancy; and to them we probably owe these characteristics of modern composition. . . . To all this I add that to read the Latin and Greek authors in their original is a sublime luxury; and I deem luxury in science to be at least as justifiable as in architecture, painting, gardening, or the other arts. I enjoy Homer in his own language infinitely beyond Pope's translation of him, and both beyond the dull narrative of the same events by Dares Phrygius; and it is an innocent enjoyment. I thank on my knees him [Jefferson's father] who directed my early education for having put into my possession this rich source of delight; and I would not exchange it for anything which I could then have acquired, and have not since acquired.[10]

Ossian's poems . . . have been and will, I think, during my life, continue to be to me the sources of daily and exalted pleasures. The tender and sublime emotions of the mind were never before so wrought up by the human hand. I am not ashamed to own that I think this rude bard of the North the greatest poet that has ever existed. Merely for the pleasure of reading his works, I am become desirous of learning the language in which he sung, and of possessing his songs in their original [Gaelic]. . . . Manuscript copies of any which are in print, it would at any time give me the greatest happiness to receive. The glow of one warm thought is to me worth more than money.[11]

The great eclipse of 1778 from Monticello

We were much disappointed in Virginia generally on the day of the great eclipse, which proved to be cloudy. In Williamsburg, where it was total, I understood only the beginning was seen. At this place, which is lat. 38°8′, and longitude west from Williamsburg, about 1°45′, as is conjectured, 11 digits only were supposed to be covered. It was not seen at all until the moon had advanced nearly one third over the sun's disc. Afterwards it was seen at intervals through the whole. The egress particularly was visible.

It proved, however, of little use to me, for want of a timepiece that could be depended on, which circumstance . . . has induced me to trouble you [David Rittenhouse] with this letter, to remind you of your kind promise of making me an accurate clock, which, being intended for astronomical purposes only, I would have divested of all apparatus for striking, or for any other purpose, which, by increasing its complication, might disturb its accuracy.

A companion to it for keeping seconds, and which might be moved easily, would greatly add to its value. The theodolite, for which I also spoke to you, I can now dispense with, having since purchased a most excellent one.[12]

Music the favorite passion of my soul

Music . . . is the favorite passion of my soul, and fortune has cast my lot in a country where it is in a state of deplorable barbarism. . . . The bounds of an American fortune will not admit the indulgence of a domestic band of musicians, yet I have thought that a passion for music might be reconciled with that economy which we are obliged to observe.

I retain among my domestic servants a gardener, a weaver, a cabinet-maker, and a stone-cutter, to which I would add a vigneron. In a country where, like [Italy], music is cultivated and practiced by every class of men, I suppose there might be found persons of these trades who could perform on the French horn, clarinet, or hautboy, and bassoon, so that one might have a band of two French horns, two clarinets, two hautboys, and a bassoon without enlarging their domestic expenses. A certainty of employment for half a dozen years, and at the end of that time to find them, if they choose, a conveyance to their own country, might induce them to come here on reasonable wages. . . . Sobriety and good nature would be desirable parts of their characters.[13]

Notes on Virginia

In the year 1781 I . . . received a letter from M. de Marbois, of the French legation in Philadelphia, . . . addressing to me a number of queries relative to the State of Virginia. I had always made it a practice whenever an opportunity occurred of obtaining any information of our country which might be of use to me in any station, public or private, to commit it to writing. These memoranda were on loose paper. . . . I thought this a good occasion to embody their substance, which I did in the order of Mr. Marbois' queries, so as to answer his wish, and to arrange them for my own use. Some friends . . . wished for copies. . . . I therefore corrected and enlarged them, and had two hundred copies printed under the title of 'Notes on Virginia.'

I gave a very few copies to some particular friends in Europe. . . . A European copy, by the death of the owner, got into the hands of a bookseller, who engaged its translation, and when ready for the press communicated his intentions and manuscript to me, suggesting that I should correct it, without asking any other permission for the publication. I never had seen so wretched an attempt at translation. Interverted, abridged, mutilated, and often reversing the sense of the original, I found it a blotch of errors from beginning to end. I corrected some of the most material, and in that form it was printed in French. A London bookseller, on seeing the translation, requested me to permit him to print the English original. I thought it best to do so to let the world see that it was not really so bad as the French translation had made it appear.[14]

Architecture in Virginia: a critique

The private buildings are very rarely constructed of stone or brick, much the greatest portion being of scantling and boards, plastered with lime. It is impossible to devise things more ugly, uncomfortable, and happily more perishable. There are two or three plans, on one of which, according to its size, most of the houses in the state are built. The poorest people build huts of logs, laid horizontally in pens, stopping the interstices with mud. These are warmer in winter and cooler in summer than the more expensive construction of scantling and plank. . . . The only public buildings worthy of mention are the capitol, the palace, the college, and the hospital for lunatics, all of them in Williamsburg. . . .

The capitol is a light and airy structure, with a portico in front of two orders, the lower of which, being Doric, is tolerably just in its proportions and ornaments, save only that the intercolonations are too large. The upper is Ionic, much too small for that on which it is mounted, its ornaments not proper to the order, nor proportioned within themselves. It is crowned with a pediment which is too high for its span. Yet, on the whole, it is the most pleasing piece of architecture we have. The palace is not handsome without, but it is spacious and commodious within, is prettily situated, and with the grounds annexed to it, it is capable of being made an elegant seat. The college and hospital are rude, mis-shapen piles, which, but that they have roofs, would be taken for brick-kilns.

There are no other public buildings but churches and court houses, in which no attempts are made at elegance. Indeed, it would not be easy to execute such an attempt, as a workman could scarcely be found capable of drawing an order. The genius of architecture seems to have shed its maledictions over this land. . . . Perhaps a spark may fall on some young subjects of natural taste, kindle up their genius, and produce a reformation in this elegant and useful art.[15]

Harpers Ferry: a war between rivers and mountains

The passage of the Potomac through the Blue Ridge is, perhaps, one of the most stupendous scenes in nature. You stand on a very high point of land. On your right comes up the Shenandoah, having ranged along the foot of the mountain a hundred miles to seek a vent. On your left approaches the Potomac, in quest of a passage also. In the moment of their junction they rush together against the mountain, rend it asunder, and pass off to the sea. The first glance of this scene hurries our senses into the opinion that this earth has been created in time, that the mountains were formed first, that the rivers began to flow afterwards, that in this place, particularly, they have been dammed up by the Blue Ridge of mountains, and have formed an ocean which filled the whole valley; that continuing to rise they have at length broken over at this spot, and have torn the mountain down from its summit to its base. The piles of rock on each hand, but particularly on the Shenandoah, the evident marks of their disrupture and avulsion from their beds by the most powerful agents of nature, corroborate the impression.

But the distant finishing which nature has given to the picture is of a very different character. It is a true contrast to the foreground. It is as placid and delightful as that is wild and tremendous. For the mountain being cloven asunder, she presents to your eye, through the cleft, a small catch of smooth blue horizon, at an infinite distance in the plain country, inviting you, as it were, from the riot and tumult roaring around, to pass through the breach and

participate of the calm below. . . . This scene is worth a voyage
across the Atlantic. Yet here, as in the neighborhood of the Natural
Bridge, are people who have passed their lives within half a dozen
miles, and have never been to survey these monuments of a war
between rivers and mountains which must have shaken the earth
itself to its centre.[16]

So beautiful an arch!

The Natural Bridge, the most sublime of nature's works, . . . is
on the ascent of a hill which seems to have been cloven through its
length by some great convulsion. The fissure, just at the bridge, is,
by some admeasurements, two hundred and seventy feet deep, by
others only two hundred and five. It is about forty-five feet wide
at the bottom and ninety feet at the top; this of course determines
the length of the bridge, and its height from the water. . . . Though
the sides of this bridge are provided in some parts with a parapet of
fixed rocks, yet few men have resolution to walk to them and look
over into the abyss. You involuntarily fall on your hands and feet.
creep to the parapet, and peep over it. Looking down from this
height about a minute gave me a violent headache. If the view
from the top be painful and intolerable, that from below is delightful in an equal extreme. It is impossible for the emotions
arising from the sublime to be felt beyond what they are here; so
beautiful an arch, so elevated, so light, and springing as it were up
to heaven![17]

Farmers are God's chosen people

Those who labor in the earth are the chosen people of God, if
ever He had a chosen people, whose breasts He has made His
peculiar deposit for substantial and genuine virtue. It is the focus
in which He keeps alive that sacred fire which otherwise might
escape from the face of the earth. Corruption of morals in the mass
of cultivators is a phenomenon of which no age nor nation has
furnished an example. It is the mark set on those who, not looking
up to heaven, to their own soil and industry, as does the husband-
man, for their subsistence, depend for it on casualties and caprice
of customers. Dependence begets subservience and venality, suf-
focates the germ of virtue, and prepares fit tools for the designs of
ambition. . . .

Generally speaking, the proportion which the aggregate of the other classes of citizens bears in any state to that of its husbandmen is the proportion of its unsound to its healthy parts, and is a good enough barometer whereby to measure its degree of corruption. While we have land to labor, then, let us never wish to see our citizens occupied at a workbench, or twirling a distaff. Carpenters, masons, smiths, are wanting in husbandry; but, for the general operations of manufacture, let our workshops remain in Europe.[18]

Slavery: I tremble for my country

There must doubtless be an unhappy influence on the manners of our people produced by the existence of slavery among us. The whole commerce between master and slave is a perpetual exercise of the most boisterous passions, the most unremitting despotism on the one part, and degrading submissions on the other. Our children see this, and learn to imitate it. . . . The parent storms, the child looks on, catches the lineaments of wrath, puts on the same airs in the circle of smaller slaves, gives a loose to the worst of passions and thus nursed, educated, and daily exercised in tyranny, cannot but be stamped by it with odious peculiarities. . . . And can the liberties of a nation be thought secure when we have removed their only firm basis, a conviction in the minds of the people that these liberties are of the gift of God? That they are not to be violated but with His wrath?

Indeed I tremble for my country when I reflect that God is just; that his justice cannot sleep forever; that considering numbers, nature and natural means only, a revolution of the wheel of fortune, an exchange of situation is among possible events; that it may become probable by supernatural interference! The Almighty has no attribute which can take side with us in such a contest. But it is impossible to be temperate and to pursue this subject through the various considerations of policy, of morals, of history natural and civil. We must be contented to hope they will force their way into everyone's mind. I think a change already perceptible. . . . The spirit of the master is abating, that of the slave rising from the dust, his condition mollifying, the way I hope preparing, under the auspices of heaven, for a total emancipation, and that this is disposed in the order of events to be with the consent of the masters rather than by their extirpation.[19]

The climate of Virginia

Journals of observation on the quantity of rain and degrees of heat being lengthy, confused, and too minute to produce general and distinct ideas, I have taken five years' observations, to wit, from 1772 to 1777, made in Williamsburg and its neighborhood, have reduced them to an average for every month in the year, and stated their averages, . . . adding an analytical view of the winds during the same period. . . . The difference of temperature of the air at the seacoast or on the Chesapeake Bay and at the Alleghany has not been ascertained, but contemporary observations made at Williamsburg . . . and at Monticello, which is on the most eastern ridge of the mountains, called the Southwest, where they are intersected by the Rivanna, have furnished a ratio by which that difference may in some degree be conjectured.

These observations make the difference . . . to be on an average $6\frac{1}{3}$ degrees of Fahrenheit's thermometer. . . . The averaged and almost unvaried difference of the height of mercury in the barometer, at those two places, was .784 of an inch, the atmosphere at Monticello being so much the lightest, that is to say, about one-thirty-seventh of its whole weight. It should be observed, however, that the hill of Monticello is of five hundred feet perpendicular height above the river which washes its base. This position being nearly central between our northern and southern boundaries, and between the bay and Alleghany, may be considered as furnishing the best average of the temperature of our climate. . . .

But a more remarkable difference is in the winds. . . . By reducing nine months' observations at Monticello . . . and by reducing in like manner an equal number of observations, to wit, four hundred and twenty-one . . . at Williamsburg, . . . it may be seen that the southwest wind prevails equally at both places; that the northeast is, next to this, the principal wind towards the seacoast, and the northwest is the predominant wind at the mountains.

The difference between these two winds to sensation, and in fact, is very great. The northeast is loaded with vapor, insomuch that the salt-makers have found that their crystals would not shoot while that blows; it brings a distressing chill, and is heavy and oppressive to the spirits. The northwest is dry, cooling, elastic, and animating. The eastern and southeastern breezes . . . have advanced into the country very sensibly within the memory of people now living. . . . As the lands become more cleared it is probable that they will extend still further westward.[20]

The whimsical mountain

Monticello . . . affords an opportunity of seeing a phenomenon which is rare at land, though frequent at sea. The seamen call it *looming*. Philosophy is as yet in the rear of the seamen, for so far from having accounted for it she has not given it a name. Its principal effect is to make distant objects appear larger, in opposition to the general law of vision by which they are diminished. I knew an instance at Yorktown, from whence the water prospect eastwardly is without termination, wherein a canoe with three men at a great distance was taken for a ship with its three masts. I am little acquainted with the phenomenon as it shows itself at sea, but at Monticello it is familiar.

There is a solitary mountain about forty miles off in the south whose natural shape, as presented to view there, is a regular cone; but by the effect of looming it sometimes subsides almost totally in the horizon; sometimes it rises more acute and more elevated; sometimes it is hemispherical; and sometimes its sides are perpendicular, its top flat, and as broad as its base. In short, it assumes at times the most whimsical shapes and all these perhaps successively in the same morning.[21]

An Indian mound on the Rivanna

There being [an Indian mound] in my neighborhood, I wished to satisfy myself whether any, and which, of these [conflicting opinions as to their origin] were just. For this purpose I determined to open and examine it thoroughly. It was situated on the low grounds of the Rivanna, about two miles above its principal fork, and opposite to some hills on which had been an Indian town. It was of spheroidical form, of about forty feet diameter at the base, and had been of about twelve feet altitude, though now reduced by the plough to seven and a half. . . .

I . . . came to collections of human bones at different depths from six inches to three feet below the surface. These were lying

in the utmost confusion, some vertical, some oblique, some horizontal, and directed to every point of the compass, entangled and
held together in clusters by the earth. . . . I conjectured that in this
barrow might have been a thousand skeletons. Everyone will
readily seize the circumstances above related, which militate
against the opinion that it covered the bones only of persons fallen
in battle; and against the tradition, also, [that] the bodies were
placed upright, and touching each other.[22]

America's natural history

The opinion advanced by the Count de Buffon is, 1. That the
animals common to both the old and new world are smaller in the
latter. 2. That those peculiar to the new are on a smaller scale.
3. That those which have been domesticated in both have de-
generated in America; and, 4. That on the whole it exhibits fewer
species. . . . Let us then take a comparative view of the quadrupeds
of Europe and America. . . .

The result of this view . . . is that of twenty-six quadrupeds
common to both countries, seven are said to be larger in America,
seven of equal size, and twelve not sufficiently examined. . . .
Proceeding to the . . . animals found in one of the two countries
only, . . . [we find] that there are eighteen quadrupeds peculiar
to Europe; more than four times as many, to wit, seventy-four,
peculiar to America. . . . That some of [those quadrupeds domesticated in both continents] in some parts of America have become
less than their original stock is doubtless true, and the reason is very
obvious. In a thinly-peopled country the spontaneous productions
of the forests and waste fields are sufficient to support indifferently
the domestic animals of the farmer. . . . With those individuals
in America where necessity or curiosity has produced equal attention, as in Europe, to the nourishment of animals, the horses,
cattle, sheep, and hogs of one continent are as large as those of the
other. . . .

We may conclude . . . that the third member of Monsieur de
Buffon's assertion . . . is as probably wrong as the first and second
were certainly so. That the last part of it is erroneous, which af-
firms that the species of American quadrupeds are comparatively
few, is evident. . . .

New World man not inferior to the European

Hitherto I have considered this hypothesis as applied to brute animals only, and not in its extension to the man of America, whether aboriginal or transplanted. It is the opinion of Monsieur de Buffon that the former furnishes no exception. . . . Of the Indians of South America I know nothing; for I would not honor with the appellation of knowledge what I derive from the fables published of them. These I believe to be just as true as the fables of Aesop. . . . The Indian of North America being more within our reach, I can speak of him . . . in contradiction to this representation. . . .

Were we to compare them in their present state with the Europeans north of the Alps when the Roman arms and arts first crossed those mountains the comparison would be unequal, because at the time those parts of Europe were swarming with numbers; because numbers produce emulation, and multiply the chances of improvement, and one improvement begets another. Yet I may safely ask, how many good poets, how many able mathematicians, how many great inventors in arts and sciences had Europe north of the Alps then produced? And it was sixteen centuries after this before a Newton could be formed.

I do not mean to deny that there are varieties in the race of man distinguished by their powers both of body and mind. I believe there are, as I see to be the case in the races of other animals. I only mean to suggest a doubt whether the bulk and faculties of animals depend on the side of the Atlantic on which their food happens to grow, or which furnishes the elements of which they are compounded. Whether Nature has enlisted herself as a Cis- or Trans-Atlantic partisan. I am induced to suspect there has been more eloquence than sound reasoning displayed in support of this theory; that it is one of those cases where the judgment has been seduced by a glowing pen; and whilst I render every tribute of honor and esteem to the celebrated zoologist who has added, and is still adding, so many precious things to the treasures of science, I must doubt whether in this instance he has not cherished error also by lending her for a moment his vivid imagination and bewitching tongue.

The genius of America

So far the Count de Buffon has carried this new theory of the tendency of Nature to belittle her productions on this side of the Atlantic. Its application to the race of whites transplanted from Europe remained for the Abbé Raynal. . . . 'America has not yet produced one good poet.' When we shall have existed as a people as long as the Greeks did before they produced a Homer, the Romans a Virgil, the French a Racine and Voltaire, the English a Shakespeare and Milton, should this reproach be still true, we will inquire from what unfriendly causes it has proceeded, that the other countries of Europe and quarters of the earth shall not have inscribed any name on the roll of poets.

But neither has America produced 'one able mathematician, one man of genius in a single art or a single science.' In war we have produced a Washington, whose memory will be adored while liberty shall have votaries, whose name shall triumph over time, and will in future ages assume its just station among the most celebrated worthies of the world, when that wretched philosophy shall be forgotten which would have arranged him among the degeneracies of nature. In physics we have produced a Franklin, than whom no one of the present age has made more important discoveries, nor has enriched philosophy with more, or more ingenious, solutions of the phenomena of nature. We have supposed Mr. [David] Rittenhouse second to no astronomer living; that in genius he must be the first, because he is self-taught. As an artist he has exhibited as great a proof of mechanical genius as the world has ever produced. He has not indeed made a world; but [with his model of the planetary system] he has by imitation approached nearer its Maker than any man who has lived from the creation to this day.

As in philosophy and war, so in government, in oratory, in painting, in the plastic art, we might show that America, though but a child of yesterday, has already given hopeful proofs of genius, as well as of the nobler kinds, which arouse the best feelings of man, which call him into action, which substantiate his freedom and conduct him to happiness, as of the subordinate, which serve to amuse him only. We therefore suppose that this reproach is as unjust as it is unkind; and that of the geniuses which adorn the present age America contributes its full share.[23]

My children: births, and deaths

Martha Jefferson was born September 27, 1772, at 1 o'clock A.M.

Jane Randolph Jefferson, born April 3, 1774, at 11 o'clock A.M. She died September ——, 1775.

A son, born May 28, 1777, at 10 o'clock P.M. Died June 14, at 10 o'clock and 20 minutes P.M.

Mary Jefferson, born August 1, 1778, at 1 o'clock and 30 minutes A.M. Died April 17, 1804, between 8 and 9 A.M.

A daughter, born in Richmond, November 3, 1780, at 10 o'clock and 45 minutes P.M. Died April 15, 1781, at 10 o'clock A.M.

Lucy Elizabeth Jefferson, born May 8, 1782, at 1 o'clock A.M. Died ——, 1784.[24]

Dreadful suspense closed by catastrophe

Mrs. Jefferson has added [May 8, 1782] another daughter to our family. She has been ever since and still continues very dangerously ill.[25]

My history ... would have been as happy a one as I could have asked could the objects of my affection have been immortal. But all the favors of fortune have been embittered by domestic losses. Of six children I have lost four, and finally their mother [Mrs. Jefferson died September 6, 1782].[26]

Your friendly letters [those of Chastellux] found me a little emerging from the stupor of mind which had rendered me as dead to the world as she was whose loss occasioned it. Your letter recalled to my memory that there were persons still living of much value to me. If you should have thought me remiss ... you will, I am sure, ascribe it to its true cause, the state of dreadful suspense in which I had been kept all the summer, and the catastrophe which closed it. Before that event my scheme of life had been determined. I had ... rested all prospects of future happiness on domestic and literary objects. A single event wiped away all my plans, and left me a blank which I had not the spirits to fill up.[27]

Loving advice to a motherless daughter

The conviction that you [Martha] would be more improved in the situation I have placed you than if still with me, has solaced me on my parting with you, which my love for you has rendered a difficult thing. The acquirements which I hope you will make under the tutors I have provided for you will render you more worthy of my love; and if they cannot increase it, they will prevent its diminution. Consider the good lady who has taken you under her roof . . . as your mother, as the only person to whom, since the loss with which Heaven has pleased to afflict you, you can now look up; and that her displeasure or disapprobation, on any occasion, will be an immense misfortune, which, should you be so unhappy as to incur by any unguarded act, think no concession too much to regain her good-will.

With respect to the distribution of your time, the following is what I should approve:

From 8 to 10, practice music.

From 10 to 1, dance one day and draw another.

From 1 to 2, draw on the day you dance, and write a letter next day.

From 3 to 4, read French.

From 4 to 5, exercise yourself in music.

From 5 till bedtime, read English, write, etc. . . .

I expect you will write me by every post. Inform me what books you read, what tunes you learn, and enclose me your best copy of every lesson in drawing. . . . Take care that you never spell a word wrong. Always before you write a word consider how it is spelt, and, if you do not remember it, turn to a dictionary. It produces great praise to a lady to spell well.

I have placed my happiness on seeing you good and accomplished, and no distress this world can now bring on me would equal that of your disappointing my hopes. If you love me, then strive to be good under every situation and to all living creatures, and to acquire those accomplishments which I have put in your power, and which will go far towards insuring you the warmest love of your affectionate father.[28]

Good taste, and the graver sciences

I omitted [dear Martha] to advise you on the subject of dress. . . .
I do not wish you to be gaily clothed at this time of life [she was
then eleven years old], but that what you wear should be fine of
its kind. But, above all things, and at all times, let your clothes be
clean, whole, and properly put on. . . . Nothing is so disgusting to
our sex as a want of cleanliness and delicacy in yours. I hope,
therefore, the moment you rise from bed your first work will be to
dress yourself in such style as that you may be seen by any gentleman without his being able to discover a pin amiss or any other
circumstance of neatness wanting.[29]

The plan of reading which I have formed for [Martha] is considerably different from that which I think would be most proper
for her sex in any other country than America. I am obliged to
extend my views beyond herself, and consider her as the head of a
little family of her own. The chance that in marriage she will draw
a blockhead I calculate at about fourteen to one, and of course that
the education of her family will probably rest on her own ideas and
directions without assistance. With the poets and prose writers I
shall therefore combine a certain extent of reading in the graver
sciences. However . . . her time in Philadelphia will be chiefly
occupied in acquiring a little taste and execution in such of the fine
arts as she could not prosecute to equal advantage in a more retired situation.[30]

Source of happiness henceforth

You ask me to write you long letters. I will do it, my dear
[Martha], on condition you will read them from time to time, and
practice what they inculcate. Their precepts will be dictated by
experience, by a perfect knowledge of the situation in which you
will be placed, and by the fondest love for you. This it is which
makes me wish to see you more qualified than common. My expectations from you are high, yet not higher than you may attain.
Industry and resolution are all that are wanting. Nobody in this
world can make me so happy, or so miserable, as you. . . . To your
sister [Mary] and yourself I look to render the evening of my life
serene and contented. Its morning has been clouded by loss after
loss, till I have nothing left but you.[31]

CHAPTER III

Revolutionist

THOMAS JEFFERSON began his political career in 1769, and he began it characteristically by striking a blow for freedom. He was twenty-six, a lawyer of two years' standing, when at his first session in the colonial House of Burgesses he attempted to make it legally possible for owners to emancipate their slaves. Jefferson did not succeed. Indeed, nothing liberal could expect success, he tells us, under the imperial system of George the Third and his Tory ministers, to whose unwarrantable assumptions of right over British America he traces the seeds of the Revolutionary War.

At this same session a step towards the American Revolution was taken when Jefferson and his fellow burgesses committed Virginia, the largest and most populous of the colonies, to the support of Massachusetts in opposition to the Townsend revenue acts. These parliamentary duties on tea and other imports had reopened the controversy over taxation begun by the Stamp Act of 1765. At Williamsburg the burgesses defiantly asserted the right of self-taxation, the right to petition for redress of grievances, and the right of the colonies to unite in such petitions. Lord Botetourt, the royal governor, promptly dissolved the assembly. But on the next day young Jefferson and his colleagues met in the Apollo Room of the Raleigh Tavern, and there they pledged themselves to a boycott of British imports until the offensive acts were repealed.

This was the first of many such rebellious meetings in the Raleigh Tavern, where in carefree days Jefferson had danced with Rebecca Burwell. During these years of protest against the continuing encroachments of Tory Britain, the younger and more radical burgesses were led by Patrick Henry, with his Homeric oratory, and by young Jefferson, with his scholarly and eloquent pen. Jefferson's famous pamphlet of 1774, *A Summary View of the Rights of British America*, was the boldest declaration of American rights that had yet been written. Even the Virginia convention found it much too radical. Yet within two years Jefferson was to give its philosophy classic expression in the Declaration of Independence.

In his *Summary View* the young lawyer from Albemarle cut through the murky fog of legalistic quibbling and bluntly denied Parliament any control whatsoever over the colonies. Exercising their natural rights, he declared, the colonists had migrated to the New World and there set up governments independent of Parliament. Since their only bond with Britain was a common executive in the person of the king, all British laws touching American trade and manufactures were wanton assaults upon natural and constitutional rights. Jefferson specified these parliamentary usurpations, and against King George himself he listed grievances which were later to appear in the Declaration of Independence. In forthright and eloquent language he admonished and warned and threatened George the Third that unless these acts were revoked, and unless these grievances ceased, he would suffer the loss of his American dominions.

This widely read pamphlet was soon followed by Jefferson's *Reply to Lord North*, another masterly expression of American rights, in which he rejected the unsatisfactory proposals of King George's prime minister. These writings brought him to the forefront of Revolutionary politics. When he entered the Continental Congress at Philadelphia in 1775, his colleagues promptly called upon him to help draft a declaration of the causes and necessity of taking up arms. Blood in defense of American rights had already been shed. New England's embattled farmers were then besieging the British troops in Boston. Although Jefferson's ideas were again considered too radical, some of them were incorporated in the draft finally prepared by John Dickinson of Pennsylvania. The concluding paragraphs, which Jefferson claimed as his own, were thoroughly Jeffersonian in tone and style and force; and it was these concluding paragraphs which inspired the American troops encamped about Boston to shout out their approval in 'thundering huzzas.'

Meanwhile the skirmishes at Lexington and Concord had been followed by the battle of Bunker Hill. And in Virginia the royal governor, Lord Dunmore, had commenced hostilities, attempted to incite the slaves to revolt, and conducted himself in such a brutal and provocative manner as to arouse Jefferson's compatriots to 'a perfect frenzy.' In especially revealing letters to John Randolph, a Tory kinsman, Jefferson had expressed his hope that the wisdom of Great Britain would 'ere long put an end to this unnatural contest.' But all hopes of reconciliation were rudely crushed. A bloody campaign was about to open. 'Under the fostering hand' of George the Third a fight for redress of grievances was fast changing into a war for independence. Such was the situation in the fall of 1775, as described by the young Virginian, who six years before had entered the colonial House of Burgesses and struck his first blow at the imperial system of George the Third.

Politics in the royal colony of Virginia

In 1769 I became a member of the legislature by the choice of the county in which I live, and so continued until it was closed by the Revolution. I made one effort in that body for the permission of the emancipation of slaves, which was rejected, and indeed during the regal government nothing liberal could expect success. Our minds were circumscribed within narrow limits by a habitual belief that it was our duty to be subordinate to the mother country in all matters of government, to direct all our labors in subservience to her interests, and even to observe a bigoted intolerance for all religions but hers.

The difficulties with our representatives were of habit and despair, not of reflection and conviction. Experience soon proved that they could bring their minds to rights on the first summons of their attention. But the King's Council, which acted as another house of legislature, held their places at will, and were in most humble obedience to that will; the Governor too, who had a negative on our laws, held by the same tenure, and with still greater devotedness to it; and, last of all, the Royal negative closed the last door to every hope of amelioration.[1]

The seeds of war

The seeds of the war are here traced to their true source. The Tory education of the King was the first preparation for that change in the British government which that party never ceases to wish. This naturally insured Tory administrations during his life. At the moment he came to the throne ... the assumptions of unwarrantable right over America commenced. They were so signal, and followed one another so close, as to prove they were part of a system either to reduce it under absolute subjection, and thereby make it an instrument for attempts on Britain itself, or to sever it from Britain so that it might not be a weight in the Whig scale. This latter alternative, however, was not considered as the one which would take place. They knew so little of America that they thought it unable to encounter the little finger of Great Britain.[2]

The question, who commenced the Revolution? is as difficult as that of the first inventors of a thousand good things. For example, who first discovered the principle of gravity? Not Newton; for Galileo, who died the year Newton was born, had measured its force in the descent of gravid bodies. ... The fact is that one new idea leads to another, that to a third, and so on through a course of time until someone, with whom no one of these ideas was original, combines all together and produces what is justly called a new invention.

I suppose it would be as difficult to trace our Revolution to its first embryo. ... The truth, I suppose, is that the opposition in every colony began whenever the encroachment was presented to it. This question of priority is as the inquiry would be, who first of the three hundred Spartans offered his name to Leonidas?[3]

Young radicals seize command

In May, 1769, a meeting of the General Assembly was called by the Governor, Lord Botetourt, ... and to that meeting became known the joint resolutions and address of the Lords and Commons of 1768–9, on the proceedings in Massachusetts. Counter-resolutions and an address to the King by the House of Burgesses were agreed to with little opposition, and a spirit manifestly displayed itself of considering the cause of Massachusetts as a common one. The Governor dissolved us, but we met the next day in the Apollo [Room] of the Raleigh Tavern, formed ourselves into a voluntary convention, drew up articles of association against the use of any merchandise imported from Great Britain, signed and recommended them to the people, repaired to our several counties, and were re-elected without any other exception than of the very few who had declined assent to our proceedings.

Nothing of particular excitement occurring for a considerable time, our countrymen seemed to fall into a state of insensibility to our situation. The duty on tea, not yet repealed, and the Declaratory Act of a right in the British Parliament to bind us by their laws in all cases whatsoever still suspended over us. But a court of inquiry held in Rhode Island in 1772, with a power to send persons to England to be tried for offenses committed here, was considered at our session of the spring of 1773 as demanding attention.

Not thinking our old and leading members up to the point of forwardness and zeal which the times required, Mr. [Patrick] Henry, Richard Henry Lee, Francis L. Lee, Mr. [Dabney] Carr and myself agreed to meet in the evening, in a private room of the Raleigh, to consult on the state of things. There may have been a member or two more whom I do not recollect.

For continental unity of action

We were all sensible that the most urgent of all measures was that of coming to an understanding with all the other colonies to consider the British claims as a common cause to all, and to produce a unity of action; and, for this purpose, that a committee of correspondence in each colony would be the best instrument for intercommunication and that their first measure would probably be to propose a meeting of deputies from every colony, at some central place, who should be charged with the direction of the measures which should be taken by all.

We, therefore, drew up . . . resolutions. . . . The consulting members proposed to me to move them, but I urged that it should be done by Mr. Carr, my friend and brother-in-law, then a new member, to whom I wished an opportunity should be given of making known to the house his great worth and talents. It was so agreed; he moved them, they were agreed to *nem. con.*, and a committee of correspondence appointed of whom Peyton Randolph, the speaker, was chairman. The Governor (then Lord Dunmore) dissolved us, but the committee met the next day, prepared a circular letter to the speakers of the other colonies, inclosing to each a copy of the resolutions, and left it in charge with their chairman to forward them by expresses....

The technique of revolution

The next event which excited our sympathies for Massachusetts was the Boston Port Bill, by which that port was to be shut up on the 1st of June, 1774. This arrived while we were in session in the spring of that year.

The lead in the House on these subjects being no longer left to the old members, Mr. Henry, R. H. Lee, Fr. L. Lee, three or four other members whom I do not recollect, and myself, agreeing that we must boldly take an unequivocal stand in the line with Massachusetts, determined to meet and consult on the proper measures in the council-chamber, for the benefit of the library in that room. We were under conviction of the necessity of arousing our people from the lethargy into which they had fallen as to passing events, and thought that the appointment of a day of general fasting and prayer would be most likely to call up and alarm their attention.

No example of such a solemnity had existed since the days of our distresses in the war of '55, since which a new generation had grown up. With the help therefore of Rushworth [compiler of documents relative to the English civil war of 1642–1649 between Charles I and Parliament], whom we rummaged over for the revolutionary precedents and forms of the Puritans of that day preserved by him, we cooked up a resolution, somewhat modernizing their phrases, for appointing the 1st day of June, on which the Port Bill was to commence, for a day of fasting, humiliation, and prayer to implore Heaven to avert from us the evils of civil war, to inspire us with firmness in support of our rights, and to turn the hearts of the King and Parliament to moderation and justice.

To give greater emphasis to our proposition, we agreed to wait the next morning on Mr. [Robert Carter] Nicholas, whose grave and religious character was more in unison with the tone of our resolution, and to solicit him to move it. We accordingly went to him in the morning. He moved it the same day; the 1st of June was proposed; and it passed without opposition. The Governor dissolved us, as usual.

Like a shock of electricity

We retired to the Apollo, as before, agreed to an association, and instructed the committee of correspondence to propose to the corresponding committees of the other colonies to appoint deputies to meet in Congress at such place, *annually*, as should be convenient, to direct from time to time the measures required by the general interest; and we declared that an attack on any one colony should be considered as an attack on the whole. This was in May [of 1774]. We further recommended to the several counties to elect deputies to meet at Williamsburg the 1st of August ensuing, to consider the state of the colony, and particularly to appoint delegates to a general Congress, should that measure be acceded to by the committees of correspondence generally. It was acceded to; Philadelphia was appointed for the place, and the 5th of September for the time of the meeting.

We returned home and in our several counties invited the clergy to meet assemblies of the people on the 1st of June to perform the ceremonies of the day, and to address to them discourses suited to the occasion. The people met generally, with anxiety and alarm in their countenances, and the effect of the day through the whole colony was like a shock of electricity, arousing every man and placing him erect and solidly on his centre. They chose, universally, delegates for the convention. Being elected one for my own county, I prepared a draught of instructions to be given to the delegates whom we should send to the Congress, which I meant to propose at our meeting.

Basic rights of British America

In this I took the ground that, from the beginning, I had thought the only one orthodox or tenable, which was that the relation between Great Britain and these colonies was exactly the same as that of England and Scotland after the accession of James and until the union, and the same as her present relations with Hanover, having the same executive chief but no other necessary political connection; and that our emigration from England to this country gave her no more rights over us than the emigrations of the Danes and Saxons gave to the present authorities of the mother country over England.

In this doctrine, however, I had never been able to get anyone to agree with me but Mr. Wythe. He concurred in it from the first dawn of the question, What was the political relation between us and England? Our other patriots, Randolph, the Lees, Nicholas, Pendleton, stopped at the half-way house of John Dickinson, who admitted that England had a right to regulate our commerce and to lay duties on it for the purposes of regulation but not of raising revenue. But for this ground there was no foundation in compact in any acknowledged principles of colonization nor in reason, expatriation being a natural right and acted on as such by all nations in all ages.

I set out for Williamsburg some days before that appointed for our meeting, but was taken ill of a dysentery on the road and was unable to proceed. I sent on, therefore, to Williamsburg two copies of my draught, the one under cover to Peyton Randolph, who I knew would be in the chair of the convention, the other to Patrick Henry. Whether Mr. Henry disapproved the ground taken, or was too lazy to read it (for he was the laziest man in reading I ever knew) I never learned, but he communicated it to nobody.

Peyton Randolph informed the convention he had received such a paper from a member prevented by sickness from offering it in his place, and he laid it on the table for perusal. It was read generally by the members, approved by many, though thought too bold for the present state of things; but they printed it in pamphlet form under the title of 'A Summary View of the Rights of British America.' [4]

The God who gave us life gave us liberty

These are our grievances [concluded Jefferson's *Summary View*], which we have thus laid before his Majesty with that freedom of language and sentiment which becomes a free people claiming their rights as derived from the laws of nature and not as the gift of their Chief Magistrate. Let those flatter who fear; it is not an American art. To give praise where it is not due might be well from the venal, but would ill beseem those who are asserting the rights of human nature. They know, and will therefore say, that Kings are the servants, not the proprietors of the people. Open your breast, Sire, to liberal and expanded thought. Let not the name of George the Third be a blot on the page of history.... The whole art of government consists in the art of being honest. Only aim to do your duty, and mankind will give you credit where you fail. No longer persevere in sacrificing the rights of one part of the empire to the inordinate desires of another; but deal out to all equal and impartial right. Let no act be passed by any one legislature which may infringe on the rights and liberties of another.

This is the important post in which fortune has placed you, holding the balance of a great, if a well-poised empire. This, Sire, is the advice of your great American council, on the observance of which may perhaps depend your felicity and future fame and the preservation of that harmony which alone can continue, both to Great Britain and America, the reciprocal advantages of their connection.

It is neither our wish nor our interest to separate from her. We are willing, on our part, to sacrifice everything which reason can ask to the restoration of that tranquillity for which all must wish. On their part, let them be ready to establish union on a generous plan. Let them name their terms, but let them be just. Accept of every commercial preference it is in our power to give, for such things as we can raise for their use, or they make for ours. But let them not think to exclude us from going to other markets to dispose of those commodities which they cannot use, nor to supply those wants which they cannot supply. Still less let it be proposed that our properties, within our own territories, shall be taxed or regulated by any power on earth but our own. The God who gave us life gave us liberty at the same time; the hand of force may destroy but cannot disjoin them.

This, Sire, is our last, our determined resolution. And that you will be pleased to interpose, with that efficacy which your earnest endeavors may insure, to procure redress of these our great grievances, to quiet the minds of your subjects in British America against any apprehensions of future encroachment, to establish fraternal love and harmony through the whole empire, and that that may continue to the latest ages of time, is the fervent prayer of all British America.[5]

For this pamphlet, 'honored' as an arch rebel

It found its way to England, was taken up by the opposition, interpolated a little by Mr. [Edmund] Burke so as to make it answer opposition purposes, and in that form ran rapidly through several editions. . . . I was informed afterwards by Peyton Randolph that it had procured me the honor of having my name inserted in a long list of proscriptions, enrolled in a bill of attainder commenced in one of the Houses of Parliament but suppressed in embryo by the hasty step of events, which warned them to be a little cautious. . . . The names, I think, were about twenty which he repeated to me, but I recollect those only of Hancock, the two Adamses, Peyton Randolph himself, Patrick Henry, and myself.

The convention met on the 1st of August, renewed their association, appointed delegates to the [Continental] Congress, gave them instructions very temperately and properly expressed both as to style and matter, and they repaired to Philadelphia at the time appointed. The splendid proceedings of that Congress at their first session belong to general history, are known to every one, and need not therefore be noted here. They terminated their session on the 26th of October, to meet again on the 10th of May ensuing.

The convention at their ensuing session of March, '75 approved of the proceedings of Congress, thanked their delegates, and reappointed the same persons to represent the colony at the meeting to be held in May; and foreseeing the probability that Peyton Randolph, their president, and speaker also of the House of Burgesses, might be called off, they added me, in that event, to the delegation.[6]

Meanwhile at Lexington and Concord the die is cast

Within this week [May 7, 1775] we have received the unhappy news of an action of considerable magnitude between the King's troops and our brethren of Boston, in which it is said five hundred of the former, with the Earl of Percy, are slain. . . . This accident has cut off our last hope of reconciliation, and a frenzy of revenge seems to have seized all ranks of people. It is a lamentable circumstance that the only mediatory power acknowledged by both parties, instead of leading to a reconciliation his divided people, should pursue the incendiary purpose of still blowing up the flames, as we find him constantly doing in every speech and declaration. This may, perhaps, be intended to intimidate into acquiescence, but the effect has been most unfortunately otherwise. . . .

When I saw Lord Chatham's bill I entertained high hope that a reconciliation could have been brought about. . . . But the dignity of Parliament, it seems, can brook no opposition to its power. Strange that a set of men who have made sale of their virtue to the Minister should yet talk of retaining dignity! [7]

Victorious over timid, cold-water men

Mr. Randolph was, according to expectation, obliged to leave the chair of Congress to attend the General Assembly summoned by Lord Dunmore to meet on the 1st day of June, 1775. Lord North's conciliatory propositions, as they were called, had been received by the Governor, and furnished the subject for which this assembly was convened. Mr. Randolph accordingly attended, and the tenor of these propositions being generally known as having been addressed to all the governors, he was anxious that the answer of our assembly, likely to be the first, should harmonize with what he knew to be the sentiments and wishes of the body he had recently left. He feared that Mr. Nicholas, whose mind was not yet up to the mark of the times, would undertake the answer, and therefore pressed me to prepare it.

I did so, and with his aid carried it through the House, with long and doubtful scruples from Mr. Nicholas and James Mercer and a dash of cold water on it here and there enfeebling it somewhat, but finally with unanimity, or a vote approaching it. This being passed, I repaired immediately to Philadelphia and conveyed to Congress the first notice they had of it. It was entirely approved there.

I took my seat with them on the 21st of June. On the 24th a committee which had been appointed to prepare a declaration of the causes of taking up arms brought in their report (drawn, I

believe, by John Rutledge) which, not being liked, the House re-
committed it on the 26th and added Mr. [John] Dickinson and
myself to the committee. . . . I prepared a draught of the declaration committed to us. It was too strong for Mr. Dickinson. He
still retained the hope of reconciliation with the mother country
and was unwilling it should be lessened by offensive statements.
He was so honest a man, and so able a one, that he was greatly
indulged even by those who could not feel his scruples. We therefore requested him to take the paper and put it into a form he
could approve. He did so, preparing an entire new statement and
preserving of the former only the last four paragraphs and half of
the preceding one. We approved and reported it to Congress, who
accepted it.[8]

Why we take up arms

We are reduced to the alternative of choosing an unconditional
submission to the tyranny of irritated ministers, or resistance by
force. The latter is our choice. [Thus began Jefferson's paragraphs
in the Declaration of the Causes and Necessity of Taking up Arms,
of July 6, 1775.] We have counted the cost of this contest, and find
nothing so dreadful as voluntary slavery. Honor, justice, and
humanity forbid us tamely to surrender that freedom which we
received from our gallant ancestors, and which our innocent
posterity have a right to receive from us. We cannot endure the
infamy and guilt of resigning succeeding generations to that
wretchedness which inevitably awaits them if we basely entail
hereditary bondage upon them.

Our cause is just. Our union is perfect. Our internal resources
are great, and, if necessary, foreign assistance is undoubtedly attainable. We gratefully acknowledge, as signal instances of the
Divine favor towards us, that His Providence would not permit us
to be called into this severe controversy until we were grown up to
our present strength, had been previously exercised in warlike
operation, and possessed of the means of defending ourselves.
With hearts fortified with these animating reflections, we most
solemnly, before God and the world, declare that, exerting the utmost energy of those powers which our beneficent Creator hath
graciously bestowed upon us, the arms we have been compelled
by our enemies to assume we will, in defiance of every hazard, with

unabating firmness and perseverance, employ for the preservation
of our liberties; being with one mind resolved to die freemen rather
than to live slaves.

We fight not for glory or conquest

Lest this declaration should disquiet the minds of our friends and
fellow-subjects in any part of the empire, we assure them that we
mean not to dissolve that union which has so long and so happily
subsisted between us and which we sincerely wish to see restored.
Necessity has not yet driven us into that desperate measure, or
induced us to excite any other nation to war against them. We
have not raised armies with ambitious designs of separating from
Great Britain and establishing independent states. We fight not
for glory or for conquest. We exhibit to mankind the remarkable
spectacle of a people attacked by unprovoked enemies, without
any imputation or even suspicion of offense. They boast of their
privileges and civilization, and yet proffer no milder conditions than
servitude or death.

In our native land, in defense of the freedom that is our birth-
right and which we ever enjoyed till the late violation of it; for the
protection of our property, acquired solely by the honest industry
of our forefathers and ourselves; against violence actually offered;
we have taken up arms. We shall lay them down when hostilities
shall cease on the part of the aggressors and all danger of their
being renewed shall be removed, and not before.

With a humble confidence in the mercies of the supreme and
impartial Judge and Ruler of the Universe, we most devoutly implore His divine goodness to protect us happily through this great
conflict, to dispose our adversaries to reconciliation on reasonable
terms, and thereby to relieve the empire from the calamities of
civil war.[9]

Bunker Hill and those intrepid Yankees

Our accounts of the battle . . . have become clear, and greatly to
our satisfaction. Contrary to what usually happens, the first accounts were below truth; and it is now certain that the regulars
have had between 1200 and 1400 killed and wounded in that engagement, and that of these 500 were killed. Major Pitcairn is
among the slain, at which everybody rejoices, as he was the com-

manding officer at Lexington, was the first who fired his own piece there and gave the command to fire. . . .

The New Englanders are fitting out light vessels of war, by which it is hoped we shall not only clear the seas and bays here of everything below the size of a ship of war, but that they will visit the coasts of Europe and distress the British trade in every part of the world. The adventurous genius and intrepidity of those people is amazing. They are now intent on burning Boston as a hive which gives cover to regulars; and none are more bent upon it than the very people who came out of it and whose prosperity lies there.[10]

To a Tory friend: will it be everlasting avulsion?

I am sorry the situation of our country should render it not eligible to you to remain longer in it [wrote Jefferson to John Randolph in August of 1775]. I hope the returning wisdom of Great Britain will ere long put an end to this unnatural contest. There may be people to whose tempers and dispositions contention is pleasing and who, therefore, wish a continuance of confusion, but to me it is of all states but one the most horrid. My first wish is a restoration of our just rights; my second, a return of the happy period when, consistently with duty, I may withdraw myself totally from the public stage and pass the rest of my days in domestic ease and tranquillity, banishing every desire of ever hearing what passes in the world. Perhaps (for the latter adds considerably to the warmth of the former wish), looking with fondness towards a reconciliation with Great Britain, I cannot help hoping you may be able to contribute towards expediting this good work. . . .

I wish no false sense of honor, no ignorance of our real intentions, no vain hope that partial concessions of right will be accepted, may induce the Ministry to trifle with accommodation till it shall be out of their power ever to accommodate. If, indeed, Great Britain disjoined from her colonies be a match for the most potent nations of Europe, with the colonies thrown into their scale they may go on securely. But if they are not assured of this, it would be certainly unwise, by trying the event of another campaign, to risk our accepting a foreign aid which, perhaps, may not be obtainable but on condition of everlasting avulsion from Great Britain.

This would be thought a hard condition to those who still wish for reunion with their parent country. I am sincerely one of those, and would rather be in dependence on Great Britain, properly limited, than on any nation on earth, or than on no nation. But I am one of those, too, who, rather than submit to the rights of legislating for us assumed by the British Parliament, and which late experience has shown they will so cruelly exercise, would lend my hand to sink the whole Island in the ocean.[11]

I speak the sentiments of America

You will have heard, before this reaches you, that Lord Dunmore has commenced hostilities in Virginia [he wrote John Randolph in November of 1775]. That people bore with everything till he attempted to burn the town of Hampton. They opposed and repelled him, with considerable loss on his side and none on ours. It has raised our countrymen into a perfect frenzy. It is an immense misfortune to the whole empire to have a King of such a disposition at such a time. We are told, and everything proves it true, that he is the bitterest enemy we have. . . . In an earlier part of this contest our petitions told him that from our King there was but one appeal. The admonition was despised, and that appeal forced on us. To undo his empire he has but one truth more to learn, that after colonies have drawn the sword there is but one step more they can take. That step is now pressed upon us by the measures adopted, as if they were afraid we would not take it.

Believe me, dear sir, there is not in the British Empire a man who more cordially loves a union with Great Britain than I do. But by the God that made me, I will cease to exist before I yield to a connection on such terms as the British Parliament propose; and in this I think I speak the sentiments of America.

We want neither inducement nor power to declare and assert a separation. It is will alone which is wanting, and that is growing apace under the fostering hand of our King. One bloody campaign will probably decide, everlastingly, our future course; and I am sorry to find a bloody campaign is decided on. If our winds and waters should not combine to rescue their shores from slavery, and General Howe's reinforcements should arrive in safety, we have hopes he will be inspirited to come out of Boston and take another drubbing; and we must drub him soundly before the sceptred tyrant will know we are not mere brutes, to crouch under his hand and kiss the rod with which he designs to scourge us.[12]

CHAPTER IV

Liberty and the Pursuit of Happiness

IMPELLED by provocative events, the movement for independence gathered headway during the winter of 1775–1776. Brushing aside 'olive branch petitions,' King George and his Tory Parliament declared the colonists in a state of rebellion, prohibited all trade with them, bombarded and burned their seaport towns, and hired German mercenaries to assist in crushing them into submission. The Americans were no less aggressive. They captured the forts of Ticonderoga and Crown Point, invaded Canada, and compelled Sir William Howe to evacuate the town of Boston. By May of 1776 the British colonies, led by Virginia, were snapping the last political ties with Great Britain and transforming themselves into American commonwealths.

After a year of civil war, and after a decade of unavailing protest, Jefferson and the other radicals in the Continental Congress at Philadelphia now pressed for a clear-cut declaration of American independence. The Virginia delegation brought the great question to a head on June 7, 1776, when it moved 'that these United Colonies are, and of right ought to be, free and independent states.' Since the debates revealed that some of the colonies 'were not yet ripe for falling from the parent stem,' as Jefferson noted, the momentous decision was not made until July 2. Meanwhile a committee of five was appointed to prepare a formal Declaration of Independence. On this committee were such eminent men as the venerable Benjamin Franklin and John Adams, the fiery Whig from Massachusetts. Its chairman was Thomas Jefferson, who had just turned thirty-three.

Why was so young a man placed at the head of so important a committee, and why did his colleagues unanimously insist that he alone should undertake the drafting of the Great Declaration? Because Jefferson already had 'the reputation of a masterly pen,' answered John Adams; 'a reputation for literature, science, and a happy talent of composition.' The tall, raw-boned, clear-eyed Virginian who had entered Congress the year before was modest, reserved, and no orator, said Adams. But 'he was so frank, explicit, and decisive upon committees and in conversation, . . . that he soon seized upon my heart.' Young Jefferson's *Summary View of the Rights of British America* and his other writings were eloquent evidence of his radical Whig principles. Above all, everything he wrote was distinguished by a 'peculiar felicity of expression.'

In felicitous and imperishable prose the Declaration drafted by Jefferson and approved by Congress on July 4, 1776, announced the birth of a nation, listed the causes which brought it into being, and set forth the democratic philosophy which not only justified the embattled patriots of '76 but henceforth was to inspire Americans and all liberty-loving peoples who would fight and die if necessary for man's 'inalienable rights.' With clarity and succinctness Jefferson formulated the basic 'self-evident truths' upon which rested the Revolution and the new American republic. And he expressed these fundamental principles in ringing phrases which stirred, and would always stir, the American soul to its very depths.

Congress made a few changes in the wording of the Declaration and struck out several passages in Jefferson's long indictment of George the Third, among them his arraignment of the King for perpetuating the American slavetrade. The young author, as he tells us, writhed a little under criticism, but he was comforted by Doctor Franklin's amusing story of John Thompson, the Hatter. It was a story which Jefferson liked to tell in later years, when a proud and grateful American people treasured every incident and object associated with the Declaration of Independence.

An insight into Jefferson's everyday life during this period is given by the items in his account book, items for punch at the taverns, strings for his fiddle and toys and a doll for his daughter, maps, writing paper, a new thermometer for his daily weather observations, and a straw hat to withstand the June sun. His reminiscences about drafting the Declaration on a portable desk, of his own design, in his lodgings in the house of a Philadelphia bricklayer are likewise revealing of the small things of those momentous days when the American Charter of Freedom was being written and debated, and men bravely pledged their lives, their fortunes, and their sacred honor.

Later in life, when John Adams and Timothy Pickering of Massachusetts stated that the sentiments of the Declaration had been for two years 'hackneyed in Congress,' Jefferson said his aim had not been originality of principles but 'an expression of the American mind.' In this he succeeded most admirably. His raw materials were ideas of natural rights which had often been expressed, by John Locke, James Otis, and by many other political writers. With great literary skill he fused these raw materials into a statement of principles, a creed of Americanism, which was truly 'the genuine effusion of the soul of our country.' It was also characteristically Jeffersonian. Man's right to 'life, liberty, and property,' for example, had become a commonplace expression of Revolutionary pamphleteers. But in the Great Declaration drafted by Thomas Jefferson, who was always to put human rights above property rights, the expression significantly was transformed into 'life, liberty, and the pursuit of happiness.'

Shall America now declare herself independent?

On the 15th of May, 1776, the convention of Virginia instructed their delegates in Congress to propose to that body to declare the colonies independent of Great Britain, and appointed a committee to prepare a declaration of rights and plan of government.

In Congress, Friday, June 7, 1776. The delegates from Virginia moved, in obedience to instructions from their constituents, that the Congress should declare that these United Colonies are, and of right ought to be, free and independent states, that they are absolved from all allegiance to the British crown, and that all political connection between them and the state of Great Britain is, and ought to be, totally dissolved; that measures should be immediately taken for procuring the assistance of foreign powers, and a Confederation be formed to bind the colonies more closely together.

The House being obliged to attend at that time to some other business, the proposition was referred to the next day, when the members were ordered to attend punctually at ten o'clock.

Saturday, June 8. They proceeded to take it into consideration and referred it to a committee of the whole, into which they immediately resolved themselves, and passed that day and Monday, the 10th, in debating the subject.

It was argued by Wilson, Robert R. Livingston, Edward Rutledge, Dickinson, and others that, though they were friends to the measures themselves and saw the impossibility that we should ever again be united with Great Britain, yet they were against adopting them at this time. . . .

On the other side, it was urged by John Adams, Lee, Wythe, and others, that no gentleman had argued against the policy or the right of separation from Britain, nor had supposed it possible we should ever renew our connection; that they had only opposed its being now declared. . . .

Drafting the Declaration

It appearing in the course of these debates that the colonies of New York, New Jersey, Pennsylvania, Delaware, Maryland, and South Carolina were not yet matured for falling from the parent stem, but that they were fast advancing to that state, it was thought most prudent to wait a while for them, and to postpone the final decision to July 1st; but, that this might occasion as little delay as possible, a committee was appointed to prepare a Declaration of Independence. The committee were John Adams, Dr. Franklin, Roger Sherman, Robert R. Livingston, and myself. Committees were also appointed, at the same time, to prepare a plan of confederation for the colonies, and to state the terms proper to be proposed for foreign alliance.

The committee for drawing the Declaration of Independence desired me to do it. It was accordingly done, and being approved by them, I reported it to the House on Friday, the 28th of June, when it was read and ordered to lie on the table.[1]

The committee of five met; no such thing as a subcommittee was proposed, but they unanimously pressed on myself alone to undertake the draught. I consented; I drew it, but before I reported it to the committee, I communicated it *separately* to Dr. Franklin and Mr. Adams, requesting their corrections, because they were the two members of whose judgments and amendments I wished most to have the benefit before presenting it to the committee. ... Their alterations were two or three only, and merely verbal. I then wrote a fair copy, reported it to the committee, and from them, unaltered, to Congress.[2]

Independence decided upon, July 2, 1776

On Monday, the 1st of July, the House resolved itself into a committee of the whole and resumed the consideration of the original motion made by the delegates from Virginia, which, being again debated through the day, was carried in the affirmative by the votes of New Hampshire, Connecticut, Massachusetts, Rhode Island, New Jersey, Maryland, Virginia, North Carolina, and Georgia. South Carolina and Pennsylvania voted against it. Delaware had but two members present, and they were divided. The delegates from New York declared they were for it themselves, and were assured their constituents were for it, but that their instructions having been drawn near a twelvemonth before, when reconciliation was still the general object, they were enjoined by them to do nothing which should impede that object. ...

The committee rose and reported their resolution to the House. Mr. Edward Rutledge of South Carolina then requested the determination might be put off to the next day, as he believed his colleagues, though they disapproved of the resolution, would then join in it for the sake of unanimity. The ultimate question, whether the House would agree to the resolution of the committee, was accordingly postponed to the next day [July 2], when it was again moved, and South Carolina concurred in voting for it. In the meantime a third member had come post from the Delaware counties, and turned the vote of that colony in favor of the resolution. Members of a different sentiment attending that morning from Pennsylvania also, her vote was changed, so that the whole twelve colonies who were authorized to vote at all gave their voices for it; and within a few days the convention of New York approved of it and thus supplied the void occasioned by the withdrawing of her delegates from the vote.

The Declaration approved on July 4th

Congress proceeded the same day to consider the Declaration of Independence, which had been reported and lain on the table the Friday preceding, and on Monday referred to a committee of the whole.

The pusillanimous idea that we had friends in England worth keeping terms with still haunted the minds of many. For this reason those passages which conveyed censures on the people of England were struck out, lest they should give them offence. The clause, too, reprobating the enslaving the inhabitants of Africa was struck out in complaisance to South Carolina and Georgia, who had never attempted to restrain the importation of slaves, and who, on the contrary, still wished to continue it. Our Northern brethren also, I believe, felt a little tender under those censures; for though their people had very few slaves themselves, yet they had been pretty considerable carriers of them to others.

The debates, having taken up the greater parts of the 2d, 3d, and 4th days of July, were, on the evening of the last, closed; the Declaration was reported by the committee [and] agreed to by the House. . . .

The Declaration as written and as approved

As the sentiments of men are known not only by what they receive, but what they reject also, I will state the form of the Declaration as originally reported. The parts struck out by Congress shall be distinguished by [brackets] and those inserted by them shall be [distinguished by italics]:

A DECLARATION BY THE REPRESENTATIVES OF THE UNITED STATES OF AMERICA, IN [GENERAL] CONGRESS ASSEMBLED

When in the course of human events it becomes necessary for one people to dissolve the political bands which have connected them with another, and to assume among the powers of the earth the separate and equal station to which the laws of nature and of nature's God entitle them, a decent respect to the opinions of mankind requires that they should declare the causes which impel them to the separation.

We hold these truths to be self-evident: that all men are created equal; that they are endowed by their Creator with [inherent and] *certain* inalienable rights; that among these are life, liberty, and the pursuit of happiness; that to secure these rights, governments are instituted among men, deriving their just powers from the consent of the governed; that whenever any form of government becomes destructive of these ends, it is the right of the people to alter or to abolish it, and to institute new government, laying its foundation on such principles, and organizing its powers in such form, as to them shall seem most likely to effect their safety and happiness. Prudence, indeed, will dictate that governments long established should not be changed for light and transient causes; and accordingly all experience hath shown that mankind are more disposed to suffer while evils are sufferable, than to right themselves by abolishing the forms to which they are accustomed. But when a long train of abuses and usurpations, [begun at a distinguished period and] pursuing invariably the same object, evinces a design to reduce them under absolute despotism, it is their right, it is their duty to throw off such government, and to provide new guards for their future security. Such has been the patient sufferance of these colonies; and such is now the necessity which constrains them to [expunge] *alter* their former systems of government. The history of the present King of Great Britain is a history of [unremitting] *repeated* injuries and usurpations, [among which appears no solitary fact to contradict the uniform tenor of the rest, but all have] *all having* in direct object the establishment of an absolute tyranny over these states. To prove this, let facts be submitted to a candid world [for the truth of which we pledge a faith yet unsullied by falsehood].

He has refused his assent to laws the most wholesome and necessary for the public good.

He has forbidden his governors to pass laws of immediate and pressing importance, unless suspended in their operation till his assent should be obtained; and, when so suspended, he has utterly neglected to attend to them.

He has refused to pass other laws for the accommodation of large districts of people unless those people would relinquish the right of representation in the legislature, a right inestimable to them, and formidable to tyrants only.

He has called together legislative bodies at places unusual, uncomfortable, and distant from the depository of their public records, for the sole purpose of fatiguing them into compliance with his measures.

He has dissolved representative houses repeatedly [and continually] for opposing with manly firmness his invasions on the rights of the people.

He has refused for a long time after such dissolutions to cause others to be elected, whereby the legislative powers, incapable of annihilation, have returned to the people at large for their exercise, the state remaining, in the meantime, exposed to all the dangers of invasion from without and convulsions within.

He has endeavored to prevent the population of these states; for that purpose obstructing the laws for naturalization of foreigners, refusing to pass others to encourage their migrations hither, and raising the conditions of new appropriations of lands.

He has [suffered] *obstructed* the administration of justice [totally to cease in some of these states] *by* refusing his assent to laws for establishing judiciary powers.

He has made [our] judges dependent on his will alone for the tenure of their offices, and the amount and payment of their salaries.

He has erected a multitude of new offices, [by a self-assumed power] and sent hither swarms of new officers to harass our people and eat out their substance.

He has kept among us in times of peace standing armies [and ships of war] without the consent of our legislatures.

He has affected to render the military independent of, and superior to, the civil power.

He has combined with others to subject us to a jurisdiction foreign to our constitutions and unacknowledged by our laws, giving his assent to their acts of pretended legislation for quartering large bodies of armed troops among us; for protecting them by a mock trial from punishment for any murders which they should commit on the inhabitants of these states; for cutting off our trade with all parts of the world; for imposing taxes on us without our consent; for depriving us *in many cases* of the benefits of trial by jury; for transporting us beyond seas to be tried for pretended offences; for abolishing the free system of English laws in a neighboring province, establishing therein an arbitrary government, and enlarging its boundaries, so as to render it at once an example and fit instrument for introducing the same absolute rule into these [states] *colonies*; for taking away our charters, abolishing our most valuable laws, and altering fundamentally the forms of our governments; for suspending our own legislatures, and declaring themselves invested with power to legislate for us in all cases whatsoever.

He has abdicated government here [withdrawing his governors, and declaring us out of his allegiance and protection] *by declaring us out of his protection, and waging war against us.*

He has plundered our seas, ravaged our coasts, burnt our towns, and destroyed the lives of our people.

He is at this time transporting large armies of foreign mercenaries to complete the works of death, desolation, and tyranny already begun with circumstances of cruelty and perfidy *scarcely paralleled in the most barbarous ages, and totally* unworthy the head of a civilized nation.

He has constrained our fellow citizens taken captive on the high seas to bear arms against their country, to become the executioners of their friends and brethren, or to fall themselves by their hands.

He has *excited domestic insurrection among us, and has* endeavored to bring on the inhabitants of our frontiers, the merciless Indian savages, whose known rule of warfare is an undistinguished destruction of all ages, sexes, and conditions [of existence].

[He has incited treasonable insurrections of our fellow citizens, with the allurements of forefeiture and confiscation of our property.

[He has waged cruel war against human nature itself, violating its most sacred rights of life and liberty in the persons of a distant people who never offended him, captivating and carrying them into slavery in another hemisphere, or to incur miserable death in their transportation thither. This piratical warfare, the opprobrium of INFIDEL powers, is the warfare of the CHRISTIAN king of Great Britain. Determined to keep open a market where MEN should be bought and sold, he has prostituted his negative for suppressing every legislative attempt to prohibit or to restrain this execrable commerce. And that this assemblage of horrors might want no fact of distinguished die, he is now exciting those very people to rise in arms among us, and to purchase that liberty of which he has deprived them, by murdering the people on whom he also obtruded them: thus paying off former crimes committed against the LIBERTIES of one people, with crimes which he urges them to commit against the LIVES of another.]

In every stage of these oppressions we have petitioned for redress in the most humble terms: our repeated petitions have been answered only by repeated injuries.

A prince whose character is thus marked by every act which may define a tyrant is unfit to be the ruler of a *free* people [who mean to be free. Future ages will scarcely believe that the hardiness of one man adventured, within the short compass of twelve years only, to lay a foundation so broad and so undisguised for tyranny over a people fostered and fixed in principles of freedom].

Nor have we been wanting in attentions to our British brethren. We have warned them from time to time of attempts by their legislature to extend [a] *an unwarrantable* jurisdiction over [these our states] *us*. We have reminded them of the circumstances of our emigration and settlement here, [no one of which could warrant so strange a pretension: that these were effected at the expense of our own blood and treasure, unassisted by the wealth or the strength of Great Britain: that in constituting indeed our several forms of government, we had adopted one common king, thereby laying a foundation for perpetual league and amity with them: but that submission to their parliament was no part of our constitution, nor ever in idea, if history may be credited: and,] we *have* appealed to their native justice and magnanimity [as well as to] *and we have conjured them by* the ties of our common kindred to disavow these usurpations which [were likely to] *would inevitably* interrupt our connection and correspondence. They too have been deaf to the voice of justice and of consanguinity, [and when occasions have been given them, by the regular course of their laws, of removing from their councils the disturbers of our harmony, they have, by their free election, re-established them in power. At this very time too, they are permitting their chief magistrate to send over not only soldiers of our common blood, but Scotch and foreign mercenaries to invade and destroy us. These facts have given the last stab to agonizing affection, and manly spirit bids us to renounce forever these unfeeling brethren. We must endeavor to forget our former love for them, and hold them as we hold the rest of mankind, enemies in war, in peace friends. We might have been a free and a great people together; but a communication of grandeur and of freedom, it seems, is below their dignity. Be it so, since they will have it. The road to happiness and to glory is open to us, too. We will tread it apart from them, and] *we must therefore* acquiesce in the necessity which denounces our [eternal] separation *and hold them as we hold the rest of mankind, enemies in war, in peace friends!*

We, therefore, the representatives of the United States of America in General Congress assembled, *appealing to the supreme judge of the world for the rectitude of our intentions,* do in the name, and by the authority of the good people of these [states reject and renounce all allegiance and subjection to the kings of Great Britain and all others who may hereafter claim by, through or under them; we utterly dissolve all political connection which may heretofore have subsisted between us and the people or parliament of Great Britain: and finally we do assert and declare these colonies to be free and independent states,] *colonies, solemnly publish and declare, that these united colonies are, and of right ought to be, free and independent states; that they are absolved from all allegiance to the British crown, and that all political connection between them and the state of Great Britain is, and ought to be, totally dissolved;* and that as free and independent states they have full power to levy war, conclude peace, contract alliances, establish commerce, and to do all other acts and things which independent states may of right do.

And for the support of this declaration, *with a firm reliance on the protection of divine providence,* we mutually pledge to each other our lives, our fortunes, and our sacred honor.[3]

An expression of the American mind

All American Whigs thought alike on these subjects. When forced, therefore, to resort to arms for redress, an appeal to the tribunal of the world was deemed proper for our justification. This was the object of the Declaration of Independence. Not to find out new principles or new arguments never before thought of, not merely to say things which had never been said before; but to place before mankind the common sense of the subject, in terms so plain and firm as to command their assent, and to justify ourselves in the independent stand we are compelled to take.

Neither aiming at originality of principle or sentiment, nor yet copied from any particular and previous writing, it was intended to be an expression of the American mind and to give to that expression the proper tone and spirit called for by the occasion. All its authority rests then on the harmonizing sentiments of the day, whether expressed in conversation, in letters, printed essays, or in the elementary books of public right, as Aristotle, Cicero, Locke, Sidney, etc. [4]

[Timothy] Pickering's observations and Mr. [John] Adams' in addition, 'that it contained no new ideas, that it is a commonplace compilation, its sentiments hackneyed in Congress for two years before, and its essence contained in Otis' pamphlet,' may all be true. Of that I am not to be the judge. Richard Henry Lee charged it as copied from Locke's treatise on government. Otis' pamphlet I never saw, and whether I had gathered my ideas from reading or reflection I do not know.

I know only that I turned to neither book nor pamphlet while writing it. I did not consider it as any part of my charge to invent new ideas altogether and to offer no sentiment which had ever been expressed before. Had Mr. Adams been so restrained, Congress would have lost the benefit of his bold and impressive advocations of the rights of revolution. For no man's confident and fervid addresses more than Mr. Adams' encouraged and supported us through the difficulties surrounding us, which, like the ceaseless action of gravity, weighed on us by night and by day. Yet, on the same ground, we may ask what of these elevated thoughts was new, or can be affirmed never before to have entered the conceptions of man?

Writhing a little under criticism

Whether, also, the sentiments of independence and the reasons for declaring it, which make so great a portion of the instrument, had been hackneyed in Congress for two years before the 4th of July, '76, or this dictum also of Mr. Adams be another slip of memory, let history say. This, however, I will say for Mr. Adams, that he supported the Declaration with zeal and ability, fighting fearlessly for every word of it.

As to myself, I thought it a duty to be on that occasion a passive auditor of the opinions of others, more impartial judges than I could be of its merits or demerits. During the debate I was sitting by Doctor Franklin, and he observed that I was writhing a little under the acrimonious criticisms on some of its parts; and it was on that occasion, that by way of comfort, he told me the story of John Thompson, the hatter, and his new sign.[5]

Old Doctor Franklin tells a comforting story

'I have made it a rule,' said he, 'whenever in my power, to avoid becoming the draughtsman of papers to be reviewed by a public body. I took my lesson from an incident which I will relate to you.

'When I was a journeyman printer, one of my companions, an apprentice hatter, having served out his time was about to open shop for himself. His first concern was to have a handsome sign-board with a proper inscription. He composed it in these words, "John Thompson, *Hatter, makes and sells hats for ready money,*" with a figure of a hat subjoined. But he thought he would submit it to his friends for their amendments. The first he showed it to thought the word "*Hatter*" tautologous, because followed by the words "makes hats" which show he was a hatter. It was struck out. The next observed that the word "*makes*" might as well be omitted, because his customers would not care who made the hats. If good and to their mind, they would buy by whomsoever made. He struck it out. A third said he thought the words "*for ready money*" were use-less, as it was not the custom of the place to sell on credit. Everyone who purchased expected to pay. They were parted with, and the inscription now stood, "John Thompson sells hats." "*Sells hats!*" says his next friend. "Why nobody will expect you to give them away. What then is the use of that word?" It was stricken out, and "*hats*" followed it, the rather as there was one painted on the board. So the inscription was reduced ultimately to "John Thompson" with the figure of a hat subjoined.'[6]

Small things as well as great

May 18, 1776. Paid at Smith's for punch 2/6. May 20, Paid for paper 9d. Paid for toothbrush 8/6. Received of Willing & Morris 300 dollars delegate money.... Paid Jefferies repairing watch, etc. 21/. May 23, Took lodgings at Graaf's. May 24, Paid a barber 13d. Paid Hillegas for fiddlestrings 27/. May 27, Paid for toys 1/7. Paid Randolph for 8 days lodging 40/. Paid for a relisher at Clarke's 2/. May 28, Paid for a doll 2/. May 31, Gave a tumbler 4d. Paid for silver cover to an ivory book 45/.

June 1, Paid for paper 2/6. Paid Bradford for a map 8/6. Paid for seeing a monkey 1/. June 4, Paid Graaf one week's lodging 35/. Paid for ½ lb. tea and canister 20/. Paid for wafers 4d. Paid at Duff's for punch 2/. June 5, Paid at Greentree's, dinner and club 7/. June 7, Paid for shoes for Bob [his servant] 8/. June 9, Paid for 7 washballs 10/6. Paid for stockings for Bob 7/. Paid Mrs. Graaf one week's lodging 35/. June 18, Paid for a nest of trunks 7/6. June 19, Paid Greentree for wine 6/. June 20, Paid Aitkin for lining a map 5/. June 22, Paid Sparhawk for pair spurs 25/. June 25, Paid for a straw hat 10/. June 27, Paid Byrne for 6 weeks shaving and [hair] dressing 30/. June 30, Paid Sparhawk for a pencil 1/6, a map 7/6.

July 4, Paid Sparhawk for a thermometer £3–15. Paid for 7 pair women's gloves 27/. Gave in charity 1/6.[7]

The Declaration written in the house of a bricklayer

The paper of July 4th, 1776, was but the Declaration, the genuine effusion of the soul of our country at that time. Small things may, perhaps, like the relics of saints, help to nourish our devotion to this holy bond of our Union and keep it longer alive and warm in our affections. This effect may give importance to circumstances however small. At the time of writing that instrument, I lodged in the house of a Mr. Graaf, a new brick house, three stories high, of which I rented the second floor, consisting of a parlor and bedroom, ready furnished. In that parlor I wrote habitually and in it wrote this paper particularly.

So far I state from written proofs in my possession. The proprietor, Graaf, was a young man, son of a German, and then newly married. I think he was a bricklayer, and that his house was on the south side of Market Street, probably between Seventh and Eighth Streets, and if not the only house on that part of the street, I am sure there were few others near it.[8]

On a plain portable writing-box

I received a letter from a friend in Philadelphia lately [in 1825] asking information of the house, and room of the house there, in which the Declaration of Independence was written, with a view to future celebrations of the Fourth of July in it. . . . If then things acquire a superstitious value because of their connection with particular persons, surely a connection with the great Charter of our Independence may give a value to what has been associated with that; and such was the idea of the enquirers after the room in which it was written.

Now I happen still to possess the writing-box on which it was written. It was made from a drawing of my own by Ben. Randall, a cabinetmaker in whose house I took my first lodgings on my arrival in Philadelphia in May, 1776, and I have used it ever since. It claims no merit of particular beauty. It is plain, neat, convenient, and, taking no more room on the writing table than a moderate quarto volume, it yet displays itself sufficiently for any writing. . . . Its imaginary value will increase with years, . . . and another half-century . . . may see it carried in the procession of our nation's birthday as the relics of the saints are in those of the Church.[9]

To sum up: the case against George the Third

The following is an epitome of the first sixteen years of his reign: The colonies were taxed internally and externally; their essential interests sacrificed to individuals in Great Britain; their legislatures suspended; charters annulled; trials by juries taken away; their persons subjected to transportation across the Atlantic, and to trial before foreign judicatories; their supplications for redress thought beneath answer; themselves published as cowards in the councils of their mother country and courts of Europe; armed troops sent among them to enforce submission to these violences; and actual hostilities commenced against them. No alternative was presented but resistance or unconditional submission. Between these could be no hesitation. They closed in the appeal to arms. They declared themselves independent states. They confederated together into one great republic.[10]

I pray God that these principles may be eternal

Timothy [Pickering] thinks the instrument the better for having a fourth of it expunged. . . . In other words, that the Declaration, as being a libel on the government of England, composed in times of passion, should now be buried in utter oblivion, to spare the feelings of our English friends and Angloman fellow-citizens.

But it is not to wound them that we wish to keep it in mind, but to cherish the principles of the instrument in the bosoms of our own citizens; and it is a heavenly comfort to see that these principles are yet so strongly felt. . . . I pray God that these principles may be eternal.[11]

CHAPTER V

Fighting for Man's Inalienable Rights

FOR Thomas Jefferson the American Revolution was far more than a war for independence from Great Britain. Three months after writing the Great Declaration he returned to Virginia to fight on the home front for man's 'inalienable rights.' He was tremendously in earnest. He passionately believed in the democratic philosophy of the Declaration, and he worked unceasingly for social reforms 'by which every fibre would be eradicated of ancient or future aristocracy.' The idealist now became the man of action, the leader of a bloodless social revolution.

Young Jefferson struck at the economic foundations of a self-perpetuating aristocracy when he proposed the abolition of entails and primogeniture. By holding their vast estates in 'fee tail' instead of 'fee simple,' and by devising them to the eldest son, the great families of colonial Virginia had been enabled to transmit their property undivided and undiminished from one generation to another. Jefferson would break up these privileged hereditary estates, bring about a wider distribution of property, and thus make an opening for 'the aristocracy of virtue and talent.' In spite of the deep antagonism of large landholders, who regarded the master of Monticello as a traitor to his class, as a radical 'leveler,' he succeeded in doing away with these props of economic privilege and oligarchical rule.

In demanding the end of spiritual tyranny as embodied in the tax-supported state church, the young reformer brought on the severest contests in which he was ever engaged. It took three years of persistent struggle to overthrow the Anglican Church. Separation of church and state was achieved, but a further struggle had to be fought before Jefferson's famous bill for establishing complete religious freedom was enacted. His arguments against the folly of coercing men's minds and consciences have an eloquence and cogency which insure him a high place among the champions of intellectual and spiritual liberty. He himself considered his bill for religious freedom as ranking in importance with the Declaration of Independence.

This was but one of the many bills which made up the revised legal code. It was but one of the many reforms Jefferson had in mind when he called for the remodeling of the whole legal structure and its adaptation 'in all its parts with a single eye to reason and the good of those for whose government it was framed.'

Prominent in this general reformation was his plan for a broad system of public education, embracing free elementary schools, academies, and a university, with provision for the education of youths of genius at the public expense. This was a subject dear to Jefferson's heart. Throughout his life he was to 'preach a crusade against ignorance,' stressing the vital importance of general education. There could be no surer foundation for the preservation of the people's freedom and happiness. Only an educated people could understand their rights, maintain them, and provide for the successful functioning of a democratic republic, in which 'the influence over government must be shared by all the people.'

Such were some of the major objectives of Jefferson's campaign in the former royal colony of Virginia to bring about 'the republican change on democratic principles.' Although his comprehensive program was not fully realized, these years were among the most significant and fruitful of his whole career. From 1776 to 1779 he rallied and led the progressive forces, developed and applied a political philosophy based on the 'self-evident truths' of the Declaration of 1776, and succeeded not only in effecting a social revolution in Virginia but in giving great impetus to the democratic movement throughout the new American republic.

The way opened for a great social revolution

Our Revolution . . . presented us an album on which we were free to write what we pleased. We had no occasion to search into musty records, to hunt up royal parchments, or to investigate the laws and institutions of a semi-barbarous ancestry. We appealed to those of nature, and found them engraved on our hearts. Yet we did not avail ourselves of all the advantages of our position. We had never been permitted to exercise self-government. When forced to assume it, we were novices in its science. Its principles and forms had entered little into our former education. We established, however, some, although not all its important principles.[1]

I knew that our legislation under the regal government had many very vicious points which urgently required reformation, and I thought I could be of more use in forwarding that work. I therefore retired from my seat in Congress on the 2d of September [1776], resigned it, and took my place in the legislature of my state on the 7th of October. On the 11th I moved for leave to bring in a bill for the establishment of courts of justice, the organization of which was of importance. I drew the bill; it was approved by the committee, reported, and passed, after going through its due course. On the 12th I obtained leave to bring in a bill declaring tenants in tail to hold their lands in fee simple.

A leveling blow at hereditary aristocracy

In the earlier times of the colony when lands were to be obtained for little or nothing, some provident individuals procured large grants; and, desirous of founding great families for themselves, settled them on their descendants in fee tail. The transmission of this property from generation to generation, in the same name, raised up a distinct set of familes who, being privileged by law in the perpetuation of their wealth, were thus formed into a patrician order, distinguished by the splendor and luxury of their establishments. From this order, too, the king habitually selected his Counsellors of State; the hope of which distinction devoted the whole corps to the interests and will of the crown.

To annul this privilege and, instead of an aristocracy of wealth of more harm and danger than benefit to society, to make an opening for the aristocracy of virtue and talent, which Nature has wisely provided for the direction of the interests of society and scattered with equal hand through all its conditions, was deemed essential to a well-ordered republic. To effect it no violence was necessary, no deprivation of natural right, but rather an enlargement of it by a repeal of the law. For this would authorize the present holder to divide the property among his children equally, as his affections were divided; and would place them, by natural generation, on the level of their fellow citizens.

Edmund Pendleton, able opponent

But this repeal was strongly opposed by Mr. Pendleton, who was zealously attached to ancient establishments; and who, taken all in all, was the ablest man in debate I have ever met with. He had not indeed the poetical fancy of Mr. [Patrick] Henry, his sublime imagination, his lofty and overwhelming diction; but he was cool, smooth and persuasive; his language flowing, chaste and embellished; his conceptions quick, acute and full of resource; never vanquished: for if he lost the main battle, he returned upon you, and regained so much of it as to make it a drawn one, by dexterous manoeuvres, skirmishes in detail, and the recovery of small advantages which, little singly, were important all together. You never knew when you were clear of him, but were harassed by his perseverance until the patience was worn down of all who had less of it than himself. Add to this that he was one of the most virtuous and benevolent of men, the kindest friend, the most amiable and pleasant of companions, which ensured a favorable reception to whatever came from him.

Finding that the general principle of entails could not be maintained, he took his stand on an amendment which he proposed, instead of an absolute abolition to permit the tenant in tail to convey in fee simple if he chose it; and he was within a few votes of saving so much of the old law. But the bill passed finally for entire abolition.

In that one of the bills for organizing our judiciary system which proposed a court of chancery, I had provided for a trial by jury of all matters of fact, in that as well as in the courts of law. He defeated it by the introduction of four words only, '*if either party choose.*' The consequence has been, that as no suitor will say to his judge, 'Sir, I distrust you, give me a jury,' juries are rarely, I might say perhaps never, seen in that court but when called for by the Chancellor of his own accord.

Importation of slaves prohibited

The first establishment in Virginia which became permanent was made in 1607. I have found no mention of negroes in the colony until about 1650. The first brought here as slaves were by a Dutch ship; after which the English commenced the trade and continued it until the Revolutionary War. That suspended, *ipso facto*, their further importation for the present, and the business of the war pressing constantly on the legislature, this subject was not acted on finally until the year '78 when I brought in a bill to prevent their further importation. This passed without opposition and stopped the increase of the evil by importation, leaving to future efforts its final eradication.

The struggle against spiritual tyranny

The first settlers of this colony were Englishmen, loyal subjects to their king and church, and the grant to Sir Walter Raleigh contained an express proviso that their laws 'should not be against the true Christian faith, now professed in the Church of England.' As soon as the state of the colony admitted, it was divided into parishes, in each of which was established a minister of the Anglican Church endowed with a fixed salary, in tobacco, a glebe house and land with the other necessary appendages. To meet these expenses all the inhabitants of the parishes were assessed whether they were or not members of the established church. . . .

By the time of the Revolution a majority of the inhabitants had become dissenters from the established church but were still obliged to pay contributions to support the pastors of the minority. This unrighteous compulsion to maintain teachers of what they deemed religious errors was grievously felt during the regal government, and without a hope of relief. But the first republican legislature which met in '76 was crowded with petitions to abolish this spiritual tyranny. These brought on the severest contests in which I have ever been engaged.

Our great opponents were Mr. Pendleton and Robert Carter Nicholas, honest men but zealous churchmen. The petitions were referred to the committee of the whole house on the state of the country; and, after desperate contests in that committee, almost daily from the 11th of October to the 5th of December, we prevailed so far only as to repeal the laws which rendered criminal the maintenance of any [dissenting] religious opinions, the forbearance of repairing to church, or the exercise of any [other] mode of worship; and further, to exempt dissenters from contributions to the support of the established church; and to suspend, only until the next session, levies on the members of that church for the salaries of their own incumbents. For although the majority of our citizens were dissenters, as has been observed, a majority of the legislature were churchmen. Among these, however, were some reasonable and liberal men who enabled us, on some points, to obtain feeble majorities.

Church separated from state

But our opponents carried, in the general resolutions of the committee of November 19, a declaration that religious assemblies ought to be regulated, and that provision ought to be made for continuing the succession of the clergy and superintending their conduct. And in the bill now passed was inserted an express reservation of the question whether a general assessment should not be established by law on everyone to the support of the pastor of his choice, or whether all should be left to voluntary contributions; and on this question, debated at every session from '76 to '79 (some of our dissenting allies, having now secured their particular object, going over to the advocates of a general assessment), we could only obtain a suspension from session to session until '79, when the question against a general assessment was finally carried and the establishment of the Anglican Church entirely put down.[2]

But religious freedom not yet achieved

Statutory oppressions in religion being thus wiped away, we remain at present [1781] under those only imposed by the common law or by our own acts of assembly. At the common law, *heresy* was a capital offense, punishable by burning. . . . By our own act of assembly of 1705, chapter 30, if a person brought up in the Christian religion denies the being of a God, or the Trinity, or asserts there are more gods than one, or denies the Christian religion to be true, or the scriptures to be of divine authority, he is punishable on the first offense by incapacity to hold any office or employment ecclesiastical, civil, or military; on the second by disability to sue, to take any gift or legacy, to be guardian, executor, or administrator, and by three years' imprisonment without bail.

A father's right to the custody of his own children being founded in law on his right of guardianship, this being taken away they may of course be severed from him and put by the authority of a court into more orthodox hands. This is a summary view of that religious slavery under which a people have been willing to remain who have lavished their lives and fortunes for the establshment of their civil freedom.

The folly of coercing men's minds and consciences

The error seems not sufficiently eradicated that the operations of the mind as well as the acts of the body are subject to the coercion of the laws. But our rulers can have no authority over such natural rights, only as we have submitted to them. The rights of conscience we never submitted, we could not submit. We are answerable for them to our God. The legitimate powers of government extend to such acts only as are injurious to others. But it does me no injury for my neighbor to say there are twenty gods, or no God. It neither picks my pocket nor breaks my leg. If it be said his testimony in a court of justice cannot be relied on, reject it then, and be the stigma on him. Constraint may make him worse by making him a hypocrite, but it will never make him a truer man. It may fix him obstinately in his errors, but will not cure them.

Reason and free inquiry are the only effectual agents against error. Give a loose to them, they will support the true religion by bringing every false one to their tribunal, to the test of their investigation. They are the natural enemies of error, and of error only. Had not the Roman government permitted free inquiry, Christianity could never have been introduced. Had not free inquiry been indulged at the era of the Reformation, the corruptions of Christianity could not have been purged away. If it be restrained now, the present corruptions will be protected and new ones encouraged.

Truth can stand by itself

Was the government to prescribe to us our medicine and diet, our bodies would be in such keeping as our souls are now. Thus in France the emetic was once forbidden as a medicine, and the potato as an article of food. Government is just as infallible, too, when it fixes systems in physics. Galileo was sent to the Inquisition for affirming that the earth was a sphere; the government had declared it to be as flat as a trencher, and Galileo was obliged to abjure his error. This error, however, at length prevailed, the earth became a globe, and Descartes declared it was whirled round its axis by a vortex. The government in which he lived was wise enough to see that this was no question of civil jurisdiction, or we should all have been involved by authority in vortices. In fact, the vortices have been exploded, and the Newtonian principle of gravitation is now more firmly established, on the basis of reason, than it would be were the government to step in and to make it an article of necessary faith. Reason and experiment have been indulged, and error has fled before them. It is error alone which needs the support of government. Truth can stand by itself.

The tragic absurdity of uniformity

Subject opinion to coercion: whom will you make your inquisitors? Fallible men, men governed by bad passions, by private as well as public reasons. And why subject it to coercion? To produce uniformity. But is uniformity of opinion desirable? No more than of face and stature. Introduce the bed of Procrustes then, and as there is danger that the large men may beat the small, make us all of a size, by lopping the former and stretching the latter. Difference of opinion is advantageous in religion. The several sects perform the office of a *censor morum* over each other. Is uniformity attainable? Millions of innocent men, women, and children, since the introduction of Christianity, have been burnt, tortured, fined, imprisoned; yet we have not advanced one inch towards uniformity.

What has been the effect of coercion? To make one half the world fools, and the other half hypocrites. To support roguery and error all over the earth. Let us reflect that it is inhabited by a thousand millions of people. That these profess probably a thousand different systems of religion. That ours is but one of that thousand. That if there be but one right, and ours that one, we should wish to see the nine hundred and ninety-nine wandering sects gathered into the fold of truth. But against such a majority we cannot effect this by force. Reason and persuasion are the only practicable instruments. To make way for these, free inquiry must be indulged; and how can we wish others to indulge it while we refuse it ourselves?

Let us experiment

But every state, says an inquisitor, has established some religion. No two, say I, have established the same. Is this a proof of the infallibility of establishments? Our sister states of Pennsylvania and New York, however, have long subsisted without any establishment at all. The experiment was new and doubtful when they made it. It has answered beyond conception. They flourish infinitely. Religion is well supported; of various kinds indeed, but all good enough; all sufficient to preserve peace and order; or if a sect arises whose tenets would subvert morals, good sense has fair play, and reasons and laughs it out of doors without suffering the state to be troubled with it. . . . They have made the happy discovery that the way to silence religious disputes is to take no notice of them. Let us too give this experiment fair play, and get rid, while we may, of those tyrannical laws.

It is true we are as yet secured against them by the spirit of the times. I doubt whether the people of this country would suffer an execution for heresy, or a three years' imprisonment for not comprehending the mysteries of the Trinity. But is the spirit of the people an infallible, a permanent reliance? Is it government? Is this the kind of protection we receive in return for the rights we give up? Besides, the spirit of the times may alter, will alter. Our rulers will become corrupt, our people careless. A single zealot may commence persecutor, and better men be his victims.

It can never be too often repeated that the time for fixing every essential right on a legal basis is while our rulers are honest, and ourselves united. From the conclusion of this war we shall be going downhill. It will not then be necessary to resort every moment to the people for support. They will be forgotten, therefore, and their rights disregarded. They will forget themselves but in the sole faculty of making money, and will never think of uniting to effect a due respect for their rights. The shackles, therefore, which shall not be knocked off at the conclusion of this war will remain on us long, will be made heavier and heavier, till our rights shall revive or expire in a convulsion.[3]

A general attack on the old order

In giving this account of the laws of which I was myself the mover and draughtsman, I by no means mean to claim to myself the merit of obtaining their passage. I had many occasional and strenuous coadjutors in debate, and [along with George Wythe and young James Madison] one, most steadfast, able and zealous, who was himself a host. This was George Mason, a man of the first order of wisdom among those who acted on the theatre of the Revolution, of expansive mind, profound judgment, cogent in argument, learned in the lore of our former constitution, and earnest for the republican change on democratic principles. . . .

So far we were proceeding in the details of reformation only, selecting points of legislation prominent in character and principle, urgent, and indicative of the strength of the general pulse of reformation. When I left Congress in '76 it was in the persuasion that our whole code must be reviewed, adapted to our republican form of government; and, now that we had no negatives of Councils, Governors, and Kings to restrain us from doing right, it should be corrected in all its parts with a single eye to reason and the good of those for whose government it was framed. Early, therefore, in the session of '76, to which I returned, I moved and presented a bill for the revision of the laws, which was passed on the 24th of October; and on the 5th of November, Mr. Pendleton, Mr. Wythe, George Mason, Thomas L. Lee. and myself were appointed a committee to execute the work. . . .

Another blow at landed aristocracy

When we proceeded to the distribution of the work, Mr. Mason excused himself, as, being no lawyer, he felt himself unqualified for the work, and he resigned soon after. Mr. Lee excused himself on the same ground, and died, indeed, in a short time. The other two gentlemen, therefore, and myself divided the work among us. The common law and statutes to the 4 James I (when our separate legislature was established) were assigned to me; the British statutes from that period to the present day to Mr. Wythe; and the Virginia laws to Mr. Pendleton.

As the law of descents and the criminal law fell of course within my portion, I wished the committee to settle the leading principles of these as a guide for me in framing them; and with respect to the first I proposed to abolish the law of primogeniture and to make real estate descendible in parcenary to the next of kin, as personal property is, by the statute of distribution.

Mr. Pendleton wished to preserve the right of primogeniture, but seeing at once that that could not prevail, he proposed we should adopt the Hebrew principle and give a double portion to the elder son. I observed that if the eldest son could eat twice as much or do double work, it might be a natural evidence of his right to a double portion; but being on a par in his powers and wants with his brothers and sisters he should be on a par also in the partition of the patrimony; and such was the decision of the other members.

The revised code completed

On the subject of the criminal law all were agreed that the punishment of death should be abolished except for treason and murder; and that for other felonies should be substituted hard labor in the public works. . . . I thought it would be useful also . . . to reform the style of the later British statutes and of our own acts of assembly, which, from their verbosity, their endless tautologies, their involutions of case within case and parenthesis within parenthesis, and their multiplied efforts at certainty by *saids* and *aforesaids*, by *ors* and by *ands*, to make them more plain, are really rendered more perplexed and incomprehensible, not only to common readers, but to the lawyers themselves.

We were employed in this work . . . to February, 1779, when we met at Williamsburg, that is to say, Mr. Pendleton, Mr. Wythe and myself; and meeting day by day, we examined critically our several parts sentence by sentence, scrutinizing and amending, until we had agreed on the whole. We then returned home, had fair copies made of our several parts, which were reported to the General Assembly, June 18, 1779. . . . We had in this work brought so much of the common law as it was thought necessary to alter, all the British statutes from Magna Charta to the present day and all the laws of Virginia from the establishment of our legislature . . . which we thought should be retained, within the compass of one hundred and twenty-six bills, making a printed folio of ninety pages only.

Some bills were taken out, occasionally from time to time, and passed; but the main body of the work was not entered on by the legislature until after the general peace, in 1785, when, by the unwearied exertions of Mr. Madison in opposition to the endless quibbles, chicaneries, perversions, vexations and delays of lawyers and demi-lawyers, most of the bills were passed by the legislature, with little alteration.

A broad mantle protecting mind and conscience

The bill for establishing religious freedom, the principles of which had to a certain degree been enacted before, I had drawn in all the latitude of reason and right. It still met with opposition, but with some mutilations in the preamble it was finally passed [in 1786]; and a singular proposition proved that its protection of opinion was meant to be universal.

Where the preamble declares that coercion is a departure from the plan of the holy author of our religion, an amendment was proposed, by inserting the words 'Jesus Christ,' so that it should read, 'a departure from the plan of Jesus Christ, the holy author of our religion'; the insertion was rejected by a great majority, in proof that they meant to comprehend within the mantle of its protection the Jew and the Gentile, the Christian and Mahometan, the Hindoo, and infidel of every denomination.[4]

The Statute of Virginia for Religious Freedom

Well aware that the opinions and belief of men depend not on their own will, but follow involuntarily the evidence proposed to their minds; that Almighty God hath created the mind free, and manifested His supreme will that free it shall remain by making it altogether insusceptible of restraint; that all attempts to influence it by temporal punishments, or burdens, or by civil incapacitations, tend only to beget habits of hypocrisy and meanness, and are a departure from the plan of the holy author of our religion. . . .

That to compel a man to furnish contributions of money for the propagation of opinions which he disbelieves and abhors is sinful and tyrannical; . . . that our civil rights have no dependence on our religious opinions, any more than our opinions in physics or geometry; . . . that the opinions of men are not the object of civil government, nor under its jurisdiction; . . . that it is time enough for the rightful purposes of civil government for its officers to interfere when principles break out into overt acts against peace and good order; and finally, that truth is great and will prevail if left to herself; that she is the proper and sufficient antagonist to error, and has nothing to fear from the conflict unless by human interposition disarmed of her natural weapons, free argument and debate, errors ceasing to be dangerous when it is permitted freely to contradict them.

We the General Assembly of Virginia do enact that no man shall be compelled to frequent or support any religious worship, place, or ministry whatsoever, nor shall be enforced, restrained, molested, or burdened in his body or goods, or shall otherwise suffer, on account of his religious opinions or belief; but that all men shall be free to profess, and by argument to maintain, their opinions in matters of religion, and that the same shall in no wise diminish, enlarge, or affect their civil capacities.[5]

A pioneer system of public education

We thought that on this subject a systematical plan of general education should be proposed, and I was requested to undertake it. I accordingly prepared three bills for the revisal, proposing three distinct grades of education, reaching all classes. 1st. Elementary schools, for all children generally, rich and poor. 2d. Colleges, for a middle degree of instruction, calculated for the common purposes of life, and such as would be desirable for all who were in easy circumstances. And, 3d, an ultimate grade for teaching the sciences generally, and in their highest degree.

The first bill proposed to lay off every county into hundreds, or

wards, of a proper size and population for a school, in which reading, writing, and common arithmetic should be taught; and that
the whole state should be divided into twenty-four districts, in each
of which should be a school for classical learning, grammar, geography, and the higher branches of numerical arithmetic. The
second bill proposed to amend the constitution of William and
Mary College, to enlarge its sphere of science, and to make it in
fact a university. The third was for the establishment of a library
[a public library which would include a public art gallery].[6]

Geniuses raked from the rubbish

This [first] bill proposes to lay off every county into small districts of five or six miles square, called hundreds, and in each of
them to establish a school for teaching reading, writing, and
arithmetic. The tutor to be supported by the hundred, and every
person in it entitled to send their children three years gratis, and
as much longer as they please, paying for it. These schools to be
under a visitor who is annually to choose the boy of best genius in
the school, of those whose parents are too poor to give them further
education, and to send him forward to one of the grammar schools,
of which twenty are proposed to be erected in different parts of the
country, for teaching Greek, Latin, geography, and the higher
branches of numerical arithmetic.

Of the boys thus sent in one year, trial is to be made at the
grammar schools one or two years, and the best genius of the whole
selected and continued six years, and the residue dismissed. By
this means twenty of the best geniuses will be raked from the rub-
bish annually, and be instructed at the public expense so far as
the grammar schools go. At the end of six years' instruction, one
half are to be discontinued (from among whom the grammar
schools will probably be supplied with future masters); and the
other half, who are to be chosen for the superiority of their parts and
disposition, are to be sent and continued three years in the study
of such sciences as they shall choose at William and Mary College. . . .

Preach a crusade against ignorance

The general objects of this law are to provide an education adapted
to the years, to the capacity, and the condition of everyone, and

directed to their freedom and happiness.... By that part of our plan which prescribes the selection of the youths of genius from among the classes of the poor, we hope to avail the state of those talents which nature has sown as liberally among the poor as the rich, but which perish without use if not sought for and cultivated. But of the views of this law none is more important, none more legitimate, than that of rendering the people the safe, as they are the ultimate, guardians of their own liberty.

For this purpose the reading in the first stage, where *they* will receive their whole education, is proposed ... to be chiefly historical. History by apprizing them of the past will enable them to judge of the future; it will avail them of the experience of other times and other nations; it will qualify them as judges of the actions and designs of men; it will enable them to know ambition under every disguise it may assume, and, knowing it, to defeat its views.

In every government on earth is some trace of human weakness, some germ of corruption and degeneracy, which cunning will discover and wickedness insensibly open, cultivate, and improve. Every government degenerates when trusted to the rulers of the people alone. The people themselves therefore are its only safe depositories. And to render even them safe, their minds must be improved to a certain degree.[7]

I think by far the most important bill in our whole code is that for the diffusion of knowledge among the people. No other sure foundation can be devised for the preservation of freedom and happiness.... Preach, my dear sir [George Wythe], a crusade against ignorance; establish and improve the law for educating the common people. Let our countrymen know ... that the tax which will be paid for this purpose is not more than the thousandth part of what will be paid to kings, priests, and nobles who will rise up among us if we leave the people in ignorance.[8]

Government for and by all the people

An amendment of our constitution must here come in aid of the public education. The influence over government must be shared among all the people ... [extending the limited suffrage now existing by which] the majority of the men in the state who pay and fight for its support are unrepresented in the legislature, the roll of freeholders entitled to vote not including generally the half of those on the roll of the militia or of the tax-gatherers. . . .

If every individual which composes their mass participates of the ultimate authority, the government will be safe, because the corrupting the whole mass will exceed any private resources of wealth and public ones cannot be provided but by levies on the people. In this case every man would have to pay his own price. The government of Great Britain has been corrupted because but one man in ten has a right to vote for members of Parliament. The sellers of the government, therefore, get nine-tenths of their price clear. It has been thought that corruption is restrained by confining the right of suffrage to a few of the wealthier of the people; but it would be more effectually restrained by an extension of that right to such members as would bid defiance to the means of corruption.[9]

Obstructed by jealousy and selfishness

These bills were not acted on until the . . . year '96, and then only so much of the first as provided for elementary schools. The College of William and Mary was an establishment purely of the Church of England . . . and one of its fundamental objects was declared to be to raise up ministers for that church. The religious jealousies, therefore, of all the dissenters took alarm lest this might give an ascendancy to the Anglican sect, and refused acting on the bill. Its local eccentricity, too, and unhealthy autumnal climate, lessened the general inclination towards it.

And in the Elementary bill they inserted a provision which completely defeated it; for they left it to the court of each county to determine for itself when this act should be carried into execution within their county. One provision of the bill was that the expenses of these schools should be borne by the inhabitants of the county, everyone in proportion to his general tax-rate. This would throw on wealth the education of the poor; and the justices, being generally of the more wealthy class, were unwilling to incur that burden, and I believe it was not suffered to commence in a single county. I shall recur again to this subject towards the close of my story. . . .

The sacred cause of emancipation

The bill on the subject of slaves was a mere digest of the existing laws respecting them, without any intimation of a plan for a future and general emancipation. It was thought better that this should be kept back, and attempted only by way of amendment whenever the bill should be brought on. The principles of the amendment, however, were agreed on, that is to say, the freedom of all born after a certain day, and deportation at a proper age. But it was found that the public mind would not yet bear the proposition. . . . Yet the day is not distant when it must bear and adopt it, or worse will follow.

Nothing is more certainly written in the book of fate than that these people are to be free; nor is it less certain that the two races, equally free, cannot live in the same government. Nature, habit, opinion have drawn indelible lines of distinction between them. It is still in our power to direct the process of emancipation and deportation, peaceably and in such slow degree as that the evil will wear off insensibly and their place be, *pari passu*, filled up by free white laborers. If, on the contrary, it is left to force itself on, human nature must shudder at the prospect.[10]

Northward of the Chesapeake . . . there being but few slaves, they can easily disencumber themselves of them. . . . In Virginia . . . the sacred side [of emancipation] is gaining daily recruits from the influx into office of young men, grown and growing up. These have sucked in the principles of liberty, as it were, with their mother's milk; and it is to them I look with anxiety to turn the fate of this question. . . . The College of William and Mary . . . is the place where are collected together all the young men of Virginia under preparation for public life. They are there under the direction (most of them) of . . . Mr. Wythe, . . . whose sentiments on the subject of slavery are unequivocal.[11]

A God of justice and exterminating thunder

What a stupendous, what an incomprehensible machine is man! who can endure toil, famine, stripes, imprisonment, and death itself in vindication of his own liberty, and the next moment be deaf to all those motives whose power supported him through his trial and inflict on his fellow men a bondage one hour of which is fraught with more misery than ages of that which he rose in rebellion to oppose. But we must await with patience the workings of an over-ruling Providence, and hope that that is preparing the deliverance of these, our suffering brethren. When the measure of their tears shall be full, when their groans shall have involved heaven itself in darkness, doubtless a God of justice will awaken to their distress, and by diffusing light and liberality among their oppressors, or, at length, by his exterminating thunder manifest his attention to the things of this world, and that they are not left to the guidance of a blind fatality.[12]

All this a foundation truly republican

I considered four of these bills, passed or reported, as forming a system by which every fibre would be eradicated of ancient or future aristocracy and a foundation laid for a government truly republican. The repeal of the laws of entail would prevent the accumulation and perpetuation of wealth in select families, and preserve the soil of the country from being daily more and more absorbed in mortmain. The abolition of primogeniture, and equal partition of inheritances, removed the feudal and unnatural distinctions which made one member of every family rich and all the rest poor, substituting equal partition, the best of all agrarian laws. The restoration of the rights of conscience relieved the people from taxation for the support of a religion not theirs; for the establishment was truly of the religion of the rich, the dissenting sects being entirely composed of the less wealthy people, and these, by the bill for a general education, would be qualified to understand their rights, to maintain them, and to exercise with intelligence their parts in self-government; and all this would be effected without the violation of a single natural right of any one individual citizen.[13]

A bloodless social revolution

The people seem to have laid aside the monarchical and taken up the republican government with as much ease as would have attended their throwing off an old and putting on a new suit of clothes. Not a single throe has attended this important transformation. A half-dozen aristocratical gentlemen, agonizing under the loss of pre-eminence, have sometimes ventured their sarcasms on our political metamorphosis. They have been thought fitter objects of pity than of punishment. We are, at present, in the complete and quiet exercise of well-organized government.[14]

It is comfortable to see the standard of reason at length erected after so many ages during which the human mind has been held in vassalage by kings, priests, and nobles; and it is honorable for us to have produced the first legislature who had the courage to declare that the reason of man may be trusted with the formation of his own opinions.[15]

CHAPTER VI

War Governor

JEFFERSON was thirty-six, the leader of the democratic forces, when he was elected Governor of Virginia in 1779. His position, especially after his re-election in 1780, was one of exceptional difficulty. From the beginning of the Revolution his state had given generously of troops and supplies to Washington's army in the north. Now, with the British under Lord Cornwallis invading the Carolinas and advancing on Virginia, the young Governor was forced to drain off more men and equipment to the defending army in the south. Further, Virginia's western frontier was menaced by the British and Indians, and her seaboard was not only harassed by British expeditionary forces but successfully invaded by the traitor Benedict Arnold, who penetrated up the James River as far as the new capital of Richmond.

As governor of an invaded and war-exhausted state Jefferson struggled as best he could against tremendous obstacles: the want of arms, money, and essential supplies; the disaffection of the Tories; the dependence upon short-term and untried militia. Virginia's plight became desperate when Cornwallis in May of 1781 effected a junction with Arnold. Opposed only by militia and a small detachment of Continentals under Lafayette, the British ravaged the state with fire and sword during the months preceding their surrender that fall at Yorktown. Jefferson himself, as he tells us, suffered severe property losses, and he came very near being captured when Colonel Tarleton made his famous raid on Charlottesville in June of 1781.

At this crisis, just as his second term was about to expire, he was shocked into angry protest by the clamor for a dictator with un-limited power, the very thought of which was treason against democracy, treason against mankind in general. He keenly re-sented criticism of his military measures during the invasion, and his resentment continued even after the legislature unanimously and warmly commended his services as war governor.

His bitterness at the time (accentuated by the death of his wife in 1782) made him vow never again to enter politics. But he was soon prevailed upon to serve in the Confederation Congress. Here he made two important national contributions. He provided a coinage system for the new republic, and he set forth, in his report on the territories, the vital principle of federal union: that new states should be added to the original thirteen on the basis of ab-solute equality. His attempt to exclude slavery forever from all the territories, from the Lakes to the Gulf, was defeated by only one vote. It was a dramatic event in America's history, fraught with terrible significance for her future. The fate of unborn millions depended upon the tongue of one man, 'and Heaven was silent in that awful moment!'

Again his thoughts turned to retirement at his beloved Monti-cello, and he urged his friends, James Monroe, William Short, and James Madison, to establish themselves near him. But once again he heeded the call of public duty. In 1784 as a minister plenipo-tentiary he sailed to France, and there, at last, he was to recover fully from the strain of these war years.

Governor of Virginia

On the 1st of June, 1779, I was appointed Governor of the Com-monwealth, and retired from the legislature. . . . Being now, as it were, identified with the Commonwealth itself, to write my own history during the two years of my administration would be to write the public history of that portion of the Revolution within this state. This has been done by others, and particularly by Mr. Girardin, who wrote his *Continuation of Burk's History of Virginia* while at Milton, in this neighborhood, had free access to all my papers while composing it, and has given as faithful an account as I could myself.[1]

Soldiers without guns

There is really nothing to oppose the progress of the enemy
northward but the cautious principles of the military art [he wrote
General George Washington in June of 1780]. North Carolina is
without arms. We do not abound. Those we have are freely im-
parted to them, but such is the state of their resources that they
have not yet been able to move a single musket from this state to
theirs. All the wagons we can collect have been furnished to the
Marquis de Kalb, and are assembling for the march of twenty-five
hundred militia under General Stevens. . . . I have written to Congress to hasten supplies of arms and military stores for the Southern
States, and particularly to aid us with cartridge paper and cartridge
boxes, the want of which articles, small as they are, renders our
stores useless. The want of money cramps every effort.[2]

The numbers of regulars and militia ordered from this state into
the southern service are about seven thousand. I trust we may
count that fifty-five hundred will actually proceed; but we have
arms for three thousand only. . . . We are still more destitute of
clothing, tents, and wagons for our troops. The southern army
suffers for provisions, which we could plentifully supply were it
possible to find means of transportation.[3]

The British invade, and the Tories make trouble

I have this morning [October 22, 1780] received certain information of the arrival of a hostile fleet in our bay of about sixty sail. . . .
We are endeavoring to collect as large a body to oppose them as
we can arm; this will be lamentably inadequate if the enemy be in
any force. It is mortifying to suppose that a people able and
zealous to contend with the enemy should be reduced to fold their
arms for want of the means of defense. . . . Of the troops we shall
raise there is not a single man who ever saw the face of an enemy.[4]

A very dangerous insurrection in Pittsylvania was prevented a
few days ago by being discovered three days before it was to take
place. The ringleaders were seized in their beds. This dangerous
fire is only smothered; when it will break out seems to depend altogether on events. . . . The rest of the state turns out with a spirit
and alacrity which makes me perfectly happy. If they had arms

BUST OF JEFFERSON. Done in Paris by Jean Antoine Houdon in 1789

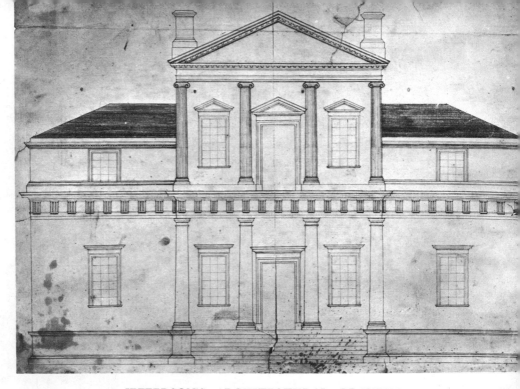

JEFFERSON'S ARCHITECTURAL DRAWING
FOR MONTICELLO. Drawn before March of 1771

HIS FLOOR PLAN FOR MONTICELLO. Drawn before March of 1771

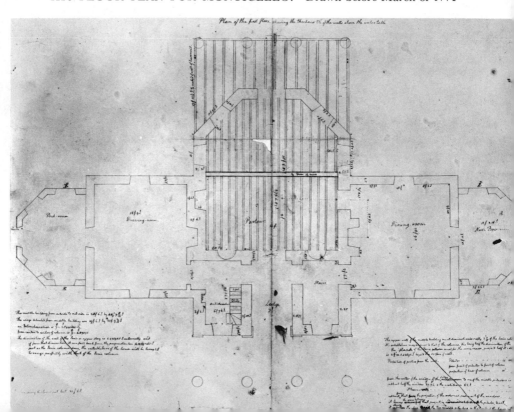

MARIA COSWAY.　A Self-Portrait, 1787

THE MAISON CARRÉE AT NÎMES

THE VIRGINIA STATE CAPITOL AT RICHMOND
Designed by Jefferson in 1786, after the Maison Carrée

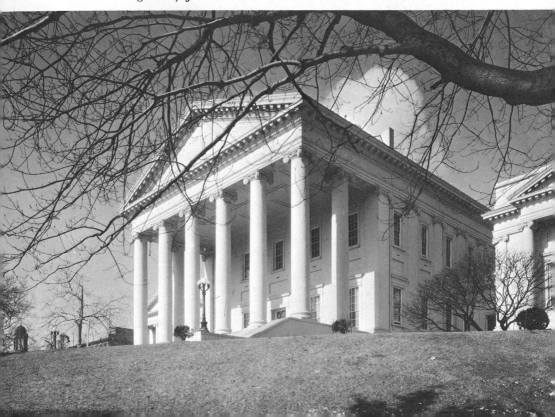

there is no effort either of public or private enemies in this state which would give any apprehensions. Our whole arms are or will be in the hands of the force now assembling. Were any disaster to befall these, we have no other resource but a few scattered squirrel guns, rifles, etc., in the hands of the western people.[5]

An intercepted courier; offensive defense

Two or three days ago a British emissary from Portsmouth [Virginia] was taken endeavoring to proceed towards Carolina. On a proposal to search him they observed him to put his hand in his pocket and put something to his mouth like a quid of tobacco. On examination it was found to be a letter, of which the enclosed is a copy, written on silk paper, rolled up in goldbeater's skin, and nicely tied at each end, the whole not larger than a goose quill. By this you will find our conjectures verified that they expected to meet with Lord Cornwallis in the neighborhood at least of this country.[6]

A powerful army forming by our enemies in the south renders it necessary for us to reserve as much of our militia as possible free to act in that quarter. At the same time we have reason to believe that a very extensive combination of British and Indian savages is preparing to invest our western frontier. To prevent the cruel murders and devastations which attend the latter species of war, and at the same time to prevent its producing a powerful diversion of our force from the southern quarter, in which they mean to make their principal effort and where alone success can be decisive of their ultimate object, it becomes necessary that we aim the first stroke in the western country and throw the enemy under the embarrassments of a defensive war rather than labor under them ourselves. We have therefore determined that an expedition shall be undertaken under [George Rogers Clark] . . . into the hostile country beyond the Ohio, the principal object of which is to be the reduction of the British post at Detroit and incidental to it the acquiring possession of Lake Erie. . . .

If that post be reduced we shall be quiet in future on our frontier, and thereby immense treasures of blood and money be saved; we shall be at leisure to turn our whole force to the rescue of our eastern country from subjugation; we shall divert through our own

country a branch of commerce [furs] which the European states
have thought worthy of the most important struggles and sacrifices;
and in the event of peace on terms which have been contemplated
by some powers, we shall form to the American Union a barrier
against the dangerous extension of the British Province of Canada
and add to the empire of liberty an extensive and fertile country,
thereby converting dangerous enemies into valuable friends.[7]

Benedict Arnold harasses Virginia

Twenty-seven sail of vessels had entered the capes [on December
30, 1780]. . . . We immediately dispatched General Nelson to the
lower country with power to call on the militia in that quarter. . . .
It was ascertained that they were enemies and had advanced up
James River. . . .

They marched from Westover at two o'clock in the afternoon of
[January] 4th, and entered Richmond at one o'clock in the afternoon of the 5th. A regiment of infantry and about thirty horse
continued on, without halting, to the foundry. They burnt that,
the boring mill, the magazine, and two other houses, and proceeded to Westham; but nothing being in their power there, they
retired to Richmond. The next morning they burnt some buildings
of public and private property, with what stores remained in them,
destroyed a great quantity of private stores, and about twelve
o'clock retired towards Westover, where they encamped. . . .

Their numbers, from the best intelligence I have had, are about
fifteen hundred infantry and, as to their cavalry, accounts vary
from fifty to one hundred and twenty; the whole commanded by
the parricide Arnold.[8]

Five thousand guineas for his capture

It is above all things desirable to drag [Benedict Arnold] from
those under whose wing he is now sheltered. On his march to and
from this place [Richmond] I am certain it might have been done
with facility by men of enterprise and firmness. I think it may still
be done, though perhaps not quite so easily. Having peculiar
confidence in the men from the western side of the mountains, I
meant, as soon as they should come down, to get the enterprise
proposed to a chosen number of them, . . . and engage them to
undertake to seize and bring off this greatest of all traitors.

Whether this may be best effected by their going in as friends and awaiting their opportunity, or otherwise, is left to themselves. The smaller the number the better.... Every necessary caution must be used..., as should they be taken the laws of war will justify against them the most rigorous sentence. I will undertake, if they are successful in bringing him off alive, that they shall receive five thousand guineas reward among them. And to men formed for such an enterprise it must be a great incitement to know that their names will be recorded with glory in history.[9]

Knocking at the door of Congress

The situation of affairs here and in Carolina is such as must shortly turn up important events one way or the other.... I learn that Lord Cornwallis... had burned his own wagons to enable himself to move with facility, had pressed on... and was still advancing [towards Virginia].... I have been knocking at the door of Congress for aids of all kinds, but especially of arms, ever since the middle of summer.... Justice indeed requires that we should be aided powerfully. Yet if they would repay us the arms we have lent them, we should give the enemy trouble, though abandoned to ourselves.[10]

Every moment... brings us new proofs that we must be aided by [our] northern brethren. Perhaps they are aiding us and we may not be informed of it. I think near half the enemy's force are now in Virginia and the states south of that. Is half the burden of opposition to rest on Virginia and North Carolina? [11]

Naked militia, and mutineers

The nakedness of the militia on service near Williamsburg and want of shoes is such as to have produced murmurings almost amounting to mutinies, and... there is no hope of being able longer to keep them in service. The precedent of an actual mutiny would be so mischievous as to induce us to believe an accommodation to their present temper most prudent.[12] Mild laws, a people not used to prompt obedience, a want of provisions of war and means of procuring them, render our orders often ineffectual, oblige us to temporize, and when we cannot accomplish an object in one way to attempt it in another.[13]

I am sorry such a spirit of disobedience has shown itself. . . . It must be subdued. Laws made by common consent must not be trampled on by individuals. It is very much the good to force the unworthy into their due share of contributions to the public support, otherwise the burden on them will become oppressive indeed. . . . Men on horseback have been found the most certain instruments of public punishment. Their best way too, perhaps, is not to go against the mutineers when embodied, which would bring on perhaps an open rebellion or bloodshed most certainly, but when they shall have dispersed, to go and take them out of their beds, singly and without noise, or if they be not found the first time, to go again and again so that they may never be able to remain in quiet at home.[14]

Bravery of raw militia

The enemy after leaving Williamsburg . . . marched up to Petersburg, where they were received by Major General Baron Steuben with a body of militia somewhat under one thousand, who, though the enemy were twenty-three hundred strong, disputed the ground very handsomely two hours, during which time the enemy gained only one mile, and that by inches. Our troops were then ordered to retire over a bridge, which they did in perfectly good order. Our loss was between sixty and seventy, killed, wounded, and taken. The enemy's is unknown, but it must be equal to ours; for their own honor they must confess this, as they broke twice and ran like sheep till supported by fresh troops. . . .

By this time Major General Marquis Fayette, having been advised of our danger, had by forced marches got here with his detachment of Continental troops; and reinforcements of militia having also come in, the enemy, finding we were able to meet them on equal footing, thought proper to burn the warehouses and tobacco at Manchester and retire to Warwick, where they did the same.

Ill armed and untried militia who never before saw the face of an enemy have at times during the course of this war given occasions of exultation to our enemies, but they afforded us while at Warwick a little satisfaction in the same way. Six or eight hundred of their picked men of light infantry with General Arnold at their head, having crossed the river from Warwick, fled from a patrol of sixteen horse, every man into his boat as he could, some pushing north, some south, as their fears drove them.[15]

Virginia's desperate plight

A powerful enterprise meditated by the northwestern savages has obliged this state to have an army of between two and three thousand men collected at this time at the Ohio. The Cherokees on our southwestern corner take off the aid of our most valuable counties in that quarter. To support General Greene and prevent the enemy entering our country on the south, we are obliged to send the whole of our regulars and continual reliefs of militia, and on our seaboard an enemy three thousand strong is firmly posted, has totally shut up the only door we had to commerce for either private or public purposes, and lays us under the necessity of keeping up two armies of militia to prevent their ravaging the adjacent country. Notwithstanding all this I believe from what I have lately seen that we should be substantially safe were our citizens armed, but we have not as many arms as we have enemies in the state. . . .

Should a superiority on the Continental seas be obtained by [the French] fleet, it will save everything from north to south; if the detachments of the British army can once be insulated, they will be whittled down by the militia, by famine, by sickness and desertion, to nothing. If they can be prevented availing themselves of an army flying on the wings of the wind to relieve the laboring part, acting in New York this week, in Portsmouth the next, in Charleston the third, the Continental war would be totally changed, and a single campaign would strip them of the labors and laurels of half a dozen.[16]

Virginians look to their Washington

I make no doubt you [General Washington] will have heard . . . of the junction of Lord Cornwallis with the force at Petersburg under Arnold. . . . Your Excellency will judge from this state of things, and from what you know of our country, what it may probably suffer during the present campaign. Should the enemy be able to produce no opportunity of annihilating [Lafayette's small detachment of Continentals], a small proportion of their force may yet restrain his movements effectually while the greater part [are] employed in detachment to waste an unarmed country, and lead the minds of the people to acquiesce under those events which they see no human power prepared to ward off. . . .

Were it possible for this circumstance to justify in your Excellency a determination to lend us your personal aid, it is evident from the universal voice that the presence of their beloved countryman, whose talents have so long been successfully employed in establishing the freedom of kindred states, to whose person they have still flattered themselves they retained some right, and have ever looked up as their *dernier resort* in distress; that your appearance among them, I say, would restore full confidence of salvation, and would render them equal to whatever is not impossible.[17]

General Nelson becomes governor

Lord Cornwallis about the middle of May [1781] joining the main southern armies, M. de Lafayette was obliged to retire. The enemy crossed the river and advanced up into the country about fifty miles, and within thirty miles of Charlottesville, at which place the legislature being to meet in June, the Governor [that is, Jefferson himself] proceeded to his seat at Monticello, two or three miles from it.

His office was now near expiring; the country under invasion by a powerful army, no services but military of any avail, unprepared by his line of life and education for the command of armies, he believed it right not to stand in the way of talents better fitted than his own to the circumstances under which the country was placed. He therefore himself proposed to his friends in the legislature that General [Thomas] Nelson, who commanded the militia of the state, should be appointed governor, as he was sensible that the union of the civil and military power in the same hands at this time would greatly facilitate military measures. This appointment accordingly took place on the 12th of June, 1781.[18]

A dictator would be treason!

Our circumstances being much distressed, it was proposed . . . to create a *dictator*, invested with every power legislative, executive, and judiciary, civil and military, of life and of death, over our persons and over our properties; ... and wanted a few votes only of being passed. One who entered into this contest from a pure love of liberty and a sense of injured rights, who determined to make every sacrifice, and to meet every danger, for the re-establishment of those rights on a firm basis, who did not mean to expend his blood and substance for the wretched purpose of changing this master for that, but to place the powers of governing him in a plurality of hands of his own choice, so that the corrupt will of no one man might in future oppress him, must stand confounded and dismayed when he is told that a considerable portion of that plurality had meditated the surrender of them into a single hand, and, in lieu of a limited monarch, to deliver him over to a despotic one! ...

Was it from the necessity of the case? ... It was belied by the event. ... The very thought alone was treason against the people, was treason against mankind in general, as riveting forever the chains which bow down their necks, by giving to their oppressors a proof, which they would have trumpeted through the universe, of the imbecility of republican government in times of pressing danger to shield them from harm. Those who assume the right of giving away the reins of government in any case must be sure that the herd whom they hand on to the rods and hatchet of the dictator will lay their necks on the block when he shall nod to them. But if our assemblies supposed such a resignation in the people I hope they mistook their character.[19]

Tarleton's raid: I was no Don Quixote

Learning that the legislature was in session at Charlottesville, [Lord Cornwallis] detached Colonel Tarleton with his legion of horse to surprise them. As he was passing through Louisa on the evening of the 3d of June, he was observed by a Mr. Jouett who, suspecting the object, set out immediately for Charlottesville and, knowing the byways of the neighborhood, passed the enemy's encampment, rode all night, and before sunrise of the 4th called at Monticello with notice of what he had seen, and passed on to Charlottesville to notify the members of the legislature. The Speakers of the two Houses and some other members were lodging with us. I ordered a carriage to be ready to carry off my family; we breakfasted at leisure with our guests; and after breakfast they had gone to Charlottesville when a neighbor rode up full speed to inform me that a troop of horse was then ascending the hill to the house. I instantly sent off my family and, after a short delay for some pressing arrangements, I mounted my horse and, knowing that in the public road I should be liable to fall in with the enemy, I went through the woods and joined my family at the house of a friend, where we dined.

Would it be believed, were it not known, that this flight from a troop of horse whose whole legion, too, was within supporting distance, has been the subject with party writers of volumes of reproach on me, serious or sarcastic? That it has been sung in verse, and said in humble prose, that forgetting the noble example of the hero of La Mancha and his windmills, I declined a combat singly against a troop, in which victory would have been so glorious? Forgetting, themselves, at the same time, that I was not provided with the enchanted arms of the Knight, nor even with his helmet of Mambrino. These closet heroes, forsooth, would have disdained the shelter of a wood, even singly and unarmed, against a legion of armed enemies.[20]

Tarleton was genteel; Cornwallis wantonly plundered

I did not suffer by [Banastre Tarleton]. On the contrary, he behaved very genteelly with me. . . . He dispatched a troop of horse under Captain McLeod with the double object of taking me prisoner . . . and of remaining there in *vidette*, my house commanding a view of ten or twelve counties round about. He gave strict orders to Captain McLeod to suffer nothing to be injured. . . . McLeod preserved everything with sacred care during about eighteen hours that he remained there. . . .

Lord Cornwallis . . . encamped his army . . . all along the main James River to a seat of mine called Elk Hill, . . . his own headquarters being in my house at that place. . . . He destroyed all my growing crops of corn and tobacco; he burned all my barns containing the same articles of the last year, having first taken what he wanted; he used, as was to be expected, all my stocks of cattle, sheep, and hogs for the sustenance of his army, and carried off all the horses capable of service; of those too young for service he cut the throats; and he burned all the fences on the plantation so as to leave it an absolute waste. He carried off also about thirty slaves. Had this been to give them freedom he would have done right; but it was to consign them to inevitable death from the smallpox and putrid fever then raging in his camp. This I knew afterwards to have been the fate of twenty-seven of them. . . .

Virginia wasted by fire and sword

I relate these things on my own knowledge in a great degree, as I was on the ground soon after he left it. He treated the rest of the neighborhood somewhat in the same style, but not with that spirit of total extermination with which he seemed to rage over my possessions. Wherever he went the dwelling houses were plundered of everything that could be carried off. Lord Cornwallis's character in England would forbid the belief that he shared in the plunder, but that his table was served with the plate thus pillaged from private houses can be proved by many hundred eyewitnesses.

From an estimate I made at that time on the best information I could collect, I supposed the State of Virginia lost under Lord Cornwallis's hands that year about thirty thousand slaves, and that of these about twenty-seven thousand died of the smallpox and camp fever. . . . History will never relate the horrors committed by the British army in the *Southern States* of America. They raged in Virginia six months only, from the middle of April to the middle of October, 1781, when they were all taken prisoners [at Yorktown], and I give you a faithful specimen of their transactions for ten days of that time, and on one spot only. *Ex pede Herculem.* I suppose their whole devastations during those six months amounted to about three millions sterling.[21]

Services as war governor unanimously commended

Some members [of the legislature] had not been at Richmond at the time of Arnold's enterprise. One of these, George Nicholas, a very honest and able man, then, however, young and ardent, supposing that there had been some remissness in the measures of the Executive on that occasion, moved for an inquiry. . . . Mr. Nicholas, however, before the day, became better satisfied as to what had been done and did not appear to bring forward the inquiry; and in a publication, several years after, he made honorable acknowledgment of the erroneous views he had entertained on those transactions. I therefore read in my place the inquiries he had proposed to make, and stated the justifications of the Executive. And ... 'The following resolution was *unanimously* agreed to by both Houses of the General Assembly of Virginia, December the 19th, 1781.

'*Resolved*, That the sincere thanks of the General Assembly be given to our former Governor, Thomas Jefferson, Esquire, for his impartial, upright, and attentive administration whilst in office. The Assembly wish in the strongest manner to declare the high opinion they entertain of Mr. Jefferson's ability, rectitude, and integrity as Chief Magistrate of this Commonwealth, and mean, by thus publicly avowing their opinion, to obviate and to remove all unmerited censure.' [22]

After Yorktown: America as I hope to see it

Young as we are, and with such a country before us to fill with people and with happiness, we should point in that direction the whole generative force of nature, wasting none of it in efforts of mutual destruction. It should be our endeavor to cultivate the peace and friendship of every nation, even of that which has injured us most. ... Our interest will be to throw open the doors of commerce, and to knock off all its shackles, giving perfect freedom to all persons for the vent of whatever they may choose to bring into our ports, and asking the same in theirs. Never was so much false arithmetic employed on any subject as that which has been employed to persuade nations that it is their interest to go to war. Were the money which it has cost to gain ... a little town, or a little territory, the right to cut wood here or to catch fish there, expended in improving what they already possess, in making roads, opening rivers, building ports, improving the arts, and finding employment for their idle poor, it would render them much stronger, much wealthier and happier. This I hope will be our wisdom.[23]

In Congress, 1783–84: a new coinage system

On the 6th of [June, 1783] I was appointed by the legislature a delegate to Congress, the appointment to take place on the 1st of November ensuing. . . . I accordingly left home on the 16th of October, arrived at Trenton, where Congress was sitting, on the 3d of November, and took my seat on the 4th, on which day Congress adjourned to meet at Annapolis on the 26th. . . .

They, as early as January 7, 1782, had turned their attention to the moneys current in the several states, and had directed the Financier, Robert Morris, to report to them a table of rates. . . . That officer . . . went into the consideration of the necessity of establishing a standard of value with us, and of the adoption of a money unit. . . . The general views of the Financier were sound, and the principle was ingenious on which he proposed to found his unit; but it was too minute for ordinary use, too laborious for computation either by the head or in figures.

The price of a loaf of bread, 1/20 of a dollar, would be 72 units. A pound of butter, 1/5 of a dollar, 288 units. A horse or bullock, of eighty dollars value, would require a notation of six figures, to wit, 115,200; and the public debt, suppose of eighty millions, would require twelve figures, to wit, 115,200,000,000 units. Such a system of money-arithmetic would be entirely unmanageable for the common purposes of society.

I proposed, therefore, instead of this, to adopt the dollar as our unit of account and payment, and that its divisions and subdivisions should be in the decimal ratio. I wrote some notes on the subject. . . . The Financier [disagreed}. . . . I replied to this, and printed my notes and reply on a flying sheet which I put into the hands of the members of Congress for consideration, and the Committee agreed to report on my principle. This was adopted the ensuing year, and is the system which now prevails.[24]

A stronger government needed

The crippled state of Congress is not new to you [George Washington]. We have only nine states present, eight of whom are represented by two members each, and of course on all great questions not only a unanimity of states but of members is necessary — a unanimity which can never be obtained on a matter of any importance. The consequence is that we are wasting our time and labor in vain efforts to do business.[25]

I see the best effects produced by sending our young statesmen here. They see the affairs of the Confederacy from a high ground; they learn the importance of the Union and befriend federal measures when they return. Those who never come here see our affairs insulated, pursue a system of jealousy and self-interest, and distract the Union as much as they can.[26]

I find the conviction growing strongly that nothing can preserve our Confederacy unless the band of Union, their common council, be strengthened.[27]

Basic principles of federal union

The Committee ... have agreed [to Jefferson's plan] that so much of the territory ceded or to be ceded by individual states to the United States ... shall be divided into distinct states. . . . Provided that both the temporary and permanent governments be established on these principles as their basis:

1. That they shall forever remain a part of this Confederacy of the United States of America.

2. That in their persons, property, and territory they shall be subject to the government of the United States in Congress assembled, and to the Articles of Confederation in all those cases in which the original states shall be so subject.

3. That they shall be subject to pay a part of the federal debts, contracted or to be contracted, to be apportioned on them by Congress according to the same common rule and measure by which the apportionments thereof shall be made on the other states.

4. That their respective governments shall be in republican forms and shall admit no person to be a citizen who holds any hereditary title.

5. That after the year 1800 of the Christian era there shall be neither slavery nor involuntary servitude in any of the said states. . . .

That whensoever any of the said states shall have, of free inhabitants, as many as shall then be in any one the least numerous

of the thirteen original states, such state shall be admitted . . . on
an equal footing with the said original states.[28]

One vote alone retained slavery in the territories

The act of Congress [the Ordinance of 1784, affecting all the
territories, from the Great Lakes to the Gulf of Mexico] . . . shows
how and when they shall be taken into the Union. . . . You will
observe two clauses struck out of the report, the first respecting
hereditary honors, the second slavery. The first was done not from
an approbation of such honors, but because it was thought an im-
proper place to encounter them. The second was lost by an individual vote only. Ten states were present. The four Eastern
States, New York, and Pennsylvania, were for the clause. Jersey
would have been for it, but there were but two members, one of
whom was sick in his chambers. South Carolina, Maryland, and
! Virginia ! voted against it. North Carolina was divided, as would
have been Virginia had not one of its delegates been sick in bed.[29]

The voice of a single individual of the state which was divided,
or of one of those which were of the negative, would have prevented
this abominable crime from spreading itself over the new country.
Thus we see the fate of millions unborn hanging on the tongue of
one man, and Heaven was silent in that awful moment! But it is
to be hoped it will not always be silent, and that the friends to the
rights of human nature will in the end prevail.[30]

Considers retiring to Monticello

Monroe is buying land almost adjoining me. [William] Short
will do the same. What would I not give if you [Madison] could
fall into the circle. With such a society I could once more venture
home and lay myself up for the residue of life, quitting all its contentions, which grow daily more and more insupportable. Think
of it. To render it practicable only requires you to think it so.
Life is of no value but as it brings us gratifications. Among the
most valuable of these is rational society. It informs the mind,
sweetens the temper, cheers our spirits, and promotes health.[31]

Would you but make it a 'partie quarrée,' I should believe that
life had still some happiness in store for me. Agreeable society is
the first essential in constituting the happiness, and, of course, the

value of our existence. And it is a circumstance worthy great attention when we are making first our choice of a residence. Weigh well the value of this against the difference in pecuniary interest, and ask yourself which will add most to the sum of your felicity through life. I think that weighing them in this balance your decision will be favorable to all our prayers. . . . I view the prospect of this society as inestimable.[32]

But goes to France as a minister plenipotentiary

On the 7th of May [1784] Congress resolved that a minister plenipotentiary should be appointed, in addition to Mr. Adams and Dr. Franklin, for negotiating treaties of commerce with foreign nations, and I was elected to that duty. I accordingly left Annapolis on the 11th, took with me my eldest daughter then at Philadelphia . . . , and proceeded to Boston in quest of a passage. While passing through the different states I made a point of informing myself of the state of the commerce of each; went on to New Hampshire with the same view, and returned to Boston.

Thence I sailed on the 5th of July in the *Ceres*, a merchant ship of Mr. Nathaniel Tracey, bound to Cowes. He was himself a passenger, and, after a pleasant voyage of nineteen days from land to land, we arrived at Cowes on the 26th. I was detained there a few days by the indisposition of my daughter. On the 30th we embarked for Havre, arrived there on the 31st, left it on the 3d of August, and arrived at Paris on the 6th. I called immediately on Dr. Franklin, at Passy, communicated to him our charge, and we wrote to Mr. Adams, then at The Hague, to join us at Paris.[33]

CHAPTER VII

An American in Paris

FROM his arrival in Paris in August of 1784 until his departure in the fall of 1789, Thomas Jefferson served his country with ability as a diplomat, first as a special envoy and then, for four years, as Benjamin Franklin's successor as American minister to France. His diplomatic duties, as he tells us, were chiefly directed to the winning of preferential treatment for America's commerce. Although France was friendly enough, his sensitive American pride was stung again and again by 'the present disrespect of the nations of Europe' for an upstart New World republic. Great Britain was especially hostile, as he discovered when he went to London in 1786 to aid John Adams in his negotiations at the court of 'mulish' George the Third. Against the Barbary pirates Jefferson urged war rather than the payment of tribute, but the United States was then so weak that it was unable to furnish a single warship to carry out his policy of naval protection for America's commerce and seamen.

These North African pirates were a source of worry when he had his little daughter Polly (Mary) sail from Virginia and join him and her sister Patsy (Martha) in Paris. He looked after his two little girls with tender concern. And he displayed his zealous Americanism not only in advising Patsy to conquer her studies with American self-reliance but in contrasting the domestic felicities of home with the daily activities of a Parisienne, and in listing the disadvantages of a European education for his countrymen. Yet he loved the French people with all his heart, and he enjoyed the intellectual and artistic circles into which he had been introduced by Franklin and Lafayette. He loved Paris with its theatres and concerts and bookstalls, its shops (in which he purchased corsets for John Adams' daughter), and its Bois de Boulogne, in which during his daily walk or ride he thought warmly of absent friends and reflected on such matters as the latest creation of Houdon or David, an improvement in quilling the harpsichord, or the essay on English prosody which he was writing for his old friend, Chastellux, with whom at Monticello he had once spent a night discussing the poetry of Ossian around a punch-bowl.

From Paris he sent informative 'crumbs of science' to learned friends at home. He considered phosphoric matches a beautiful discovery, differed with Count de Buffon as to the future of chemistry, noted the pioneer work being done in aerial navigation, and was impressed with the advantages of mass-production methods applied to industry. He forced Buffon to alter his views on natural history, and he collected useful plants and animals to colonize in America. He found time, also, to contrive a portable copying-press, to design a phaeton, to make a map of his native state for the Paris edition of his *Notes on Virginia*, and to draw up the architectural plans for the Virginia capitol at Richmond.

Thus he happily cultivated his scientific and artistic interests, and delighted in the social amenities of Paris. But such pleasures did not blind him to the fate of the common man in the monarchical Old World. Throughout his stay abroad Jefferson was a critical observer, and what he saw of 'the vaunted scene of Europe' only deepened and intensified his democratic Americanism.

Behold me on the vaunted scene of Europe!

Behold me at length on the vaunted scene of Europe! It is not necessary for your information that I should enter into details concerning it. But you are, perhaps, curious to know how this new scene has struck a savage of the mountains of America. Not advantageously, I assure you. I find the general fate of humanity here most deplorable. The truth of Voltaire's observation offers itself perpetually, that every man here must be either the hammer or the anvil. It is a true picture of that country to which they say we shall pass hereafter, and where we are to see God and his angels in splendor, and crowds of the damned trampled under their feet.

While the great mass of the people are thus suffering under physical and moral oppression . . . intrigues of love occupy the younger, and those of ambition the elder part, of the great. Conjugal love having no existence among them, domestic happiness, of which that is the basis, is utterly unknown. In lieu of this are substituted pursuits which nourish and invigorate all our bad passions, and which offer only moments of ecstasy amidst days and months of restlessness and torment. Much, very much inferior, this, to the tranquil, permanent felicity with which domestic society in America blesses most of its inhabitants, leaving them to follow steadily those pursuits which health and reason approve, and rendering truly delicious the intervals of those pursuits.

Polite manners and the fine arts

In science the mass of the people are two centuries behind ours; their literati half a dozen years before us. Books really good acquire just reputation in that time, and so become known to us and communicate to us all their advances in knowledge. Is not this delay compensated by our being placed out of the reach of that swarm of nonsensical publications which issues daily from a thousand presses, and perishes almost in issuing? With respect to what are termed polite manners, without sacrificing too much the sincerity of language I would wish my countrymen to adopt just so much of European politeness as to be ready to make all those little sacrifices of self which really render European manners amiable and relieve society from the disagreeable scenes to which rudeness often subjects it. Here it seems that a man might pass a life without encountering a single rudeness. In the pleasures of the table they are far before us, because with good taste they unite temperance. They do not terminate the most sociable meals by transforming themselves into brutes. I have never yet seen a man drunk in France, even among the lowest of the people.

Were I to proceed to tell you how much I enjoy their architecture, sculpture, painting, music, I should want words. It is in these arts they shine. The last of them, particularly, is an enjoyment the deprivation of which with us cannot be calculated. I am almost ready to say it is the only thing which from my heart I envy them, and which, in spite of all the authority of the Decalogue, I do covet. But I am running on in an estimate of things [which can only reveal] that I have brought with me all the prejudices of country, habit, and age.[1]

Treaty-making with John Adams and Dr. Franklin

Mr. Adams soon joined us at Paris, and our first employment was to prepare a general form to be proposed to such nations as were disposed to treat with us. . . . We inserted . . . an article exempting from capture by the public or private armed ships of either belligerent, when at war, all merchant vessels and their cargoes employed merely in carrying on the commerce between nations, . . . with a provision against the molestation of fishermen, husbandmen, citizens unarmed and following their occupations in unfortified places; for the humane treatment of prisoners of war; the abolition of contraband of war, which exposes merchant vessels to such vexatious and ruinous detentions and abuses; and for the principle of free bottoms, free goods. . . .

Without urging, we sounded the ministers of the several European nations at the court of Versailles on their dispositions towards mutual commerce, and the expediency of encouraging it by the protection of a treaty. Old Frederic of Prussia met us cordially, and without hesitation. . . . Denmark and Tuscany entered also into negotiations with us. Other powers appearing indifferent, we did not think it proper to press them. They seemed, in fact, to know little about us but as rebels who had been successful in throwing off the yoke of the mother country. They were ignorant of our commerce, which had been always monopolized by England, and of the exchange of articles it might offer advantageously to both parties. They were inclined, therefore, to stand aloof until they could see better what relations might be usefully instituted with us. . . .

Succeeds, but does not replace, Benjamin Franklin

Mr. Adams, being appointed Minister Plenipotentiary of the United States to London, left us in June, and in July, 1785, Dr. Franklin returned to America, and I was appointed his successor at Paris.[2]

There appeared to me more respect and veneration attached to the character of Dr. Franklin in France than to that of any other person in the same country, foreign or native. I had opportunities of knowing particularly how far these sentiments were felt by the foreign ambassadors and ministers at the court of Versailles. The fable of his capture by the Algerines, propagated by the English newspapers, excited no uneasiness, as it was seen at once to be a dish cooked up to the palate of their readers. But nothing could exceed the anxiety of his diplomatic brethren on a subsequent report of his death which, though premature, bore some marks of authenticity.... When he left Passy it seemed as if the village had lost its patriarch. On taking leave of the court, which he did by letter, the King ordered him to be handsomely complimented, and furnished him with a litter and mules of his own, the only kind of conveyance the state of his health could bear....

The succession to Dr. Franklin at the court of France was an excellent school of humility. On being presented to anyone as the minister of America, the common place question used in such cases was 'C'est vous, Monsieur, qui remplace le Docteur Franklin?' — 'It is you, sir, who replace Dr. Franklin?' I generally answered, 'No one can replace him, sir; I am only his successor.' [3]

My duties at Paris were confined to a few objects: the receipt of our whale-oils, salted fish, and salted meats on favorable terms; the admission of our rice on equal terms with that of Piedmont, Egypt, and the Levant; a mitigation of the monopolies of our tobacco by the Farmers-General; and a free admission of our productions into their islands were the principal commercial objects which required attention; and on these occasions I was powerfully aided by all the influence and the energies of the Marquis de Lafayette, who proved himself equally zealous for the friendship and welfare of both nations; and in justice I must also say that I found the government entirely disposed to befriend us on all occasions, and to yield us every indulgence not absolutely injurious to themselves. [4]

The author of the Declaration meets 'mulish' George III

In February, 1786, Mr. Adams wrote to me pressingly to join him in London immediately, as he thought he discovered there some symptoms of better disposition towards us. . . . I accordingly left Paris on the 1st of March, and on my arrival in London we agreed on a very summary form of treaty, proposing an exchange of citizenship for our citizens, our ships, and our productions generally, except as to office. On my presentation, as usual, to the King and Queen at their levées, it was impossible for anything to be more ungracious than their notice of Mr. Adams and myself. I saw at once that the ulcerations in the narrow mind of that mulish being left nothing to be expected on the subject of my attendance. . . . After staying there seven weeks [unavailingly] I left London the 26th, arrived at Paris on the 30th of April.[5]

That nation hate us, their ministers hate us, and their King more than all other men. They have the impudence to avow this. . . . Our overtures of commercial arrangements have been treated with a derision which shows their firm persuasion that we shall never unite to suppress their commerce, or even to impede it. I think their hostility towards us is much more deeply rooted at present than during the war.[6] We are young and can survive them; but their rotten machine must crush under the trial. . . . I shall not wonder to see the scenes of ancient Rome and Carthage renewed in our day. . . . Peace and friendship with all mankind is our wisest policy; and I wish we may be permitted to pursue it. But the temper and folly of our enemies may not leave this in our choice.[7]

War, not tribute, for the Barbary pirates

We have taken some pains to find out the sums which the nations of Europe give to the Barbary States to purchase their peace. They will not tell this, yet from some glimmerings it appears to be very considerable, and I do expect that they would tax us at one, two, or perhaps three hundred thousand dollars a year. Surely our people will not give this. Would it not be better to offer them an equal treaty; if they refuse, why not go to war with them? . . . We ought to begin a naval power if we mean to carry on our own commerce. Can we begin it on a more honorable occasion, or with a weaker foe? I am of opinion Paul Jones with half a dozen frigates would totally destroy their commerce.[8]

We have two plans to pursue. The one to carry nothing for ourselves, and thereby render ourselves invulnerable to the European states, the other (which our country will be for) is to carry as much as possible. But this will require a protecting force on the sea. Otherwise the smallest power in Europe, every one which possesses a single ship of the line, may dictate to us and enforce their demands by captures on our commerce. Some naval force then is necessary if we mean to be commercial. . . . Be assured that the present disrespect of the nations of Europe for us will inevitably bring on insults which must involve us in war. A coward is much more exposed to quarrels than a man of spirit.[9]

I was very unwilling that we should acquiesce in the European humiliation of paying a tribute to those [North African] pirates, and endeavored to form an association of the powers subject to habitual depredations from them. I accordingly prepared, and proposed . . . articles . . . for concerted operation among the powers at war with the piratical states of Barbary . . . beginning with the Algerines. . . . It was expected [that our American Confederation] would contribute a frigate, and its expenses, to be in constant cruise. But . . . their recommendatory powers for obtaining contributions were so openly neglected by the several states that they declined an engagement which they were conscious they could not fulfill with punctuality; and so it fell through.[10]

The pirates must not capture my dear child

I must now repeat my wish to have Polly [Mary] sent to me next summer. This, however, must depend on the circumstance of a good vessel sailing from Virginia in the months of April, May, June, or July. I would not have her set out sooner or later on account of the equinoxes. The vessel should have performed one voyage at least, but not be more than four or five years old. . . . My anxieties on this subject could induce me to endless details. . . . I will only add that I would rather live a year longer without her than have her trusted to any but a good ship and a summer passage. Patsy [Martha] is well. She speaks French as easily as English; while [David] Humphreys [Secretary of Legation], [William] Short [private secretary], and myself are scarcely better at it than when we landed.[11]

To the cautions . . . suggested I am obliged to add another. . . .
The Algerines this fall took two vessels from us and now have
twenty-two of our citizens in slavery. . . . I do not think the insurance against them on vessels coming to France will be worth
one-half per cent, but who can estimate the value of a half per cent
on the fate of a child? My mind revolts at the possibility of a
capture, so that unless you hear from myself — not trusting the
information of any other person on earth — that peace is made
with the Algerines, do not send her but in a vessel of French or
English property; for these vessels alone are safe from prize by the
barbarians.[12]

My dear Polly is safely arrived here, and in good health. She
had got so attached to Captain Ramsay that they were obliged to
decoy her from him. She stayed three weeks in London with Mrs.
[John] Adams, and had got up such an attachment to her that she
refused to come with the person I sent for her. After some days she
was prevailed on to come. She did not know either her sister or
myself, but soon renewed her acquaintance and attachment. She
is now in the same convent [the Abbaye de Panthemont] with her
sister, and will come to see me once or twice a week. It is a house
of education altogether, the best in France, and at which the best
masters attend. There are in it as many Protestants as Catholics,
and not a word is ever spoken to them on the subject of religion.[13]

Conquer Livy, dear Patsy, with American resolution

I do not like your saying that you are unable to read the ancient
print of your Livy but with the aid of your master. We are always
equal to what we undertake with resolution. A little degree of this
will enable you to decipher your Livy. If you always lean on your
master you will never be able to proceed without him. It is part
of the American character to consider nothing as desperate, to
surmount every difficulty by resolution and contrivance. In
Europe there are shops for every want; its inhabitants, therefore,
have no idea that their wants can be supplied otherwise. Remote
from all other aid, we are obliged to invent and to execute; to find
means within ourselves, and not to lean on others. Consider, therefore, the conquering your Livy as an exercise in the habit of sur-
mounting difficulties, a habit which will be necessary to you in the

country where you are to live, and without which you will be thought a very helpless animal, and less esteemed. Music, drawing, books, invention, and exercise will be so many resources to you against ennui. But there are others which, to this object, add that of utility. These are the needle and domestic economy. The latter you cannot learn here.[14]

The day of a Parisienne

At eleven o'clock it is day, *chez madame*. The curtains are drawn. Propped on bolsters and pillows, and her head scratched into a little order, the bulletins of the sick are read, and the billets of the well. She writes to some of her acquaintance, and receives the visits of others. If the morning is not very thronged she is able to get out and hobble round the cage of the Palais Royal; but she must hobble quickly, for the coiffeur's turn is come, and a tremendous turn it is! Happy if he does not make her arrive when dinner is half over! The torpitude of digestion a little passed, she flutters half an hour through the streets by way of paying visits, and then to the spectacles. These finished, another half-hour is devoted to dodging in and out of the doors of her very sincere friends, and away to supper. After supper, cards; and after cards, bed; to rise at noon the next day and to tread, like a mill horse, the same trodden circle over again.

Thus the days of life are consumed, one by one, without an object beyond the present moment; ever flying from the ennui of that, yet carrying it with us; eternally in pursuit of happiness, which keeps eternally before us. If death or bankruptcy happen to trip us out of the circle, it is matter for the buzz of the evening, and is completely forgotten by the next morning. In America, on the other hand, the society of your husband, the fond cares for the children, the arrangements of the house, the improvements of the grounds, fill every moment with a healthy and a useful activity. Every exertion is encouraging because to present amusement it joins the promise of some future good. The intervals of leisure are filled by the society of real friends, whose affections are not thinned to cobweb by being spread over a thousand objects. This is the picture, in the light it is presented to my mind.[15]

Foreign education: pardon my zealous Americanism

Let us view the disadvantages of sending a youth to Europe. To enumerate them all would require a volume. I will select a few. If he goes to England, he learns drinking, horse racing, and boxing. These are the peculiarities of English education. The following circumstances are common to education in that and the other countries of Europe. He acquires a fondness for European luxury and dissipation and a contempt for the simplicity of his own country; he is fascinated with the privileges of the European aristocrats, and sees with abhorrence the lovely equality which the poor enjoy with the rich in his own country; he contracts a partiality for aristocracy and monarchy; he forms foreign friendships which will never be useful to him and loses the seasons of life for forming in his own country those friendships which, of all others, are the most faithful and permanent; he is led by the strongest of all the human passions into a spirit for female intrigue, destructive of his own and others' happiness, or a passion for whores, destructive of his health, and, in both cases, learns to consider fidelity to the marriage bed as an ungentlemanly practice and inconsistent with happiness. . . .

It appears to me, then, that an American coming to Europe for education loses in his knowledge, in his morals, in his health, in his habits, and in his happiness. I had entertained only doubts on this head before I came to Europe: what I see and hear since I came here proves more than I had even suspected. . . . Did you [John Bannister, Jr., a young Virginian] expect by so short a question to draw such a sermon on yourself? I daresay you did not. But the consequences of foreign education are alarming to me, as an American. I sin, therefore, through zeal whenever I enter on the subject. You are sufficiently American to pardon me for it.[16]

I love the French people with all my heart

I consider your boasts of the splendor of your city and of its superb hackney coaches as a flout [Jefferson wrote Mrs. John Adams, wife of the American minister at London]. . . . I would not give the polite, self-denying, feeling, hospitable, good-humored people of this country, and their amiability in every point of view (though it must be confessed our streets are somewhat dirty, and our fiacres rather indifferent), for ten such races of rich, proud, hectoring, swearing, squibbing, carnivorous animals as those among whom you are.... I do love this *people* with all my heart, and think that with a better religion, a better form of government and their present governors, their condition and country would be most enviable. I pray you to observe that I have used the term *people* and that this is a noun of the masculine as well as feminine gender.[17]

I fancy it must be the quantity of animal food eaten by the English which renders their character insusceptible of civilization. I suspect it is in their kitchens and not in their churches that their reformation must be worked, and that missionaries of that description from hence would avail more than those who should endeavor to tame them by precepts of religion or philosophy.[18] Their mechanics certainly exceed all others in some lines. But be just to [Frenchmen]. They have not patience, it is true, to set rubbing a piece of steel from morning till night, as a lethargic Englishman will do, full charged with porter. But do not their benevolence, their cheerfulness, their amiability ... compensate their want of patience? [19]

The workmen of Paris are making rapid strides towards English perfection [he wrote Mrs. William Bingham, an American friend]. ... Commission me to have you a phaeton made, and, if it is not as much handsomer than a London one, as that is than a fiacre, send it back to me. Shall I fill the box with caps, bonnets, etc.? Not of my own choosing, but — I was going to say, of Mademoiselle Bertin's, forgetting for the moment that she ... is a bankrupt. They shall be chosen then by whom you please; or, if you are altogether nonplussed by her eclipse, we will call an *Assemblée des Notables* to help you out of the difficulty, as is now the fashion.[20]

A courtier elegantly presents two pairs of corsets

Mr. Jefferson has the honor to present his compliments to Mrs. Smith [John Adams's daughter] and to send her the two pair of corsets she desired. He wishes they may be suitable, as Mrs. Smith omitted to send her measure. Times are altered since Mademoiselle de Sanson had the honor of knowing her; should they be too small, however, she will be so good as to lay them by a while. There are ebbs as well as flows in this world. When the mountain refused to come to Mahomet, he went to the mountain. Mr. Jefferson wishes Mrs. Smith a happy New Year, and abundance of happier ones still to follow it. He begs leave to assure her of his esteem and respect, and that he shall always be happy to be rendered useful to her by being charged with her commands.[21]

My foolish heart; music and the arts

Many motives, my dear Madam [Mrs. Angelica Church, a friend in London whose little daughter Kitty was visiting the Jeffersons], authorize me to write to you, but none more than this, that I esteem you infinitely. Yet I have thought it safe to get Kitty to write also, that her letter may seem as a passport to mine, and shed on it the *suave odeur* of those warm emotions it will excite in your breast. When we have long expected the visit of a dear friend, he is welcome when he comes, and all who come with him. I present myself then under the wing of Kitty, though she thinks herself under mine. She is here at this instant, well, cheerful, and chattering French to her doll and her friend Polly. We want your presence to round the little family circle, to enliven the Sunday's dinner, which is not less a holiday to me than to the girls. We talk of you, we think of you, and try to enjoy your company by the force of imagination; and were the force of that sufficient, you would be with me every day. Worn down every morning with writing on business, I sally at twelve o'clock into the Bois de Boulogne and unbind my labors by thinking on my friends; and could I write as I ride, and give them my thoughts warm as they flow from the heart, my friends would see what a foolish heart it is.[22]

A new theatre is established..., that of the Opéra Buffons, where Italian operas are given, and good music.... Paris is every day enlarging and beautifying.... Fine boulevards within and without the walls... will afford beautiful rides round the city of between fifteen and twenty miles in circuit.... We have nothing new and excellent in... painting. In fact, I do not feel an interest in any pencil but that of David.[23] [As to modern dress for Houdon's statue of General Washington] I found it strongly the sentiment of

West, Copley, Trumbull, and Brown, in London; after which it would be ridiculous to add that it was my own. I think a modern in an antique dress as just an object of ridicule as a Hercules or Marius with a periwig and a *chapeau bras*.[24] Houdon only stopped a moment . . . , so that I have not yet had an opportunity of asking his opinion of the improvement [for the harpsichord]. . . . He is among the foremost, or, perhaps, the foremost artist in the world.[25]

Poetry, and crumbs of science

A daily habit of walking in the Bois de Boulogne gave me an opportunity of turning this subject [the measure of English verse] in my mind. . . . Error is the stuff of which the web of life is woven and he who lives longest and wisest is only able to weave out the more of it. I began with the design of converting you [Chastellux] to my opinion that the arrangement of long and short syllables into regular feet constituted the harmony of English verse. I ended by discovering that you were right in denying that proposition. The next object was to find out the real circumstance which gives harmony to English poetry and laws to those who make it. I present you with the result [a long essay, 'Thoughts on English Prosody,' in which Jefferson maintained in opposition to Dr. Samuel Johnson that the real basis of English poetry was not quantity but emphasis and accent].[26]

As you [the president of William and Mary College] seem willing to accept of the crumbs of science on which we are subsisting here, it is with pleasure I continue to hand them on. . . . Herschel's volcano in the moon you have doubtless heard of, and placed among the other vagaries of a head which seems not organized for sound induction. . . . Dr. Ingenhouse had discovered, as he supposed, from experiment, that vegetation might be promoted by occasioning streams of the electrical fluid to pass through a plant. . . . Speaking one day with Monsieur de Buffon on the present ardor of chemical inquiry, he affected to consider chemistry but as cookery, and to place the toils of the laboratory on a footing with those of the kitchen. I think it, on the contrary, among the most useful of sciences, and big with future discoveries for the utility and safety of the human race.[27]

Phosphoric matches... are a beautiful discovery and very useful, especially to heads which like... mine cannot at all times be got to sleep. The convenience of lighting a candle without getting out of bed, of sealing letters without calling a servant, of kindling a fire without flint, steel, punk, etc., are of value.[28]

An accident has happened here which will probably damp the ardor with which aerial navigation has been pursued. Monsieur Pilatre de Rozière had been attending many months at Boulogne a fair wind to cross the Channel in a balloon which was compounded of one of inflammable air, and another called a Montgolfier with rarefied air only. He at length thought the wind fair and with a companion ascended. After proceeding a proper direction about two leagues, the wind changed and brought them again over the French coast. Being at the height of about six thousand feet, some accident, unknown, burst the balloon of inflammable air, and the Montgolfier being unequal alone to sustain their weight, they precipitated from that height to the earth, and were crushed to atoms.[29]

An improvement... here in the construction of muskets... consists in the making every part of them so exactly alike that what belongs to any one may be used for every other musket in the magazine.... Supposing it might be useful in the United States, I went to the workman. He presented me the parts of fifty locks taken to pieces, and arranged in compartments. I put several together myself, taking pieces at hazard as they came to hand, and they fitted in the most perfect manner. The advantages of this... are evident.[30]

America should be great in science

What a field have we at our doors to signalize ourselves in! The botany of America is far from being exhausted, its mineralogy is untouched, and its natural history or zoology totally mistaken and misrepresented.... It is the work to which the young men whom you [at Harvard] are forming should lay their hands. We have spent the prime of our lives in procuring them the precious blessing of liberty. Let them spend theirs in showing that it is the great parent of *science* and of virtue; and that a nation will be great in both always in proportion as it is free.[31]

M. de Buffon ... did not know our panther. I gave him the
stripped skin of one I bought in Philadelphia, and it presents him a
new species, which will appear in his next volumes. I have convinced him that our deer is not a Chevreuil. ... He has never seen
the horns of what we call the elk.[32]

I am happy to be able to present to you [M. de Buffon] at this
moment the bones and skin of a moose, the horns of another individual of the same species, the horns of the caribou, the elk, the
deer, the spiked horned buck, and the roebuck of America. ... I
really suspect you will find that the moose, the round-horned elk,
and the American deer are species not existing in Europe.[33]

Colonizing European plants and animals

We are probably far from possessing, as yet, all the articles of
culture for which nature has fitted our country. To find out these
will require abundance of unsuccessful experiments. ... I send ...
some seeds of a grass found very useful in the southern parts of
Europe. ... It is called by the names of Sulla, and Spanish St.
Foin, and is the *Hedysarum coronarium* of Linnaeus.[34] I am satisfied
that the rice of Lombardy is of a different species from [that of
South Carolina]. The exportation of it in the husk being prohibited, I could not bring with me but as much as my pockets
would hold, which I have sent to [the South Carolina] society of
agriculture. It may serve to raise seed from.[35] M. Malsherbes ...
is making for me a collection of the vines from which ... the most
valuable wines of this country are made. Another gentleman is
collecting for me the best eating grapes. I propose also to colonize
their hare, rabbit, red and gray partridge, pheasants of different
kinds, and some other birds.[36] I am persuaded there are many
parts of our lower country where the olive tree might be raised,
which is assuredly the richest gift of heaven. I can scarcely except
bread.[37]

Copy-press, and design for a phaeton

Having a great desire to have a portable copying machine, and
being satisfied from some experiments that the principle of the large
machine might be applied in a small one, I planned one when in
England, and had it made. It answers perfectly. I have since set

a workman to making them here, and they are in such demand
that he has his hands full. Being assured that you [Madison] will
be pleased to have one when you shall have tried its convenience, I
send you one.[38]

You have had great reason, my dear sir [Baron de Geismar, a
European friend], to wonder that you have been so long receiving
an answer to your request relative to the drawing of a cabriolet and
phaeton. Your object was to have such drawings as that a workman
could work by them. A painter's eye draught would not have
answered this purpose, and, indeed, to be sure of having them
done with the accuracy necessary to guide a workman, I could
depend on nobody but myself. But the work was to be done
principally in an open court and there came on between two and
three months of such intense cold as rendered this impossible.
Since the season has become milder I have devoted such little
scraps of time to this object as I was master of, and I now enclose
you the drawings. They are made with such scrupulous exactness
in every part that your workman may safely rely on them.[39]

For Virginia a map, and design for the state capitol

A copy of my *Notes on Virginia* got into the hands of a bookseller who was about publishing a very abominable translation of
them when the Abbé Morellet . . . diverted him from it by undertaking to translate it for him. They will thus appear in French in
spite of my precautions. The Abbé engaged me to make a map. . . .
Though it is on a scale of only an inch to twenty miles, it is as
particular as the four-sheet maps from which it is taken, and I
answer for the exactness of the reduction. I have supplied some
new places, though the first object which induced me to undertake
it was to make a map for my book.[40]

I was written to in 1785 . . . by directors appointed to superintend
the building of a capitol in Richmond. . . . Thinking it a favorable
opportunity of introducing into the state an example of architecture
in the classic style of antiquity, and the Maison Carrée of Nîmes
an ancient Roman temple, being considered as the most perfect
model existing of what may be called Cubic architecture, I applied
to M. Clerisseau, who had published drawings of the antiquities
to Nîmes, to have me a model of the building made in stucco, only

changing the order from Corinthian to Ionic, on account of the difficulty of the Corinthian capitals. . . . To adapt the exterior to our use, I drew a plan for the interior, with the apartments necessary for legislative, executive, and judiciary purposes; and accommodated in their size and distribution to the form and dimensions of the building. These were forwarded to the directors in 1786, and were carried into execution.[41]

CHAPTER VIII

My Head and My Heart

IN THE summer of 1786 through John Trumbull, the American artist, Jefferson met Richard Cosway and his beautiful young wife Maria, both of whom were well-known English painters. Maria Cosway, born and brought up in Italy, was gifted and charming, distinguished not only as a painter but as a musician. During the Cosways' short stay in Paris Jefferson became very much attached to her. When she returned to England in October of 1786 he wrote her a long and affectionate letter in the form of an essay on friendship, which he called a 'Dialogue between my Head and my Heart.' Of all the thousands of his letters this one to Maria Cosway, with its informative autobiographical detail and its description of the conflict between the emotional and intellectual sides of his character, is one of the most interesting, and certainly the most self-revealing.

His long letter to Mrs. Cosway was written with his left hand. His right wrist had been fractured in a fall the month before. It continued to give him pain, and on the advice of physicians he decided to try the waters at Aix, in Provence. Leaving Paris in the spring of 1787, he made a three months' tour of southern France and northern Italy. As was his custom when traveling, he filled his notebooks with observations on whatever might be useful in America. But in his letters he expressed his delight at the beauty of the countryside, the cloudless skies with nightingales in full chorus, and the remains of Roman grandeur such as the Maison Carrée at Nîmes (his model for the Virginia capitol), at which he rapturously gazed for hours 'like a lover at his mistress.'

On this tour, and throughout his stay abroad, he was deeply concerned with the welfare of the common people. His first-hand observations of the wretched condition of the many, contrasted with the privileged position of the few, caused him to lash out at kings, nobles, and priests as 'an abandoned confederacy against the happiness of the mass of the people.' When conservatives at home were seriously alarmed by the rioting of debt-ridden Massachusetts farmers, and voiced their distrust of democracy, Jefferson retained his confidence in the ability of the people to rule themselves, and even declared that a little rebellion now and then was a good thing. He welcomed the bloodless reform in America accomplished by the Constitution of 1787, although he disapproved of the perpetual re-eligibility of the President to office and insisted upon a Bill of Rights. He welcomed the reform movement in France, and he thought that bloody disorders might be avoided if Lafayette and other leaders followed his advice of moderation, of compromise and gradual gains. But this was not to be. On the eve of his departure for the United States in 1789 the attack on the Bastille in Paris took place, and the world-shattering French Revolution began its violent course.

On leaving France after five years' residence in that 'great and good country,' Jefferson paid a gracious tribute to its people and from the bottom of his heart wished success to its Revolution. With a heightened appreciation of his native country and of the rôle it was destined to play in the history of mankind, he returned to America and to the Monticello he had so vividly described to Maria Cosway.

The charming Maria Cosway leaves Paris

Having performed the last sad office of handing you into your carriage at the pavillon de St. Denis, and seen the wheels get actually into motion, I turned on my heel and walked, more dead than alive, to the opposite door where my own was awaiting me. Mr. Danquerville was missing. He was sought for, found, and dragged down stairs. We were crammed into the carriage, like recruits for the Bastille, and not having soul enough to give orders to the coachman, he presumed Paris our destination, and drove off. After a considerable interval, silence was broke with a '*Je suis vraiment affligé du départ de ces bons gens.*'

This was a signal for a mutual confession of distress. We began immediately to talk of Mr. and Mrs. Cosway, of their goodness, their talents, their amiability; and, though we spoke of nothing else, we seemed hardly to have entered into the matter, when the coachman announced the rue St. Denis, and that we were opposite Mr. Danquerville's. He insisted on descending there, and traversing a short passage to his lodgings. I was carried home. Seated by my fireside, solitary and sad, the following dialogue took place between my Head and my Heart.

Dialogue between my Head and my Heart

Head. Well, friend, you seem to be in a pretty trim.

Heart. I am indeed the most wretched of all earthly beings. Overwhelmed with grief, every fibre of my frame distended beyond its natural powers to bear, I would willingly meet whatever catastrophe should leave me no more to feel, or to fear.

Head. These are the eternal consequences of your warmth and precipitation. This is one of the scrapes into which you are ever leading us. You confess your follies, indeed; but still you hug and cherish them; and no reformation can be hoped where there is no repentance.

Heart. Oh, my friend! this is no moment to upbraid my foibles. I am rent into fragments by the force of my grief! If you have any balm, pour it into my wounds; if none, do not harrow them by new torments. Spare me in this awful moment! At any other, I will attend with patience to your admonitions.

Head. On the contrary, I never found that the moment of triumph, with you, was the moment of attention to my admonitions. While suffering under your follies, you may perhaps be made sensible of them, but the paroxysm over, you fancy it can never return. Harsh, therefore, as the medicine may be, it is my office to administer it. You will be pleased to remember that when our friend Trumbull used to be telling us of the merits and talents of these good people, I never ceased whispering to you that we had no occasion for new acquaintances; that the greater their merits and talents, the more dangerous their friendship to our tranquillity, because the regret at parting would be greater.

The Heart disdains diagrams and crotchets

Heart. Accordingly, sir, this acquaintance was not the consequence of my doings. It was one of your projects which threw us in the way of it. It was you, remember, and not I, who desired the meeting at Legrand and Motinos. I never trouble myself with domes nor arches. The Halle aux Bleds might have rotted down before I should have gone to see it. But you, forsooth, who are eternally getting us to sleep with your diagrams and crotchets, must go and examine this wonderful piece of architecture; and when you had seen it, oh! it was the most superb thing on earth! What you had seen there was worth all you had yet seen in Paris! I thought so, too. But I meant it of the lady and gentleman to whom we had been presented; and not of a parcel of sticks and chips put together in pens. You, then, sir, and not I, have been the cause of the present distress.

Head. It would have been happy for you if my diagrams and crotchets had gotten you to sleep on that day, as you are pleased to say they eternally do. My visit to Legrand and Motinos had public utility for its object. A market is to be built in Richmond. What a commodious plan is that of Legrand and Motinos; especially if we put on it the noble dome of the Halle aux Bleds. If such a bridge as they showed us can be thrown across the Schuylkill at Philadelphia, the floating bridges taken up, and the navigation of that river opened, what a copious resource will be added, of wood and provisions, to warm and feed the poor of that city!

While I was occupied with these objects, you were dilating with your new acquaintances and contriving how to prevent a separation from them. Every soul of you had an engagement for the day. Yet all these were to be sacrificed that you might dine together. Lying messengers were to be despatched into every quarter of the city, with apologies for your breach of engagement. You, particularly, had the effrontery to send word to the Duchess Danville that, on the moment we were setting out to dine with her, despatches came to hand which required immediate attention. You wanted me to invent a more ingenious excuse; but I knew you were getting into a scrape, and I would have nothing to do with it. Well; after dinner to St. Cloud, from St. Cloud to Ruggieri's, from Ruggieri's to Krumfoltz; and if the day had been as long as a Lapland summer day, you would still have contrived means among you to have filled it.

That beautiful day we went to St. Germains

Heart. Oh! my dear friend, how you have revived me by recalling to my mind the transactions of that day! How well I remember them all, and that, when I came home at night and looked back to the morning, it seemed to have been a month agone. Go on, then, like a kind comforter, and paint to me the day we went to St. Germains. How beautiful was every object! the Port de Reuilly, the hills along the Seine, the rainbows of the machine of Marly, the terrace of St. Germains, the châteaux, the gardens, the statues of Marly, the pavillon of Lucienne. Recollect, too, Madrid, Bagatelle, the King's garden, the Dessert. How grand the idea excited by the remains of such a column! The spiral staircase, too, was beautiful.

Every moment was filled with something agreeable. The wheels of time moved on with a rapidity of which those of our carriage gave but a faint idea. And yet, in the evening, when one took a retrospect of the day, what a mass of happiness had we travelled over! Retrace all those scenes to me, my good companion, and I will forgive the unkindness with which you were chiding me. The day we went to St. Germains was a little too warm, I think; was it not?

Head. Thou art the most incorrigible of all the beings that ever sinned! I reminded you of the follies of the first day, intending to deduce from thence some useful lessons for you; but instead of listening to them, you kindle at the recollection, you retrace the whole series with a fondness which shows you want nothing, but the opportunity, to act it over again.

The pangs of separation

I often told you, during its course, that you were imprudently engaging your affections under circumstances that must have cost you a great deal of pain; that the persons, indeed, were of the greatest merit, possessing good sense, good humor, honest hearts, honest manners, and eminence in a lovely art; that the lady had, moreover, qualities and accomplishments belonging to her sex which might form a chapter apart for her, such as music, modesty, beauty, and that softness of disposition which is the ornament of her sex and charm of ours; but that all these considerations would increase the pang of separation; that their stay here was to be short; that you rack our whole system when you are parted from those you love, complaining that such a separation is worse than death, inasmuch as this ends our sufferings, whereas that only begins them; and that the separation would, in this instance, be the more severe, as you would probably never see them again.

Heart. But they told me they would come back again the next year.

Head. But in the meantime see what you suffer; and their return, too, depends on so many circumstances, that if you had a grain of prudence you would not count upon it. Upon the whole it is improbable, and therefore you should abandon the idea of ever seeing them again.

Heart. May heaven abandon me if I do!

Head. Very well. Suppose, then, they come back. They are to stay two months, and, when these are expired, what is to follow? Perhaps you flatter yourself they may come to America?

Maria might visit our own dear Monticello

Heart. God only knows what is to happen. I see nothing impossible in that supposition; and I see things wonderfully contrived, sometimes, to make us happy. Where could they find such objects as in America for the exercise of their enchanting art? especially the lady, who paints landscapes so inimitably. She wants only subjects worthy of immortality to render her pencil immortal. The Falling Spring, the Cascade of Niagara, the passage of the Potomac through the Blue Mountains, the Natural Bridge; it is worth a voyage across the Atlantic to see these objects; much more to paint, and make them, and thereby ourselves, known to all ages. And our own dear Monticello; where has nature spread so rich a mantle under the eye? mountains, forests, rocks, rivers. With what majesty do we there ride above the storms! How sublime to look down into the workhouse of nature, to see her clouds, hail, snow, rain, thunder, all fabricated at our feet! and the glorious sun, when rising as if out of a distant water, just gilding the tops of the mountains, and giving life to all nature!

I hope in God no circumstance may ever make either seek an asylum from grief! With what sincere sympathy I would open every cell of my composition, to receive the effusion of their woes! I would pour my tears into their wounds; and if a drop of balm could be found on the top of the Cordilleras, or at the remotest sources of the Missouri, I would go thither myself to seek and to bring it. Deeply practised in the school of affliction, the human heart knows no joy which I have not lost, no sorrow of which I have not drunk! Fortune can present no grief of unknown form to me! Who, then, can so softly bind up the wound of another as he who has felt the same wound himself? But heaven forbid they should ever know a sorrow! Let us turn over another leaf, for this has distracted me.

Americans are not a lawless banditti

Head. Well. Let us put this possibility to trial then on another point. When you consider the character which is given of our country by the lying newspapers of London and their credulous copiers in other countries; when you reflect that all Europe is made to believe we are a lawless banditti, in a state of absolute anarchy, cutting one another's throats, and plundering without distinction, how could you expect that any reasonable creature would venture among us?

Heart. But you and I know that all this is false: that there is not a country on earth where there is greater tranquillity; where the laws are milder, or better obeyed; where everyone is more attentive to his own business, or meddles less with that of others; where strangers are better received, more hospitably treated, and with a more sacred respect.

Head. True, you and I know this, but your friends do not know it.

Heart. But they are sensible people, who think for themselves. They will ask of impartial foreigners who have been among us whether they saw or heard on the spot any instance of anarchy.

They will judge, too, that a people occupied as we are in opening rivers, digging navigable canals, making roads, building public schools, establishing academies, erecting busts and statues to our great men, protecting religious freedom, abolishing sanguinary punishments, reforming and improving our laws in general; they will judge, I say, for themselves, whether these are not the occupations of a people at their ease; whether this is not better evidence of our true state than a London newspaper hired to lie, and from which no truth can ever be extracted but by reversing everything it says.

The Head coldly lectures on friendship

Head. I did not begin this lecture, my friend, with a view to learn from you what America is doing. Let us return, then, to our point. I wish to make you sensible how imprudent it is to place your affections, without reserve, on objects you must so soon lose, and whose loss, when it comes, must cost you such severe pangs. Remember the last night. You knew your friends were to leave Paris today. This was enough to throw you into agonies. All night you tossed us from one side of the bed to the other; no sleep, no rest. The poor crippled wrist, too, never left one moment in the same position; now up, now down, now here, now there; was it to be wondered at if its pains returned? The surgeon then was to be called, and to be rated as an ignoramus because he could not divine the cause of this extraordinary change.

In fine, my friend, you must mend your manners. This is not a world to live at random in, as you do. To avoid those eternal distresses to which you are forever exposing us, you must learn to look forward before you take a step which may interest our peace. Everything in this world is matter of calculation. Advance then with caution, the balance in your hand. Put into one scale the pleasures which any object may offer; but put fairly into the other the pains which are to follow, and see which preponderates. The making an acquaintance is not a matter of indifference. When a new one is proposed to you, view it all round. Consider what advantages it presents, and to what inconveniences it may expose you. Do not bite at the bait of pleasure till you know there is no hook beneath it. The art of life is the art of avoiding pain; and he is the best pilot who steers clearest of the rocks and shoals with which it is beset. Pleasure is always before us, but misfortune is at our side; while running after that, this arrests us.

The most effectual means of being secure against pain is to retire within ourselves and to suffice for our own happiness. Those which depend on ourselves are the only pleasures a wise man will count on, for nothing is ours which another may deprive us of. Hence the inestimable value of intellectual pleasures. Ever in our power, always leading us to something new, never cloying, we ride serene and sublime above the concerns of this mortal world, contemplating truth and nature, matter and motion, the laws which bind up their existence, and that Eternal Being who made and bound them up by those laws. Let this be our employ. Leave the bustle and tumult of society to those who have not talents to occupy themselves without them.

Friendship is but another name for an alliance with the follies and the misfortunes of others. Our own share of miseries is sufficient; why enter then as volunteers into those of another? Is there so little gall poured into our cup that we must need help to drink that of our neighbor? A friend dies or leaves us: we feel as if a limb was cut off. He is sick: we must watch over him, and participate of his pains. His fortune is shipwrecked: ours must be laid under contribution. He loses a child, a parent, or a partner: we must mourn the loss as if it were our own.

The Heart warmly defends itself

Heart. And what more sublime delight than to mingle tears with one whom the hand of heaven hath smitten! to watch over the bed of sickness, and to beguile its tedious and its painful moments! to share our bread with one to whom misfortune has left none! This world abounds indeed with misery; to lighten its burden, we must divide it with one another. But let us now try the virtue of your mathematical balance, and as you have put into one scale the burdens of friendship, let me put its comforts into the other. When languishing then under disease, how grateful is the solace of our friends! how are we penetrated with their assiduities and attentions! how much are we supported by their encouragements and kind offices! When heaven has taken from us some object of our love, how sweet is it to have a bosom whereon to recline our heads, and into which we may pour the torrent of our tears! Grief, with such a comfort, is almost a luxury!

In a life where we are perpetually exposed to want and accident, yours is a wonderful proposition, to insulate ourselves, to retire from all aid, and to wrap ourselves in the mantle of self-sufficiency! For, assuredly, nobody will care for him who cares for nobody. But friendship is precious, not only in the shade but in the sunshine of life; and thanks to a benevolent arrangement of things the greater part of life is sunshine. I will recur for proof to the days we have lately passed. On these, indeed, the sun shone brightly. How gay did the face of nature appear! Hills, valleys, châteaux, gardens, rivers, every object wore its liveliest hue! Whence did they borrow it? From the presence of our charming companion. They were pleasing, because she seemed pleased. Alone, the scene would have been dull and insipid: the participation of it with her gave it relish.

Let the gloomy monk, sequestered from the world, seek unsocial pleasures in the bottom of his cell! Let the sublimated philosopher grasp visionary happiness, while pursuing phantoms dressed in the garb of truth! Their supreme wisdom is supreme folly; and they mistake for happiness the mere absence of pain. Had they ever felt the solid pleasure of one generous spasm of the heart, they would exchange for it all the frigid speculations of their lives, which you have been vaunting in such elevated terms. Believe me, then, my friend, that that is a miserable arithmetic which could estimate friendship at nothing, or at less than nothing.

Respect for you has induced me to enter into this discussion, and to hear principles uttered which I detest and abjure. Respect for myself now obliges me to recall you into the proper limits of your office. When nature assigned us the same habitation, she gave us over it a divided empire. To you she allotted the field of science; to me that of morals. When the circle is to be squared or the orbit of a comet to be traced, when the arch of greatest strength or the solid of least resistance is to be investigated, take up the problem; it is yours; nature has given me no cognizance of it. In like manner, in denying to you the feelings of sympathy, of benevolence, of gratitude, of justice, of love, of friendship, she has excluded you from their control. To these she has adapted the mechanism of the heart. Morals were too essential to the happiness of man to be risked on the uncertain combinations of the head. She laid their foundation, therefore, in sentiment, not in science. That she gave to all, as necessary to all; this to a few only, as sufficing with a few.

The weary soldier and the begging woman

I know, indeed, that you pretend authority to the sovereign control of our conduct in all its parts; and a respect for your grave saws and maxims, a desire to do what is right, has sometimes induced me to conform to your counsels. A few facts, however, which I can readily recall to your memory, will suffice to prove to you that nature has not organized you for our moral direction. When the poor, wearied soldier whom we overtook at Chickahominy, with his pack on his back, begged us to let him get up behind our chariot, you began to calculate that the road was full of soldiers, and that if all should be taken up, our horses would fail in their journey. We drove on therefore. But, soon becoming sensible you had made me do wrong, that, though we cannot relieve all the distressed, we should relieve as many as we can, I turned about to take up the soldier; but he had entered a byepath, and was no more to be found; and from that moment to this I could never find him out, to ask his forgiveness.

Again, when the poor woman came to ask a charity in Philadelphia, you whispered that she looked like a drunkard, and that half a dollar was enough to give her for the ale-house. Those who want the dispositions to give easily find reasons why they ought not to give. When I sought her out afterwards, and did what I should have done at first, you know that she employed the money immediately towards placing her child at school.

Hearts, not heads, won our Revolution

If our country when pressed with wrongs at the point of the bayonet had been governed by its heads instead of its hearts, where should we have been now? Hanging on a gallows as high as Haman's. You began to calculate and to compare wealth and numbers; we threw up a few pulsations of our blood, we supplied enthusiasm against wealth and numbers, we put our existence to the hazard when the hazard seemed against us, and we saved our country, justifying, at the same time, the ways of Providence whose precept is to do always what is right and leave the issue to Him.

In short, my friend, as far as my recollection serves me, I do not know that I ever did a good thing on your suggestion, or a dirty one without it. I do forever, then, disclaim your interference in my province. Fill paper as you please with triangles and squares; try how many ways you can hang and combine them together. I shall never envy nor control your sublime delights. But leave me to decide when and where friendships are to be contracted.

You say I contract them at random. So you said the woman at Philadelphia was a drunkard. I receive none into my esteem till I know they are worthy of it. Wealth, title, office are no recommendations to my friendship. On the contrary, great good qualities are requisite to make amends for their having wealth, title, and office. You confess that in the present case I could not have made a worthier choice. You only object that I was so soon to lose them. We are not immortal ourselves, my friend; how can we expect our enjoyments to be so? We have no rose without its thorn; no pleasure without alloy. It is the law of our existence, and we must acquiesce. It is the condition annexed to all our pleasures, not by us who receive, but by Him who gives them.

The pleasures of friendship outweigh the pains

True, this condition is pressing cruelly on me at this moment. I feel more fit for death than life. But when I look back on the pleasures of which it is the consequence, I am conscious they were worth the price I am paying. Notwithstanding your endeavors, too, to damp my hopes, I comfort myself with expectations of their promised return. Hope is sweeter than despair; and they were too good to mean to deceive me. 'In the summer,' said the gentleman; but 'In the spring,' said the lady; and I should love her forever, were it only for that!

Know, then, my friend, that I have taken these good people into my bosom; that I have lodged them in the warmest cell I could find; that I love them and will continue to love them through life; that if fortune should dispose them on one side the globe, and me on the other, my affections shall pervade its whole mass to reach

them. Knowing then my determination, attempt not to disturb
it. If you can at any time furnish matter for their amusement, it
will be the office of a good neighbor to do it. I will in like manner
seize any occasion which may offer to do the like good turn for you
with Condorcet, Rittenhouse, Madison, La Cretelle, or any other
of those worthy sons of science whom you so justly prize.

Let your letters be brimful of affection

I thought this a favorable proposition whereon to rest the issue
of the dialogue. So I put an end to it by calling for my nightcap.
Methinks I hear you wish to heaven I had called a little sooner,
and so spared you the ennui of such a sermon. I did not interrupt
them sooner, because I was in a mood for hearing sermons. You
too were the subject; and on such a thesis I never think the theme
long, not even if I am to write it, and that slowly and awkwardly,
as now, with the left hand. But that you may not be discouraged
from a correspondence which begins so formidably, I will promise
you on my honor that my future letters shall be of a reasonable
length. I will even agree to express but half my esteem for you,
for fear of cloying you with too full a dose. But, on your part, no
curtailing. If your letters are as long as the Bible they will appear
short to me. Only let them be brimful of affection. I shall read
them with the dispositions with which Arlequin, in *Les deux billets*,
spelt the words '*je t'aime*,' and wished that the whole alphabet
had entered into their composition.

We have had incessant rains since your departure. These make
me fear for your health, as well as that you had an uncomfortable
journey. The same cause has prevented me from being able to
give you any account of your friends here. . . . De la Tude comes
sometimes to take family soup with me, and entertains me with
anecdotes of his five and thirty years' imprisonment. How fertile is
the mind of man which can make the Bastille and dungeon of
Vincennes yield interesting anecdotes! You know this was for
making four verses on Madame de Pompadour. . . . I have read the
memoir of his three escapes.

As to myself, my health is good, except my wrist which mends
slowly, and my mind which mends not at all, but broods constantly
over your departure. The lateness of the season obliges me to

decline my journey into the south of France. Present me in the most friendly terms to Mr. Cosway, and receive me into your own recollection with a partiality and warmth proportioned not to my own poor merit, but to the sentiments of sincere affection and esteem with which I have the honor to be, my dear Madam, your most obedient humble servant.[1]

Bring me, in return, happy days!

Just as I had sealed the enclosed, I received a letter of a good length, dated Antwerp, with your [Mrs. Cosway's] name at the bottom. I prepared myself for a feast. . . . I found that your name was to four lines only, instead of four pages. I thank you for the four lines, however, because they prove you think of me; little, indeed, but better little than none. To show how much I think of you, I send you the enclosed letter of three sheets of paper, being a history of the evening I parted with you. But how expect you should read a letter of three mortal sheets of paper? I will tell you. Divide it into six doses of half a sheet each, and every day, when the toilette begins, take a dose, that is to say, read half a sheet. By this means it will have the only merit its length and dullness can aspire to, that of assisting your *coiffeuse* to procure you six good naps of sleep. I will even allow you twelve days to get through it, holding you rigorously to one condition only, that is, that at whatever hour you receive this, you do not break the seal of the enclosed till the next toilette. . . .

I send you the song I promised. Bring me in return the subject, *Jours heureux!* Were I a songster, I should sing it all to these words: '*Dans ces lieux qu'elle tarde à se rendre!*' Learn it, I pray you, and sing it with feeling. My right hand presents its devoirs to you, and sees, with great indignation, the left supplanting it in a correspondence so much valued.[2]

A journey to southern France and northern Italy

In a former letter I mentioned . . . the dislocation of my wrist. I can make not the least use of it except for the single article of writing, though it is going on five months since the accident happened. I have great anxieties lest I should never recover any considerable use of it. I shall, by the advice of my surgeons, set out in a fortnight for the waters of Aix, in Provence. I choose these out of several they proposed to me because if they fail to be effectual my journey will not be useless altogether. It will give me an opportunity of examining the canal of Languedoc, and . . . to make the tour of the ports concerned in commerce with us.[3]

At Nîmes: in love with the Maison Carrée

Here I am, Madam [Comtesse de Tessé, an aunt of Lafayette] gazing whole hours at the Maison Carrée, like a lover at his mistress. The stocking weavers and silk spinners around it consider me a hypochondriac Englishman about to write with a pistol the last chapter of his history. This is the second time I have been in love since I left Paris. The first was with a Diana at the Château de Laye-Epinaye in Beaujolais, a delicious morsel of sculpture by M. A. Slodtz. This, you will say, was in rule, to fall in love with a female beauty; but with a house! it is out of all precedent. No, Madam, it is not without a precedent in my own history. While in Paris I was violently smitten with the Hôtel de Salm, and used to go to the Tuileries almost daily to look at it. The *loueuse des chaises*, inattentive to my passion, never had the complaisance to place a chair there, so that, sitting on the parapet and twisting my neck round to see the object of my admiration, I generally left it with a *torti-colli*.

From Lyons to Nîmes I have been nourished with the remains of Roman grandeur. . . . From a correspondent at Nîmes you will not expect news. Were I to attempt to give you news, I should tell you stories one thousand years old. I should detail to you the intrigues of the courts of the Caesars, how they affect us here, the oppressions of their praetors, prefects, etc. I am immersed in antiquities from morning to night. For me the city of Rome is actually existing in all the splendor of its empire. I am filled with alarms for the event of the irruptions daily making on us by the Goths, the Visigoths, Ostrogoths, and Vandals, lest they should reconquer us to our original barbarism. If I am sometimes induced to look forward to the eighteenth century, it is only when recalled to it by the recollection of your goodness and friendship.[4]

Cloudless skies and nightingales in full chorus

I write you, my dear Patsy, from the canal of Languedoc, on which I am at present sailing, as I have been for a week past, cloudless skies above, limpid waters below, and on each hand a row of nightingales in full chorus. This delightful bird had given me a rich treat before, at the fountain of Vaucluse. After visiting the tomb of Laura at Avignon I went to see this fountain — a noble one of itself, and rendered famous forever by the songs of Petrarch, who lived near it. I arrived there somewhat fatigued and sat down by the fountain to repose myself. It gushes, of the size of a river, from a secluded valley of the mountains, the ruins of Petrarch's château being perched on a rock two hundred feet perpendicular above. To add to the enchantment of the scene, every tree and bush was filled with nightingales in full song. . . . As you have trees in the garden of the convent there might be nightingales in them, and this is the season of their song. Endeavor, my dear, to make yourself acquainted with the music of this bird, that when you return to your own country you may be able to estimate its merit in comparison with that of the mocking-bird.[5]

Privileged orders and the misery of the masses

I am constantly roving about to see what I have never seen before, and shall never see again. In the great cities I go to see what travellers think alone worthy of being seen; but I make a job of it, and generally gulp it all down in a day. On the other hand I am never satiated with rambling through the fields and farms, examining the culture and cultivators with a degree of curiosity which makes some take me to be a fool, and others to be much wiser than I am. . . . I have often wished for you [Lafayette]. . . . It will be a great comfort to you to know, from your own inspection, the condition of all the provinces of your own country. . . . And to do it most effectually you must be absolutely incognito, you must ferret the people out of their hovels as I have done, look into their kettles, eat their bread, loll on their beds under pretence of resting yourself, but in fact to find if they are soft. You will feel a sublime pleasure in the course of this investigation, and a sublimer one hereafter when you shall be able to apply your knowledge to the softening of their beds or the throwing a morsel of meat into their kettles of vegetables.[6]

The property of this country is absolutely concentrated in a very few hands. . . . The consequences of this enormous inequality producing so much misery to the bulk of mankind, legislators cannot invent too many devices for subdividing property. . . . Whenever there is in any country uncultivated lands and unemployed poor, it is clear that the laws of property have been so far extended as to violate natural right. The earth is given as a common stock for man to labor and live on. If for the encouragement of industry we allow it to be appropriated, we must take care that other employment be provided to those excluded from the appropriation. If we do not, the fundamental right to labor the earth returns to the unemployed.[7]

If anybody thinks that kings, nobles, or priests are good conservators of the public happiness, send them here. It is the best school in the universe to cure them of that folly. They will see here, with their own eyes, that these descriptions of men are an abandoned confederacy against the happiness of the mass of the people. The omnipotence of their effect cannot be better proved than in this country particularly, where, notwithstanding the finest soil upon earth, the finest climate under heaven, and a people of the most benevolent, the most gay and amiable character of which the human form is susceptible; where such a people, I say, surrounded by so many blessings from nature, are yet loaded with misery by kings, nobles, and priests, and by them alone.[8] Every earthly advantage combined [is] insufficient to prevent this scourge from rendering existence a curse to twenty-four out of twenty-five parts of the inhabitants of this country.[9]

A little rebellion now and then a good thing

Some tumultuous meetings of the people have taken place in the Eastern States [the rioting of debt-ridden farmers in Massachusetts, in 1786, called 'Shays's Rebellion']. . . . Their principal demand was a respite in the judiciary proceedings. No injury was done . . . nor did the tumult continue twenty-four hours in any one in-

stance. . . . These people are not entirely without excuse.[10] The
way to prevent these irregular interpositions of the people is to
give them full information of their affairs. . . . If once they become
inattentive to the public affairs, . . . Congress and Assemblies,
judges and governors shall all become wolves. It seems to be the
law of our general nature, in spite of individual exceptions; and
experience declares that man is the only animal which devours its
own kind, for I can apply no milder term to the governments of
Europe, and to the general prey of the rich on the poor.[11] I hold
it that a little rebellion now and then is a good thing, and as necessary in the political world as storms in the physical. . . . It is a
medicine necessary for the sound health of government.[12]

God forbid we should ever be twenty years without such a rebellion. The people cannot be all, and always, well informed. The
part which is wrong will be discontented in proportion to the
importance of the facts they misconceive. If they remain quiet
under such misconceptions it is a lethargy, the forerunner of death
to the public liberty. . . . Let them take arms. The remedy is to
set them right as to facts, pardon and pacify them. What signify
a few lives lost in a century or two? The tree of liberty must be
refreshed from time to time with the blood of patriots and tyrants.
It is its natural manure.[13]

Educate and inform the whole mass of the people. Enable them
to see that it is their interest to preserve peace and order, and they
will preserve them. And it requires no very high degree of education to convince them of this. They are the only sure reliance for
the preservation of our liberty. After all, it is my principle that the
will of the majority should prevail. If they approve the proposed
Constitution in all its parts, I shall concur in it cheerfully, in hopes
they will amend it whenever they shall find it works wrong.[14]

The Constitution of 1787: bloodless reform

I approved, from the first moment, of the great mass of what
is in the new Constitution: the consolidation of the government;
the organization into executive, legislative, and judiciary; the sub-
division of the legislative; the happy compromise of interests between the great and little states, by the different manner of voting
in the different Houses; the voting by persons instead of states; the

qualified negative on laws given to the executive, which, however, I should have liked better if associated with the judiciary also, as in New York; and the power of taxation. I thought at first that the latter might have been limited. . . .

What I disapproved, from the first moment also, was the want of a bill of rights to guard liberty against the legislative as well as the executive branches of the government, that is to say, to secure freedom in religion, freedom of the press, freedom from monopolies, freedom from unlawful imprisonment, freedom from a permanent military, and a trial by jury in all cases determinable by the laws of the land. I disapproved, also, the perpetual re-eligibility of the President. To these points of disapprobation I adhere. . . . I suppose the majority of the United States are of my opinion [that a bill of rights] should now be annexed. . . . With respect to the re-eligibility of the President, . . . indeed, since the thing is established, I would wish it not to be altered during the life of our great leader [Washington].[15]

We can surely boast of having set the world a beautiful example of a government reformed by reason alone, without bloodshed. But the world is too far oppressed to profit by the example. On this side of the Atlantic the blood of the people is become an inheritance, and those who fatten on it will not relinquish it easily. The struggle in this country is, as yet, of doubtful issue.[16]

A bloody revolution begins in France

The American war seems first to have awakened the thinking part of this nation in general from the sleep of despotism in which they were sunk. The officers too who had been to America were mostly young men, less shackled by habit and prejudice, and more ready to assent to the dictates of common sense and common right. They came back impressed with these. The press, notwithstanding its shackles, began to disseminate them; conversation, too, assumed new freedom; politics became the theme of all societies, male and female, and a very extensive and zealous party was formed, which may be called the Patriotic party, who, sensible of the abusive government under which they lived, longed for occasions of reforming it.[17]

I was much acquainted with the leading patriots of the [National]

Assembly. Being from a country which had successfully passed through a similar reformation, they were disposed to my acquaintance, and had some confidence in me. I urged, most strenuously, an immediate compromise; to secure what the government was [in June of 1789] ready to yield, and trust to future occasions for what might still be wanting. It was well understood that the King would grant, at this time: 1. freedom of the person by habeas corpus, 2. freedom of conscience, 3. freedom of the press, 4. trial by jury, 5. a representative legislature, 6. annual meetings, 7. the origination of laws, 8. the exclusive right of taxation and appropriation, and 9. the responsibility of ministers; and with the exercise of these powers they could obtain, in future, whatever might be further necessary to improve and preserve their constitution. They thought otherwise, however, and events have proved their lamentable error. . . .

The fall of the Bastille

The King was [on July 11, 1789] completely in the hands of men the principal among whom had been noted, through their lives, for the Turkish despotism of their characters. . . . The news of this change [of ministry, and the plan to crush the revolution with foreign troops] began to be known at Paris about one or two o'clock. In the afternoon a body of about one hundred German cavalry were advanced and drawn up in the Place Louis XV, and about two hundred Swiss posted at a little distance in their rear. This drew people to the spot who thus accidentally found themselves in front of the troops, merely at first as spectators, but as their numbers increased their indignation rose. They retired a few steps and posted themselves on and behind large piles of stones, large and small, collected in that place for a bridge which was to be built adjacent to it.

In this position, happening to be in my carriage on a visit, I passed through the lane they had formed, without interruption. But the moment after I had passed the people attacked the cavalry with stones. They charged, but the advantageous position of the people and the showers of stones obliged the horse to retire and quit the field altogether, leaving one of their number on the ground, and the Swiss in the rear not moving to their aid. This was the signal for universal insurrection, and this body of cavalry, to avoid being massacred, retired towards Versailles.

The people now armed themselves with such weapons as they could find in armorers' shops and private houses, and with bludgeons; and were roaming all night, through all parts of the city, without any decided object. The next day (the 13th), the Assembly pressed on the King to send away the troops, to permit the bourgeoisie of Paris to arm for the preservation of order in the city, and offered to send a deputation from their body to tranquillize them; but their propositions were refused. . . . The city committee determined to raise forty-eight thousand bourgeoisie, or rather to restrain their numbers to forty-eight thousand. On the 14th they sent one of their members (Monsieur de Corny) to the Hôtel des Invalides to ask arms for their Garde Bourgeoisie. He was followed by, and he found there, a great collection of people. The Governor of the Invalides came out and represented the impossibility of his delivering arms without the orders of those from whom he received them. De Corny advised the people then to retire, and retired himself; but the people took possession of the arms. It was remarkable that not only the Invalides themselves made no opposition, but that a body of five thousand foreign troops, within four hundred yards, never stirred. M. de Corny and five others were then sent to ask arms of M. de Launay, Governor of the Bastille. They found a great collection of people already before the place, and they immediately planted a flag of truce, which was answered by a like flag hoisted on the parapet. The deputation prevailed on the people to fall back a little, advanced themselves to make their demand of the Governor, and in that instant a discharge from the Bastille killed four persons of those nearest to the deputies. The deputies retired. I happened to be at the house of M. de Corny when he returned to it, and received from him a narrative of these transactions.

On the retirement of the deputies the people rushed forward, and almost in an instant were in possession of a fortification of infinite strength, defended by one hundred men, which in other times had stood several regular sieges and had never been taken. How they forced their entrance has never been explained. They took all the arms, discharged the prisoners and such of the garrison as were not killed in the first moment of fury, carried the Governor and Lieutenant Governor to the Place de Grève (the place of public execution), cut off their heads and sent them through the city, in triumph, to the Palais Royal. . . .

The decapitation of De Launay worked powerfully through the night on the whole Aristocratic party, insomuch that in the morning those of the greatest influence on the Count d'Artois represented to him the absolute necessity that the King should give up everything to the Assembly. This according with the dispositions of the King, he went about eleven o'clock, accompanied only by his brothers, to the Assembly, and there read them a speech in which he asked their interposition to re-establish order. . . .

Marie Antoinette

The King was now become a passive machine in the hands of the National Assembly, and had he been left to himself he would have willingly acquiesced in whatever they should devise as best for the nation. . . . But he had a Queen of absolute sway over his weak mind and timid virtue, and of a character the reverse of his in all points, . . . proud, disdainful of restraint, indignant at all obstacles to her will, eager in the pursuit of pleasure, and firm enough to hold to her desires or perish in the wreck. Her inordinate gambling and dissipations . . . had been a sensible item in the exhaustion of the treasury which called into action the reforming hand of the nation; and her opposition to it, her inflexible perverseness and dauntless spirit, led herself to the guillotine, drew the King on with her, and plunged the world into crimes and calamities which will forever stain the pages of modern history. I have ever believed that had there been no Queen there would have been no revolution. . . .

As yet we are but in the first chapter of its history. The appeal to the rights of man which had been made in the United States was taken up by France first of the European nations. From her the spirit has spread. . . . The tyrants . . . have allied indeed against it; but it is irresistible . . . and the condition of man through the civilized world will be finally and greatly ameliorated. . . .

A parting tribute to the French

I had been more than a year soliciting leave to go home, with a view to place my daughters in the society and care of their friends, and to return for a short time to my station at Paris. But . . . it was not till the last of August [1789] that I received the permission I had asked. And here I cannot leave this great and good country without expressing my sense of its pre-eminence of character among the nations of the earth. A more benevolent people I have never known, nor greater warmth and devotedness in their select friendships. Their kindness and accommodation to strangers is unparalleled, and the hospitality of Paris is beyond anything I had conceived to be practicable in a large city. Their eminence, too, in science, the communicative dispositions of their scientific men, the politeness of the general manners, the ease and vivacity of their conversation, give a charm to their society to be found nowhere else. In a comparison of this with other countries we have the proof of primacy which was given to Themistocles after the battle of Salamis. Every general voted to himself the first reward of valor, and the second to Themistocles. So, ask the travelled inhabitant of any nation, in what country on earth would you rather live? Certainly in my own, where are all my friends, my relations, and the earliest and sweetest affections and recollections of my life. Which would be your second choice? France.[18]

All my wishes end where I hope my days will end

I am savage enough to prefer the woods, the wilds, and the independence of Monticello to all the brilliant pleasures of this gay capital. I shall, therefore, rejoin myself to my native country with new attachments and with exaggerated esteem for its advantages; for though there is less wealth there, there is more freedom, more ease, and less misery.[19] I am as happy nowhere else, and in no other society, and all my wishes end, where I hope my days will end, at Monticello. Too many scenes of happiness mingle themselves with all the recollections of my native woods and fields to suffer them to be supplanted in my affection by any other.[20]

On the 26th of September [1789] I left Paris for Havre, where I was detained by contrary winds until the 8th of October. On that day, and the 9th, I crossed over to Cowes, where I had engaged the *Clermont*, Captain Colley, to touch for me. She did so, but here again we were detained by contrary winds until the 22d, when we embarked, and landed at Norfolk on the 23d of November. . . . I arrived at Monticello on the 23d of December.[21]

CHAPTER IX

Washington's Secretary of State

UPON his return from France in December of 1789, Jefferson at the insistence of President Washington accepted the appointment of Secretary of State in the new government set up under the Constitution. When he entered upon his duties in March of 1790 he was shocked by the anti-democratic, 'monarchical' views of influential Americans, who found a very able and aggressive leader in Alexander Hamilton, Washington's Secretary of the Treasury. Of Washington's devotion to republicanism he had no doubt, as he tells us in his excellent brief sketch of that great man. But Hamilton, in his opinion, which of course was colored by the ensuing partisan strife, 'was not only a monarchist but for a monarchy bottomed on corruption.'

When he arrived in New York Hamilton's plan for funding the debt at par had already passed. Although the funding plan was invaluable in placing the credit of the new government on a firm foundation, it had enabled speculators to reap a golden harvest, and a strong opposition to the commercial-financial interests of the Northern cities had developed in the agrarian South. This opposition threatened another of Hamilton's plans: the assumption of the state debts by the general government. Upon Jefferson's arrival Hamilton appealed to him for aid. Impressed by the argument that the Union itself was at stake, and not then fully aware of Hamilton's politico-economic views, Jefferson arranged the famous bargain of 1790 by which the assumption was passed and the federal capital, after ten years at Philadelphia, was located permanently on the banks of the Potomac. With the chartering of the

Bank of the United States in 1791, against which Jefferson opposed his strict-constructionist interpretation of the Constitution, the party division in the new republic took shape between Jefferson's democratic Republicans and Hamilton's 'monarchical' Federalists.

In foreign affairs, Secretary Jefferson watched with great interest the struggle for the rights of man in France, advocated commercial retaliation against nations maintaining trade barriers against the United States, and attempted to get from Spain not only the right of freely navigating the Mississippi (then the western boundary of the republic) but the cession of Spanish New Orleans. In masterly fashion he presented the American arraignment of Great Britain for failure to execute the Treaty of Peace of 1783, notably by not evacuating British frontier garrisons on American soil from Lake Champlain to Lake Michigan. A sore problem for the young nation, hemmed in on the north by Britain's Canada and on the south and west by Spain's Floridas and vast Louisiana territory, was the aid and incitement given by the agents of these powers to hostile Indians. In 1790, when a war between Spain and Britain seemed likely (although it did not take place), Jefferson showed the caliber of his diplomacy by his bold and well-conceived plans for winning advantages from 'the follies of the Old World.'

Meanwhile the opposition to Hamilton's policies gained headway. Stating in detail the grounds for that opposition, and noting that the division was not only one of political sentiment and economic interest but also of geography, Jefferson urged Washington to give up his idea of retiring at the end of his first term. He was very much relieved when the President consented to stand for re-election in 1792, because only the assurance of having Washington at the helm for four years more would remove the threat of that 'incalculable evil,' the breaking up of the new and still precarious American Union.

Secretary of State

On my way home ... I received a letter from the President, General Washington, by express, covering an appointment to be Secretary of State. I received it with real regret. My wish had been

to return to Paris, where I had left my household establishment as
if there myself, and to see the end of the Revolution, which I then
thought would be certainly and happily closed in less than a year.
I then meant to return home, to withdraw from political life, into
which I had been impressed by the circumstances of the times, to
sink into the bosom of my family and friends, and to devote myself
to studies more congenial to my mind. In my answer of December
15th I expressed these dispositions candidly to the President...
but assured him that... I would sacrifice my own inclinations
without hesitation...; this I left to his decision. I arrived at Monticello on the 23d of December, where I received a second letter
from the President, expressing his continued wish that I should
take my station there.... This silenced my reluctance, and I
accepted the new appointment.

In the interval of my stay at home my eldest daughter had been
happily married to the eldest son of the Tuckahoe branch of Randolphs, a young gentleman [Thomas Mann Randolph] of genius,
science, and honorable mind, who afterwards filled a dignified
station in the general government and the most dignified in his
own state. I left Monticello on the first of March, 1790, for New
York. At Philadelphia I called on the venerable and beloved
Franklin. He was then on the bed of sickness from which he never
rose. My recent return from a country in which he had left so
many friends, and the perilous convulsions to which they had been
exposed, revived all his anxieties to know what part they had
taken, what had been their course, and what their fate. He went
over all in succession with a rapidity and animation almost too
much for his strength.... I arrived at New York on the 21st of
March, where Congress was in session.[1]

New York City in March of 1790

I arrived here... after as laborious a journey of a fortnight
from Richmond as I ever went through; resting only one day at
Alexandria, and another at Baltimore. I found my carriage and
horses at Alexandria, but a snow of eighteen inches deep falling
the same night, I saw the impossibility of getting on in my own
carriage, so left it there to be sent to me by water, and had my
horses led on to this place, taking my passage in the stage, though

relieving myself a little sometimes by mounting my horse. The roads through the whole way were so bad that we could never go more than three miles an hour, sometimes not more than two, and in the night but one. My first object was to look out a house in the Broadway, if possible, as being the centre of my business. Finding none there vacant for the present I have taken a small one in Maiden Lane.[2]

Behold me, my dear friend [Lafayette], elected Secretary of State, instead of returning to the far more agreeable position which placed me in the daily participation of your friendship. . . . Wherever I am, or ever shall be, I shall be sincere in my friendship to you and to your nation. I think with others that nations are to be governed with regard to their own interests, but I am convinced that it is their interest in the long run to be grateful, faithful to their engagements, even in the worst of circumstances, and honorable and generous always. If I had not known that the head of our government was in these sentiments, and that his national and private ethics were the same, I would never have been where I am. . . . Our last news from Paris is of the 8th of January. So far it seemed that your revolution had got along with a steady pace, meeting indeed occasional difficulties and dangers, but we are not to expect to be translated from despotism to liberty in a feather-bed.[3]

Mortified by monarchical tendencies

Here, certainly, I found a state of things which, of all I had ever contemplated, I the least expected. I had left France in the first year of her revolution, in the fervor of natural rights and zeal for reformation. My conscientious devotion to these rights could not be heightened, but it had been aroused and excited by daily exercise. The President received me cordially, and my colleagues and the circle of principal citizens apparently with welcome. The courtesies of dinner parties given me, as a stranger newly arrived among them, placed me at once in their familiar society. But I cannot describe the wonder and mortification with which the table conversations filled me.

Politics were the chief topic, and a preference of kingly over republican government was evidently the favorite sentiment. An apostate I could not be, nor yet a hypocrite; and I found myself for the most part the only advocate on the republican side of the question, unless among the guests there chanced to be some member of that party from the legislative Houses.[4] The furthest that anyone would go in support of the republican features of our new government would be to say, 'The present Constitution is well as a beginning, and may be allowed a fair trial; but it is, in fact, only a stepping-stone to something better.'[5]

I took occasion at various times of expressing to General Washington my disappointment at these symptoms of a change of principle, and that I thought them encouraged by the forms and ceremonies which I found prevailing . . . the levees, birthdays, the pompous cavalcade to the State House on the meeting of Congress, the formal speech from the throne, the procession of Congress in a body to re-echo the speech in an answer, etc., etc. . . . not at all in character with the simplicity of republican government, and looking as if wistfully to those of European courts.[6]

The first public ball which took place after the President's arrival there, Colonel Humphreys, Colonel W. S. Smith, and Mrs. Knox [wife of the Secretary of War] were to arrange the ceremonials. These arrangements were as follows: A sofa at the head of the room, raised on several steps, whereon the President and Mrs. Washington were to be seated. The gentlemen were to dance in swords. Each one when going to dance was to lead his partner to the foot of the sofa, make a low obeisance to the President and his lady, then go and dance, and when done bring his partner again to the foot of the sofa for new obeisances, and then to retire to their chairs. . . .

Mrs. Knox contrived to come with the President, and to follow him and Mrs. Washington to their destination, and she had the design of forcing an invitation from the President to a seat on the sofa. She mounted up the steps after them unbidden, but unfortunately the wicked sofa was so short that when the President and Mrs. Washington were seated there was not room for a third person; she was obliged, therefore, to descend in the face of the company, and to sit where she could. In other respects the ceremony was conducted rigorously according to the arrangements, and the President made to pass an evening which his good sense rendered a very miserable one to him.[7]

Alexander Hamilton's funding plan

Hamilton's financial system had then passed. It had two objects: 1st, as a puzzle, to exclude popular understanding and inquiry; 2d, as a machine for the corruption of the legislature, for he avowed the opinion that man could be governed by one of two motives only, force or interest; force, he observed, in this country was out of the question, and the interests, therefore, of the members must be laid hold of to keep the legislative in unison with the executive. And with grief and shame it must be acknowledged that his machine was not without effect; that even in this, the birth of our government, some members were found sordid enough to bend their duty to their interests, and to look after personal rather than public good.

It is well known that during the war the greatest difficulty we encountered was the want of money or means to pay our soldiers who fought, or our farmers, manufacturers, and merchants who furnished the necessary supplies of food and clothing for them. After the expedient of paper money had exhausted itself, certificates of debt were given to the individual creditors, with assurance of payment so soon as the United States should be able. But the distresses of these people often obliged them to part with these for the half, the fifth, and even a tenth of their value; and speculators had made a trade of cozening them from the holders by the most fraudulent practices, and persuasions that they would never be paid. In the bill for funding and paying these, Hamilton made no difference between the original holders and the fraudulent purchasers of this paper. Great and just repugnance arose at putting these two classes of creditors on the same footing, and great exertions were used to pay the former the full value, and to the latter, the price only which they had paid, with interest. But this would have prevented the game which was to be played, and for which the minds of greedy members were already tutored and prepared.

When the trial of strength on these several efforts had indicated the form in which the bill would finally pass, this being known within doors sooner than without, and especially than to those who were in distant parts of the Union, the base scramble began. Couriers and relay horses by land, and swift sailing pilot boats by sea, were flying in all directions. Active partners and agents were associated and employed in every state, town, and country neighborhood, and this paper was bought up at five shillings, and even as low as two shillings in the pound, before the holder knew that Congress had already provided for its redemption at par. Immense sums were thus filched from the poor and ignorant, and fortunes accumulated by those who had themselves been poor enough before. Men thus enriched by the dexterity of a leader would follow of course the chief who was leading them to fortune, and become the zealous instruments of all his enterprises.

Assumption of debts of the states

This game was over, and another was on the carpet at the moment of my arrival; and to this I was most ignorantly and innocently made to hold the candle. This fiscal manoeuvre is well known by the name of the Assumption. Independently of the debts of Congress, the states had during the war contracted separate and heavy debts . . .; and the more debt Hamilton could rake up, the more plunder for his mercenaries. This money, whether wisely or foolishly spent, was pretended to have been spent for general pur- poses, and ought, therefore, to be paid from the general purse. But it was objected that nobody knew what these debts were, what their amount, or what their proofs. No matter; we will guess them to be twenty millions. But of these twenty millions, we do not know how much should be reimbursed to one state, or how much to another. No matter; we will guess. And so another scramble was set on foot among the several states, and some got much, some little, some nothing. But the main object was obtained, the phalanx of the Treasury was reinforced by additional recruits. This measure produced the most bitter and angry contest ever known in Congress, before or since the union of the states. I arrived in the midst of it. But a stranger to the ground, a stranger to the actors on it, so long absent as to have lost all familiarity with the subject, and as yet unaware of its object, I took no concern in it.

Hamilton appeals for aid

The great and trying question, however, was lost in the House of Representatives. So high were the feuds excited by this subject that on its rejection business was suspended. . . . The Eastern members, particularly, who . . . were the principal gamblers in these scenes, threatened a secession and dissolution. Hamilton was in despair. As I was going to the President's one day, I met him in the street. He walked me backwards and forwards before the President's door for half an hour. He painted pathetically the temper into which the legislature had been wrought; the disgust of those who were called the creditor states; the danger of the *secession* of their members, and the separation of the states. He observed that the members of the administration ought to act in concert; that though this question was not of my department, yet a common duty should make it a common concern; that . . . it was probable that an appeal from me to the judgment and discretion of some of my friends might effect a change in the vote, and the machine of government, now suspended, might be again set into motion.

I told him that I was really a stranger to the whole subject; that not having yet informed myself of the system of finances adopted, I knew not how far this was a necessary sequence; that undoubtedly if its rejection endangered a dissolution of our Union at this incipient stage, I should deem that the most unfortunate of all consequences, to avert which all partial and temporary evils should be yielded. I proposed to him, however, to dine with me the next day, and I would invite another friend or two, bring them into conference together, and I thought it impossible that reasonable men, consulting together coolly, could fail, by some mutual sacrifices of opinion, to form a compromise which was to save the Union.

The bitter pill sweetened

The discussion took place. I could take no part in it but an exhortatory one, because I was a stranger to the circumstances which should govern it. But it was finally agreed that . . . the preservation of the Union and of concord among the states was more important, and that therefore it would be better that the vote of rejection should be rescinded, to effect which some members should change their votes. But it was observed that this pill would be peculiarly bitter to the Southern States, and that some con-

comitant measure should be adopted to sweeten it a little to them.
There had before been propositions to fix the seat of government
either at Philadelphia, or at Georgetown on the Potomac; and it
was thought that by giving it to Philadelphia for ten years, and to
Georgetown permanently afterwards, this might, as an anodyne,
calm in some degree the ferment which might be excited by the
other measure alone.

So two of the Potomac members (White and Lee, but White with
a revulsion of stomach almost convulsive) agreed to change their
votes, and Hamilton undertook to carry the other point. In doing
this, the influence he had established over the Eastern members,
with the agency of Robert Morris with those of the Middle States,
effected this side of the engagement; and so the Assumption was
passed, and twenty millions of stock divided among favored states,
and thrown in as a pabulum to the stockjobbing herd. This added
to the number of votaries to the Treasury, and made its chief
[Hamilton] the master of every vote in the legislature which might
give to the government the direction suited to his political views.

Division into Republicans and Federalists

I know well, and so must be understood, that nothing like a
majority in Congress had yielded to this corruption. Far from it.
But a division, not very unequal, had already taken place in the
honest part of that body between the parties styled Republican and
Federal. The latter being monarchists in principle adhered to
Hamilton of course as their leader in that principle, and this mer-
cenary phalanx added to them insured him always a majority in
both Houses; so that the whole action of legislature was now under
the direction of the Treasury. Still the machine was not complete.
The effect of the funding system and of the Assumption would be
temporary; it would be lost with the loss of the individual members
whom it has enriched, and some engine of influence more permanent must be contrived while these myrmidons were yet in place
to carry it through all opposition. This engine was the Bank of
the United States [modeled after the Bank of England, and char-
tered by Congress in 1791]. . . .

Here then was the real ground of the opposition which was made
to the course of administration. Its object was to preserve the

legislature pure and independent of the executive, to restrain the administration to republican forms and principles, and not permit the Constitution to be construed into a monarchy, and to be warped, in practice, into all the principles and pollutions of their favorite English model. Nor was this an opposition to General Washington. He was true to the republican charge confided to him; and has solemnly and repeatedly protested to me, in our conversations, that he would lose the last drop of his blood in support of it; and he did this the oftener and with the more earnestness because he knew my suspicions of Hamilton's designs against it, and wished to quiet them. For he was not aware of the drift or of the effect of Hamilton's schemes. Unversed in financial projects and calculations and budgets, his approbation of them was bottomed on his confidence in the man.[8]

Pen-portrait of Washington

Perhaps the strongest feature in his character was prudence, never acting until every circumstance, every consideration, was maturely weighed; refraining if he saw a doubt, but, when once decided, going through with his purpose whatever obstacles opposed. His integrity was most pure, his justice the most inflexible I have ever known, no motives of interest or consanguinity, of friendship or hatred, being able to bias his decision. He was, indeed, in every sense of the words, a wise, a good, and a great man. His temper was naturally irritable and high-toned, but reflection and resolution had obtained a firm and habitual ascendancy over it. If ever, however, it broke its bonds, he was most tremendous in his wrath. In his expenses he was honorable but exact, liberal in contributions to whatever promised utility but frowning and unyielding on all visionary projects and all unworthy calls on his charity. His heart was not warm in its affections, but he exactly calculated every man's value and gave him a solid esteem proportioned to it.

His person . . . was fine, his stature exactly what one would wish, his deportment easy, erect and noble; the best horseman of his age, and the most graceful figure that could be seen on horseback. Although in the circle of his friends, where he might be unreserved with safety, he took a free share in conversation, his colloquial

talents were not above mediocrity, possessing neither copiousness
of ideas nor fluency of words. In public, when called on for a
sudden opinion, he was unready, short, and embarrassed. Yet he
wrote readily, rather diffusely, in an easy and correct style. This
he had acquired by conversation with the world, for his education
was merely reading, writing, and common arithmetic, to which
he added surveying at a later day. His time was employed in action
chiefly, reading little, and that only in agriculture and English
history. . . .

On the whole, his character was, in its mass, perfect, in nothing
bad, in few points indifferent; and it may truly be said that never
did nature and fortune combine more perfectly to make a man
great, and to place him in the same constellation with whatever
worthies have merited from man an everlasting remembrance. For
his was the singular destiny and merit of leading the armies of his
country successfully through an arduous war for the establishment
of its independence; of conducting its councils through the birth
of a government, new in its forms and principles, until it had settled
down into a quiet and orderly train; and of scrupulously obeying
the laws through the whole of his career, civil and military, of which
the history of the world furnishes no other example. . . .

I am satisfied the great body of Republicans think of him as
I do. . . . We knew his honesty, the wiles with which he was encom-
passed, and that age had already begun to relax the firmness of
his purposes; and I am convinced he is more deeply seated in the
love and gratitude of the Republicans than in the Pharisaical
homage of the Federal monarchists. For he was no monarchist
from preference of his judgment. The soundness of that gave him
correct views of the rights of man, and his severe justice devoted
him to them.[9]

The character of Hamilton

But Hamilton was not only a monarchist but for a monarchy
bottomed on corruption. In proof of this I will relate an anecdote
for the truth of which I attest the God who made me. [At a dinner
I gave in 1791] after the cloth was removed . . . conversation
began . . . and by some circumstance was led to the British constitution, on which Mr. Adams [John Adams, then Vice President]

observed, 'Purge that constitution of its corruption, and give to its popular branch equality of representation, and it would be the most perfect constitution ever devised by the wit of man.' Hamilton paused and said, 'Purge it of its corruption, and give to its popular branch equality of representation, and it would become an *impracticable* government; as it stands at present, with all its supposed defects, it is the most perfect government which ever existed.' [10] Another incident took place on the same occasion which will further delineate Mr. Hamilton's political principles. The room being hung around with a collection of the portraits of remarkable men, among them were those of Bacon, Newton, and Locke, Hamilton asked me who they were. I told him they were my trinity of the three greatest men the world had ever produced, naming them. He paused for some time: 'The greatest man,' said he, 'that ever lived was Julius Caesar.' [11]

Hamilton was, indeed, a singular character. Of acute understanding, disinterested, honest, and honorable in all private transactions, amiable in society, and duly valuing virtue in private life, yet so bewitched and perverted by the British example as to be under thorough conviction that corruption was essential to the government of a nation.[12]

The Constitution interpreted; farmers vs. stockjobbers

I consider the foundation of the Constitution as laid on this ground: That 'all powers not delegated to the United States by the Constitution, nor prohibited by it to the states, are reserved to the states or to the people.' (XIIth amendment.) To take a single step beyond the boundaries thus specially drawn around the powers of Congress is to take possession of a boundless field of power no longer susceptible of any definition.

The incorporation of a bank, and the powers assumed by this bill [to charter Hamilton's Bank of the United States], have not, in my opinion, been delegated to the United States by the Constitution. They are not among the powers specially enumerated. . . . Still less are these powers covered by any other of the special enumerations. Nor are they within either of the general phrases, which are the two following: 1. To lay taxes to provide for the general welfare of the United States, that is to say, 'to lay taxes for

the purpose of providing for the general welfare.' For the laying of
taxes is the *power*, and the general welfare the *purpose* for which the
power is to be exercised.... They are not ... *to do anything they
please* to provide for the general welfare, but only to *lay taxes* for
that purpose.... 2. The second general phrase is, 'to make all
laws *necessary* and proper for carrying into execution the enumerated
powers.' But they can all be carried into execution without a
bank. ... The present is the case of a right remaining exclusively
with the states, and consequently one of those intended by the
Constitution to be placed under its protection.[13]

What is said in our country of the fiscal arrangements now
going on? I really fear their effect when I consider the present
temper of the Southern States.... However, all will pass — the
excise will pass — the bank will pass. The only corrective of what
is corrupt ... will be the augmentation of the ... agricultural
representation, which may put that interest above that of the
stockjobbers.[14]

A wave of financial speculation

The bank filled and overflowed in the moment it was opened.
Instead of twenty thousand shares, twenty-four thousand were
offered, and a great many unpresented who had not suspected that
so much haste was necessary. Thus it is that we shall be paying
thirteen per cent per annum for eight millions of paper money
instead of having that circulation of gold and silver for nothing.
Experience has proved to us that a dollar of silver disappears for
every dollar of paper emitted; and, for the paper emitted from the
bank, seven per cent profits will be received by the subscribers for
it as bank paper ... and six per cent on the public paper of which
it is the representative. ... It is impossible to say where the appetite
for gambling will stop. The land office, the federal town, certain
schemes of manufacture, are all likely to be converted into aliment
for that rage.[15]

What do you think of this scrippomany? Ships are lying idle at
the wharfs, buildings are stopped, capitals withdrawn from commerce, manufactures, arts, and agriculture to be employed in
gambling, and the tide of public prosperity almost unparalleled
in any country is arrested in its course, and suppressed by the rage

of getting rich in a day. No mortal can tell where this will stop; for the spirit of gaming, when once it has seized a subject, is incurable. The tailor who has made thousands in one day, though he has lost them the next, can never again be content with the slow and moderate earnings of his needle. Nothing can exceed the public felicity, if our papers are to be believed, because our papers are under the orders of our scripmen. I imagine, however, we shall hear that all the cash has quitted the extremities of the nation, and accumulated here. That produce and property fall to half price there, and the same things rise to double price here.[16]

This nefarious business is becoming more and more the public detestation, and cannot fail, when the knowledge of it shall be sufficiently extended, to tumble its authors headlong from their heights. Money is leaving the remoter parts of the Union and flowing to this place to purchase paper; and here, a paper medium supplying its place, it is shipped off in exchange for luxuries. The value of property is necessarily falling in the places left bare of money. In Virginia, for instance, property has fallen 25 per cent in the last twelve months.[17]

Bursting of the paper bubble

At length our paper bubble is burst. The failure of Duer, in New York, soon brought on others, and these still more, like ninepins knocking one another down, till at that place the bankruptcy is become general, every man concerned in paper being broke, and most of the tradesmen and farmers who had been laying down money, having been tempted by these speculators to lend it to them at an interest of from 3 to 6 per cent a month, have lost the whole. It is computed there is a dead loss at New York of about 5 millions of dollars, which is reckoned the value of all the buildings of the city; so that if the whole town had been burnt to the ground it would have been just the measure of the present calamity. . . . In the meantime, buildings and other improvements are suspended. Workmen turned adrift. Country produce not to be sold at any price. . . . Notwithstanding the magnitude of this calamity, every newspaper almost is silent on it.[18]

No man of reflection who had ever attended to the South Sea Bubble in England, or that of Law in France, and who applied the lessons of the past to the present time, could fail to foresee the issue though he might not calculate the moment at which it would happen. The evidences of the public debt are solid and sacred. I presume there is not a man in the United States who would not part with his last shilling to pay them. But all that stuff called scrip, of whatever description, was folly or roguery.[19]

Fattening on the follies of the Old World

I look with great anxiety for the firm establishment of the new government in France, being perfectly convinced that if it takes place there it will spread sooner or later all over Europe. On the contrary, a check there would retard the revival of liberty in other countries. I consider the establishment and success of their government as necessary to stay up our own and to prevent it from falling back to that kind of a half-way house, the English constitution.[20]

I participate fully [in the] indignation at the trammels imposed on our commerce with Great Britain. Some attempts have been made in Congress, and others are still making, to meet their restrictions by effectual restriction on our part. It was proposed to double the foreign tonnage [duties] for a certain time, and after that to prohibit the exportation of our commodities in the vessels of nations not in treaty with us. This has been rejected. . . . If the war between Spain and England [over claims to the Pacific Northwest] takes place, I think France will inevitably be involved in it. In that case I hope the new world will fatten on the follies of the old.[21]

Spain must give us free use of the Mississippi

The present appearances of war between our two neighbors, Spain and England, cannot but excite all our attention. . . . The unsettled state of our dispute with Spain [over the navigation of the Mississippi] may give a turn to it very different from what we would wish. . . . You [American chargé at Madrid] know that the navigation cannot be practiced without a port where the sea and river vessels may meet and exchange loads. . . . The fixing on a proper port, and the degree of freedom it is to enjoy in its operations, will require negotiation, and be governed by events. There is danger, indeed, that even the unavoidable delay of sending a negotiator here may render the mission too late for the preservation of peace. It is impossible to answer for the forbearance of our Western citizens. We endeavor to quiet them with the expectation of an attainment of their rights by peaceable means. But should they in a moment of impatience hazard others, there is no saying how far we may be led; for neither themselves nor their rights will ever be abandoned by us.

You will be pleased to observe that we press these matters warmly and firmly under this idea that the war between Spain and Great Britain will be begun before you receive this; and such a moment must not be lost. But should an accommodation take place we retain, indeed, the same object and the same resolutions unalterably; but your discretion will suggest that in that event they must be pressed more softly, and that patience and persuasion must temper your conferences till either these may prevail or some other circumstance turn up which may enable us to use other means for the attainment of an object which we are determined, in the end, to obtain at every risk.[22]

Will France aid us in obtaining Spanish New Orleans?

France will be called into the war as an ally, and not on any pretence of the quarrel being in any degree her own. She may reasonably require, then, that Spain should do everything which depends on her to lessen the number of her enemies. She cannot doubt that we shall be of that number if she does not yield our right to the common use of the Mississippi, and the means of using and securing it. You [American chargé at Paris] will observe we state in general the necessity not only of our having a port near the mouth of the river (without which we could make no use of the navigation at all) but of its being so well separated from the territories of Spain and her jurisdiction as not to engender daily disputes and broils between us [which] it is certain . . . will end in war. Hence the necessity of a well-defined separation. Nature has decided what shall be the geography of that in the end, whatever it might be in the beginning, by cutting off from the adjacent countries of Florida and Louisiana . . . a long and narrow slip of land called the Island of New Orleans.

The idea of ceding this could not be hazarded to Spain, in the first step; it would be too disagreeable at first view, because this island, with its town, constitutes at present their principal settlement. . . . Reason and events, however, may, by little and little, familiarize them to it. . . . I suppose this idea too much even for the Count de Montmorin [French foreign minister] at first. . . . On the whole, in the event of war, it is left to the judgment of the Marquis de Lafayette and yourself how far you will develop the ideas, now communicated, to the Count de Montmorin, and how far you will suffer them to be developed to the Spanish Court.[23]

Justice from Britain if we remain neutral

On [Great Britain's] own proposal formally to exchange a minister we sent them one. They have taken no notice of that, and talk of agreeing to exchange one now, as if the idea were new. Besides what they are saying to you [American agent at London] they are talking to us through Quebec; but so informally that they may disavow it when they please. . . . They talk of a minister, a treaty of commerce *and alliance*. If the object of the latter be honorable, it is useless; if dishonorable, inadmissible. These tamperings prove they view a war as very possible; and some symptoms indicate designs against the Spanish possessions adjoining us [the Floridas, from Key West to New Orleans, and the great province of Louisiana, from the Mississippi to the Rockies]. The consequences of their acquiring all the country on our frontier from the St. Croix to the St. Mary's are too obvious to you to need development. You will readily see the dangers which would then environ us. We wish you, therefore, to intimate to them that we cannot be indifferent to enterprises of this kind. That we should contemplate a change of neighbors with extreme uneasiness; and that a due balance on our borders is not less desirable to us than a balance of power in Europe has always appeared to them. We wish to be neutral, and we will be so, *if they will execute the treaty* [of peace, of 1783] *fairly, and attempt no conquests adjoining us.*[24]

The provisional and definitive treaties, in their 7th article, stipulated that his 'Britannic Majesty should, with all convenient speed, and without causing any destruction, or *carrying away any negroes, or other property*, of the American inhabitants, *withdraw all his armies, garrisons, and fleets, from the said United States,* and from every port, place, and harbor, within the same.'

But the British garrisons were not withdrawn with all convenient speed, nor have ever yet been withdrawn from Michilimackinac, on Lake Michigan; Detroit, on the strait of Lakes Erie and Huron; Fort Erie, on Lake Erie; Niagara, Oswego, on Lake Ontario; Oswegatchie, on the River St. Lawrence; Pointe-au-Fer, and Dutchman's Point, on Lake Champlain. 2d. The British officers have undertaken to exercise a jurisdiction over the country and inhabitants in the vicinities of those forts; and, 3d, they have excluded the citizens of the United States from navigating, even on our side of the middle line of the rivers and lakes established as a boundary between the two nations.

By these proceedings we have been intercepted entirely from the commerce of furs with the Indian nations to the northward — a commerce which had ever been of great importance to the United States, not only for its intrinsic value but as it was the means of cherishing peace with those Indians, and of superseding the necessity of that expensive warfare we have been obliged to carry on with them during the time that these posts have been in other hands.[25]

Northwestern Indians, and the British

Our news from the westward is disagreeable. Constant murders committing by the Indians, and their combination threatens to be more and more extensive. I hope we shall give them a thorough drubbing this summer, and then change our tomahawk into a golden chain of friendship. The most economical as well as most humane conduct towards them is to bribe them into peace, and to retain them in peace by eternal bribes. The expedition this year would have served for presents on the most liberal scale for one hundred years; nor shall we otherwise ever get rid of an army, or of our debt. The least rag of Indian depredation will be an excuse to raise troops for those who love to have troops, and for those who think that a public debt is a good thing.[26]

The Indian war calls for sensible exertions. It would have been a trifle had we only avowed enemies to contend with. The British court have disavowed all aid to the Indians. Whatever may have been their orders in that direction, the Indians are fully and notoriously supplied by their agents with everything necessary to carry on the war. Time will show how all this is to end.[27]

Southwestern Indians, and the Spaniards

We have been constantly endeavoring by every possible means to keep peace with the Creeks ... and ... we have constantly endeavored to keep them at peace with the Spanish settlements also; ... Spain on the contrary, or at least the officers of her governments, ... have excited them and the other Southern Indians to commence a war against us, have furnished them with arms and ammunitions for the express purpose of carrying on that war; and prevented the Creeks from running the boundary which would have removed the cause of difference from between us.[28]

We love and we value peace; we know its blessings from experience. We abhor the follies of war and are not untried in its distresses and calamities. Unmeddling with the affairs of other nations, we had hoped that our distance and our dispositions would have left us free, in the example and indulgence of peace with all the world. We had with sincere and particular dispositions courted and cultivated the friendship of Spain. ... If we are disappointed in this appeal, if we are to be forced into a contrary order of things, our mind is made up. We shall meet it with firmness. The necessity of our position will supersede all appeal to calculation now, as it has done heretofore. We confide in our own strength without boasting of it; we respect that of others without fearing it. If we cannot otherwise prevail on the Creeks to discontinue their depredations, we will attack them in force. If Spain chooses to consider our defense against savage butchery as a cause of war to her, we must meet her also in war, with regret but without fear; and we shall be happier, to the last moment, to repair with her to the tribunal of peace and reason.[29]

Conquest and commerce

If there be one principle more deeply rooted than any other in the mind of every American, it is that we should have nothing to do with conquest. As to commerce, indeed, we have strong sensations. In casting our eyes over the earth, we see no instance of a nation forbidden, as we are, by foreign powers to deal with neighbors [European colonies in America], and obliged, with them, to carry into another hemisphere the mutual supplies necessary to relieve mutual wants. . . . An exchange of surpluses and wants between neighbor nations is both a right and a duty under the moral law. . . . Circumstances sometimes require that rights the most unquestionable should be advanced with delicacy. It would seem that the one now spoken of would need only a mention to be assented to by any unprejudiced mind; but with respect to America, Europeans in general have been too long in the habit of confounding force with right. . . . In policy, if not in justice, they should be disposed to avoid oppression, which, falling on us, as well as on their colonies, might tempt us to act together.[30]

Instead of embarrassing commerce under piles of regulating laws, duties, and prohibitions, could it be relieved from all its shackles in all parts of the world, could every country be employed in producing that which nature has best fitted it to produce, and each be free to exchange with others mutual surpluses for mutual wants, the greatest mass possible would then be produced of those things which contribute to human life and human happiness; the numbers of mankind would be increased, and their condition bettered. . . . But should any nation, contrary to our wishes, suppose it may better find its advantages by continuing its system of prohibitions, duties, and regulations, it behooves us to protect our citizens, their commerce and navigation, by counter prohibitions, duties, and regulations, also.[31]

Washington should serve a second term

When you [Washington] first mentioned to me your purpose of retiring from the government, though I felt all the magnitude of the event, I was in a considerable degree silent. I knew that, to such a mind as yours, persuasion was idle and impertinent; that before forming your decision you had weighed all the reasons for and against the measure, had made up your mind on full view of them, and that there could be little hope of changing the result. Pursuing my reflections, too, I knew we were some day to try to walk alone, and if the essay should be made while you should be alive and looking on, we should derive confidence from that circumstance, and resource, if it failed. The public mind, too, was calm and confident, and therefore in a favorable state for making the experiment. Had no change of circumstances intervened, I should not, with any hopes of success, have now ventured to propose to you a change of purpose. But the public mind is no longer confident and serene; and that from causes in which you are no ways personally mixed. . . .

It has been urged . . . that a public debt, greater than we can possibly pay before other causes of adding new debt to it will occur, has been artificially created by adding together the whole amount of the debtor and creditor sides of accounts, instead of only taking their balances, which could have been paid off in a short time; that this accumulation of debt has taken forever out of our power those easy sources of revenue which, applied to the ordinary necessities and exigencies of government, would have answered them habitually, and covered us from habitual murmurings against taxes and tax-gatherers, reserving extraordinary calls for those extraordinary occasions which would animate the people to meet them; that . . . we are already obliged to strain the impost till it produces clamor, and will produce evasion and war on our own citizens to collect it, and even to resort to an *excise* law of odious character with the people, partial in its operation, unproductive unless enforced by arbitrary and vexatious means, and committing the authority of the government in parts where resistance is most probable and coercion least practicable. . . .

I tremble at the threat of disunion

They think the ten or twelve per cent annual profit paid to the lenders of this paper medium taken out of the pockets of the people, who would have had without interest the coin it is banishing; that all the capital employed in paper speculation is barren and useless, producing, like that on a gaming table, no accession to itself, and is withdrawn from commerce and agriculture, where it would have produced addition to the common mass; that it nourishes in our citizens habits of vice and idleness instead of industry and morality; that it has furnished effectual means of corrupting such a portion of the legislature as turns the balance between the honest voters, whichever way it is directed; that this corrupt squadron, deciding the voice of the legislature, have manifested their dispositions to get rid of the limitations imposed by the Constitution on the general legislature, limitations on the faith of which the states acceded to that instrument; that the ultimate object of all this is to prepare the way for a change from the present republican form of government to that of a monarchy, of which the English constitution is to be the model; that this was contemplated by the convention is no secret, because its partisans have made more of it. To effect it then was impracticable, but they are still eager after their object, and are predisposing everything for its ultimate attainment. . . .

The only hope of safety hangs now on the numerous representation which is to come forward the ensuing year. . . . It is expected the great mass will form an accession to the Republican Party. . . . True wisdom would direct that they should be temperate and peaceable; but the division of sentiment and interest happens unfortunately to be so geographical that no mortal can say that what is most wise and temperate would prevail against what is most easy and obvious. I can scarcely contemplate a more incalculable evil than the breaking of the Union into two or more parts. . . . And this is the event at which I tremble, and to prevent which I consider your continuing at the head of affairs as of the last importance. The confidence of the whole Union is centred in you. Your being at the helm will be more than an answer to every argument which can be used to alarm and lead the people in any quarter into violence and secession. North and South will hang together if they have you to hang on.[32]

CHAPTER X

The Thorny Path of Neutrality

WHILE serving as America's first Secretary of State Jefferson found relief from the bitterness of party strife in his many non-political interests. With his friend James Madison (who in Congress led the fight against Hamilton's Federalists) he made a vacation tour to the north in 1791, collected botanical specimens, fished, and rambled about. He aided L'Enfant in planning the new Federal City at Washington, and his architectural tastes influenced the style of the President's House and the Capitol. Since one of his duties was the issuing of patents, he spent happy hours examining drawings of inventions, including that of Eli Whitney's cotton gin. He tried to have Congress extend the decimal system to weights and measures, and he imported for cultivation in the United States olive trees and upland rice, believing that the greatest service one could render his country was the introduction of a useful plant.

From the capital city of Philadelphia he wrote frequent and affectionate letters to his family at Monticello, to Maria (as Mary was called after her stay in Paris), and to Martha and her husband, Thomas Mann Randolph. Again and again he expressed his deep longing to retire to his mountaintop. Subjected to Hamilton's newspaper attacks and involved in 'the heats and tumults of conflicting parties,' it was only at the urgent insistence of President Washington that he remained in office until the last day of 1793.

In that tumultuous year of 1793 events abroad had a powerful impact upon the United States. The establishment of the French Republic and the execution of the French king was followed, in February of 1793, by the opening of the great war waged by Great

Britain and the combined monarchs of Europe against republican France. At home, the struggle between pro-French Jeffersonians and pro-British Hamiltonians became intensified, and Washington's administration was confronted with grave problems of neutrality.

Although Jefferson deplored the excesses of the French Revolution, he rejoiced at every step in its progress. He was convinced that the cause of liberty and self-government at home and throughout the world was involved in the success or failure of a France dedicated to Liberty, Equality, and Fraternity. As Secretary of State he urged recognition of the French Republic (against the advice of Hamilton), and he established the permanent American principle that recognition should be accorded any new government which rested upon the consent of the people. As Secretary of State, also, it fell to him to develop the system of American neutrality, and to maintain it at home as well as against the two great belligerents.

This was a most difficult task. Yet he executed it with marked ability and with the most scrupulous fidelity, in spite of his own private sympathies for France and in spite of the pro-British subserviency of Hamilton, against whom he was 'daily pitted in the Cabinet.' He protested against Britain's captures of American ships, impressment of American seamen, and her anti-neutral edict declaring foodstuffs contraband of war. Yet at the same time he combatted the privateering activities of pro-French Americans against British shipping, and in August of 1793 he demanded the recall of Citizen Genet, the first minister from the French Republic. His vigorous assertion of American rights in the Genet affair gave the lie to the Federalist charge that he was more French than American, and won the respect of his most carping critics.

In thus upholding his country's rights and sovereignty against the assaults of both belligerents, Jefferson laid down a policy by which neutral America for the next twenty years attempted to avoid being plunged into the great European war: a war 'with which we meddle not, and which we wish to avoid if justice to all parties and from all parties will enable us to avoid it.'

A vacation tour, botanizing and fishing

Mr. Madison and myself . . . have visited . . . the principal scenes
of General Burgoyne's misfortunes, . . . the encampments at Saratoga and ground where the British piled their arms, and the field
of the battle of Bennington. . . . We have also visited Forts William
Henry and George, Ticonderoga, Crown Point, etc., which have
been scenes of blood from a very early part of our history. We were
more pleased, however, with the botanical objects which continu-
ally presented themselves: . . . the sugar maple in vast abundance;
the silver fir, white pine, pitch pine, spruce pine, a shrub with
decumbent stems which they call juniper, an azalea very different
from the nudiflora, with very large clusters of flowers, more thickly
set on the branches, of a deeper red, and high pink-fragrance. It is
the richest shrub I have seen. The honeysuckle of the gardens
growing wild on the banks of Lake George, the paper-birch, an
aspen with a velvet leaf, a shrub-willow with downy catkins, a wild
gooseberry, the wild cherry with single fruit (not the bunch cherry),
strawberries in abundance.[1]

Lake George is, without comparison, the most beautiful water
I ever saw; formed by a contour of mountains into a basin thirty-
five miles long, and from two or four miles broad, finely interspersed
with islands, its water limpid as crystal, and the mountainsides
covered with rich groves of thuja, silver fir, white pine, aspen, and
paper-birch down to the water-edge; here and there precipices of
rock to checker the scene and save it from monotony. An abundance of speckled trout, salmon trout, bass, and other fish with which
it is stored have added to our other amusements the sport of taking
them.[2]

Planning the new Federal City at Washington

I have examined my papers and found the plans of Frankfort-
on-the-Mayne, Carlsruhe, Amsterdam, Strasburg, Paris, Orléans,
Bordeaux, Lyons, Montpelier, Marseilles, Turin, and Milan, which
I send in a roll by the post. They are on large and accurate scales,
having been procured by me while in those respective cities myself.
As they are connected with the notes I made in my travels, and
often necessary to explain them to myself, I will beg your care of

them, and to return them when no longer useful to you [Major L'Enfant].[3]

I should propose . . . that no street be narrower than one hundred feet, with footways of fifteen feet. Where a street is long and level, it might be one hundred and twenty feet wide. I should prefer squares of at least two hundred yards every way, which will be about eight acres each. . . . I doubt much whether the obligation to build the houses at a given distance from the street contributes to its beauty. It produces a disgusting monotony; all persons make this complaint against Philadelphia. . . . In Paris it is forbidden to build a house beyond a given height; and it is admitted to be a good restriction. It keeps down the price of ground, keeps the houses low and convenient, and the streets light and airy. Fires are much more manageable where houses are low.[4]

Whenever it is proposed to prepare plans for the Capitol I should prefer the adoption of some one of the models of antiquity which have had the approbation of thousands of years; and for the President's house I should prefer the celebrated fronts of modern buildings which have already received the approbation of all good judges. Such are the Galérie du Louvre, the Gardes Meubles, and two fronts of the Hôtel de Salm.[5] While in Europe I selected about a dozen or two of the handsomest fronts of private buildings, of which I have the plates. Perhaps it might decide the taste of the new town were these to be engraved here and distributed gratis among the inhabitants of Georgetown. The expense would be trifling.[6]

Doctor [William] Thornton's plan of a Capitol has been produced, and has so captivated the eyes and judgment of all as to leave no doubt . . . of its preference over all which have been produced. . . . It is simple, noble, beautiful, excellently distributed, and moderate in size.[7]

Cotton gin and decimals; the greatest of all services

An act of Congress authorizing the issuing of patents for new discoveries has given a spring to invention beyond my conception. Being an instrument in granting the patents, I am acquainted with their discoveries. Many of them indeed are trifling, but there are some of great consequence. . . . Yesterday the man who built the famous bridge from Boston to Charlestown was with me, asking a patent for a pile engine of his own construction.[8]

Your [Eli Whitney's] drawing of the cotton gin was received. . . . As the State of Virginia, of which I am, carries on household manufactures of cotton to a great extent, as I also do myself, and one of our great embarrassments is the clearing the cotton of the seed, I feel a considerable interest in the success of your invention for family use. Permit me therefore to ask information from you on these points. Has the machine been thoroughly tried in the ginning of cotton, or is it yet but a machine of theory? What quantity of cotton has it cleaned on an average of several days, and worked by hand, and how many hands? What will be the cost of one of them made to be worked by hand? Favorable answers to these questions would induce me to engage one of them.[9]

The experiment made by Congress . . . that there should be one money of account and payment through the United States, and that its parts and multiples should be in a decimal ratio, has obtained such general approbation, both at home and abroad, that nothing seems wanting but the actual coinage to banish the discordant pounds, shillings, pence, and farthings of the different states, and to establish in their stead the new denominations. Is it in contemplation . . . to extend a like improvement to our measures and weights, and to arrange them also in a decimal ratio? The facility which this would introduce into the vulgar arithmetic would unquestionably be soon and sensibly felt by the whole mass of the people. . . . Let the foot be divided into 10 inches; the inch into 10 lines; the line into 10 points. Let 10 feet make a decad; 10 decads one rood; 10 roods a furlong; 10 furlongs a mile.[10]

I have arrived at Baltimore from Marseilles forty olive trees of the best kind from Marseilles, and a box of seed, the latter to raise stocks, and the former, cuttings to engraft on the stocks. I am ordering them on instantly to Charleston. . . . Another cargo is on its way from Bordeaux, so that I hope to secure the commencement of this culture, and from the best species.[11] In 1790 I got a cask of heavy upland rice from the River Denbigh, in Africa, . . . in hopes it might supersede the culture of the wet rice which renders South Carolina and Georgia so pestilential through the summer. It . . . has spread in the upper parts of Georgia so as to have become almost general, and is highly prized. Perhaps it may answer in Tennessee and Kentucky. The greatest service which can be rendered any country is to add a useful plant to its culture, especially a bread grain; next in value to bread is oil.[12]

Philadelphia bonnets; Socrates on a stick

I inclose you [Martha] the *Magasin des Modes* of July. My furniture is arrived from Paris, but... my house [at Philadelphia, the capital from 1790 to 1800] will not be ready to receive them for some weeks.[13] Petit [his French steward while in Paris] arrived here three or four days ago, and accosted me with an assurance that he was come *pour rester toujours avec moi.* The principal small news he brings is that Panthemont [where Patsy and Polly had been placed while in Paris] is one of the convents to be kept up for education, that the old Abbess is living, ... that some of the nuns have chosen to rejoin the world, others to stay.[14] Perhaps you think you have nothing to say to me. It is a great deal to say you are all well; or that one has a cold, another a fever, etc.; besides that, there is not a sprig of grass that shoots uninteresting to me, nor anything that moves, from yourself down to Bergère and Grizzle [the shepherd dogs brought back from France].[15]

Instead of waiting to send the two veils for your sister and yourself round with the other things, I inclose them with this letter. Observe that one of the strings is to be drawn tight round the root of the crown of the hat, and the veil then falling over the brim of the hat is drawn by the lower string as tight or loose as you please round the neck. When the veil is not chosen to be down, the lower string is also tied round the root of the crown, so as to give it the appearance of a puffed bandage for the hat.[16]

My dear Martha, having no particular subject for a letter I find none more soothing to my mind than to indulge itself in expressions of the love I bear you, and the delight with which I recall the various scenes through which we have passed together in our wanderings over the world. These reveries alleviate the toils and inquietudes of my present situation, and leave me always impressed with the desire of being at home once more and of exchanging labor, envy, and malice for ease, domestic occupation, and domestic love and society; where I may once more be happy with you, with

Mr. Randolph and dear little Anne [his first grandchild], with whom even Socrates might ride on a stick without being ridiculous.[17]

I wrote you in my last that the frogs had begun their songs on the 7th; since that the bluebirds saluted us on the 17th; the weeping willow began to leaf on the 18th; the lilac and gooseberry on the 25th, and the golden willow on the 26th. I inclose for your sister three kinds of flowering beans, very beautiful and very rare. She must plant and nourish them with her own hand this year in order to save enough seeds for herself and me.[18] I believe you knew Otchakitz, the Indian who lived with the Marquis de Lafayette. He came here lately with some deputies from his nation, and died here of pleurisy. I was at his funeral yesterday; he was buried standing up, according to their manner.[19] One of the Indian chiefs now here, whom you may remember to have seen at Monticello a day or two before Tarleton drove us off, remembers you, and enquired after you. He is of the Pioria nation; perhaps you may recollect that he gave our name to an infant son he then had with him, and who, he now tells me, is a fine lad.[20] We were entertained here lately with the ascent of Mr. Blanchard in a balloon. The security of the thing appeared so great that everybody is wishing for a balloon to travel in. I wish for one sincerely, as instead of ten days I should be within five hours of home.[21]

Next year we will sow our cabbages together

My head has been so full of farming ... that I could not resist the addressing my last weekly letters to Mr. Randolph, and boring him with my plans. Maria [Polly] writes to you today.... She passes two or three days in the week with me, under the trees, for I never go into the house [on the banks of the Schuylkill, taken for the summer] but at the hour of bed. I never before knew the full value of trees. My house is entirely embosomed in high plane trees, with good grass below; and under them I breakfast, dine, write, read, and receive my company. What would I not give that the trees planted nearest round the house at Monticello were full grown.[22]

I sincerely congratulate you on the arrival of the mocking-bird. Learn all the children to venerate it as a superior being in the form of a bird, or as a being which will haunt them if any harm is done to itself or its eggs.[23] It is a relief to be withdrawn from the torment of the scenes amidst which we are. Spectators of the heats and tumults of conflicting parties, we cannot help participating of their feelings. I should envy you the tranquil occupations of your situation were it not that I value your happiness more than my own, but I too shall have my turn. The ensuing year will be the longest of my life, and the last of such hateful labors; the next we will sow our cabbages together.[24]

Subjected to Hamilton's attacks

On accepting the office I am in, I knew I was to set myself up as a butt of reproach not only for my own errors, but for the errors of those who would undertake to judge me. . . . I have therefore to console myself that obloquy has begun upon me so late as to spare me a longer interval of satisfaction than expected; and that however ardently my retirement to my own home and my own affairs may be wished for by others, as the author says, there is no one of them who feels the wish once where I do a thousand times.[25]

Though I see the pen of the Secretary of the Treasury plainly in the attack on me, yet, since he has not chosen to put his name to it, I am not free to notice it as his. I have preserved through life a resolution, set in a very early part of it, never to write in a public paper without subscribing my name; and to engage openly an adversary who does not let himself be seen is staking all against nothing. The indecency, too, of newspaper squabbling between two public ministers, besides my own sense of it, has drawn something like an injunction from another quarter. Every fact alleged . . . as to myself is false, and can be proved so; and perhaps will be one day.[26]

That I have ever intrigued . . . to defeat the plans of the Secretary of the Treasury . . . is contrary to all truth [he wrote President Washington in September of 1792]. . . . That I have utterly, in my private conversations, disapproved of the system of the Secretary of the Treasury I acknowledge and avow; and this was not merely a speculative difference. His system flowed from principles adverse to liberty, and was calculated to undermine and demolish the Republic. . . .

When I came into this office, it was with a resolution to retire from it as soon as I could with decency. It pretty early appeared to me that the proper moment would be the first of those epochs at which the Constitution seems to have contemplated a periodical change or renewal of the public servants. . . . I look to that period with the longing of a wave-worn mariner who has at length the land in view, and shall count the days and hours which still lie between me and it. . . .

I am more desirous to predispose everything for the repose to which I am withdrawing than expose it to be disturbed by newspaper contests. If these, however, cannot be avoided altogether, yet a regard for your [Washington's] quiet will be a sufficient motive for my deferring it till I become merely a private citizen. . . . I may then, too, avoid the charge of misapplying that time which now, belonging to those who employ me, should be wholly devoted to their service. . . . To a thorough disregard of the honors and emoluments of office I join as great a value for the esteem of my countrymen, and conscious of having merited it by an integrity which cannot be reproached, and by an enthusiastic devotion to their rights and liberty, I will not suffer my retirement to be clouded by the slanders of a man whose history, from the moment at which history can stoop to notice him, is a tissue of machinations against the liberty of the country which has not only received and given him bread but heaped its honors on his head. Still, however, I repeat the hope that it will not be necessary to make such an appeal.[27]

Washington persuades him not to resign

This morning [October 1, 1792] at Mount Vernon I had the following conversation with the President. He opened it by expressing his regret at the resolution in which I appeared so fixed . . . of retiring from public affairs. He said that he should be extremely sorry . . . and that he could not see where he should find another character to fill my office. . . . He then expressed his concern at the difference . . . between the Secretary of the Treasury and myself . . . and he wished he could be the mediator to put an end to it. That he thought it important to preserve the check of my opinions in the Administration, in order to keep things in their proper channel,

and prevent them from going too far. That as to the idea of transforming this government into a monarchy, he did not believe there
were ten men in the United States whose opinions were worth attention who entertained such a thought.

I told him there were many more than he imagined . . .; that the
Secretary of the Treasury was one of these. That I had heard him
say that this Constitution was a shilly-shally thing, of mere milk
and water, which could not last, and was only good as a step to
something better. That when we reflected that he had endeavored
in the [Constitutional] Convention to make an English constitution
of it, and when failing in that, we saw all his measures tending to
bring it to the same thing, it was natural for us to be jealous; and
particularly when we saw that these measures had established
corruption in the legislature, where there was a squadron devoted
to the nod of the Treasury, doing whatever he had directed, and
ready to do what he should direct. . . .

He said, that as to that interested spirit in the legislature, it was
what could not be avoided in any government unless we were to
exclude particular descriptions of men, such as the holders of the
funds, from all office. . . . He touched on the merits of the funding
system, observed there was a difference of opinion about it, some
thinking it very bad, others very good; that experience was the
only criterion of right which he knew, and this alone would decide
which opinion was right. That for himself, he had seen our affairs
desperate and our credit lost, and that this was in a sudden and
extraordinary degree raised to the highest pitch. I told him, all
that was ever necessary to establish our credit was an efficient
government and an honest one, declaring it would sacredly pay
our debts, laying taxes for this purpose, and applying them to it.
I avoided going further into the subject. He finished by another
exhortation to me not to decide too positively on retirement, and
here we were called to breakfast.[28]

Zealous for the rights of man

Would you [Thomas Paine] believe it possible that in this country there should be high and important characters who need your
lessons in republicanism, and who do not heed them? It is but too
true that we have a sect preaching up and pouting after an English

constitution of king, lords, and commons, and whose heads are itching for crowns, coronets, and mitres. But our people, my good friend, are firm and unanimous in their principles of republicanism, and there is no better proof of it than that they love what you write and read it with delight. The printers season every newspaper with extracts from your last, as they did before from your first part, of the *Rights of Man*. They have both served here to separate the wheat from the chaff, and to prove that though the latter appears on the surface, it is on the surface only. The bulk below is sound and pure. Go on then in doing with your pen what in other times was done with the sword: show that reformation is more practicable by operating on the mind than on the body of man.[29]

France becomes a republic

We are now under the first impression of the news of the King's flight from Paris, and his recapture. It would be unfortunate were it in the power of any one man to defeat the issue of so beautiful a revolution.[30] Such are the fruits of that form of government which heaps importance on idiots, and of which the Tories of the present day are trying to preach into our favor. I still hope the French Revolution will issue happily. I feel that the permanence of our own leans in some degree on that; and that a failure there would be a powerful argument to prove there must be a failure here.[31]

We have just received here [March, 1793] the news of the decapitation of the King of France. Should the present foment in Europe not produce republics everywhere, it will at least soften the monarchical governments by rendering monarchs amenable to punishment like other criminals, and doing away that . . . insolence and oppression, the inviolability of the king's person.[32] During the transition from the late form of government to the re-establishment of some other legitimate authority . . . you [American minister at Paris] may have been at a loss to determine with whom business might be done. . . . We surely cannot deny to any nation that right whereon our own government is founded, that every one may govern itself according to whatever form it pleases, and change these forms at its own will; and that it may transact its business with foreign nations through whatever organ it thinks proper, whether King, Convention, Assembly, Committee, President, or anything else it may choose. The will of the nation is the only thing essential to be regarded.[33]

Bloodshed justified; the spirit of '76 rekindled

In the struggle [in France] which was necessary, many guilty persons fell without the forms of trial, and with them some innocent. These I deplore as much as anybody, and shall deplore some of them to the day of my death. But I deplore them as I should have done had they fallen in battle. It was necessary to use the arm of the people, a machine not quite so blind as balls and bombs, but blind to a certain degree. A few of their cordial friends met at their hands the fate of enemies. But time and truth will rescue and embalm their memories, while their posterity will be enjoying that very liberty for which they would never have hesitated to offer up their lives. The liberty of the whole earth was depending on the issue of the contest, and was ever such a prize won with so little innocent blood?

My own affections have been deeply wounded by some of the martyrs to this cause, but rather than it should have failed, I would have seen half the earth desolated. Were there but an Adam and an Eve left in every country, and left free, it would be better than as it now is. I have expressed ... my sentiments because they are really those of ninety-nine in a hundred of our citizens. The universal feasts and rejoicings which have lately been had, on account of the successes of the French [against the combined monarchs of Europe], showed the genuine effusions of their hearts.[34]

All the old spirit of 1776, rekindling the newspapers from Boston to Charleston, proves this; and even the monocrat papers are obliged to publish the most furious philippics against England. A French frigate took a British prize off the capes of Delaware the other day and sent her up here. Upon her coming into sight, thousands and thousands of the *yeomanry* of the city crowded and covered the wharves. Never before was such a crowd seen there; and when the British colors were seen *reversed*, and the French flying above them, they burst into peals of exultation.

Party divisions; daily pitted like two cocks

I wish we may be able to repress the spirit of the people within the limits of a fair neutrality. In the meantime, Hamilton is panic-struck if we refuse our breech to every kick which Great Britain may choose to give it. He is for proclaiming at once the most abject principles, such as would invite and merit habitual insults; and indeed every inch of ground must be fought in our councils to desperation in order to hold up the face of even a sneaking neutrality. ... Some propositions have come from him which would astonish Mr. Pitt himself with their boldness. If we preserve even a sneaking neutrality, we shall be indebted for it to the President and not to his counsellors. ... Great Britain has as yet not condescended to notice us in any way ..., no answer of any kind to a single complaint for the daily violations committed on our sailors and ships. Indeed, we promise beforehand so fast that she has not time to ask anything.[35] In these discussions, Hamilton and myself were daily pitted in the Cabinet like two cocks.[36]

If anything prevents it being a mere English neutrality, it will be that the penchant of the President is not that way, and, above all, the ardent spirit of our constituents. The line is now drawn so clearly as to show on one side: 1. The fashionable circles of Philadelphia, New York, Boston, and Charleston; natural aristocrats. 2. Merchants trading on British capital. 3. Paper [money] men. All the old Tories are found in some one of the three descriptions. On the other side are: 1. Merchants trading on their own capital. 2. Irish merchants. 3. Tradesmen, mechanics, farmers, and every other possible description of our citizens.[37]

With respect to our conduct as a neutral nation, it is marked out in our treaties with France and Holland, two of the belligerent powers; and as the duties of neutrality require an *equal* conduct to both parties, we should, on that ground, act on the same principles towards Great Britain. We presume that this would be satisfactory to her because of its equality, and because she too has sanctioned the same principles in her treaty with France. ... You [American minister at London] are desired to persevere till you obtain a regulation to guard our vessels from having their hands impressed, and to inhibit the British navy officers from taking them under the pretext of their being British subjects. There appears but one practical rule, that the vessel being American shall be conclusive evidence that the hands are so to a certain number, proportioned to her tonnage.[38]

Citizen Genet; neutrality a thorny path

It was suspected that there was not a clear mind in the President's counsellors to receive Genet [Citizen Edmond Genet, minister from the French Republic, who arrived in Philadelphia in May of 1793]. The citizens, however, determined to receive him. . . . A vast concourse of people attended him. . . . It is impossible for anything to be more affectionate, more magnanimous, than the purport of his mission. We know [said Genet] that under present circumstances we have a right to call upon [America] for the guarantee of our islands [in the West Indies, under the Franco-American Treaty of 1778]. But we do not desire it. We wish you to do nothing but what is for your own good. . . . Cherish your own peace and prosperity. You have expressed a willingness to enter into a more liberal treaty of commerce with us; I bring full powers . . . to form such a treaty. . . . In short, he offers everything and asks nothing. Yet I know the offers will be opposed, and suspect they will not be accepted. . . . It is impossible . . . to conceive what is passing in our conclave; and it is evident that one or two, at least, under the pretense of avoiding war on the one side have no great antipathy to run foul of it on the other, and to make a part in the confederacy of princes against human liberty.[39]

The war . . . embarrasses our government daily and immensely. The predilection of our citizens for France renders it very difficult to suppress their attempts to cruise against the English on the ocean, and to do justice to the latter in cases where they are entitled to it.[40]

Never in my opinion was so calamitous an appointment made as that of the present Minister of France here [he wrote in July of 1793]. Hot-headed, all imagination, no judgment, passionate, disrespectful and even indecent towards the President in his written as well as verbal communications, talking of appeals from him to Congress, from them to the people, urging the most unreasonable and groundless propositions, and in the most dictatorial style, etc., etc., etc. . . . He renders my position immensely difficult.[41]

The grossly arrogant Genet must be recalled

Mr. Genet had been then but a little time with us; and but a little more was necessary to develop in him a character and conduct so unexpected and so extraordinary as to place us in the most distressing dilemma between our regard for his nation, which is constant and sincere, and a regard for our laws. . . . When the government forbids their citizens to arm and engage in the war, he undertakes to arm and engage them. When they forbid vessels to be fitted in their ports for cruising on nations with whom they are at peace, he commissions them to fit and cruise. When they forbid an unceded jurisdiction to be exercised within their territory by foreign agents, he undertakes to uphold that exercise, and to avow it openly.

. . . The *Little Sarah* or *Little Democrat* [privateer] was armed, equipped, and manned in the port of Philadelphia under the very eye of the government, as if meant to insult it. Having fallen down the river, and being evidently on the point of departure for a cruise, Mr. Genet was desired in my letter of July the 12th [1793], on the part of the President, to detain her till some inquiry and determination on the case should be had. Yet within three or four days after, she was sent out by orders from Mr. Genet himself, and is at this time cruising on our coasts, as appears by the protest of the master of one of our vessels maltreated by her. . . .

Mr. Genet, not content with using our force, whether we will or not, in the military line against nations with whom we are at peace, undertakes also to direct the civil government; and particularly for the executive and legislative bodies to pronounce what powers may or may not be exercised by the one or the other. . . . We draw a veil over the sensations which these expressions excite. No words can render them; but they will not escape the sensibility of a friendly and magnanimous nation, who will do us justice. . . . Conscious, on our part, of the same friendly and sincere dispositions, we can with truth affirm, both for our nation and government, that we have never omitted a reasonable occasion of manifesting them. . . . And for these things he rewards us by endeavors to excite discord and distrust between our citizens and those whom they have entrusted with their government, between the different branches of our government, between our nation and his.

But none of these things, we hope, will be found in his power. That friendship which dictates to us to bear with his conduct yet a while, lest the interests of his nation here should suffer injury, will hasten them to replace an agent whose dispositions are such a mis-

representation of theirs, and whose continuance here is inconsistent
with order, peace, respect, and that friendly correspondence which
we hope will ever subsist between the two nations.[42]

Genet condemned generally; British captures

The indications from different parts of the continent are already
sufficient to show that the mass of the Republican interest has no
hesitation to disapprove of this intermeddling by a foreigner, and
the more readily as his object was evidently, contrary to his pro-
fessions, to force us into the war.[43] His conduct has given room for
the enemies of liberty and of France to come forward in a state of
acrimony against that nation which they never would have dared
to have done. The disapprobation of the agent mingles with the
reprehension of his nation.... However, the people going right
themselves, if they always see their Republican advocates with
them, an accidental meeting with the monocrats will not be a
coalescence.[44]

It is an essential character of neutrality to furnish no aids (not
stipulated by treaty) to one party which we are not equally ready
to furnish to the other. If we permit corn [grain] to be sent to Great
Britain and her friends, we are equally bound to permit it to France.
To restrain it would be a partiality which might lead to war with
France; and between restraining it ourselves, and permitting her
enemies to restrain it unrightfully, is no difference.... Thus we
should see ourselves plunged by this unauthorized act of Great
Britain into a war with which we meddle not, and which we wish
to avoid if justice to all parties and from all parties will enable us to
avoid it.

In the case where we found ourselves obliged by treaty to withhold from the enemies of France the right of arming in our ports, we
thought ourselves in justice bound to withhold the same right from
France also, and we did it. Were we to withhold from her supplies
of provisions, we should in like manner be bound to withhold them
from her enemies also; and thus shut to ourselves all the ports of
Europe where corn is in demand, or make ourselves parties in the
war. This is a dilemma which Great Britain has no right to force
upon us, and for which no pretext can be found in any part of our
conduct. She may, indeed, feel the desire of starving an enemy

nation; but she can have no right of doing it at our loss, nor of making us the instruments of it.[45]

I am going back to Virginia

Your letter [that of Mrs. Angelica Church, about Jefferson's friends in Paris] gives me the first information that our dear friend Madame de Corny has been, as to her fortune, among the victims of the times. Sad times indeed! and much lamented victim! . . . And Madame Cosway in a convent! I knew that to much goodness of heart she joined enthusiasm and religion; but I thought that very enthusiasm would have prevented her from shutting up her adoration of the God of the universe within the walls of a cloister; that she would rather have sought the *mountaintop*. How happy should I be that it were *mine* that you, she, and Madame de Corny would seek. . . .

I am going to Virginia. I have at length become able to fix that to the beginning of the new year. I am then to be liberated from the hated occupations of politics and to remain in the bosom of my family, my farm, and my books. I have my house to build [that is, remodeling Monticello], my fields to farm, and to watch for the happiness of those who labor for mine. I have one daughter married to a man of science, sense, virtue, and competence; in whom indeed I have nothing more to wish. They live with me. If the other [Maria] shall be as fortunate, in due process of time I shall imagine myself as blessed as the most blessed of the patriarchs.[46]

In every bud that opens, in every breath that blows

Having had the honor of communicating to you [President Washington] . . . my purpose of retiring from the office of Secretary of State at the end of the month of September, you were pleased, for particular reasons, to wish its postponement to the close of the year. That term being now arrived, and my propensities to retirement becoming daily more and more irresistible, I now [December 31, 1793] take the liberty of resigning the office into your hands. . . . I carry into my retirement a lively sense of your goodness, and shall continue gratefully to remember it.[47]

I have now been in the public service four and twenty years. . . . I have served my tour. . . . There has been a time when . . . perhaps the esteem of the world was of higher value in my eye than everything in it. But age, experience, and reflection, preserving to that only its due value, have set a higher on tranquillity. The motion of my blood no longer keeps time with the tumult of the world. It leads me to seek happiness in the lap and love of my family, in the society of my neighbors and my books, in the wholesome occupations of my farm and my affairs, in an interest or affection in every bud that opens, in every breath that blows around me, in an entire freedom of rest, of motion, of thought, owing account to myself alone of my hours and actions.[48]

CHAPTER XI

The Struggle for Democracy

WHEN Thomas Jefferson returned to Monticello in January of 1794 he declared that he was through, once and for all, with public affairs. Happy again as a Virginia planter, he occupied himself with restoring his neglected farms, remodeling and putting a dome on Monticello, developing his new trade of nail-making, and inventing a plough which became world-famous. As to politics, he tried to confine himself to a 'pious ejaculation' now and then for the cause of embattled democracy.

It was not long, however, before he was giving advice and encouragement to Madison and others in their fight against the Federalists, the 'Anglican monarchical aristocratical party.' He was indignant at attempts to suppress the political clubs called Democratic Societies, and alarmed at the huge army of fifteen thousand men sent to crush a few Western farmers who had rioted against Hamilton's excise tax on their whiskey. Infamous and execrable, in his opinion, was the treaty negotiated with Great Britain in 1794 by John Jay, in which Jay acquiesced in British maritime practices and thus gave an offended France a pretext for similar depredations upon American commerce.

In 1796 the Republicans drafted Jefferson as their presidential candidate against Federalist John Adams. Since he received the second largest number of votes (68 to Adams' 71), under the system then prevailing he was elected Vice President. From this vantage point he organized and directed the democratic forces during the four stormy years of Adams' administration.

At his first session in Philadelphia there was strong Federalist pressure for war with France. Party passions ran high, but in the end Adams decided to send special envoys to negotiate differences at Paris. During this and other lulls in the political storm Jefferson found time to write an account of the *Megalonyx Jeffersoni* for the American Philosophical Society (of which he was president from 1797 to 1815), to devise new uses for the steam engine, and to compile a Parliamentary Manual for Congress. But most of his time, perforce, was spent in welding together the farmers, planters, and artisans of the country (which was then overwhelmingly agricultural) into a hard-hitting opposition party, and in waging a desperate struggle for democratic and constitutional rights against a Federalist party made arrogant by the X, Y, Z affair.

In the spring of 1798 President Adams made known that his special envoys to Paris had been refused official recognition, and that French agents (whom he called 'X, Y, and Z') had demanded as the price of diplomatic relations a loan to France and bribes for Talleyrand and other members of the French Directory. War hysteria seized the nation. Army and navy measures, taxes and loans, were rushed through Congress, and an undeclared naval war was begun against the French Republic. The Federalists then passed the repressive Alien and Sedition Acts. At his own discretion President Adams could now imprison or banish 'alien enemies,' and naturalization now became possible only after fourteen years' residence for exiled English and Irish liberals, who had a way of becoming Jeffersonian editors and politicians. Most detestable of all was the Sedition Act, which attempted to crush all political opposition by making criticism of Federalist officials or policies a crime. A Tory reign of terror now ensued. Jefferson was grossly abused, his colleagues were mobbed, and 'seditious' Republican editors were clapped into jail.

With great courage, skill, and energy Jefferson directed the Republican counter-attack, a campaign which was fought for two years and ended in his election to the presidency. Against the centralizing and dictatorial encroachments of Federalism he himself wrote the Kentucky Resolutions, which declared the Alien and Sedition Acts unconstitutional, in violation of the Bill of Rights and the rights of the states. He made full use of the press, and he took advantage of dissensions among the Federalists when Adams made peace with France. But the Federalists, the self-styled party of 'the rich, wise, and well-born,' were still formidable. Although Jefferson defeated John Adams in the hard-fought and scurrilous presidential contest of 1800, his opponents desperately tried to thwart the will of the people. Both he and Aaron Burr, his running-mate, had received the same number of electoral votes, and under the Constitution (until amended in 1804) this tie left the final decision to the House of Representatives. The Federalist leaders of the House intrigued and schemed to make Burr President. Thirty-six ballots were cast before Jefferson's victory was assured. It was glorious news to all friends of the rights of man. The 'Revolution of 1800' had succeeded, and throughout the young republic democratic Americans triumphantly sang

> 'Rejoice! Columbia's sons rejoice!
> To tyrants never bend the knee,
> But join with heart, and soul, and voice,
> For JEFFERSON and LIBERTY.'

I have laid up my Rosinante in his stall

I return to farming with an ardor which I scarcely knew in my youth, and which has got the better entirely of my love of study. Instead of writing ten or twelve letters a day, which I have been in the habit of doing as a thing of course, I put off answering my letters now, farmer-like, till a rainy day, and then find it sometimes postponed by other necessary occupations.[1] I think it is Montaigne who has said that ignorance is the softest pillow on which a man can rest his head. I am sure it is true as to everything political, and shall endeavor to estrange myself to everything of that character.[2] I have laid up my Rosinante in his stall.[3]

If you [William B. Giles, a Virginia politician] visit me as a farmer, it must be as a co-disciple; for I am but a learner; an eager one indeed, but yet desperate, being too old now to learn a new art. However, I am as much delighted and occupied with it as if I was the greatest adept. I shall talk with you about it from morning till night, and put you on very short allowance as to political aliment. Now and then a pious ejaculation for the French and Dutch republicans, returning with due dispatch to clover, potatoes, wheat, etc.[4]

Over the foreign powers I am convinced [the French] will triumph complete, and I cannot but hope that that triumph, and the consequent disgrace of the invading tyrants, is destined, in order of events, to kindle the wrath of the people of Europe against those who have dared to embroil them in such wickedness, and to bring at length kings, nobles, and priests to the scaffolds which they have been so long deluging with human blood. I am still warm whenever I think of these scoundrels, though I do it as seldom as I can, preferring infinitely to contemplate the tranquil growth of my lucerne and potatoes.[5]

My estate is a large one for the country, to wit, upwards of ten thousand acres of valuable land on the navigable parts of James River and two hundred negroes, and not a shilling out of it is or ever was under any incumbrance for debt.[6] I find on a more minute examination of my lands than the short visits heretofore made to them permitted that a ten years' abandonment of them to the ravages of overseers has brought on them a degree of degradation far beyond what I had expected. As this obliges me to adopt a milder course of cropping, so I find that they have enabled me to do it by having opened a great deal of lands during my absence. I have therefore determined on a division of my farm into six fields, to be put under this rotation: first year, wheat; second, corn, potatoes, peas; third, rye or wheat, according to circumstances; fourth and fifth, clover where the fields will bring it, and buckwheat dressings where they will not; sixth, folding, and buckwheat dressings. But it will take me from three to six years to get this plan under way.[7]

Invention of a world-famous plough

Since my retirement ... I have made researches into nothing but what is connected with agriculture. In this way, I have a little matter to communicate [to the American Philosophical Society], and will do it ere long. It is the form of a mould-board *of least resistance*. I had some years ago conceived the principles of it. ... I have since reduced the thing to practice, and have reason to believe the theory fully confirmed.[8]

I have imagined and executed a mould-board which may be mathematically demonstrated to be perfect, as far as perfection depends on mathematical principles, and one great circumstance in its favor is that it may be made by the most bungling carpenter, and cannot possibly vary a hair's breadth in its form but by gross negligence. . . . It is on the principle of two wedges combined at right angles, the first in the direct line of the furrow to raise the turf gradually, the other across the furrow to turn it over gradually. For both these purposes the wedge is the instrument of the least resistance.[9] It has been greatly approved [at Philadelphia], as it has been before by some very good judges at my house, where I have used it . . . with entire approbation.[10]

Remodeling Monticello; my new trade of nail-making

We have had a fine winter. Wheat looks well. Corn is scarce and dear. Twenty-two shillings here, thirty shillings in Amherst. Our blossoms are but just opening. I have begun the demolition of my house, and hope to get through its re-edification in the course of the summer.[11] I had hoped . . . to have finished the walls of my house in the autumn, and to have covered it early in winter. But we did not finish them at all. I have to resume the work, therefore, in the spring, and to take off the roof of the old part during the summer, to cover the whole.[12]

On returning home after an absence of ten years, I found my farms so much deranged that I saw evidently they would be a burden to me instead of a support till I could regenerate them; and consequently that it was necessary for me to find some other resource in the meantime. I thought for a while of taking up the manufacture of potash, which requires but small advances of money. I concluded at length however to begin a manufacture of nails, which needs little or no capital. . . . My new trade of nail-making is to me in this country what an additional title of nobility or the ensigns of a new order are in Europe.[13]

Democratic Societies and the Whiskey Rebellion

The denunciation of the Democratic Societies is one of the extraordinary acts of boldness of which we have seen so many from the faction of monocrats. It is wonderful, indeed, that the President should have permitted himself to be the organ of such an attack on the freedom of discussion, the freedom of writing, printing, and publishing. It must be a matter of rare curiosity to get at the modifications of these rights proposed by them, and to see what line their ingenuity would draw between democratical societies, whose avowed object is the nourishment of the republican principles of our Constitution, and the Society of the Cincinnati, a *self-created* one carving out for itself hereditary distinctions, lowering over our Constitution eternally, meeting together in all parts of the Union, periodically, with closed doors, accumulating a capital in their separate treasury, corresponding secretly and regularly, and of which society the very persons denouncing the democrats are themselves the fathers, founders, and high officers. Their sight must be perfectly dazzled by the glittering of crowns and coronets not to see the extravagance of the proposition to suppress the friends of general freedom, while those who wish to confine that freedom to the few are permitted to go on in their principles and practices. . . .

And with respect to the transactions against the Excise Law [Hamilton's tax on whiskey] . . . we know of none which, according to the definitions of law, have been anything more than riotous. . . . The information of our militia returned from the westward is uniform that though the people there let them pass quietly they were objects of their laughter, not of their fear; that one thousand men could have cut off their whole force in a thousand places of the Alleghany; that their detestation of the Excise Law is universal, and has now associated to it a detestation of the government; and that a separation [of the Western people], which was perhaps a very distant and problematical event, is now near and certain, and determined in the mind of every man.[14]

Jay's Treaty; Anglomen vs. farmers and laborers

The most remarkable political occurrence with us has been the treaty with England, of which no man in the United States has had the effrontery to affirm that it was not a very bad one except Alexander Hamilton.[15] I [think] the treaty an execrable thing. . . . I trust the popular branch of our Legislature will disapprove of it, and thus rid us of this infamous act, which is really nothing more than a treaty of alliance between England and the Anglomen of this country against the Legislature and people of the United States.[16]

Though the Anglomen have in the end got their treaty through, and so far have triumphed over the cause of republicanism, yet it has been to them a dear-bought victory. It has given the most radical shock to their party which it has ever received. . . . They see that nothing can support them but the colossus of the President's merits with the people, and the moment he retires, that his successor, if a monocrat, will be overborne by the republican sense of his constituents; if a Republican, he will of course give fair play to that sense, and lead things into the channel of harmony between the governors and governed. In the meantime, patience.[17]

The aspect of our politics has wonderfully changed since you [Philip Mazzei] left us. In place of that noble love of liberty and republican government which carried us triumphantly through the war, an Anglican monarchical aristocratical party has sprung up whose avowed object is to draw over us the substance, as they have already done the forms, of the British government. The main body of our citizens, however, remain true to their republican principles. . . . Against us are the Executive, the Judiciary, two out of three branches of the Legislature, all the officers of the government, all who want to be officers, all timid men who prefer the calm of despotism to the boisterous sea of liberty, British merchants and Americans trading on British capital, speculators and holders in the banks and public funds, a contrivance invented for the purposes of corruption, and for assimilating us in all things to the rotten as well as the sound parts of the British model.

It would give you a fever were I to name to you the apostates who have gone over to these heresies, men who were Samsons in the field and Solomons in the council, but who have had their heads shorn by the harlot England. In short, we are likely to preserve the liberty we have obtained only by unremitting labors and perils. But we shall preserve it. . . . We have only to awake and snap the Lilliputian cords with which they have been entangling us during the first sleep which succeeded our labors.[18]

The Republican part of our Union comprehends 1. The entire

body of landholders throughout the United States. 2. The body of laborers, not being landholders, whether in husbanding or the arts. The latter is to the aggregate of the [Federalists] probably as five hundred to one; but their wealth is not as disproportionate, though it is also greatly superior, and is in truth the foundation of that of their antagonists. Trifling as are the numbers of the anti-Republican party there are circumstances which give them an appearance of strength and numbers. They all live in cities together and can act in a body readily, and at all times; they give chief employment to the newspapers, and therefore have most of them under their command.[19]

Elected Vice President in 1796

I had retired after five and twenty years of constant occupation in public affairs, and total abandonment of my own. I retired much poorer than when I entered the public service, and desired nothing but rest and oblivion. My name, however, was again brought forward, without concert or expectation on my part (on my salvation I declare it).[20]

It seems possible, from what we hear of the votes at the late election, that [I may be] in Philadelphia about the beginning of March, exactly in that character which, if I were to reappear at Philadelphia, I would prefer to all others [that is, as Vice President].[21] I know the difficulty of obtaining belief to one's declarations of a disinclination to honors ... but no arguments were wanting to reconcile me to a relinquishment of the first office or acquiescence under the second.[22] I have no wish to meddle again in public affairs, ... least of all at a moment when the storm is about to burst which has been conjuring up for four years past. If I am to act, however, a more tranquil and unoffending station could not have been found for me. ... It will give me philosophical evenings in the winter, and rural days in summer.[23] The second office of the government is honorable and easy, the first is but a splendid misery.[24]

My letters inform me that Mr. Adams speaks of me with great friendship, and with satisfaction in the prospect of administering the government in concurrence with me. I am glad of the first information, because though I saw that our ancient friendship was affected by a little leaven, produced partly by his constitution, partly by the contrivance of others, yet I never felt a diminution of confidence in his integrity, and retained a solid affection for him. His principles of government I knew to be changed, but conscientiously changed. As to my participating in the administration, if by that he meant the executive cabinet, both duty and inclination will shut that door to me. I cannot have a wish to see the scenes of 1793 revived as to myself, and to descend daily into the arena like a gladiator, to suffer martyrdom in every conflict.[25]

I do not believe Mr. Adams wishes war with France; nor do I believe he will truckle to England as servilely as has been done. If he assumes this front at once, and shows that he means to attend to self-respect and national dignity with both the nations, perhaps the depredations of both on our commerce may be amicably arrested.[26]

The Federalists prepare for war with France

The President's speech [of May, 1797] you will have seen; and how far its aspect was turned towards war. Our opinion here is that the Executive had that in contemplation, and were not without expectation that the Legislature might catch the flame. A powerful part of that has shown a disposition to go all lengths with the Executive.... They have voted the completing and manning the three frigates, and going on with the fortifications. The Senate have gone much further, they have brought in bills for buying more armed vessels, sending them and the frigates out as convoys to our trade, raising more cavalry, more artillerists, and providing a great army, to come into active service only if necessary.[27]

Those who have no wish but for the peace of their country, and its independence of all foreign influence, have a hard struggle indeed, overwhelmed by a cry as loud and imposing as if it were true, of being under French influence, and this raised by a faction composed of English subjects residing among us, or such as are English in all their relations and sentiments.[28]

I do sincerely wish ... that we could take our stand on a ground perfectly neutral and independent towards all nations. It has been my constant object through my public life; and with respect to the English and French, particularly, I have too often expressed to the former my wishes and made to them propositions verbally and in writing, officially and privately, to official and private characters, for them to doubt of my views, if they would be content with equality. . . . But they have wished a monopoly of commerce and influence with us; and they have in fact obtained it.[29]

Peace is undoubtedly at present the first object of our nation. . . . The insults and injuries committed on us by both the belligerent parties from the beginning of 1793 to this day, and still continuing, cannot now be wiped off by engaging in war with one of them. . . . Our countrymen have divided themselves by such strong affections to the French and the English that nothing will secure us internally but a divorce from both nations.[30]

I have formerly seen warm debates and high political passions. But gentlemen of different politics would then speak to each other, and separate the business of the Senate from that of society. It is not so now. Men who have been intimate all their lives cross the streets to avoid meeting, and turn their heads another way lest they should be obliged to touch their hats. This may do for young men with whom passion is enjoyment. But it is afflicting to peaceable minds. Tranquillity is the old man's milk. I go to enjoy it in a few days, and to exchange the roar and tumult of bulls and bears for the prattle of my grandchildren.[31]

Gleams of light; the marriage of Maria

I ought oftener, my dear Martha, to receive your letters, for the very great pleasure they give me, and especially when they express your affections for me; for, though I cannot doubt, yet they are among those truths which though not doubted, we love to hear repeated. Here, too, they serve like gleams of light to cheer a dreary scene where envy, hatred, malice, revenge, and all the worst passions of men are marshalled to make one another as miserable as possible.[32]

I receive with inexpressible pleasure the information your letter contained. After your happy establishment, which has given me an inestimable friend to whom I can leave the care of everything I love, the only anxiety I had remaining was to see Maria also so associated as to ensure her happiness. She could not have been more so to my wishes if I had had the whole earth to have chosen a partner for her [Maria married John Wayles Eppes, October 13, 1797]. . . . In order to keep us all together . . . I think to open and resettle the plantation of Pantops for them. When I look to the ineffable pleasures of my family society I become more and more disgusted with the ... rancorous and malignant passions of this scene.[33]

Politics and party hatreds destroy the happiness of every being here. They seem, like salamanders, to consider fire as their element. The children, I am afraid, will have forgotten me. However, my memory may perhaps be hung on the Game of the Goose which I am to carry them. Kiss them for me.[34] I have changed my circle here according to my wish, abandoning the rich, and declining their dinners and parties, and associating entirely with the class of science.[35]

The Megalonyx Jeffersoni, and Indian vocabularies

I am [writing an account for] the Philosophical Society ... of some bones of an animal of the lion kind, but of most exaggerated size. What are we to think of a creature whose claws were eight inches long, when those of the lion are not 1½ inches; whose thighbone was 6¼ diameter, when that of the lion is not 1½ inches? Were not the things within the jurisdiction of the rule and compass, and of ocular inspection, credit to them could not be obtained. I have been disappointed in getting the femur as yet, but shall bring on the bones I have [which were discovered in Greenbrier County, Virginia] for the Society.[36] I cannot ... help believing that this animal [which was given the name of *Megalonyx Jeffersoni*], as well as the mammoth, are still existing.[37]

I have long believed we can never get any information of the ancient history of the Indians, of their descent and filiation, but from a knowledge and comparative view of their languages. I have, therefore, never failed to avail myself of any opportunity which offered of getting their vocabularies. I have now made up a large collection, and afraid to risk it any longer, lest by some accident it might be lost, I am about to print it. But I still want the great southern languages, Cherokee, Creeks, Choctaw, Chickasaw ... and I enclose ... a vocabulary of the particular words I want.[38]

Steam engines in the home; Parliamentary Manual for Congress

There is one object to which I have often wished a steam engine could be adapted. You know how desirable it is both in town and country to be able to have large reservoirs of water on the top of our houses, not only for use (by pipes) in the apartments, but as a resource against fire. This last is most especially a desideratum in the country. We might indeed have water carried from time to time in buckets to cisterns on the top of the house, but this is troublesome, and therefore we never do it — consequently we are without resource when a fire happens. Could any agent be employed which would be little or no additional expense or trouble except the first purchase, it would be done. Every family has such an agent, its kitchen fire. It is small indeed, but if its small but constant action could be accumulated so as to give a stroke from time to time which might throw ever so small a quantity of water from the bottom of the well to the top of the house (say one hundred feet), it would furnish more than would waste by evaporation, or be used by the family. ... I have imagined that the iron back of the chimney might be a cistern for holding the water, which would supply steam and would be constantly kept in a boiling state by the ordinary fire.[39]

So little has the parliamentary branch of the law been attended to, that I not only find no person here, but not even a book to aid me [in presiding over the Senate]. I had at an early period of life read a good deal on the subject, and commonplaced what I read. This commonplace has been my pillow.[40] I have here endeavored to collect and digest so much ... as is called for in ordinary practice, collating the parliamentary with the senatorial rules, both where they agree and where they vary. I have done this, as well to have them at hand for my own government, as to deposit with the Senate ... a code of rules ... the effects of which may be accuracy in business, economy of time, order, uniformity, and impartiality.[41]

Organizing the opposition

If a prospect could be once opened upon us of the penetration of truth into the Eastern States, ... we might still hope for salvation, and that it would come as of old from the east. ... Can the Middle, Southern, and Western States hold on till they awake? These are painful and doubtful questions; and if ... you [Aaron Burr of New York] can give me a comfortable solution of them it will relieve a mind devoted to the preservation of our republican government in the true form and spirit in which it was established, but almost oppressed with apprehensions that fraud will at length effect what force could not, and that what with currents and counter-currents we shall, in the end, be driven back to the land from which we launched twenty years ago. Indeed, my dear sir, we have been but a sturdy fish on the hook of a dextrous angler, who, letting us flounce till we have spent our force, brings us up at last.[42]

It is true that a party has risen up among us, or rather has come among us, which is endeavoring to separate us from all friendly connection with France, to unite our destinies with those of Great Britain, and to assimilate our government to theirs. Our lenity in permitting the return of the old Tories gave the first body to this party, . . . who, by the aid of a paper system, are enriching themselves to the ruin of our country and swaying the government by their possession of the printing presses, which their wealth commands. . . . But I flatter myself . . . the people . . . begin to see to what port their leaders were steering during their slumbers, and there is yet time to haul in if we can avoid a war with France. All can be done peaceably, by the people confining their choice of representatives and senators to persons attached to republican government and the principles of 1776, not office-hunters but farmers, whose interests are entirely agricultural. Such men are the true representatives of the great American interest, and are alone to be relied on for expressing the proper American sentiments. We owe gratitude to France, justice to England, good will to all, and subservience to none.[43]

The X, Y, Z affair, a body blow to the Republicans

The first impressions from [the dispatches of the American envoys to France, made public in April of 1798 by President Adams] are very disagreeable and confused. Reflection, however, and analysis resolve them into this: Mr. Adams' speech to Congress in May [of 1797] is deemed such a national affront that no explanation on other topics can be entered on till that, as a preliminary, is wiped away by humiliating disavowals or acknowledgments. This working hard with our envoys, and indeed seeming impracticable for want of that sort of authority, submission to a heavy amercement (upwards of a million sterling) was, at an after meeting, suggested as an alternative which might be admitted if proposed by us. These overtures had been through informal agents ['Messrs X, Y, and Z']; and . . . there were interwoven with these overtures some base propositions on the part of Talleyrand, through one of his agents, to sell his interest and influence with the Directory towards soothing difficulties with them, in consideration of a large sum (fifty thousand pounds sterling); and the arguments to which his agent resorted, to induce compliance with this demand, were very unworthy of a great nation (could they be imputed to them) and calculated to excite disgust and indignation in Americans generally, and alienation in the Republicans particularly, whom they so far mistake as to presume an attachment to France and hatred to the Federal party, and not the love of their country, to be their first passion. No difficulty was expressed towards an adjustment of all differences and misunderstandings, or even ultimately a payment for spoliations, if the insult from our Executive should be first wiped away. . . .

It is evident, however, on reflection, that these papers do not offer one motive the more for our going to war. Yet such is their effect on the minds of wavering characters that I fear that to wipe off the imputation of being French partisans they will go over to the war measures so furiously pushed by the other party. . . . The most artful misrepresentations of the contents of these papers were published yesterday, and produced such a shock in the Republican mind as had never been seen since our independence.[44]

The popular movement in the Eastern States is checked, as we expected, and war addresses are showering in from New Jersey and the great trading towns.[45] The spirit kindled up in the towns is wonderful. These . . . are pouring in their addresses, offering life and fortune. Even these addresses are not the worst things. For indiscreet declarations and expressions of passion may be pardoned to a multitude acting from the impulse of the moment. But we cannot expect a foreign nation to show that apathy to the answers of the President, which are more thrasonic than the addresses. Whatever chance for peace might have been left us after the publication of the despatches is completely lost by these answers. Nor is it France alone, but his own fellow-citizens, against whom his threats are uttered. . . . He says to the address from Newark, 'The delusions and misrepresentations which have misled so many citizens must be discountenanced by authority as well as by the citizens at large.' [46]

Undeclared naval war against France

The bill for the naval armament (twelve vessels) passed by a majority of about four to three in the House of Representatives; all restrictions on the objects for which the vessels should be used were struck out. The bill for establishing a department of Secretary of the Navy . . . prevailed by forty-seven against forty-one. . . . The provisional army of twenty thousand men will meet some difficulty. It would surely be rejected if our members were all here. Giles, Clopton, Cabell, and Nicholas have gone, and Clay goes tomorrow. . . . Parker has completely gone over to the war party. In this state of things they will carry what they please.[47]

The bill from the Senate for capturing French armed vessels found hovering on our coast was passed in two days by the lower House, without a single alteration; and the *Ganges*, a twenty-gun sloop, fell down the river instantly to go on a cruise. . . . I question if they will think a declaration of war prudent, as it might alarm, and all its effects are answered by the act authorizing captures.[48]

It is our duty still to endeavor to avoid war; but if it shall actually take place, no matter by whom brought on, we must defend ourselves. If our house be on fire, without inquiring whether it was fired from within or without, we must try to extinguish it. In that, I have no doubt we shall act as one man.[49]

A Tory reign of terror begins

At present the war hawks talk of septembrizing, deportation, and . . . quelling sedition. . . . All the firmness of the human mind is now in a state of requisition. . . . Yesterday Mr. Hillhouse laid on the table of the Senate a motion for giving power [to President Adams] to send away suspected aliens. . . . There is now only wanting . . . a sedition bill, which we shall certainly soon see proposed. The object of that is the suppression of the Whig presses. . . . If these papers fall, Republicanism will be entirely brow-beaten.[50]

Party passions are indeed high. Nobody has more reason to

know it than myself. I receive daily bitter proofs of it. . . . At this moment all the passions are boiling over, and one who keeps himself cool and clear of the contagion is so far below the point of ordinary conversation that he finds himself insulated in every society.[51]

There is no event . . . however atrocious which may not be expected. I have contemplated every event which the Maratists of the day can perpetrate, and am prepared to meet every one in such a way as shall not be derogatory either to the public liberty or my own personal honor.[52] They have brought into the lower House a sedition bill, which among other enormities undertakes to make printing certain matters [criticism of the Adams administration] criminal, though one of the amendments to the Constitution has so expressly taken religion, printing presses, etc., out of their coercion. Indeed this bill and the alien bill both are so palpably in the teeth of the Constitution as to show they mean to pay no respect to it.[53]

But disunion not the remedy

It is true that we are completely under the saddle of Massachusetts and Connecticut, and that they ride us very hard, cruelly insulting our feelings, as well as exhausting our strength and subsistence. . . . But if on a temporary superiority of the one party the other is to resort to a scission of the Union, no federal government can ever exist. If to rid ourselves of the present rule of Massachusetts and Connecticut we break the Union, will the evil stop there? Suppose the New England States alone cut off, will our nature be changed? Are we not men still to the south of that, and with all the passions of men? Immediately we shall see a Pennsylvania and a Virginia party arise in the residuary confederacy, and the public mind will be distracted with the same party spirit. What a game too will the one party have in their hands by eternally threatening the other that unless they do so and so they will join their Northern neighbors. If we reduce our Union to Virginia and North Carolina, immediately the conflict will be established between the representatives of these two states, and they will end by breaking into their simple units.[54]

The Republicans counter-attack

The Alien and Sedition Laws are working hard. I fancy that some of the state legislatures will take strong ground on this occasion. For my own part, I consider those laws as merely an experiment on the American mind, to see how far it will bear an avowed violation of the Constitution. If this goes down, we shall immediately see attempted another act of Congress declaring that the President shall continue in office during life, reserving to another occasion the transfer of the succession to his heirs, and the establishment of the Senate for life.[55]

I enclose . . . a copy of the draught of the Kentucky Resolutions [written secretly by Jefferson, declaring the Alien and Sedition Acts unconstitutional, a usurpation of the rights of the states 'altogether void and of no force']. I think we should distinctly affirm all the important principles they contain, so as to hold to that ground in future, and leave the matter in such a train as that we may not be committed absolutely to push the matter to extremities, and yet may be free to push as far as events will render prudent.[56]

Congress is daily plied with petitions against the Alien and Sedition Laws and standing armies. Several parts of [Pennsylvania] are so violent that we fear an insurrection. This will be brought about by some if they can. It is the only thing we have to fear. The appearance of an attack of force against the government would check the present current of the Middle States, and rally them around the government; whereas, if suffered to go on, it will pass on to a reformation of abuses.[57] These are the Alien and Sedition Laws, the vexations of the Stamp Act, the disgusting particularities of the direct tax, the additional army without an enemy, and recruiting officers lounging at every court house to decoy the laborer from his plough, a navy of fifty ships, five millions to be raised to build it, on the usurious interest of eight per cent, the perseverance in war on our part when the French government shows such an anxious desire to keep at peace with us, taxes of ten millions now paid by four millions of people, and yet a necessity, in a year or two, of raising five millions more for annual expenses. . . .

A recapitulation is now wanting of the whole story . . . short, simple, and levelled to every capacity . . . and so concise as, omitting nothing material, may yet be printed in handbills, of which we could print and disperse ten or twelve thousand copies under letter-covers through all the United States by the members of Congress when they return home.[58]

It is acknowledged on all hands, and declared by the insurance companies, that the British depredations during the last six months have greatly exceeded the French, yet not a word is said about it officially. However, all these things are working on the public mind.[59] We are sensible that this . . . is the season for systematic energies and sacrifices. The engine is the press. Every man must lay his purse and his pen under contribution.[60]

Adams makes peace with the French Republic

A great event was presented yesterday [February 18, 1799]. The President communicated a letter from Talleyrand [giving assurances] that *whatever* Plenipotentiary we might send to France to negotiate differences should be received with the respect due to the representative of a *free, independent, and powerful nation.* . . . In consequence of this a nomination of [a] Minister Plenipotentiary to the French Republic was yesterday sent to the Senate. This renders their efforts for war desperate and silences all further denials of the sincerity of the French government.[61]

This had evidently been kept secret from the Federalists of both Houses, as appeared by their dismay. . . . It is said they are graveled and divided [between the Adams peace-Federalists and the Hamilton war hawks].[62]

The wonderful irritation produced in the minds of our citizens by the X, Y, Z story has in a great measure subsided. . . . If we are left in peace I have no doubt the wonderful turn in the public opinion now manifestly taking place and rapidly increasing will . . . become so universal and so weighty that friendship abroad and freedom at home will be firmly established by the influence and constitutional powers of the people at large, . . . that the spirit of our citizens now rising as rapidly as it was then running crazy, and rising with a strength and majesty which show the loveliness of freedom, will make this government in practice, what it is in principle, a model for the protection of man in a state of *freedom* and *order*.[63]

Presidential candidate in 1800 against John Adams

The Federalists begin to be very seriously alarmed about their election. . . . Upon the whole, I consider it as rather more doubtful than the last election, in which I was not deceived in more than a vote or two. If Pennsylvania votes, then either Jersey or New York giving a Republican vote decides the election. If Pennsylvania does not vote, then New York determines the election. In any event, we may say that if the *city* election of New York is in favor of the Republican ticket, the issue will be Republican.[64]

We must have a 'Declaration of the principles of the Constitution' in nature of a declaration of rights, in all the points in which it has been violated. The people in the Middle States are almost rallied to Virginia already; and the Eastern States are recommencing the vibration which had been checked by X, Y, Z. North Carolina is at present in the most dangerous state. . . . The medicine for that state must be very mild and secretly administered. But nothing should be spared to give them true information.[65]

From the moment that a portion of my fellow-citizens looked towards me with a view to one of their highest offices the floodgates of calumny have been opened upon me. . . . I know that I might have filled the courts of the United States with actions for these slanders, and have ruined perhaps many persons who are not innocent. But this would be no equivalent to the loss of character. I leave them, therefore, to the reproof of their own consciences. If these do not condemn them there will yet come a day when the false witness will meet a Judge who has not slept over his slanders.

If the Reverend Cotton Mather Smith of Sharon, Connecticut, believed this as firmly as I do he would surely never have affirmed that 'I had obtained my property by fraud and robbery; that in one instance I had defrauded and robbed a widow and fatherless children of an estate, to which I was executor, of ten thousand pounds sterling, . . . and that all this could be proved.' Every tittle of it is fable, there not having existed a single circumstance of my life to which any part of it can hang. . . . My property is all patrimonial, except about seven or eight hundred pounds worth of lands purchased by myself and paid for.[66]

Eternal hostility to every form of tyranny

As to the calumny of atheism, I am so broken to calumnies of every kind . . . that I entirely disregard it. . . . It has been so impossible to contradict all their lies that I have determined to contradict none, for while I should be engaged with one they would publish twenty new ones. Thirty years of public life have enabled most of those who read newspapers to judge of one for themselves.[67]

The delusion into which the X, Y, Z plot showed it possible to push the people, the successful experiment made under the prevalence of that delusion on the clause of the Constitution which, while it secured the freedom of the press, covered also the freedom of religion, had given to the clergy a very favorite hope of obtaining an establishment of a particular form of Christianity through the United States; and as every sect believes its own form the true one, every one perhaps hoped for his own, but especially the Episcopalians and Congregationalists. The returning good sense of our country threatens abortion to their hopes, and they believe that any portion of power confided to me will be exerted in opposition to their schemes. And they believe rightly, for I have sworn upon the altar of God eternal hostility against every form of tyranny over the mind of man. But this is all they have to fear from me: and enough too in their opinion.[68]

A profession of political faith

I do . . . with sincere zeal wish an inviolable preservation of our present federal Constitution according to the true sense in which it was adopted by the states, that in which it was advocated by its friends and not that which its enemies apprehended, who therefore became its enemies; and I am opposed to the monarchizing its features by the forms of its administration with a view to conciliate a first transition to a President and Senate for life and from that to a hereditary tenure of these offices, and thus to worm out the elective principle. I am for preserving to the states the powers not yielded by them to the Union, and to the legislature of the Union its constitutional share in the division of powers; and I am not for transferring all the powers of the states to the general government, and all those of that government to the executive branch.

I am for a government rigorously frugal and simple, applying all the possible savings of the public revenue to the discharge of the national debt; and not for a multiplication of officers and salaries merely to make partisans, and for increasing by every device the public debt on the principle of its being a public blessing. I am for relying for internal defense on our militia solely, till actual invasion, and for such a naval force only as may protect our coasts and harbors from such depredations as we have experienced; and not for a standing army in time of peace which may overawe the public sentiment, nor for a navy which, by its own expenses and the eternal wars in which it will implicate us, will grind us with public burdens and sink us under them.

I am for free commerce with all nations, political connection with none, and little or no diplomatic establishment. And I am not for linking ourselves by new treaties with the quarrels of Europe, entering that field of slaughter to preserve their balance or joining in the confederacy of kings to war against the principles of liberty.

I am for freedom of religion, and against all manoeuvres to bring about a legal ascendancy of one sect over another; for freedom of the press, and against all violations of the Constitution to silence by force and not by reason the complaints or criticisms, just or unjust, of our citizens against the conduct of their agents. And I am for encouraging the progress of science in all its branches; and not for raising a hue and cry against the sacred name of philosophy, for awing the human mind by stories of rawhead and bloodybones to a distrust of its own vision and to repose implicitly on that of others, to go backwards instead of forwards to look for improvement, to believe that government, religion, morality, and every other science were in the highest perfection in ages of the darkest ignorance, and that nothing can ever be devised more perfect than what was established by our forefathers.

To these I will add that I was a sincere well-wisher to the success of the French Revolution and still wish it may end in the establishment of a free and well-ordered republic, but I have not been insensible under the atrocious depredations they have committed on our commerce. The first object of my heart is my own country. In that is embarked my family, my fortune, and my own existence.

I have not one farthing of interest, nor one fibre of attachment out of it, nor a single motive of preference of any one nation to another but in proportion as they are more or less friendly to us.[69]

The Revolution of 1800: 'A triumph of principles, Mr. Adams'

The revolution of 1800 . . . was as real a revolution in the principles of our government as that of 1776 was in its form; not effected indeed by the sword, as that, but by the rational and peaceable instrument of reform, the suffrage of the people. The nation declared its will by dismissing functionaries of one principle and electing those of another in the two branches, executive and legislature, submitted to their election. Over the judiciary department the Constitution had deprived them of their control.[70]

The nation at length passed condemnation on the political principles of the Federalists by refusing to continue Mr. Adams in the presidency. On the day on which we learned . . . the vote of the city of New York, which it was well known would decide the vote of the state, and that, again, the vote of the Union, I called on Mr. Adams on some official business. He was very sensibly affected, and accosted me with these words: 'Well, I understand that you are to beat me in this contest, and I will only say that I will be as faithful a subject as any you will have.'

'Mr. Adams,' said I, 'this is no personal contest between you and me. Two systems of principles on the subject of government divide our fellow-citizens into two parties. With one of these you concur, and I with the other. As we have been longer on the public stage than most of those now living, our names happen to be more generally known. One of these parties, therefore, has put your name at its head, the other mine. Were we both to die today, tomorrow two other names would be in the place of ours, without any change in the motion of the machinery. Its motion is from its principle, not from you or myself.'

'I believe you are right,' said he, 'that we are but passive instruments, and should not suffer this matter to affect our personal dispositions.' [71]

But victory in perilous jeopardy

The election in South Carolina has in some measure decided the great contest. . . . We believe the votes to be on the whole, Jefferson seventy-three, Burr [the Republican vice-presidential candidate] seventy-three, Adams sixty-five, Pinckney sixty-four. . . . There will be an absolute parity between the two Republican candidates. This has produced great dismay and gloom on the Republican gentlemen here [in the new capital city of Washington], and exultation in the Federalists, who openly declare they will prevent an election, and will name a president of the Senate, *pro tem*, by what they say would only be a *stretch* of the Constitution. . . . The month of February, therefore, will present us storms of a new character.[72]

We are brought into dilemma by the . . . equality of the two Republican candidates. The Federalists in Congress mean to take advantage of this, and either to prevent an election altogether, or reverse what has been understood to have been the wishes of the people as to the President and Vice President, wishes which the Constitution did not permit them specially to designate. The latter alternative still gives us a Republican administration. The former, a suspension of the federal government for want of a head. This opens to us an abyss at which every sincere patriot must shudder.[73]

We have eight votes in the House of Representatives certain and there are three other states, Maryland, Delaware, and Vermont, from either of which if a single individual comes over it settles the matter. But I am far from confiding that a single one will come over; . . . nothing seems to bend the spirit of our opponents.[74]

The tie-vote contest with Aaron Burr

This is the morning of the election by the House of Representatives [February 11, 1801]. For some time past a single individual had declared he would by his vote make up the ninth state. On Saturday last he changed, and it stands at present eight one way, six the other, and two divided. Which of the two will be elected, and whether either, I deem perfectly problematical; and my mind has long been equally made up for either of the three events.[75]

Four days of balloting have produced not a single change of a vote. . . . If they could have been permitted to pass a law for putting the government into the hands of an officer, they would certainly have prevented an election. But we thought it best to declare openly and firmly, one and all, that the day such an act passed the

Middle States would arm, and that no such usurpation, even for a single day, should be submitted to. This first shook them; and they were completely alarmed at the resource for which we declared, to wit, a convention to reorganize the government and to amend it. The very word convention gives them the horrors, as in the present democratical spirit of America they fear they should lose some of the favorite morsels of the Constitution. Many attempts have been made to obtain terms and promises from me. I have declared to them unequivocally that I would not receive the government on capitulation, that I would not go into it with my hands tied.[76]

General Armstrong tells me [February 14, 1801] that Gouverneur Morris [Federalist, of New York], in conversation with him today on the scene which is passing, expressed himself thus. 'How comes it,' said he, 'that Burr who is four hundred miles off, at Albany, has agents here at work with great activity, while Mr. Jefferson, who is on the spot, does nothing?' [77] Matthew Lyon [Jeffersonian, of Vermont] expressed his wish that everything was spoken out which was known; that it would then appear on which side there was a bidding for votes, and he declared that John Brown of Rhode Island, urging him to vote for Colonel Burr, used these words: 'What is it you want, Colonel Lyon? Is it office, is it money? Only say what you want, and you shall have it.' [78]

I will not enter the Presidency by capitulation

Coming out of the Senate chamber one day I found Gouverneur Morris on the steps. He stopped me and began a conversation on the strange and portentous state of things then existing, and went on to observe that the reasons why the minority of states was so opposed to my being elected were that they apprehended that, 1, I would turn all Federalists out of office; 2, put down the navy; 3, wipe off the public debt. That I need only to declare, or authorize my friends to declare, that I would not take these steps, and instantly the event of the election would be fixed.

I told him that I should leave the world to judge of the course I meant to pursue by that which I had pursued hitherto, believing it to be my duty to be passive and silent during the present scene; that I should certainly make no terms; should never go into the office of President by capitulation, nor with my hands tied by any conditions which should hinder me from pursuing the measures which I should deem for the public good. It was understood that Gouverneur Morris had entirely the direction of the vote of Lewis Morris of Vermont, who, by coming over to Matthew Lyon, would have added another vote and decided the election.

About the same time I called on Mr. Adams. We conversed on the state of things. I observed to him that a very dangerous experiment was then in contemplation to defeat the presidential election by an act of Congress declaring the right of the Senate to name a president of the Senate, to devolve on him the government during any interregnum; that such a measure would probably produce resistance by force, and incalculable consequences, which it would be in his power to prevent by negativing such an act. He seemed to think such an act justifiable, and observed it was in my power to fix the election by a word in an instant, by declaring I would not turn out the Federal officers, nor put down the navy, nor spunge the national debt. Finding his mind made up as to the usurpation of the government by the president of the Senate, I urged it no further, observed the world must judge as to myself of the future by the past, and turned the conversation to something else.[79]

Victory, on the thirty-sixth ballot

After exactly a week's balloting there at length appeared ten states for me, four for Burr, and two voted blanks. This was done without a single vote coming over. Morris of Vermont withdrew, so that Lyon's vote became that of the state.... Mr. Huger of South Carolina (who had constantly voted for me) withdrew by agreement, his colleagues agreeing in that case to put in blanks. Bayard, the sole member of Delaware, voted blank. They had before deliberated whether they would come over in a body, when they saw they could not force Burr on the Republicans, or keep their body entire and unbroken to act in phalanx on such ground of opposition as they shall hereafter be able to conjure up. Their vote showed what they had decided on, and is considered as a declaration of perpetual war; but their conduct has completely left them without support.[80]

The suspension of public opinion from the 11th to the 17th [of February, 1801], the alarm into which it threw all the patriotic part of the Federalists, the danger of the dissolution of our Union, and unknown consequences of that, brought over the great body of them to wish with anxiety and solicitation for a choice to which they had before been strenuously opposed. In this state of mind they separated from their congressional leaders, and came over to us; and the manner in which the last ballot [the thirty-sixth] was given, has drawn a fixed line of separation between them and their leaders. . . . They are in a state of mind to be consolidated with us, if no intemperate measures on our part revolt them again. I am persuaded that weeks of ill-judged conduct here has strengthened us more than years of prudent and conciliatory administration could have done. If we can once more get social intercourse restored to its pristine harmony, I shall believe we have not lived in vain; and that it may, by rallying them to true republican principles, which few of them had thrown off, I sanguinely hope.[81]

Had it terminated in the elevation of Mr. Burr every Republican would, I am sure, have acquiesced in a moment, because, however it might have been variant from the intentions of the voters, yet it would have been agreeable to the Constitution. No man would more cheerfully have submitted than myself. . . . But in the event of a usurpation, I was decidedly with those who were determined not to permit it. Because that precedent once set would be artificially reproduced, and end soon in a dictator. Virginia was bristling up, I believe.[82]

We shall put our Argosy on a republican tack

The storm through which we have passed has been tremendous indeed. The tough sides of our Argosy have been thoroughly tried. Her strength has stood the waves into which she was steered with a view to sink her. We shall put her on her republican tack, and she will show by the beauty of her motion the skill of her builders. . . . A just and solid republican government maintained here will be a standing monument and example for the aim and imitation of the people of other countries; and I join . . . in the hope and belief that the . . . inquiry which has been excited among the mass of mankind by our Revolution and its consequences will ameliorate the condition of man over a great portion of the globe.

What a satisfaction have we in the contemplation of the benevolent effects of our efforts compared with those of the leaders on the other side, who have discountenanced all advances in science as dangerous innovations, have endeavored to render philosophy and republicanism terms of reproach, to persuade us that man cannot be governed but by the rod, etc. I shall have the happiness of living and dying in the contrary hope.[83]

CHAPTER XII

Philosopher-President

A T NOON on the fourth day of March, 1801, Thomas Jefferson
left his boarding-house in the new and sprawling city of
Washington and with republican simplicity walked over to the
unfinished Capitol to be inaugurated President of the United
States. There was nothing about this tall and slender man of
fifty-eight to suggest the frightful caricatures of the recent campaign. It was impossible to believe, said one Washingtonian, that
'this man so meek and mild, yet dignified in his manners, with a
voice so soft and low, with a countenance so benignant and intel-
ligent,' could be 'the violent democrat, the vulgar demagogue, the
bold atheist and profligate man I have so often heard denounced
by the Federalists.' His inaugural address of that day, and his
conduct of affairs during the eight years that followed, convinced
this Washington observer and most Americans that Thomas Jefferson was 'truly a philosopher, and truly a good man, and eminently
a great one.'

Written with the same felicity that marked his Declaration of
Independence, and setting forth 'the creed of our political faith,'
Jefferson's first inaugural address ranks with the Declaration of '76
as an expression of the spirit and aspirations of the American people.
Combining idealism with political practicality, he promptly set to
work to effectuate his principles. The policy he adopted as to
officeholders was in keeping with the conciliatory tone of the address, and it won over many of the rank-and-file Federalists. With
great satisfaction he did justice to the victims of the Alien and
Sedition Acts. He discharged every person sentenced or indicted

under that 'nullity,' the Sedition Law, and he welcomed to America's shores such distinguished aliens as Joseph Priestley, the English scientist, who had offended Federalist leaders by his liberalism in religion and politics. Ably assisted by James Madison, Secretary of State, and Swiss-born Albert Gallatin, Secretary of the Treasury, Jefferson planned his program of peace, economy, and reform, and at the Congressional session of 1801–02 very successfully translated political promises into realities.

His policy of measured reform and conciliation did much to heal the wounds inflicted by a decade of bitter partisan strife. Only the diehard Federalists remained in abusive opposition: party leaders and those who had profited by Hamilton's system, New England clergymen who continued their attacks on his supposed atheism, and 'Anglomen' who were shocked by democratic rules of etiquette which brought on a social war with the British minister and his virago of a wife.

Jefferson did away with the pomp and formality of his predecessors. He did away with the state carriage with its six horses and outriders, and rode about on horseback unattended. Instead of 'monarchical' levees he entertained almost daily at small dinner parties, at which the food was prepared by his French chef, the wines were excellent, and the conversation most stimulating. It ranged over the thousand and one things in which the host was interested: the influence of climate on temperament, city-planning, the new polygraph, or books for the Library of Congress. Since it was inevitable, in a republic of farmers, that the talk should turn to agriculture, the President would discuss crops and perhaps tell of the dam and grist-mill he was having built at Monticello.

Of all the congratulations which Jefferson received during these first years in office on the noiseless happy course, the rapid growth and great prosperity of the country under Republicanism, those which pleased him most came from his old Revolutionary friends. With them he felt that the hopes of 1776 were being realized, and that the American people in making a success of their experiment in self-government were 'acting for all mankind.'

Inaugural address, March 4, 1801

During the contest of opinion through which we have passed, the animation of discussion and of exertions has sometimes worn an aspect which might impose on strangers unused to think freely and to speak and to write what they think; but this being now decided by the voice of the nation, announced according to the rules of the Constitution, all will, of course, arrange themselves under the will of the law and unite in common efforts for the common good. All, too, will bear in mind this sacred principle, that though the will of the majority is in all cases to prevail, that will, to be rightful, must be reasonable; that the minority possess their equal rights, which equal laws must protect, and to violate which would be oppression. Let us, then, fellow-citizens, unite with one heart and one mind. Let us restore to social intercourse that harmony and affection without which liberty and even life itself are but dreary things. And let us reflect that having banished from our land that religious intolerance under which mankind so long bled and suffered, we have yet gained little if we countenance a political intolerance as despotic, as wicked, and capable of as bitter and bloody persecutions.

We are all Republicans, all Federalists

During the throes and convulsions of the ancient world, during the agonizing spasms of infuriated man seeking through blood and slaughter his long-lost liberty, it was not wonderful that the agitation of the billows should reach even this distant and peaceful shore; that this should be more felt and feared by some and less by others; that this should divide opinions as to measures of safety. But every difference of opinion is not a difference of principle. We have called by different names brethren of the same principle. We are all Republicans — we are all Federalists. If there be any among us who would wish to dissolve this Union or to change its republican form, let them stand undisturbed as monuments of the safety with which error of opinion may be tolerated where reason is left free to combat it. I know, indeed, that some honest men fear that a republican government cannot be strong; that this government is not strong enough. But would the honest patriot, in the full tide of successful experiment, abandon a government which has so far kept us free and firm, on the theoretic and visionary fear that this government, the world's best hope, may by possibility want energy to preserve itself? I trust not. I believe this, on the contrary, the strongest government on earth. I believe it is the only one where every man, at the call of the laws, would fly to the standard of the law, and would meet invasions of the public order as his own personal concern. Sometimes it is said that man cannot be trusted with the government of himself. Can he, then, be trusted with the government of others? Or have we found angels in the forms of kings to govern him? Let history answer this question.

The sum of good government

Let us then with courage and confidence pursue our own Federal and Republican principles, our attachment to our Union and representative government. Kindly separated by nature and a wide ocean from the exterminating havoc of one quarter of the globe; too high-minded to endure the degradations of the others; possessing a chosen country with room enough for our descendants to the hundredth and thousandth generation; entertaining a due sense of our equal right to the use of our own faculties, to the acquisitions of our industry, to honor and confidence from our fellow-citizens, resulting not from birth but from our actions and their sense of them; enlightened by a benign religion, professed, indeed, and practiced in various forms, yet all of them including honesty, truth, temperance, gratitude, and the love of man; acknowledging and adoring an overruling Providence which by all its dispensations proves that it delights in the happiness of man here and his greater happiness hereafter; with all these blessings, what more is necessary to make us a happy and prosperous people? Still one thing more, fellow-citizens — a wise and frugal government which shall restrain men from injuring one another, which shall leave them otherwise free to regulate their own pursuits of industry and improvement, and shall not take from the mouth of labor the bread it has earned. This is the sum of good government, and this is necessary to close the circle of our felicities.

Creed of our political faith

About to enter, fellow-citizens, on the exercise of duties which comprehend everything dear and valuable to you, it is proper that you should understand what I deem the essential principles of our government, and consequently those which ought to shape its administration. I will compress them within the narrowest compass they will bear, stating the general principle but not all its limitations.

Equal and exact justice to all men, of whatever state or persuasion, religious or political; peace, commerce, and honest friendship with all nations — entangling alliances with none; the support of the state governments in all their rights, as the most competent administrations for our domestic concerns and the surest bulwarks against anti-republican tendencies; the preservation of the general government in its whole constitutional vigor, as the sheet anchor of our peace at home and safety abroad; a jealous care of the right of election by the people — a mild and safe corrective of abuses which are lopped by the sword of revolution where peaceable remedies are unprovided; absolute acquiescence in the decisions of the majority, the vital principle of republics, from which there is no appeal but to force, the vital principle and immediate parent of despotism; a well-disciplined militia — our best reliance in peace and for the first moments of war, till regulars may relieve them; the supremacy of the civil over the military authority; economy in the public expense, that labor may be lightly burdened; the honest payment of our debts and sacred preservation of the public faith; encouragement of agriculture, and of commerce as its handmaid; the diffusion of information and the arraignment of all abuses at the bar of public reason; freedom of religion; freedom of the press; freedom of person under the protection of the habeas corpus; and trial by juries impartially selected.

These principles form the bright constellation which has gone before us and guided our steps through an age of revolution and reformation. The wisdom of our sages and the blood of our heroes have been devoted to their attainment. They should be the creed of our political faith — the text of civil instruction — the touchstone by which to try the services of those we trust; and should we wander from them in moments of error or alarm, let us hasten to retrace our steps and to regain the road which alone leads to peace, liberty, and safety.[1]

Union through conciliation

I am made very happy by learning that the sentiments expressed in my inaugural address gave general satisfaction, and holds out a ground on which our fellow-citizens can once more unite. I am the more pleased because these sentiments have been long and radically mine, and therefore will be pursued honestly and conscientiously.[2]

I am very much in hopes we shall be able to restore union to our country. Not indeed that the Federal leaders can be brought over. They are invincibles; but I really hope their followers may. The bulk of these last were real Republicans, carried over from us by French excesses. This induced me to offer a political creed, and to invite to conciliation first; and I am pleased to hear that these principles are recognized by them and considered as no bar of separation.[3]

I have firmly refused to follow the counsels of those who have desired the giving offices to some of their leaders in order to reconcile. I have given and will give only to Republicans, under existing circumstances. But I believe with others that deprivations of office, if made on the ground of political principles alone, would revolt our new converts, and give a body to leaders who now stand alone. Some, I know, must be made. They must be as few as possible, done gradually, and bottomed on some malversation or inherent disqualification.[4] Of the thousands of officers, therefore, in the United States, a very few individuals only, probably not twenty, will be removed.[5]

John Adams' midnight appointments

In the class of removals, however, I do not rank the new appointments which Mr. Adams crowded in with whip and spur from the twelfth of December, when the event of the election was known, and, consequently, that he was making appointments not for himself but his successor until nine o'clock of the night at twelve o'clock of which he was to go out of office.[6] Those scenes of midnight appointment . . . have been condemned by all men. The last day of

PHILOSOPHER–PRESIDENT. Portrait of Jefferson by Gilbert Stuart

117

Washington Nov. 17. 04.

I recieved last night your favor of the 14th. I continue ex-tremely satisfied with the facility of writing with the new Polygraph. Mr Hawkins's box may be considerably improved in it's form. in-stead of having it in the form Fig. 1. the upper lid should, on the hinge side, be bevilled off at a. b. thro' it's whole length (from West to East) then when you wish to use it, not for copying, but as a common writing desk, the gallows remains in it's horizontal position as a protection to the machinery, and ~~becomes~~ is more out of your way, & the lid opens before you and presents an inclined plane for writing on with a free pen as in Fig. 2. when you want to copy, it lies as in Fig. 3. ~~[illegible]~~ in this case the long-linked hinges must be left off. indeed they are always useless and in the way. if the one you are making for me is not too far advanced I should like to have it made in this way. I have taken off the long hinges of the one I have, and unscrewed the other hinges from the lid, and without bevilling it, have used & continue to use it in the way I pro-pose, & find it much more agreeable when I am not using the copying machinery, which is [illegible] half my time: so that I recommend this on experience. Accept affectionate salutations.

Fig. 1 / Fig. 2 / Fig. 3

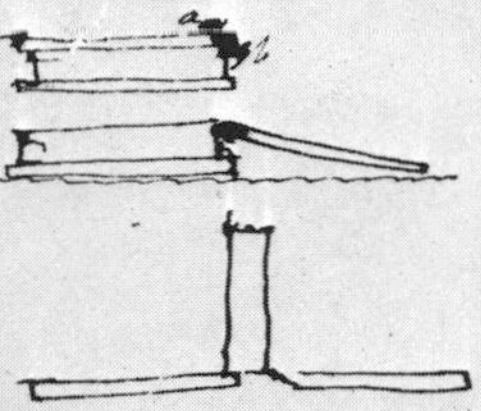

Fig. 4

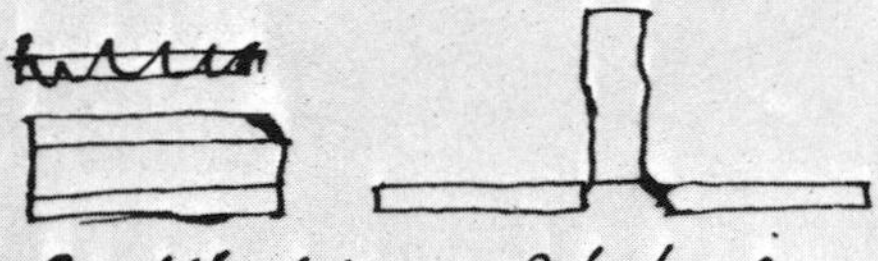

Th: Jefferson

P.S. I think it would be handsomer & take less room on the table to have no projection of either the lid or bottom, but to make it as a box, with strait ends [illegible] except one bevilled off, as Fig. 4. and so would prefer mine.

C. W. Peale esq.

IMPROVING THE POLYGRAPH. Jefferson's Letter to Charles Willson Peale, Washington, November 17, 1804

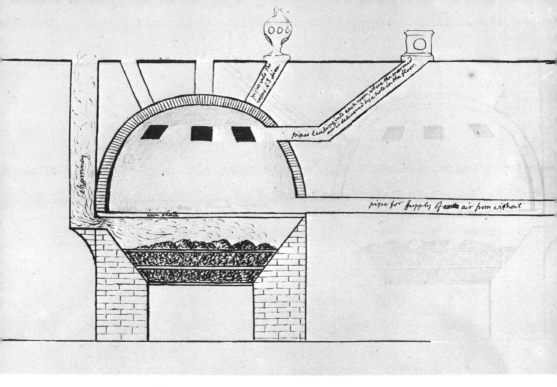

JEFFERSON'S SKETCH FOR A CENTRAL HEATING PLANT

HIS PLAN FOR THE NEW FEDERAL CITY OF WASHINGTON. Drawn about 1791

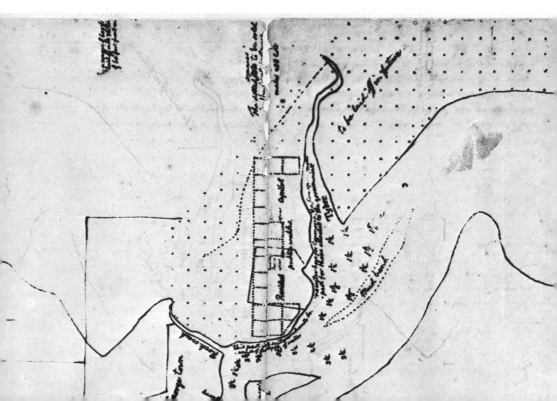

THE MEDALLION SKETCH OF JEFFERSON
Drawn about 1805 by Gilbert Stuart

his political power, the last hours, and even beyond the midnight, were employed in filling all offices, and especially permanent ones, with the bitterest Federalists, and providing for me the alternative either to execute the government by my enemies, whose study it would be to thwart and defeat all my measures, or to incur the odium of such numerous removals from office as might bear me down.[7] This outrage on decency should not have its effect, except in the life appointments which are irremovable; but as to the others I consider the nominations as nullities, and will not view the persons appointed as even candidates for *their* office, much less as possessing it by any title meriting respect.[8]

Justice to Alien and Sedition victims

The barbarians really flattered themselves they should be able to bring back the times of Vandalism, when ignorance put everything into the hands of power and priestcraft.... Those who live by mystery and charlatanerie, fearing you [Dr. Joseph Priestley] would render them useless by simplifying the Christian philosophy — the most sublime and benevolent but most perverted system that ever shone on man — endeavored to crush your well-earned and well-deserved fame. But it was the Lilliputians upon Gulliver.... It is with heartfelt satisfaction that, in the first moments of my public action, I can hail you with welcome to our land, tender to you the homage of its respect and esteem, cover you under the protection of those laws which were made for the wise and good like you, and disdain the legitimacy of that libel on legislation [the Alien Law].[9]

I discharged every person under punishment or prosecution under the Sedition Law, because I considered ... that law to be a nullity, as absolute and as palpable as if Congress had ordered us to fall down and worship a golden image; and that it was as much my duty to arrest its execution in every stage, as it would have been to have rescued from the fiery furnace those who should have been cast into it for refusing to worship the image. It was accordingly done in every instance, without asking what the offenders had done, or against whom they had offended, but whether the pains they were suffering were inflicted under the pretended Sedition Law.[10]

The judges, believing the law constitutional, had a right to pass a

sentence of fine and imprisonment, because the power was placed
in their hands by the Constitution. But the Executive, believing
the law to be unconstitutional, were bound to remit the execution
of it, because that power has been confided to them by the Constitution. That instrument meant that its coordinate branches should
be checks on each other. But the opinion which gives to the judges
the right to decide what laws are constitutional and what not, not
only for themselves in their own sphere of action but for the Legislature and Executive also, in their spheres, would make the judiciary a despotic branch.[11]

No more reform than the nation can bear

I am sensible how far I should fall short of effecting all the reformation which reason would suggest and experience approve, were I
free to do whatever I thought best; but when we reflect how difficult it is to move or inflect the great machine of society, how impossible to advance the notions of a whole people suddenly to ideal
right, we see the wisdom of Solon's remark that no more good must
be attempted than the nation can bear, and that all will be chiefly to
reform the waste of public money and thus drive away the vultures
who prey upon it, and improve some little on old routines. Some
new fences for securing constitutional rights may, with the aid of a
good Legislature, perhaps be attainable.[12]

Levees are done away. The first communication to the next
Congress will be, like all subsequent ones, by message, to which no
answer will be expected. The diplomatic establishment in Europe
will be reduced to three ministers .... The army is undergoing a
chaste reformation. The navy will be reduced to the legal establishment by the last of this month. Agencies in every department
will be revised. We shall push [Congress] to the uttermost in
economizing. A very early recommendation had been given to the
Postmaster General to employ no printer, foreigner, or Revolutionary Tory in any of his offices.[13]

The Cabinet and Washington City; a charming society

Mr. Gallatin's arrival ... renders the organization of our new
administration complete, and enables us to settle our system of
proceeding. Mr. and Mrs. Madison ... are lodging with us till

they can get a house. Great desires are expressed here that Patsy and Maria should come on.[14] I am sure my conduct must have proved, better than a thousand declarations would, that my confidence in those whom I am so happy as to have associated with me [in the Cabinet: Secretaries James Madison, State; Albert Gallatin, Treasury; Henry Dearborn, War; Robert Smith, Navy; and Levi Lincoln, the Attorney General], is unlimited, unqualified, and unabated. I am well satisfied that everything goes on with a wisdom and rectitude which I could not improve. If I had the universe to choose from, I could not change one of my associates to my better satisfaction.[15]

The residence here is very pleasant, indeed a charming society and not too much of it, all living on affectionate and unceremonious terms. It is impossible to be associated with more agreeable colleagues.[16] This may be considered as a pleasant country residence, with a number of neat little villages scattered around within the distance of a mile and a half, and furnishing a plain and substantially good society. They have begun their buildings in about four or five different points, at each of which there are buildings enough to be considered as a village. The whole population is about six thousand.[17]

Few officeholders die and none resign

I had foreseen, years ago, that the first Republican President who should come into office after all the places in the government had become exclusively occupied by Federalists would have a dreadful operation to perform. That the Republicans would consent to a continuation of everything in Federal hands was not to be expected, because neither just nor politic. On him, then, was to devolve the office of an executioner, that of lopping off. I cannot say that it has worked harder than I expected. . . . I am satisfied that the heaping of abuse on me, personally, has been with the design and the hope of provoking me to make a general sweep of all Federalists out of office. But as I have carried no passion into the execution of this disagreeable duty, I shall suffer none to be excited.[18]

Out of many thousands of officers in the United States nine only have been removed for political principle, and twelve for delinquencies chiefly pecuniary. The whole herd have squealed out as if

all their throats were cut.[19] Was it to be imagined that this monopoly of office was still to be continued in the hands of the minority?
Does it violate their *equal rights* to assert some rights in the majority
also? . . . If a due participation of office is a matter of right, how are
vacancies to be obtained? Those by death are few; by resignation,
none.[20]

Federalism entrenched in the bank and the courts

We can pay off [Hamilton's] debt in fifteen years; but we can
never get rid of his financial system. It mortifies me to be strength-
ening principles which I deem radically vicious, but this vice is en-
tailed on us by the first error.[21]

I observe an idea of establishing a branch Bank of the United
States in New Orleans. This institution is one of the most deadly
hostility existing against the principles and form of our Constitution. The nation is at this time so strong and united in its sentiments that it cannot be shaken at this moment. But . . . an institution like this, penetrating by its branches every part of the Union,
acting by command and in phalanx, may, in a critical moment, up-
set the government. I deem no government safe which is under the
vassalage of any self-constituted authorities, or any other authority
than that of the nation or its regular functionaries.

What an obstruction could not this Bank of the United States,
with all its branch banks, be in time of war! It might dictate to us
the peace we should accept, or withdraw its aids. Ought we then to
give further growth to an institution so powerful, so hostile? That it
is so hostile we know, 1, from a knowledge of the principles of the
persons composing the body of directors in every bank, principal or
branch, and those of most of the stockholders; 2, from their opposition to the measures and principles of the government and to the
election of those friendly to them; and 3, from the sentiments of the
newspapers they support. Now, while we are strong, it is the greatest duty we owe to the safety of our Constitution, to bring this
powerful enemy to a perfect subordination under its authorities.[22]

My great anxiety at present is to avail ourselves of our ascendancy
to establish good principles and good practices; to fortify Republicanism behind as many barriers as possible, that the outworks may
give time to rally and save the citadel, should that be again in

danger. On their part, they have retired into the judiciary as a stronghold. There the remains of Federalism are to be preserved and fed from the Treasury, and from that battery all the works of Republicanism are to be beaten down and erased. By a fraudulent use of the Constitution, which has made judges irremovable, they have multiplied useless judges merely to strengthen their phalanx.[23]

A winter's campaign

Our winter campaign has opened with more good humor than I expected. By sending a message instead of making a speech at the opening of the session I have prevented the bloody conflict to which the making an answer would have committed them. They consequently were able to set into real business at once, without losing ten or twelve days in combatting an answer. Hitherto there has been no disagreeable altercations. The suppression of useless offices and lopping off the parasitical plant [that is, an act increasing the number of federal judges] engrafted at the last session on the judiciary body will probably produce some. Bitter men are not pleased with the suppression of taxes. Not daring to condemn the measure, they attack the motive; and, too disingenuous to ascribe it to the honest one of freeing our citizens from unnecessary burdens and unnecessary systems of office, they ascribe it to a desire of popularity. But every honest man will suppose honest acts to flow from honest principles, and the rogues may rail without intermission.[24]

I think it an object of great importance . . . to simplify our system of finance and bring it within the comprehension of every member of Congress. Hamilton set out on a different plan. In order that he might have the entire government of his machine, he determined so to complicate it as that neither the President nor Congress should be able to understand it, or to control him. . . . We might hope to see the finances of the Union as clear and intelligible as a merchant's books, so that every member of Congress and every man of any mind in the Union should be able to comprehend them to investigate abuses and consequently to control them.[25]

Political promises become realities

The session of the first Congress convened since Republicanism has recovered its ascendancy is now drawing to a close. They will

pretty completely fulfill all the desires of the people. They have reduced the army and navy to what is barely necessary. They are dis-
arming executive patronage and preponderance by putting down
one-half the offices of the United States, which are no longer necessary. These economies have enabled them to suppress all the internal taxes and still to make such provision for the payment of their
public debt as to discharge that in eighteen years. They have lopped
off a parasite limb planted by their predecessors on their judiciary
body for party purposes; they are opening the doors of hospitality to
fugitives from the oppressions of other countries; and we have suppressed all those public forms and ceremonies which tended to
familiarize the public eye to the harbingers of another form of government. The people are nearly all united; their quondam leaders,
infuriated with the sense of their impotence, will soon be seen or
heard only in the newspapers, which serve as chimneys to carry off
noxious vapors and smoke, and all is now tranquil, firm and well, as
it should be.[26]

The Legislature . . . have carried into execution, steadily almost,
all the propositions submitted to them in my message. . . . Our
majority in the House of Representatives has been about two to one;
in the Senate, eighteen to fifteen. After another election it will be of
two to one in the Senate, and it would not be for the public good to
have it greater. A respectable minority is useful as censors. The
present one is not respectable, being the bitterest remains of the cup
of Federalism, rendered desperate and furious by despair.[27]

Diehard Federalists and the New England clergy

I have never dreamed that all opposition was to cease. The
clergy, who have missed their union with the state, the Anglomen,
who have missed their union with England, and the political adventurers, who have lost the chance of swindling and plunder in the
waste of public money, will never cease to bawl on the breaking up
of their sanctuary. But among the people the schism is healed, and
with tender treatment the wound will not reopen.[28]

From the clergy I expect no mercy. They crucified their Saviour,
who preached that their kingdom was not of this world; and all
who practice on that precept must expect the extreme of their
wrath. The laws of the present day withhold their hands from

blood; but lies and slander still remain to them.[29] But I am in hopes their good sense will dictate to them that since the mountain will not come to them, they had better go to the mountain; that they will find their interest in acquiescing in the liberty and science of their country; and that the Christian religion, when divested of the rags in which they have enveloped it, and brought to the original purity and simplicity of its benevolent institutor, is a religion of all others most friendly to liberty, science, and the freest expansion of the human mind.[30]

My religious views

My views ... are the result of a life of inquiry and reflection, and very different from that anti-Christian system imputed to me by those who know nothing of my opinions. To the corruptions of Christianity I am indeed opposed, but not to the genuine precepts of Jesus himself. I am a Christian in the only sense in which he wished anyone to be, sincerely attached to his doctrines in preference to all others, ascribing to himself every *human* excellence, and believing he never claimed any other. . . .

His parentage was obscure, his condition poor; his education null; his natural endowments great; his life correct and innocent: he was meek, benevolent, patient, firm, disinterested, and of the sublimest eloquence.

The disadvantages under which his doctrines appear are remarkable.

1. Like Socrates and Epictetus, he wrote nothing himself.

2. But he had not, like them, a Xenophon or an Arrian to write for him. I name not Plato, who only used the name of Socrates to cover the whimsies of his own brain. On the contrary, all the learned of his country, entrenched in its power and riches, were opposed to him, lest his labors should undermine their advantages; and the committing to writing his life and doctrines fell on unlettered and ignorant men who wrote, too, from memory, and not till long after the transactions had passed.

3. According to the ordinary fate of those who attempt to enlighten and reform mankind, he fell an early victim to the jealousy

and combination of the altar and the throne, at about thirty-three years of age, his reason having not yet attained the *maximum* of its energy, nor the course of his preaching, which was but of three years at most, presented occasions for developing a complete system of morals.

4. Hence the doctrines which he really delivered were defective as a whole, and fragments only of what he did deliver have come to us, mutilated, misstated, and often unintelligible.

5. They have been still more disfigured by the corruptions of schismatizing followers, who have found an interest in sophisticating and perverting the simple doctrines he taught, by engrafting on them the mysticisms of a Grecian sophist, frittering them into sub-tleties, and obscuring them with jargon, until they have caused good men to reject the whole in disgust and to view Jesus himself as an impostor.

Notwithstanding these disadvantages, a system of morals is pre-sented to us which, if filled up in the style and spirit of the rich fragments he left us, would be the most perfect and sublime that has ever been taught by man.[31]

Climate and temperament; city-planning

In no case, perhaps, does habit attach our choice or judgment more than in climate. The Canadian glows with delight in his sleigh and snow, the very idea of which gives me the shivers. The comparison of climate between Europe and North America, taking together its corresponding parts, hangs chiefly on three great points. 1. The changes between heat and cold in America are greater and more frequent. . . . 2. Our sky is always clear; that of Europe always cloudy. Hence a greater accumulation of heat here. . . . 3. The changes between wet and dry are much more frequent and sudden in Europe than in America. Though we have double the rain, it falls in half the time. Taking all these together, I prefer much the climate of the United States. . . . I think it a more cheerful one. It is our cloudless sky which has eradicated from our constitutions all disposition to hang ourselves, which we might otherwise have in-herited from our English ancestors. . . .

Experience has . . . established that [yellow fever] is originated here . . . in the lower, closer, and dirtier parts of our large cities. . . .

I have supposed it practicable to prevent its generation by building our cities on a more open plan. Take, for instance, the chequer-board for a plan. Let the black squares only be building squares, and the white ones be left open, in turf and trees. Every square of houses will be surrounded by four open squares, and every house will front an open square. The atmosphere of such a town would be . . . insusceptible of the miasmata which produce yellow fever. I have accordingly proposed that the enlargements of the city of New Orleans . . . be on this plan.[32]

The plan of the town which you [Gov. William Henry Harrison of Indiana] had done me the honor to name after me and to lay out according to an idea I had formerly expressed to you . . . I am thoroughly persuaded . . . will be found handsome and pleasant. . . . In Europe . . . they can build their town in a solid block with impunity, but here . . . ventilation is indispensably necessary.[33]

The polygraph, and books for the Library of Congress

A Mr. Hawkins . . . near Philadelphia has invented a machine which he calls a polygraph [for copying with one pen while you write with the other], and which carries two, three, or four pens. That of two pens, with which I am now writing, is best, and is so perfect that I have laid aside the copying-press . . . and write always with the polygraph. . . . The sheets which you receive are those of the copying-pen of the polygraph, not of the one with which I have written.[34]

Mr. Hawkins's box may be considerably improved. . . . The upper lid should, on the hinge side, be beveled off. . . . Then when you wish to use it, not for copying, but as a common writing desk, . . . the lid . . . presents an inclined plane for writing on with a free pen.[35] I think it the finest invention of the present age. . . . As a secretary which copies for us what we write without the power of revealing it, I find it a most precious possession to a man in public business.[36]

I have prepared a catalogue for the Library of Congress. . . . I have confined the catalogue to those branches of science which belong to the deliberations of the members as statesmen, and in these have omitted those desirable books, ancient and modern, which gentlemen generally have in their private libraries but which cannot properly claim a place in a collection made merely for the purposes of reference. . . . This catalogue . . . will enable you [Congress] to form your general plan and to select from it every year to the amount of the annual fund of those most wanting.[37]

Democratic rules of etiquette

I. In order to bring the members of society together in the first instance, the custom of the country has established that residents shall pay the first visit to strangers and, among strangers, first comers to later comers, foreign and domestic, the character of stranger ceasing after the first visits. To this rule there is a single exception. Foreign ministers, from the necessity of making themselves known, pay the first visit to the ministers of the nation, which is returned.

II. When brought together in society all are perfectly equal, whether foreign or domestic, titled or untitled, in or out of office.

All other observances are but exemplifications of these two principles. . . . To maintain the principle of equality, or of pêle mêle, and prevent the growth of precedence out of courtesy, the members of the Executive will practice at their own houses, and recommend, an adherence to the ancient usage of the country, of gentlemen in mass giving precedence to the ladies in mass in passing from one apartment where they are assembled into another.[38]

Social war with the wife of the British minister

Mr. [Anthony] Merry is with us, and we believe him to be personally as desirable a character as could have been sent us. But he is unluckily associated with one of an opposite character in every point. She has already disturbed our harmony extremely. He began by claiming the first visit from the national ministers. He corrected himself in this. But a pretension to take precedence at dinners, etc., over all others is persevered in. We have told him that the principle of society as well as of government, with us, is the equality of the individuals composing it. That no man here would come to a dinner where he was to be marked with inferiority to any other. That we might as well attempt to force our principle of equality at St. James's as he his principle of precedent here.

I had been in the habit when I invited female company (having no lady in my family) to ask one of the ladies of the four Secretaries to come and take care of my company, and as she was to do the honors of the table I handed her to dinner myself. That Mr. Merry might not construe this as giving them a precedence over Mrs. Merry, I have discontinued it. And here as well as in private houses the pêle-mêle practice is adhered to. They have got Yrujo [the Spanish minister] to take a zealous part in the claim of precedence; it has excited generally emotions of great contempt and indignation (in which the members of the Legislature participate sensibly) that the agents of foreign nations should assume to dictate to us what shall be the laws of our society.

Mrs. Merry must eat her soup at home

The consequence will be that Mr. and Mrs. Merry will put themselves into Coventry, and that he will lose the best half of his usefulness to his nation, that derived from a perfectly familiar and private intercourse with the Secretaries and myself. The latter, be assured, is a virago, and in the short course of a few weeks has established a degree of dislike among all classes which one would have thought impossible in so short a time.... I should be sorry to lose him as long as there remains a possibility of reclaiming him to the exercise of his own dispositions. If his wife perseveres, she must eat her soup at home, and we shall endeavor to draw him into society as if she did not exist. It is unfortunate that the good understanding of nations should hang on the caprice of an individual who ostensibly has nothing to do with them.[39]

Fatigues, and expenses, of White House hospitality

Four weeks tomorrow our winter campaign opens. I dread it on account of the fatigues of the table in such a round of company, which I consider as the most serious trials I undergo. I wish much to turn it over to younger hands and to be myself but a guest at the table and free to leave it as others are.... I miss you all [Martha and her family] at all times, but especially at breakfast, dinner, and the evening, when I have been used to unbend from the labors of the day.[40] I have here company enough, part of which is very friendly, part well enough disposed, part secretly hostile, and a constant succession of strangers. But this only serves to get rid of life, not to enjoy it; it is in the love of one's family only that heartfelt happiness is known. I feel it when we are all together and alone beyond what can be imagined.[41]

Analysis of Expenditures from March 4, 1801, to March 4, 1802:

Secretary...............................$	450.00	
Provisions.............................	4,504.84	
Fuel...................................	690.88	
Miscellaneous..........................	295.82	
Servants...............................	2,675.84	
Groceries (not wine)....................	2,003.71	
Wines.,...............................	2,797.28	
Stable................................	884.45	
Dress, Saddlery, etc....................	567.36	
Charities (in cash).....................	978.20	
Contingencies..........................	557.81	
Books and Stationery...................	391.30	$16,797.59
Debts prior to March 4, 1801, paid........	3,917.59	
Loans................................	170.00	
Acquisitions (lands, horses and carriages)...	4,712.74	
Building (at Monticello).................	2,076.29	
Furniture.............................	545.48	11,422.10
Household Expenses at Monticello.........	652.82	
Plantation Expenses at ditto.............	3,732.23	4,385.05
Family Aids...........................	1,030.10	1,030.10
	$33,634.84	$33,634.84

Cr.

By Salary.............................$25,000.00		
Tobacco..............................	2,974.00	
Profits of Nailery supposed about..........	533.33	
A debt contracted with J. Barnes..........	4,361.00	
	$32,868.33	
Error................................	766.51	
	$33,634.84 [42]	

Memoranda for Edmund Bacon, manager at Monticello

The first work to be done is to finish everything at the mill; to wit, the dam, the stone still wanting at the south abutment, ... making the banks of the canal secure everywhere.... The river field ... is to be planted in Quarantine corn which will be found in a tin canister in my closet.... The levelling of the garden is to be resumed. ... I have hired [nine] hands.... With these will work in common

Isaac, Charles, Ben, Shepherd, Abram, Davy, John, and Shoe-maker Phill; making a gang of 17 hands. Martin is the miller, and Jerry will drive his wagon. Those who work in the nailery are Moses, Wormley, James Hubbard, Barnaby, Isbel's Davy, Bedford John, Bedford Davy, Phill Hubbard, Bartlet, and Lewis. They are sufficient for 2 fires, five at a fire. . . . The toll of the mill is to be put away in the two garners. . . . Mr. Randolph is hopper-free and toll-free. . . .

Mrs. Randolph always chooses the clothing for the house serv-ants; that is to say, for Peter Hemings, Burwell, Edwin, Critta, and Sally. Colored plains are provided for Betty Brown, Betty Hemings, Nance, Ursula, and indeed all the others. The nailers, laborers, and hirelings may have it if they prefer it to cotton. Wool is given for stockings to those who will have it spun and knit for themselves. Fish is always to be got from Richmond. . . . After seeing what the plantation can furnish [towards the 2000 or 2500 lbs. of pork an-nually needed], and the 3 hogs at the mill, the residue must be pur-chased. In the winter a hogshead of molasses must be provided . . . to give a gill apiece to everybody once or twice a week.

Joe works with Mr. Stewart [the blacksmith, a good one but often in his cups]; John Hemings and Lewis with Mr. Dinsmore [the cabinetmaker and chief carpenter]; Burwell paints and takes care of the house. . . . Stewart and Joe do all the plantation work; and when Stewart gets into his idle frolics, it may sometimes be well for Moses or Isbel's Davy to join Joe for necessary work. The serv-ants living on the top of the mountain must have a cart-load of wood delivered at their doors once a week through the winter. . . . Mr. Bacon should not fail to come to the top of the mountain every 2 or 3 days to see that nothing is going wrong, and that the gates are in order. . . . The thorn hedges are to be kept clean wed at all times.[43]

Peace in Europe; the Barbary pirates dispersed

It is a circumstance of sincere gratification to me that . . . I am able to announce . . . that the wars and troubles which have for so many years afflicted our sister nations have at length come to an

JEFFERSON HIMSELF

end [by the Treaty of Amiens, finally concluded in March of 1802, which gave peace to Europe until May of 1803]. . . .

To this state of general peace with which we have been blessed, one only exception exists. Tripoli, the least considerable of the Barbary States, had come forward with demands unfounded either in right or in compact [which] admitted but one answer. I sent a small squadron of frigates into the Mediterranean with assurances to that power of our sincere desire to remain in peace, but with orders to protect our commerce against the threatened attack. . . . The arrival of our squadron dispelled the danger. One of the Tripolitan cruisers having fallen in with, and engaged the small schooner *Enterprise*, . . . was captured after a heavy slaughter of her men, without the loss of a single one on our part. The bravery exhibited by our citizens on that element will, I trust, be a testimony to the world that it is not the want of that virtue which makes us seek their peace. . . .

Rapid growth and great prosperity

The increase of [our] numbers during the last ten years, proceeding in geometrical ratio, promises a duplication in little more than twenty-two years. We contemplate this rapid growth, and the prospect it holds up to us, not with a view to the injuries it may enable us to do to others in some future day, but to the settlement of the extensive country still remaining vacant within our limits, to the multiplications of men susceptible of happiness, educated in the love of order, habituated to self-government, and valuing its blessings above all price.[44]

However our present interests may restrain us within our own limits, it is impossible not to look forward to distant times, when our rapid multiplication will expand itself beyond those limits and cover the whole northern, if not the southern, continent with a people speaking the same language, governed in similar forms and by similar laws; nor can we contemplate with satisfaction either blot [that is, slavery] or mixture on that surface.[45]

The receipts of external duties for [1802] have exceeded those of any former year. . . . This has enabled us to answer all the regular exigencies of government, to pay from the Treasury in one year upward of eight millions of dollars, principal and interest, of the public debt, . . . and to have now in the Treasury four millions and a half of dollars. . . . When merely by avoiding false objects of expense we are able, without a direct tax, without internal taxes, and without borrowing, to make large and effectual payments toward the discharge of our public debt and the emancipation of our posterity from that moral canker, it is an encouragement . . . of the highest order to proceed as we have begun, in substituting economy for taxation.[46]

Our noiseless happy course

The Federalists have opened all their sluices of calumny. They say we lied them out of power, and openly avow they will do the same by us. But it was not lies or arguments on our part which dethroned them, but their own foolish acts, Sedition Laws, Alien Laws, taxes, extravagances and heresies. . . . Every decent man among them revolts at [such] filth; and there cannot be a doubt that were a presidential election to come on this day they would certainly have but three New England states, . . . but three, out of sixteen states. And these three are coming up slowly.[47] I shall take no other revenge than by a steady pursuit of economy and peace, and by the establishment of Republican principles in substance and in form, to sink Federalism into an abyss from which there shall be no resurrection for it.[48]

The path we have to pursue is so quiet that we have nothing scarcely to propose to our Legislature. A noiseless course, not meddling with the affairs of others, unattractive of notice, is a mark that society is going on in happiness. If we can prevent the government from wasting the labors of the people, under the pretense of taking care of them, they must become happy. Their finances are now under such a course of application as nothing could derange but war or Federalism.[49]

Acting for all mankind

The approbation of my ancient [Revolutionary] friends is, above all things, the most grateful to my heart. They know for what objects we relinquished the delights of domestic society, tranquillity, and science, and committed ourselves to the ocean of revolution, to wear out the only life God has given us here in scenes the benefits of which will accrue only to those who follow us.[50]

In the great work which has been effected in America no individual has a right to take any great share to himself. Our people in a body are wise, because they are under the unrestrained and unperverted operation of their own understanding. . . . A nation composed of such materials, and free in all its members from distressing wants, furnishes hopeful implements for the interesting experiment of self-government; and we feel that we are acting under obligations not confined to the limits of our own society. It is impossible not to be sensible that we are acting for all mankind; that circumstances denied to others but indulged to us have imposed on us the duty of proving what is the degree of freedom and self-government in which a society may venture to leave its individual members.[51]

CHAPTER XIII

Louisiana Purchase

THE serenity that marked the beginning of Jefferson's presidency was soon rudely shattered by momentous news that threatened to change the whole destiny of the United States. Weak and decadent Spain, which had long controlled the mouth of the Mississippi, Western America's only outlet to the ocean, had secretly retroceded to a powerful and aggressive France the port of New Orleans and the vast province of Louisiana stretching from the Mississippi to the Rockies. Taking advantage of a lull in the great war, First Consul Bonaparte, dictator of France and master of Europe, was to re-establish a French empire in America which might possibly swallow up British Canada, Spanish Mexico — ultimately, perhaps, the whole New World. So great was the threat to the United States that Jefferson, who in 1801 had solemnly warned against 'entangling alliances,' in April of 1802 declared that from the moment Bonaparte took possession of New Orleans 'we must marry ourselves to the British fleet and nation.'

When the Spanish Intendant at New Orleans in October closed the river to navigation (thus violating a right granted in 1795), Western Americans demanded war and the conquest of the essential port before the arrival of Napoleon's veterans. But the Westerners, Jeffersonians to a man, acquiesced in their leader's policy of first negotiating, at Paris, for the purchase of New Orleans. Peace was his passion, as he frequently said, and he would first try every method short of war.

For months America waited in anxious suspense. Then came the news from Paris — glorious news! Faced by the prospect of a re-

newal of the European war, Napoleon in April of 1803 had sold to
the United States not only New Orleans but the whole magnificent
province of Louisiana, an uncharted wilderness empire which
doubled the area of the Republic, removed grave menaces to its
independence, secured its vital Mississippi outlet, and made possible
its greatness as a continental power. All this was obtained by
purchase, not by war; and for fifteen million dollars, which in a few
years would be repaid by tariff duties at New Orleans. It was,
Jefferson confessed, a great achievement.

Since the Constitution nowhere granted the express power of
acquiring territory, Jefferson, the advocate of strict construction, at
first thought of proposing an amendment. But this would take
precious months if not years, and from Paris came warnings that
the treaty should be promptly ratified before Bonaparte changed
his mind. Yielding to practical necessities, Jefferson and his fellow
Republicans cast aside 'metaphysical subtleties,' and on the basis of
Hamilton's doctrine of implied powers completed the stupendous
real-estate deal which gave the United States half a continent.

For months thereafter jubilant Americans acclaimed 'The Immortal Jefferson' — a Jefferson who was soon plunged into deepest
gloom by the illness and death of his younger daughter, Maria.

The Great Purchase was the high point of an administration
whose achievements he listed with pardonable pride. In spite of
the scurrilous abuse still heaped upon him by Tory reactionaries
and the 'monied corps' of the large cities, in 1804 he was overwhelmingly re-elected, carrying all but two of the seventeen states
of the Union. Immense and irresistible was the popularity of 'The
People's President.'

War clouds over Louisiana

The cession of Louisiana and the Floridas by Spain to France
works most sorely on the United States. On this subject the Secretary of State has written to you [Robert R. Livingston, American
minister at Paris] fully, yet I cannot forbear recurring to it personally, so deep is the impression it makes on my mind. It completely
reverses all the political relations of the United States and will form

a new epoch in our political course. Of all nations of any consideration France is the one which, hitherto, has offered the fewest points
on which we could have any conflict of right, and the most points of
a communion of interests. From these causes we have ever looked
to her as our *natural friend*, as one with which we never could have an
occasion of difference. Her growth, therefore, we viewed as our
own, her misfortunes ours.

There is on the globe one single spot the possessor of which is our
natural and habitual enemy. It is New Orleans, through which
the produce of three eighths of our territory must pass to market, and
from its fertility it will ere long yield more than half of our whole
produce and contain more than half of our inhabitants. France,
placing herself in that door, assumes to us the attitude of defiance.
Spain might have retained it quietly for years. Her pacific dispositions, her feeble state, would induce her to increase our facilities
there, so that her possession of the place would be hardly felt by us,
and it would not, perhaps, be very long before some circumstance
might arise which might make the cession of it to us the price of
something of more worth to her. Not so can it ever be in the hands
of France: the impetuosity of her temper, the energy and restlessness of her character placed in a point of eternal friction with us
and our character, which, though quiet and loving peace and the
pursuit of wealth, is high-minded, despising wealth in competition
with insult or injury, enterprising and energetic as any nation on
earth; these circumstances render it impossible that France and the
United States can continue long friends when they meet in so irritable a position. They, as well as we, must be blind if they do not
see this; and we must be very improvident if we do not begin to
make arrangements on that hypothesis.

We must marry ourselves to the British fleet

The day that France takes possession of New Orleans fixes the
sentence which is to restrain her forever within her low-water mark.
It seals the union of two nations who, in conjunction, can maintain
exclusive possession of the ocean. From that moment, we must
marry ourselves to the British fleet and nation. We must turn all
our attention to a maritime force, for which our resources place us
on very high ground; and having formed and connected together a

power which may render reinforcement of her settlements here impossible to France, make the first cannon which shall be fired in Europe the signal for the tearing up any settlement she may have made, and for holding the two continents of America in sequestration for the common purposes of the united British and American nations.

This is not a state of things we seek or desire. It is one which this measure, if adopted by France, forces on us as necessarily as any other cause, by the laws of nature, brings on its necessary effect. ... In that case, France will have held possession of New Orleans during the interval of a peace, long or short, at the end of which it will be wrested from her. Will this short-lived possession have been n equivalent to her for the transfer of such a weight into the scale ɔf her enemy? Will not the amalgamation of a young, thriving nation continue to that enemy the health and force which are at present so evidently on the decline? And will a few years' possession of New Orleans add equally to the strength of France? She may say she needs Louisiana for the supply of her West Indies. She does not need it in time of peace, and in war she could not depend on them because they would be so easily intercepted.

At least we must have New Orleans and the Floridas

I should suppose that all these considerations might, in some proper form, be brought into view of the government of France. Though stated by us, it ought not to give offense, because we do not bring them forward as a menace but as consequences not controllable by us, but inevitable from the course of things. ... If France considers Louisiana, however, as indispensable for her views, she might perhaps be willing to look about for arrangements which might reconcile it to our interests. If anything could do this, it would be the ceding to us the island of New Orleans and the Floridas. This would certainly, in a great degree, remove the causes of jarring and irritation between us, and perhaps for such a length of time as might produce other means of making the measure permanently conciliatory to our interests and friendships. It would, at any rate, relieve us from the necessity of taking immediate measures for countervailing such an operation by arrangements in another quarter. But still we should consider New Orleans and the Floridas as no equivalent for the risk of a quarrel with France produced by her vicinage. . . .

Every eye in the United States is now fixed on the affairs of Louisiana. Perhaps nothing since the Revolutionary War has produced more uneasy sensations through the body of the nation. . . . I have thought it not amiss, by way of supplement to the letters of the Secretary of State, to write you this private one, to impress you with the importance we affix to this transaction.[1]

The embryo of a tornado

I wish you [Du Pont de Nemours, a French friend] to be possessed of the subject because you may be able to impress on the government of France the inevitable consequences of their taking possession of Louisiana; and though, as I here mention, the cession of New Orleans and the Floridas to us would be a palliation, yet I believe it would be no more, and that this measure will cost France, and perhaps not very long hence, a war which will annihilate her on the ocean and place that element under the despotism of two nations, which I am not reconciled to the more because my own would be one of them. Add to this the exclusive appropriation of both continents of America as a consequence. I wish the present order of things to continue, and with a view to this I value highly a state of friendship between France and us. You know too well how sincere I have ever been in these dispositions to doubt them. You know, too, how much I value peace. . . .

In Europe nothing but Europe is seen, or supposed to have any right in the affairs of nations. But this little event of France's possessing herself of Louisiana, which is thrown in as nothing, as a mere make-weight in the general settlement of accounts, this speck which now appears as an almost invisible point in the horizon, is the embryo of a tornado which will burst on the countries on both sides of the Atlantic and involve in its effects their highest destinies.[2]

Spain closes the mouth of the Mississippi

The late interruption of our commerce at New Orleans by the Spanish Intendant [in October of 1802], combined with the change of proprietors which Louisiana certainly, and the Floridas possibly, are immediately to undergo, have produced a great sensation here.

... Whether we may succeed in the acquisition of the island of New Orleans and the Floridas peaceably for a price far short of the expense of a war, we cannot say. But ... nothing but the failure of every peaceable mode of redress, nothing but dire necessity, should force us from the path of peace ... to embark in the broils and contentions of Europe and become a satellite to any power there.

Yet this must be the consequence if we fail in all possible means of re-establishing our rights, were we to enter into the war alone. The Mississippi would be blockaded at least during the continuance of that war by a superior naval power, and all our Western states be deprived of their commerce unless they would surrender themselves to the blockading power. Great endeavors have been used from this quarter to inflame the Western people to take possession of New Orleans without looking forward to the use they could make of it with a blockaded river.[3]

James Monroe sent to France

The agitation of the public mind on occasion of the late suspension of our right of deposit at New Orleans is extreme. In the Western country it is natural and grounded on honest motives. In the seaports it proceeds from a desire for war, which increases the mercantile lottery; in the Federalists, generally, and especially those of Congress, the object is to force us into war if possible in order to derange our finances, or if this cannot be done, to attach the Western country to them, as their best friends, and thus get again into power. Remonstrances, memorials, etc., are now circulating through the whole of the Western country. ...

It was essential, then, to send a minister extraordinary to be joined with the ordinary one, ... well impressed with all our views and therefore qualified to meet and modify to these every form of proposition which could come from the other party. ... You [James Monroe] possessed the unlimited confidence of the administration and of the Western people and generally of the Republicans everywhere, and were you to refuse to go, no other man can be found who does this. The measure has already silenced the Federalists here. Congress will no longer be agitated by them, and the country will become calm fast as the information extends over it. All eyes, all hopes, are now fixed on you. ... For on the event of this mission depend the future destinies of this republic.[4]

Spain reopens the port; peace is my passion

For the present we have a respite on that subject, Spain having without delay restored our infracted right and assured us it is expressly saved by the instrument of her cession of Louisiana to France. Although I do not count with confidence on obtaining New Orleans from France for money, yet I am confident in the policy of putting off the day of contention for it till we have lessened the embarrassment of debt accumulated instead of being discharged by our predecessors, till we obtain more of that strength which is growing on us so rapidly, and especially till we have planted a population on the Mississippi itself sufficient to do its own work without marching men fifteen hundred miles from the Atlantic shores to perish by fatigue and unfriendly climates. This will soon take place.

In the meantime we have obtained by a peaceable appeal to justice, in four months, what we should not have obtained under seven years of war, the loss of one hundred thousand lives, a hundred millions of additional debt, many hundred millions' worth of produce and property lost for want of market, or in seeking it, and that demoralization which war superinduces on the human mind.[5]

I consider war between France and England as unavoidable. The former is much averse to it, but the latter sees her own existence to depend on a remodification of the face of Europe, over which France has extended its sway much farther since than before the Treaty of Amiens. . . . In this conflict our neutrality will be cheaply purchased by a cession of the island of New Orleans and the Floridas, because, taking part in the war, we could so certainly seize and securely hold them and more. And although it would be unwise in us to let such an opportunity pass by of obtaining the necessary accession to our territory even by force, if not obtainable otherwise, yet it is infinitely more desirable to obtain it with the blessing of neutrality rather than the curse of war.[6]

The events which have taken place in France [Bonaparte had become Consul for life and soon, in December of 1804, was to crown himself Emperor of the French] have lessened in the American mind the motives of interest which it felt in that revolution, and its amity towards that country now rests on its love of peace and commerce. We see at the same time, with great concern, the position in which Great Britain is placed, and should be sincerely afflicted were any disaster to deprive mankind of the benefit of such a bulwark against the torrent which has for some time been bearing down all before it. But her power and powers at sea seem to render everything safe in the end. Peace is our passion, and the wrongs might drive us from it. We prefer trying *ever* other just principles, right and safety, before we would recur to war.[7]

The Republic's area doubled at one stroke!

I accept with pleasure and with pleasure reciprocate ... congratulations on the acquisition of Louisiana, for it is a subject of mutual congratulation, as it interests every man of the nation. The territory acquired [in 1803 for $15,000,000, some 828,000 square miles at approximately three cents an acre], as it includes all the waters of the Missouri and Mississippi, has more than doubled the area of the United States, and the new part is not inferior to the old in soil, climate, productions, and important communications.[8]

The acquisition of New Orleans would of itself have been a great thing, as it would have insured to our Western brethren the means of exporting their produce; but that of Louisiana is inappreciable, because, giving us the sole dominion of the Mississippi, it excludes those bickerings with foreign powers which we know of a certainty would have put us at war with France immediately; and it secures to us the course of a peaceable nation. [9]

We shall get the Floridas too, in good time

The boundaries which I deem not admitting question are the high lands [the Rocky Mountains] on the western side of the Mississippi, enclosing all its waters. ... We have some claims to extend on the seacoast westwardly to the Rio Norte or Bravo [that is, the Rio Grande, in Spanish Mexico], and better; to go eastwardly to the Rio Perdido, between Mobile and Pensacola, the ancient boundary of Louisiana. These claims will be a subject of negotiation with Spain, and if, as soon as she is at war, we push them strongly with one hand, holding out a price in the other, we shall certainly obtain the Floridas, and all in good time. ...

Objections are raising to the eastward against the vast extent of our boundaries, and propositions are made to exchange Louisiana, or a part of it, for the Floridas. But, as I have said, we shall get the Floridas without, and I would not give one inch of the waters of the Mississippi to any nation, because I see in a light very important to our peace the exclusive right to its navigation and the admission of no nation into it but as into the Potomac or Delaware, with our consent and under our police. These Federalists see in this acquisition the formation of a new confederacy, embracing all the waters of the Mississippi, on both sides of it, and a separation of its eastern waters from us. These combinations depend on so many circumstances which we cannot foresee that I place little reliance on them.[10] Who can limit the extent to which the federative principle may operate effectively? The larger our association, the less will it be shaken by local passions; and, in any view, is it not better that the opposite bank of the Mississippi should be settled by our own brethren and children than by strangers of another family? [11]

Federalist grumblers; our foreign policy

These grumblers, too, are very uneasy lest the administration should share some little credit for the acquisition, the whole of which they ascribe to the accident of war. They would be cruelly mortified could they see our files from May, 1801, the first organization of the administration, but more especially from April, 1802. They would see that though we could not say when war would arise, yet we said with energy what would take place when it should arise. We did not, by our intrigues, produce the war; but we availed ourselves of it when it happened. The other party saw the case now existing, on which our representations were predicated, and the wisdom of timely sacrifice. But when these people make the war give us everything, they authorize us to ask what the war gave us in their day?

They had a war; what did they make it bring us? Instead of making our neutrality the ground of gain to their country, they were for plunging into the war. And if they were now in place, they would now be at war against . . . France. They were for making their country an appendage to England. We are friendly, cordially and conscientiously friendly, to England. We are not hostile to France. We will be rigorously just and sincerely friendly to both.[12]

We are anxious to see England maintain her standing, only wishing she would use her power on the ocean with justice. If she had done this heretofore, other nations would not have stood by and looked on with unconcern on a conflict which endangers her existence. We are not indifferent to its issue, nor should we be so on a conflict on which the existence of France should be in danger. We consider each as a necessary instrument to hold in check the disposition of the other to tyrannize over other nations.[13]

Cast aside metaphysical subtleties

This treaty must of course be laid before both Houses, because both have important functions to exercise respecting it. They, I presume, will see their duty to their country in ratifying and paying for it, so as to secure a good which would otherwise probably be never again in their power. But I suppose they must then appeal to *the nation* for an additional article to the Constitution, approving and confirming an act which the nation had not previously authorized. The Constitution has made no provision for our holding foreign territory, still less for incorporating foreign nations into our Union. The Executive, in seizing the fugitive occurrence which so much advances the good of their country, have done an act beyond the Constitution. The Legislature, in casting behind them metaphysical subtleties and risking themselves like faithful servants, must ratify and pay for it, and throw themselves on their country for doing for them unauthorized what we know they would have done for themselves had they been in a situation to do it.

It is the case of a guardian investing the money of his ward in purchasing an important adjacent territory, and saying to him when of age, I did this for your good; I pretend to no right to bind you; you may disavow me and I must get out of the scrape as I can; I thought it my duty to risk myself for you. But we shall not be disavowed by the nation, and their act of indemnity will confirm and not weaken the Constitution, by more strongly marking out its lines.[14]

Ratify before Bonaparte changes his mind

There is reason to apprehend that the government of France, perhaps not well satisfied with its bargain with us, will seize any pretext which can be laid hold of to annul the treaty. They ... render it necessary for both Houses of Congress to perform their respective parts without a day's delay, and ... that as little as possible be said as to the constitutional difficulty.[15]

I confess ... I think it important, in the present case, to set an example against broad construction, by appealing for new power to the people. If, however, our friends shall think differently, certainly I shall acquiesce with satisfaction, confiding that the good sense of our country will correct the evil of construction when it shall produce ill effects.[16] The less that is said about any constitutional difficulty, the better; and that it will be desirable for Congress to do what is necessary, *in silence*.[17]

I confess, it is a great achievement

The *dénouement* has been happy, and I confess I look to this duplication of area for the extending a government so free and economical as ours as a great achievement to the mass of happiness which is to ensue.[18] The question on its ratification in the Senate was decided by twenty-four against seven, which was ten more than enough. The vote in the House of Representatives for making provision for its execution was carried by eighty-nine against twenty-three, which was a majority of sixty-six, and the necessary bills are going through the Houses by greater majorities.[19]

Some inflexible Federalists have still ventured to brave the public opinion. It will fix their character with the world and with posterity, who, not descending to the other points of difference between us, will judge them by this fact, so palpable as to speak for itself in all times and places. ... [Our Louisiana Purchase is] a transaction replete with blessings to unborn millions of men.[20]

While the property and sovereignty of the Mississippi and its waters secure an independent outlet for the produce of the Western States, and an uncontrolled navigation through their whole course free from collision with other powers and the dangers to our peace from that source, the fertility of the country, its climate and extent, promise in due season important aids to our Treasury, an ample provision for our posterity, and a widespread field for the blessings of freedom and equal laws.[21]

Amid these triumphs, the death of Maria

The account of your illness, my dearest Maria, was known to me only this morning. Nothing but the impossibility of Congress proceeding a single step in my absence presents an insuperable bar. . . . God bless you, my ever dear daughter, and preserve you safe to the blessing of us all.[22]

Your letter . . . , my dear Martha, . . . has raised me to life again. For four days past I had gone through inexpressible anxiety. . . . Tell my dear Maria to be of good cheer, and . . . continue to let us hear of her by every post.[23]

The debility of Maria will need attention, lest a recurrence of fever should degenerate into typhus. . . . The sherry at Monticello is old and genuine, and the Pedro Ximenes much older still and stomachic. . . . The house, its contents, and appendages and servants are as freely subjected to you [Maria's husband, John Wayles Eppes] as to myself. . . . My tenderest love to Maria and Patsy, and all the young ones.[24]

My loss [in the death of Maria, April 17, 1804] is great indeed. Others may lose of their abundance, but I, of my want, have lost even the half of all I had. My evening prospects now hang on the slender thread of a single life. Perhaps I may be destined to see even this last cord of parental affection broken! The hope with which I had looked forward to the moment when, resigning public cares to younger hands, I was to retire to that domestic comfort from which the last great step is to be taken, is fearfully blighted.[25]

Fruits of the Revolution of 1800

To do without a land tax, excise, stamp tax and the other internal taxes, to supply their place by economies so as still to support the government properly and to apply $7,300,000 a year steadily to the payment of the public debt; to discontinue a great portion of the expenses on armies and navies, yet protect our country and its commerce with what remains; to purchase a country as large and more fertile than the one we possessed before, yet ask neither a new tax, nor another soldier to be added, but to provide that that country shall by its own income pay for itself before the purchase money is due; to preserve peace with all nations, and particularly an equal friendship to the two great rival powers France and England, and to maintain the credit and character of the nation in as high a degree as it has ever enjoyed, are measures which I think must reconcile the great body of those who thought themselves our enemies, but were in truth only the enemies of certain Jacobinical, atheistical, anarchical, imaginary caricatures which existed only in the land of the rawhead and bloodybones, beings created to frighten the credulous. . . .

I know indeed there are some characters who have been too prominent to retract, too proud and impassioned to relent, too greedy after office and profit to relinquish their longings, and who have covered their devotion to monarchism under the mantle of Federalism, who never can be cured of their enmities. These are incurable maniacs, for whom the hospitable doors of Bedlam are ready to open.[26]

I am happy to hear . . . that there are some at least of our monied corps who do not maintain a spirit of opposition to the national will. Every object of our wish, at home or abroad, is now satisfactorily accomplished except the reduction of this mass of anticivism which remains in our great trading towns. . . . Though not $\frac{1}{25}$ of the nation they command $\frac{3}{4}$ of its public papers. That they should acquiesce in the will of the great majority is but a reasonable expectation . . . yet . . . I am the single object of their accumulated hatred. I do not care for this now. . . . They can never now excite a pain in my mind by anything personal, but I wish to consolidate the nation, and to see these people disarmed either of the wish or the power to injure their country.[27]

Tory reactionaries, red and white

The aboriginal inhabitants . . . I have regarded with the commiseration their history inspires. Endowed with the faculties and the rights of men, breathing an ardent love of liberty and independence, and occupying a country which left them no desire but to be undisturbed, the stream of overflowing population from other regions directed itself on these shores; without power to divert or habits to contend against, they have been overwhelmed by the current or driven before it; now reduced within limits too narrow for the hunter's state, humanity enjoins us to teach them agriculture and the domestic arts. . . .

But the endeavors to enlighten them . . . are combatted by . . . the influence of interested and crafty individuals among them, who feel themselves something in the present order of things and fear to become nothing in any other. These persons inculcate a sanctimonious reverence for the customs of their ancestors; that whatsoever they did must be done through all time; that reason is a false guide, and to advance under its counsel in their physical, moral, or political condition is perilous innovation; that their duty is to remain as their Creator made them, ignorance being safety and knowledge full of danger; in short, my friends, among them is seen the action and counteraction of good sense and bigotry; they, too, have their anti-philosophers . . . who dread reformation and exert all their faculties to maintain the ascendancy of habit over the duty of improving our reason and obeying its mandates.[28]

Candidate for a second term

I sincerely regret that the unbounded calumnies of the Federal Party have obliged me to throw myself on the verdict of my country for trial, my great desire having been to retire at the end of the present term to a life of tranquillity; and it was my decided purpose when I entered into office. They force my continuance. If we can keep the vessel of state as steadily in her course for another four years, my earthly purposes will be accomplished.[29]

The spirit of republicanism is now in almost all its ancient vigor, five sixths of the people being with us. Fourteen of the seventeen states are completely with us, and two of the other three will be in one year. . . . I should have retired at the end of the first four years, but that the immense load of Tory calumnies which have been manufactured respecting me, and have filled the European market, have obliged me to appeal once more to my country for a justification. I have no fear but that I shall receive honorable testimony by their verdict on those calumnies. At the end of the next four years

I shall certainly retire. Age, inclination, and principle all dictate this.[30]

For a third term only if monarchy threatens

My opinion originally was that the President of the United States should have been elected for seven years, and forever ineligible afterwards. I have since become sensible that seven years is too long to be irremovable, and that there should be a peaceable way of withdrawing a man in midway who is doing wrong. The service for eight years, with a power to remove at the end of the first four, comes nearly to my principle as corrected by experience; and it is in adherence to that, that I determine to withdraw at the end of my second term. The danger is that the indulgence and attachments of the people will keep a man in the chair after he becomes a dotard, that re-election through life shall become habitual, and election for life follow that. General Washington set the example of voluntary retirement after eight years. I shall follow it. And a few more precedents will oppose the obstacle of habit to anyone after a while who shall endeavor to extend his term. Perhaps it may beget a disposition to establish it by an amendment of the Constitution. . . .

I had determined to declare my intention, but I have consented to be silent on the opinion of friends who think it best not to put a continuance out of my power in defiance of all circumstances. There is, however, but one circumstance which could engage my acquiescence in another election; to wit, such a division about a successor as might bring in a monarchist. But that circumstance is impossible. While, therefore, I shall make no formal declaration to the public of my purpose, I have freely let it be understood in private conversation.[31]

Overwhelmingly re-elected in 1804

The two parties which prevailed with so much violence . . . are almost wholly melted into one. At the late presidential election I have received one hundred and sixty-two votes against fourteen only [for the Federalist candidate, Charles C. Pinckney of South Carolina]. Connecticut is still Federal by a small majority; and Delaware on a poise, as she has been since 1775, and will be till

Anglomany with her yields to Americanism. Connecticut will be with us in a short time. Though the people in mass have joined us their leaders had committed themselves too far to retract. Pride keeps them hostile; they brood over their angry passions and give them vent in the newspapers which they maintain. They still make as much noise as if they were the whole nation.[32]

During this course of administration, and in order to disturb it, the artillery of the press has been levelled against us, charged with whatsoever its licentiousness could devise or dare. These abuses of an institution so important to freedom and science are deeply to be regretted, inasmuch as they tend to lessen its usefulness and to sap its safety. . . . Nor was it uninteresting to the world that an experiment should be fairly and fully made whether freedom of discussion, unaided by power, is not sufficient for the propagation and protection of truth — whether a government conducting itself in the true spirit of its constitution, with zeal and purity, and doing no act which it would be unwilling the whole world should witness, can be written down by falsehood and defamation. . . .

The experiment has been tried; . . . our fellow-citizens have looked on, cool and collected; they saw the latent source from which these outrages proceeded; they gathered around their public functionaries, and when the Constitution called them to the decision by suffrage, they pronounced their verdict, honorable to those who had served them and consolatory to the friend of man who believes he may be entrusted with his own affairs.[33]

Our business is to march straight forward to the object which has occupied us for eight and twenty years, without either turning to the right or left. . . . And when that is done you [George Clinton, the newly elected Vice President] and I may retire to the tranquillity which our years begin to call for, and review with satisfaction the efforts of the age we happened to be born in, crowned with complete success. In the hour of death we shall have the consolation to see established in the land of our fathers the most wonderful work of wisdom and disinterested patriotism that has ever yet appeared on the globe.[34]

CHAPTER XIV

Peace Is My Passion

THE prayer for peace in his second inaugural address, of
March 4, 1805, was one which Jefferson, perforce, repeated
many times during the next four years. Even then the skies of
peaceful and prosperous America were overcast by troubled relations with Spain over the vaguely defined boundaries of Louisiana,
and the renewal of the European war in 1803 had revived grave
threats to her neutral and national rights.

Jefferson, ardent expansionist, insisted that Louisiana included
West Florida (from New Orleans to Pensacola) and possibly Texas.
Further, he hoped to induce Spain to trade off East Florida (the
Florida peninsula) for spoliation claims held against her by Americans. He tried various schemes to obtain the Floridas and as much
of Texas as possible. In 1805 he thought of proposing a provisional
alliance with England, effective only if we should be forced into
war by Spain and her Napoleonic ally. Later he attempted a
peaceable accommodation by offering Spain a money payment
through France. Although unsuccessful because of the shifting
currents of European politics, he laid the basis of a policy which in
a few years was to round out the southern boundaries and make
the Gulf of Mexico an American lake.

When relations with Britain became strained because of impressments by her short-handed navy and of captures under new
principles 'interloped into the law of nations,' Jefferson resorted to
his favorite weapons of diplomacy and economic coercion. In 1806
he began negotiations at London and had Congress enact a partial
boycott against British imports (which, however, he did not put

into effect until 1807). Unfortunately, Britain refused to yield the one point on which Jefferson was adamant: the abolition of the brutal, degrading, and inhumane practice of seizing American sailors (on the pretext that they were British subjects) and impressing them into British warships. Her refusal was most ominous for future Anglo-American relations.

Meanwhile, Jefferson was intent on crushing Aaron Burr's mysterious conspiracy, 'the most extraordinary since the days of Don Quixote.' He was shocked into violent disagreement by the reasoning and tactics of Chief Justice John Marshall, diehard Federalist and his bitter personal enemy, who acquitted Burr on the ground that no overt act of treason had been proved. Most gratifying to him, however, was the striking proof which the Burr affair had given of the people's warm attachment to the Union.

In spite of foreign and domestic difficulties, the first two years of the second term were marked by a continuance of peace and of an unprecedented and widely diffused prosperity. The New World republic of farmers was the granary of the Old World belligerents. Its merchant marine, second only to Britain's in tonnage, was of meteoric growth and fabulous profits. So great was the revenue from an expanding commerce that by 1807 a surplus piled up in the Treasury, and Jefferson was able to project a grand scheme of public works, national in scope, which would cement the Union by new and indissoluble ties. If peace could be maintained, the surplus revenue would be applied to the establishment of a national university and to the building of turnpikes, canals, and other internal improvements for the more rapid development of a thriving America which Jefferson (reporting on the explorations of Meriwether Lewis and William Clark) now proudly called 'our continent.'

The philosophic President was keenly interested in every detail of the scientific survey he had directed Lewis and Clark to make of the vast wilderness world of Louisiana. He speculated whether Lewis' 'Fleecy Goat' was not really the South American llama, and he invited Doctor Wistar down from Philadelphia to inspect the bones of the 'Mammoth' which Clark had sent on to the White House. As usual, he directed farming operations and improvements at Monticello, and found time from his presidential duties to write affectionate letters to his grandchildren: to Cornelia Randolph, who had just learned to write, and to Thomas Jefferson Randolph, whom he sent off to Philadelphia for his education with an essay on the importance of good humor. Before his second term was half through he confessed that he was 'panting for retirement' to Monticello, and on the basis of both private and public considerations he discouraged demands that he should serve a third term.

In June of 1807 the British outrage on the warship *Chesapeake* brought the impressment issue to a head, and caused a nation-wide clamor for war. Resisting the clamor, Jefferson demanded reparations and the end of impressments. He obtained neither from a Tory Britain whose attitude towards the former colonies was 'unfriendly, proud, and harsh.' Before America could recover from this blow, which sounded the very depths of national humiliation, she was assailed by anti-neutral edicts of both the great belligerents. British orders-in-council and French decrees threatened to drive her commerce from the ocean or to force her into war with both powers. Jefferson's answer to these edicts was not war but the Embargo, enacted by Congress in December of 1807. By it he aimed to protect ships, cargoes, and seamen by keeping them in port. Most important, by withholding foodstuffs and other supplies from the belligerents he hoped to force them to do America justice.

The Embargo was a bold experiment in self-sacrificing economic coercion, 'the last card short of war.' Although it was violently opposed, and widely evaded, by the Federalist merchants of the Northeast, the people in 1808 showed their approval by electing to the presidency the successor Jefferson had chosen, his friend James Madison. The Embargo, however, failed to force a repeal of either the British orders or the French decrees. Jefferson privately was of the opinion that war was the only alternative (submission and tribute were not to be thought of), but after the election he followed a policy of not proposing measures which his successor would have to execute. The decision was left to Congress. In the last days of his administration the Republican Congress, frightened by threats of secession in New England, replaced the Embargo with a much weaker form of economic coercion, the Non-Intercourse Act of 1809. This reopened trade with all nations except England and France, and authorized intercourse with the belligerents only when they repealed their edicts. Meanwhile, war preparations were to be continued.

On March 4, 1809, Jefferson ended his eight years in the presidency, making way for his friend and disciple, James Madison. He regretted that he could not leave the nation under the assurance of continued peace and prosperity, but he was consoled by the belief that he had done everything in his power to secure those blessings. It was a belief held by a great many Americans, who took this occasion to review and to praise the achievements not only of his presidential years but of his forty years in public life. As he prepared to ride home to Monticello, 'a prisoner released from his chains,' his heart was warmed by the acclamations of grateful fellow-citizens throughout the Republic — the Republic he had served so long and so well.

A prayer for peace

I shall now enter on the duties to which my fellow-citizens have again called me, and shall proceed in the spirit of those principles which they have approved. . . . I shall need, therefore, all the indulgence I have heretofore experienced. . . . I shall need, too, the favor of that Being in whose hands we are, who led our forefathers, as Israel of old, from their native land and planted them in a country flowing with all the necessaries and comforts of life, who has covered our infancy with His providence and our riper years with His wisdom and power, and to whose goodness I ask you to join with me in supplications that He will so enlighten the minds of your servants, guide their councils and prosper their measures, that whatsoever they do shall result in your good, and shall secure to you the peace, friendship, and approbation of all nations.[1]

Troubled relations with Spain

With Spain our negotiations for a settlement of differences have not had a satisfactory issue. Spoliations during the former war, for which she had formally acknowledged herself responsible, have been refused to be compensated. . . . The same practices are renewed in the present war, and are already of great amount. On the Mobile our commerce passing through that river continues to be obstructed by arbitrary duties and vexatious searches. Propositions for adjusting amicably the boundaries of Louisiana have not been acceded to. . . . Inroads have been recently made into the territories of Orleans and the Mississippi, our citizens have been seized and their property plundered in the very parts of the former which had been actually delivered up by Spain, and this by the regular officers and soldiers of that government. I have therefore found it necessary at length to give orders to our troops on that frontier to be in readiness to protect our citizens, and to repel by arms any similar aggressions in future.[2]

From the papers already received [from our minister at Madrid] I infer a confident reliance on the part of Spain on the omnipotence of Bonaparte, but a desire of procrastination till peace in Europe shall leave us without an ally.[3] I am strongly impressed with a belief of hostile and treacherous intentions against us on the part of France, and that we should lose no time in securing something more than a mutual friendship with England.[4]

An attempt at further expansion

The war on the continent of Europe appears now so certain [of becoming extensive], and that peace is at least one year off, that we are now placed at our ease in point of time. We may make another effort for a peaceable accommodation with Spain without the danger of being left alone to cope with both France and Spain; and even if we are driven to war, it is now much more questionable than it was whether we had not better enter into it without fettering ourselves with an alliance [with England], that we may be free to retire whenever our terms can be obtained. . . . Our question now is, in what way to give Spain another opportunity of arrangement? Is not Paris the place? France the agent? The purchase of the Floridas the means?[5]

I proposed [to the Cabinet, November 12, 1805] we should address ourselves to France, informing her it was a last effort at amicable settlement with Spain, and offer to her or through her, 1, a sum of money for the rights of Spain east of Iberville, say the Floridas;

2, to cede the part of Louisiana from the Rio Bravo [that is, the Rio Grande] to the Guadaloupe; 3, Spain to pay within a certain time spoliations under her own flag agreed to by the convention (which we guess to be one hundred vessels, worth two millions), and those subsequent (worth as much more), and to hypothecate to us for those payments the country from Guadaloupe to Rio Bravo. . . . The first was to be the exciting motive with France, to whom Spain is in arrears for subsidies, and who will be glad also to secure us from going into the scale of England. The second, the soothing motive with Spain, which France would press bona fide because she claimed to the Rio Bravo. The third, to quiet our merchants.

It was agreed to unanimously, and the sum to be offered fixed not to exceed five million dollars. Mr. Gallatin did not like purchasing Florida under an apprehension of war, lest we should be thought in fact to purchase peace. We thought this overweighed by taking advantage of an opportunity which might not occur again of getting a country essential to our peace, and to the security of the commerce of the Mississippi.[6]

British captures and impressments

Our coasts have been infested and our harbors watched by . . . armed vessels . . . to the great annoyance and oppression of our commerce. New principles, too, have been interloped into the law of nations. . . . According to these, a belligerent [Great Britain, in capturing American vessels engaged in the indirect trade between France and Spain and their West Indian colonies] takes to himself a commerce with its own enemy which it denies to a neutral, on the ground of its aiding that enemy in the war. But reason revolts at such an inconsistency.[7]

The rights of a neutral to carry on a commercial intercourse with every part of the dominions of a belligerent, permitted by the laws of the country (with the exception of blockaded ports and contraband of war), was believed to have been decided between Great Britain and the United States by . . . the actual payment of damages . . . by . . . Great Britain for the infractions of that right. When, therefore, it was perceived that the same principle was revived with others more novel, and extending the injury, instruc-

tions were given to the Minister Plenipotentiary of the United
States at the court of London . . . to insist on the rights too evident
and too important to be surrendered. . . . On the impressment of
our seamen our remonstrances have never been intermitted. . . . The
practice, though relaxed at times in the distant seas, has been constantly pursued in those of our neighborhood.[8]

No two countries upon earth have so many points of common interest and friendship [as the United States and Great Britain], and
their rulers must be great bunglers indeed if . . . they break them
asunder. The only rivalry that can arise is on the ocean. England
may, by petty larceny thwartings, check us on that element a little,
but nothing she can do will retard us there one year's growth. We
shall be supported there by other nations and thrown into their
scale to make a part of the great counterpoise to her navy. If, on
the other hand, she is just to us, conciliatory, and encourages the
sentiment of family feelings and conduct, it cannot fail to befriend
the security of both.[9]

We sincerely wish to be honestly neutral. . . . Although our
prospect is peace, our policy and purpose is to provide for defense
by all those means to which our resources are competent.[10]

Rejection of an impossible British treaty

Our negotiators [at London, James Monroe and William
Pinkney] . . . were making up their minds to sign a treaty containing no provision against the impressment of our seamen. We
instantly, February 3d [1807], instructed them not to do so; and
that if such a treaty had been forwarded, it could not be ratified;
that therefore they must immediately resume the negotiations to
supply that defect, as a *sine qua non*. Such a treaty having come to
hand, we of course suspend it. . . . In the meantime I have, by proclamation, continued the suspension of the Non-Importation Law
[of 1806, a partial boycott against British imports], as a proof of
the continuance of friendly dispositions.[11]

I have but little expectation that the British government will
retire from their habitual wrongs in the impressment of our seamen,
and am certain that without that we will never tie up our hands by
treaty from the right of passing a non-importation or non-intercourse act to make it her interest to become just. This may bring

on a war of commercial restrictions. . . . This state of things should be understood at Paris, and every effort used . . . to accommodate our differences with Spain, under the auspices of France, with whom it is all-important that we should stand in terms of the strictest cordiality. In fact we are to depend on her and Russia for the establishment of neutral rights . . ., among which should be that of taking no persons by a belligerent out of a neutral ship unless they be the *soldiers* of an enemy.[12]

The conspiracy of former Vice President Burr

Some time in the latter part of September [1806] I received intimations that designs were in agitation in the Western country unlawful and unfriendly to the peace of the Union, and that the prime mover in these was Aaron Burr. . . . It was not until the latter part of October that the objects of the conspiracy began to be perceived, but still so blended and involved in mystery that nothing distinct could be singled out for pursuit. . . . By a letter received from [General James Wilkinson] on the 25th of November, but dated October 21st, we learn that a confidential agent of Aaron Burr had been deputed to him, with communications partly written in cipher and partly oral, explaining his designs, exaggerating his resources, and making such offers of emolument and command to engage him and the army in his unlawful enterprise as he had flattered himself would be successful. . . .

It appeared that he contemplated two distinct objects, which might be carried on either jointly or separately, and either the one or the other first, as circumstances should direct. One of these was the severance of the union of these states by the Alleghany Mountains; the other, an attack on Mexico. A third object was provided, merely ostensible, to wit: the settlement of a pretended purchase of a tract of country on the Washita, claimed by a Baron Bastrop. This was to serve as the pretext for all his preparations, an allurement for such followers as really wished to acquire settlements in that country, and a cover under which to retreat in the event of final discomfiture of both branches of his real design.

He found at once that the attachment of the Western country

to the present Union was not to be shaken; that its dissolution could not be effected with the consent of its inhabitants, and that his resources were inadequate, as yet, to effect it by force. He took his course then at once, determined to seize on New Orleans, plunder the bank there, possess himself of the military and naval stores, and proceed on his expedition to Mexico; and to this object all his means and preparations were now directed. He collected ... all the ardent, restless, desperate, and disaffected persons who were ready for any enterprise analogous to their characters. He seduced good and well-meaning citizens, some by assurances that he possessed the confidence of the government and was acting under its secret patronage, a pretense which obtained some credit from the state of our differences with Spain. ...

Orders were dispatched to every intersecting point on the Ohio and Mississippi, from Pittsburg to New Orleans, for the employment of such force either of the regulars or of the militia ... as might enable them ... to suppress effectually the further progress of the enterprise. ... Great alarm, indeed, was excited at New Orleans by the exaggerated accounts of Mr. Burr, disseminated through his emissaries, of the armies and navies he was to assemble there. General Wilkinson had arrived there himself on the 24th of November, and had immediately put into activity the resources of the place for the purpose of its defense; and on the tenth of December he was joined by his troops.[13]

Capture of 'Emperor Aaron the First'

Burr's enterprise is the most extraordinary since the days of Don Quixote. It is so extravagant that those who know his understanding would not believe it if the proofs admitted doubt. He has meant to place himself on the throne of Montezuma and extend his empire to the Alleghany, seizing on New Orleans as the instrument of compulsion for our Western States.[14]

Burr himself, after being disarmed by our endeavors of all his followers, escaped from the custody of the court of Mississippi, but was taken near Fort Stoddert [in February of 1807], making his way to Mobile, by some country people who brought him on as a prisoner to Richmond, where he is now under a course for trial.[15]

A small band of American adventurers who had fled from their debts, and who were longing to dip their hands into the mines of Mexico, enlisted in Burr's double project of attacking that country and severing our Union. Had Burr had a little success in the upper country, these parricides would have joined him. However ... a simple proclamation informing the people of these combinations ... produced an instantaneous levee en masse of our citizens wherever there appeared anything to lay hold of, and the whole was crushed in one instant. ...

Burr is now under trial ... and unless his Federal patrons give him an opportunity of running away he will unquestionably be convicted.[16] It is unfortunate that Federalism is still predominant in our judiciary department, which is consequently in opposition to the legislative and executive branches, and is able to baffle their measures often.[17]

The Federalists make Burr's cause their own

That there should be anxiety and doubt in the public mind in the present defective state of the proof is not wonderful; and this has been sedulously encouraged by the tricks of the judges to force trials before it is possible to collect the evidence, dispersed through a line of two thousand miles from Maine to Orleans. The Federalists, too, give all their aid, making Burr's cause their own, mortified only that he did not separate the Union or overturn the government, and proving that had he had a little dawn of success they would have joined him to introduce his object, their favorite monarchy, as they would any other enemy, foreign or domestic, who could rid them of this hateful republic for any other government in exchange.

The first ground of complaint was the supine inattention of the administration to a treason stalking through the land in open day. The present one, that they have crushed it before it was ripe for execution, so that no overt acts can be produced. ... Aided by no process or facilities from the *Federal* courts, but frowned on by their newborn zeal for the liberty of those whom we would not permit to overthrow the liberties of their country, we can expect no revealments from the accomplices of the chief offender. Of treasonable intentions the judges have been obliged to confess there is probable appearance. What loophole they will find in the case when it comes to trial, we cannot foresee. ...

Against Burr, personally, I never had one hostile sentiment. I never indeed thought him an honest, frank-dealing man, but considered him as a crooked gun, or other perverted machine, whose aim or shot you could never be sure of. Still, while he possessed the confidence of the nation, I thought it my duty to respect in him their confidence, and to treat him as if he deserved it.[18]

John Marshall acquits Burr: no overt act of treason proved

The scenes which have been acted at Richmond are such as have never before been exhibited in any country where all regard to public character has not yet been thrown off. They are equivalent to a proclamation of impunity to every traitorous combination which may be formed to destroy the Union; and they preserve a head for all such combinations as may be formed within, and a centre for all the intrigues and machinations which foreign governments may nourish to disturb us. However, they will produce an amendment to the Constitution which, keeping the judges independent of the executive, will not leave them so, of the nation.[19]

We had supposed we possessed fixed laws to guard us equally against treason and oppression. But it now appears we have no law but the will of the judge. Never will chicanery have a more difficult task than has been now accomplished to warp the text of the law to the will of him who is to construe it. Our case too is the more desperate as to attempt to make the law plainer by amendment is only throwing out new materials for sophistry.[20]

Confidence in the people, and a people's army

The proof we have lately seen of the innate strength of our government is one of the most remarkable which history has recorded, and shows that we are a people capable of self-government and worthy of it. The moment that a proclamation apprized our citizens that there were traitors among them, and what was their object, they [through their citizen-soldiers of the militia] rose upon them wherever they lurked and crushed by their own strength what would have produced the march of armies and civil war in any other country. The government which can wield the arm of the people must be the strongest possible.[21] The enterprise has done good by proving that the attachment of the people in the West is

as firm as that in the East to the union of our country, and by establishing a mutual and universal confidence.[22]

The classification of our militia is now the most essential thing
the United States have to do. . . . It is the real secret of Bonaparte's
success.[23] Upward of three hundred thousand able-bodied men
between the ages of eighteen and twenty-six . . . will furnish a competent number for offense or defense in any point where they may
be wanted, and will give time for raising regular forces after the
necessity of them shall become certain.[24] A militia can never be
used for distant service on any other plan, and Bonaparte will
conquer the world if they do not learn his secret of composing
armies of young men only, whose enthusiasm and health enable
them to surmount all obstacles.[25]

The spirit of this country is totally adverse to a large military
force. I have tried for two sessions to prevail on the Legislature to
let me plant thirty thousand well chosen volunteers on donation
lands on the west side of the Mississippi, as a militia always at
hand for the defense of New Orleans, but I have not yet succeeded.
. . . A great security for that country is that there is a moral certainty that neither France nor England would meddle with that
country while the present state of Europe continues, and Spain we
fear not.[26]

Meanwhile, peace and unprecedented prosperity

Wars and contentions, indeed, fill the pages of history with more
matter. But more blest is that nation whose silent course of happiness furnishes nothing for history to say. This is what I ambition
for my own country, and what it has fortunately enjoyed . . . while
Europe has been in constant volcanic eruption.[27]

These payments [of 1807], with those of the preceding five and
a half years, have extinguished of the funded debt twenty-five
millions and a half of dollars, being the whole which could be paid
or purchased within the limits of the law and of our contracts, and
have left us in the Treasury eight millions and a half of dollars.[28]
The question, therefore, now comes forward — to what . . . objects
shall these surpluses be appropriated, and the whole surplus of
impost, after the entire discharge of the public debt, . . . when the
purposes of war shall not call for them? Shall we suppress the im-

post and give that advantage to foreign over domestic manufactures? . . . Patriotism would certainly prefer its continuance
and application to the great purposes of the public education,
roads, rivers, canals, and such other objects of public improvement
as it may be thought proper to add to the constitutional enumera-
tion of federal powers. By these operations new channels of communications will be opened between the states, the lines of separation will disappear, their interests will be identified, and their
union cemented by new and indissoluble ties.

Education is here placed among the articles of public care, not
that it would be proposed to take its ordinary branches out of the
hands of private enterprise, which manages so much better all the
concerns to which it is equal; but a public institution [that is, a
national university] can alone supply those sciences which, though
rarely called for, are yet necessary to complete the circle, all the
parts of which contribute to the improvement of the country and
some of them to its preservation.[29]

Explorations of 'our continent'

The expedition of Messrs. Lewis and Clark for exploring the
River Missouri, and the best communication from that to the
Pacific Ocean, has had all the success which could have been expected. They have traced the Missouri nearly to its source, de-
scended the Columbia to the Pacific Ocean, ascertained with accuracy the geography of that interesting communication across
our continent, learned the character of the country, of its commerce
and inhabitants; and . . . have by this arduous service deserved
well of their country. . . . Very useful additions have also been made
to our knowledge of the Mississippi by Lieutenant Pike, who has
ascended to its source. . . . These important surveys, in addition to
those before possessed, furnish materials for commencing an accurate map of the Mississippi and its western waters. Some principal rivers, however, remain still to be explored.[30]

Mammoth bones in the White House

I have never known to what family you [Doctor Caspar Wistar]
ascribed the Wild Sheep, or Fleecy Goat, as Governor Lewis called

it, or the *Pogo-tragos*, if its name must be Greek. . . . If I recollect
well those horns, they, with the fleece, would induce one to suspect
it to be the Lama, or at least a *Lamae affinis.* . . .

General Clark . . . has employed ten laborers several weeks at
the Big Bone Lick and has shipped the result. . . . He has sent,
first, of the Mammoth, as he calls it, frontals, jawbones, tusks,
teeth, ribs, a thigh, and a leg, and some bones of the paw; second,
of what he calls the Elephant, a jawbone, tusks, teeth, ribs; third,
of something of the Buffalo species, a head and some other bones
unknown. . . . There is a tusk and a femur which General Clark
procured particularly at my request for a special kind of cabinet I
have at Monticello. But the great mass of the collection are mere
duplicates of what you possess at Philadelphia, of which I would
wish to make a donation to the National Institute of France, which
I believe has scarcely any specimens of the remains of these animals.
But how to make the selection without the danger of sending away
something which might be useful to our own [American Philosophi-
cal] Society? Indeed, my friend, you must give a week to this
object.[31]

The bones are spread in a large room, where you can work at
your leisure, undisturbed by any mortal, from morning till night,
taking your breakfast and dinner with us. It is a precious collection,
consisting of upwards of three hundred bones.[32]

A gold medal; and flower gardens at Monticello

I have received . . . the medal of gold by which the Society of
Agriculture at Paris have been pleased to mark their approbation
of the form of a mould-board which I had proposed; also . . . the
title of foreign associate to their Society.[33] Since the first form used,
I have made a small alteration in the form of the toe of the mould-
board which, while it preserves the principle untouched, enables
us to shorten the ploughshare six or eight inches. . . . I inclose . . . a
description of this alteration, and . . . I send . . . also . . . a model.[34]

Wormley [one of his servants at Monticello] must be directed
to weed the flower beds about the house, the nursery, the vine-
yards, and raspberry beds. . . . Put the Jenny and our two mares to
the Jack. . . . Pay great attention to the hogs and sheep. We must
get into such a stock as to have thirty killable hogs every year, and

fifty ewes. . . . The finishing everything about the mill is what I wish always to have a preference to every kind of work. Next to that my heart is most set on finishing the garden.[35]

I find that the limited number of our flower beds will too much restrain the variety of flowers in which we might wish to indulge, and therefore I have resumed an idea . . . of a winding walk surrounding the lawn before the house, with a narrow border of flowers on each side. This would give us abundant room for a great variety. . . . The hollows of the walk would give room for oval beds of flowering shrubs.[36] My old friend Thouin of the National Garden at Paris has sent me 700 species of seeds. I suppose they will contain all the fine flowers of France, and fill all the space we have for them.[37]

Mishaps on a journey; a grandchild learns to write

My journey to [Washington] was not as free from accident as usual. I was near losing Castor in the Rapidan by his lying down in the river, there waist deep, and being so embarrassed by the shafts of the carriage and harness that he was nearly drowned before the servants, jumping into the water, could lift his head out and cut him loose from the carriage. This was followed by the loss of my travelling money, I imagine as happened on the sopha in the morning I left Monticello, when it was given me again by one of the children.[38]

My dear Cornelia, . . . last night I found in a newspaper the four lines which I now inclose you; and as you are learning to write, they will be a good lesson to convince you of the importance of minding your stops in writing. I allow you a day to find out yourself how to read these lines so as to make them true. If you cannot do it in that time, you may call in assistance. At the same time, I will give you four other lines, which I learnt when I was but a little older than you, and I still remember.

> I've seen the sea all in a blaze of fire
> I've seen a house high as the moon and higher
> I've seen the sun at twelve o'clock at night
> I've seen the man who saw this wondrous sight.

All this is true, whatever you may think of it at first reading. . . . Tell your mama that I fear I shall not get away as soon as I ex-

pected. . . . Kiss her for me, and all the sisterhood. To Jefferson
I give my hand, to your papa my affectionate salutations. You
have always my love.[39]

I congratulate you, my dear Cornelia, on having acquired the
valuable art of writing. How delightful to be enabled by it to con-
verse with an absent friend as if present! To this we are indebted
for all our reading; because it must be written before we can read
it. To this we are indebted for the Iliad, the Aenead, the Colum-
biad, Henriad, Dunciad, and now, for the most glorious poem of
all, the Terrapiniad [an anti-Jefferson satire], which I now inclose
you. . . . I rejoice that you have learnt to write for another reason,
for as that is done with a goose-quill, you now know the value of a
goose, and of course you will assist Ellen in taking care of the half-
dozen very fine grey geese which I shall send by Davy.[40]

An essay on good humor

I shall be sending on to Philadelphia a grandson [Thomas Jefferson Randolph, sent for his education] of about fifteen years of
age. . . . Without that bright fancy which captivates, I am in hopes
he possesses sound judgment and much observation, and, what I
value more than all things, good humor. For thus I estimate the
qualities of the mind: 1, good humor; 2, integrity; 3, industry;
4, science. The preference of the first to the second quality may
not at first be acquiesced in; but certainly we had all rather associate with a good-humored, light-principled man than with an
ill-tempered rigorist in morality.[41]

I have mentioned good humor [my dear grandson] as one of the
preservatives of our peace and tranquillity. It is among the most
effectual, and its effect is so well imitated and aided, artificially,
by politeness, that this also becomes an acquisition of first-rate
value. In truth, politeness is artificial good humor, it covers the
natural want of it, and ends by rendering habitual a substitute
nearly equivalent to the real virtue. It is the practice of sacrificing
to those whom we meet in society all the little conveniences and
preferences which will gratify them and deprive us of nothing
worth a moment's consideration; it is the giving a pleasing and
flattering turn to our expressions which will conciliate others and
make them pleased with us as well as themselves. How cheap a

MONTICELLO, THE WEST FRONT

MONTICELLO, INTERIOR. View from the Drawing Room through the Entrance Hall and East Portico to the Valley and Mountains beyond

POPLAR FOREST, THE SOUTH FRONT

My dear Cornelia   Washington Jan. 23. 09

I recieved by the last post your letter which you desire me to answer by the succeeding one. I have accordingly set down to do it, & to find out the points in your letter to which you wish an answer. they are rather blunt & difficult to ascertain. they seem however to be these. 1. you thank me for the Terrapinias. to this I answer, you are welcome. 2. you have pasted it in a book. I answer, that is very well. 3. Virginia reads well and sends her love to me. I answer that that is best of all. that she is a very good girl, and I return her my love. your letter being now fully answered, I have only to add that I inclose you two pieces for your book; and desire you to kiss your Mama & all the young ones for me with assurances of my tenderest love.

Th: Jefferson

TO A GRANDDAUGHTER WHO HAS JUST LEARNED TO WRITE
Jefferson's Letter to Cornelia Jefferson Randolph, Washington, January 23, 1809

MARTHA JEFFERSON RANDOLPH. Portrait by Thomas Sully

price for the good will of another! When this is in return for a rude thing said by another, it brings him to his senses, it mortifies and corrects him in the most salutary way, and places him at the feet of your good nature, in the eyes of the company.

But in stating prudential rules for our government in society, I must not omit the important one of never entering into dispute or argument with another. I never saw an instance of one or two disputants convincing the other by argument. I have seen many, on their getting warm, becoming rude and shooting one another. Conviction is the effect of our own dispassionate reasoning, either in solitude, or weighing within ourselves, dispassionately, what we hear from others, standing uncommitted in argument ourselves. It was one of the rules which, above all others, made Doctor Franklin the most amiable of men in society, 'Never to contradict anybody.' If he was urged to announce an opinion, he did it rather by asking questions, as if for information, or by suggesting doubts.

When I hear another express an opinion which is not mine, I say to myself, he has a right to his opinion, as I to mine; why should I question it? His error does me no injury, and shall I become a Don Quixote, to bring all men by force of argument to one opinion? If a fact be misstated, it is probable he is gratified by a belief of it, and I have no right to deprive him of the gratification. ..

Horn-shaking political animals

There are two classes of disputants most frequently to be met with among us. The first is of young students, just entered the threshold of science, with a first view of its outlines not yet filled up with the details and modifications which a further progress would bring to their knowledge. The other consists of the ill-tempered and rude men in society who have taken up a passion for politics. . . .

You will be more exposed than others to have these animals shaking their horns at you, because of the relation in which you stand with me. Full of political venom, and willing to see me and to hate me as a chief in the antagonist party, your presence will be to them what the vomit grass is to the sick dog, a nostrum for producing ejaculation. Look upon them exactly with that eye, and pity them as objects to whom you can administer only occasional ease. My character is not within their power. It is in the hands of my fellow-citizens at large, and will be consigned to honor or infamy by the verdict of the republican mass of our country, according to what themselves will have seen, not what their enemies and mine shall have said.[42]

No third term: I am panting for retirement

I am panting for retirement, but am as yet nearly two years from that goal. The general solicitations I have received to continue another term give me great consolation, but considerations public as well as personal determine me inflexibly on that measure.[43] That I should lay down my charge at a proper season is as much a duty as to have borne it faithfully. . . . These changes are necessary, too, for the security of republican government. If some period be not fixed, either by the Constitution or by practice, to the services of the First Magistrate, his office, though nominally elective, will in fact be for life; and that will soon degenerate into an inheritance.[44] I have, therefore, requested my fellow-citizens to think of a successor for me, to whom I shall deliver the public concerns with greater joy than I received them.[45]

That some of the Federalists should prefer my continuance to the uncertainty of a successor I can readily believe. . . . There are some who know me personally and who give a credit to my intentions which they deny my understanding. Some who may fear a successor preferring a military glory of a nation to the prosperity and happiness of its individuals. But to the mass of that political sect, it is not the less true, the 4th of March, 1809, will be a day of jubilee, but it will be a day of greater joy to me.[46]

With hands as clean as they are empty

I had hoped to keep the expenses of my office within the limits of its salary, so as to apply my private income entirely to the improvement and enlargement of my estate, but I have not been able to do it.[47] I have the consolation . . . of having added nothing to my private fortune during my public service, and of retiring with hands as clean as they are empty.[48] I have now the gloomy prospect of retiring from office loaded with serious debts, which will materially affect the tranquillity of my retirement. However not being apt to deject myself with evils before they happen, I nourish the hope of getting along.[49]

I mentioned my embarrassments [my dear Martha] merely as a reason for my having been unable to assist Mr. Randolph. The economies which I may practice this year with my crops . . . will not leave serious difficulties on my hands. . . . A [return soon to a] private style of living is a thing of course, and this I shall be able to meet without interfering, as you mention, with the productions of Mr. Randolph's farms, which I wish he should be able to apply entirely to the easement of his own affairs. Indeed I know no difference between his affairs and my own. My only reason for anxiety to keep my property unimpaired is to leave it as a provision for yourselves and your family. This I trust I shall be able to do, and that we shall be able to live in the meantime in love and comfort.[50]

If I can sell the detached tracts of land I own, so as to pay the debts I have contracted here (about $10,000) and they are fully adequate to it, my wish would be to live within the income of my Albemarle possessions. They will yield $2000 rent, besides the profits of the lands and negroes of Monticello and Tufton, the toll mill, and nailery. My Bedford income [from his Poplar Forest estate in Bedford County, Virginia], about $2000 to $2500, would then be free to assist the children as they grow up and want to establish themselves. In all this I look to nothing but the happiness of yourself, Mr. Randolph, and the dear children. My own personal wants will be almost nothing beyond those of a chum of the family. My love to the children, and most of all to yourself.[51]

British outrage on the warship Chesapeake

On the 22d day of June [1807], by a formal order from the British admiral, the frigate *Chesapeake*, leaving her port for distant service, was attacked by one of those vessels which had been lying in our harbors under the indulgences of hospitality, was disabled from proceeding, had several of her crew killed, and four [impressed by the *Leopard*, the British frigate making this surprise attack]. . . . I immediately, by proclamation, interdicted our harbors and waters to all British armed vessels, forbade intercourse with them, and uncertain how far hostilities were intended, and the town of Norfolk, indeed, being threatened with immediate attack, a sufficient force was ordered for the protection of that place, and such other preparations commenced and pursued as the prospect rendered proper. An armed vessel of the United States was dispatched with instructions to our ministers at London to call on that government for the satisfaction and security required by the outrage.[52]

Never since the battle of Lexington have I seen this country in such a state of exasperation as at present, and even that did not produce such unanimity. The Federalists themselves coalesce with us as to the object, though they will return to their trade of censuring every measure taken to obtain it. 'Reparation for the past, and security for the future,' is our motto; but whether they will yield it freely or will require resort to non-intercourse, or to war, is yet to be seen. We prepare for the last. We have actually two thousand men in the field, employed chiefly in covering the exposed coast, and cutting off all supply to the British vessels.[53]

'Reparation for the past, and security for the future'

The ardor displayed by our countrymen . . . gives us the more confidence of support in the demand of *reparation* for the past and *security* for the future, that is to say, an end of impressments. If motives of either justice or interest should produce this from Great Britain, it will save a war; but if they are refused, we shall have gained time for getting in our ships and property, and at least twenty thousand seamen now afloat on the ocean, and who may man two hundred and fifty privateers. The loss of these to us would be worth to Great Britain many victories of the Nile and Trafalgar. The meantime may also be importantly employed in preparations to enable us to give quick and deep blows.[54]

They have often enough, God knows, given us cause of war before; but it has been on points which would not have united the nation. But now they have touched a chord which vibrates in every heart. Now, then, is the time to settle the old and the new.[55]

It is mortifying to wish success to Bonaparte

The new depredations committing on us, with this attack on the *Chesapeake*, and their calling on Portugal to declare on the one side or the other, . . . prove they have coolly calculated it will be to their benefit to have everything on the ocean fair prize, and to support their navy by plundering all mankind. . . . It is really mortifying that we should be forced to wish success to Bonaparte, and to look to his victories as our salvation.[56] The battle of Friedland, armistice with Russia, conquest of Prussia, will be working on the British stomach when they will receive information of the outrage they have committed on us. Yet having entered on the policy . . . of making the property of all nations lawful plunder to support a navy which their own resources cannot support, I doubt if they will readily relinquish it. That war with us had been predetermined may be fairly inferred from the diction of [Admiral] Berkley's order, . . . from its being so timed as to find us in the midst of Burr's rebellion as they expected, . . . and of the wide and sudden spread of their maritime spoliations.[57]

I never expected to be under the necessity of wishing success to Bonaparte. But the English being equally tyrannical at sea as he is on land, and that tyranny bearing on us in every point of either honor or interest, I say 'Down with England' and as for what Bonaparte is then to do to us, let us trust to the chapter of accidents. I cannot, with the Anglomen, prefer a certain present evil to a future hypothetical one.[58] We are now in hourly expectation of hearing from our ministers in London, by the return of the [dispatch vessel] *Revenge*. Whether she will bring us war or peace, or the middle state of non-intercourse, seems suspended in equal balance.[59]

Britain insists on impressments and issues new edicts

Canning's letter [George Canning, the British foreign secretary] . . . is in its aspect and style unfriendly, proud, and harsh. . . . It manifests little concern to avoid war. . . . Congress . . . will take up the question of whether War, Embargo, or Nothing shall be the course. The middle proposition is most likely. In the meantime there is a disposition, 1. to vote a sufficient number of gunboats,

2. a sufficient sum ($750,000) for defensive works, 3. to classify the militia, 4. to establish a naval militia, 5. to give a bounty in lands in Orleans on the west side of the river for a strong settlement of Americans as a militia.[60]

The British regulations had before reduced us to a direct voyage to a single port of their enemies, and it is now believed they will interdict all commerce whatever with them. A proclamation too of that government [commanding the impressment from neutral merchantmen on the high seas of all alleged British seamen] seems to have shut the door on all negotiations with us except as to the single aggression on the *Chesapeake*.

The whole world interdicted by the belligerents

The sum of these mutual enterprises on our national rights is that France and her allies, reserving for further consideration the prohibiting our carrying anything to the British territories, have virtually done it, by restraining our bringing a return cargo from them; and Great Britain, after prohibiting a great proportion of our commerce with France and her allies, is now believed to have prohibited the whole. The whole world is thus laid under interdict by these two nations, and our vessels, their cargoes and crews, are to be taken by the one or the other, for whatever place they may be destined, out of our own limits. If, therefore, on leaving our harbors we are certainly to lose them, is it not better, as to vessels, cargoes, and seamen, to keep them at home? This is submitted to the wisdom of Congress, who alone are competent to provide a remedy.[61]

These decrees and orders, taken together, want little of amounting to a declaration that every neutral vessel found on the high seas, whatsoever be her cargo and whatsoever foreign port be that of her departure or destination, shall be deemed lawful prize; and they prove, more and more, the expediency of retaining our vessels, our seamen, and property within our own harbors until the dangers to which they are exposed can be removed or lessened.[62]

Embargo of 1807, the last card short of war

The embargo keeping at home our vessels, cargoes, and seamen saves us the necessity of making their capture the cause of immediate war; for, if going to England, France had determined to take them, if to any other place, England was to take them. Till they return to some sense of moral duty, therefore, we keep within ourselves. This gives time. Time may produce peace in Europe; peace in Europe removes all causes of difference, till another European war; and by that time our debt may be paid, our revenues clear, and our strength increased.[63]

The embargo appears to be approved, even by the Federalists of every quarter except [New England]. The alternative was between that and war, and in fact it is the last card we have to play, short of war. But if peace does not take place in Europe, and if France and England will not consent to withdraw the operation of their decrees and orders from us, when Congress shall meet in December [of 1808] they will have to consider at what point of time the embargo, continued, becomes a greater evil than war.[64]

Nothing just or temperate has been omitted on our part to retard or to avoid this unprofitable alternative. Our situation will be the more singular as we may have to choose between two enemies who have both furnished cause of war. With one of them we could never come into contact; with the other great injuries may be mutually inflicted and received. Let us still hope to avoid, while we prepare to meet them.[65]

It is very evident that our embargo, added to the exclusions from the Continent, will be most heavily felt in England and Ireland. Liverpool is remonstrating and endeavoring to get the other ports into motion. . . . Congress has just passed an additional embargo law, on which if we act as boldly as I am disposed to do, we can make it effectual. . . . It will show our people that while the embargo gives us double rations, it is starving our enemies.[66] In the meantime [with the American market closed to Britain] great advances are making in the establishment of manufactures.[67]

Federalist merchants oppose and evade the Embargo

They are now playing a game of the most mischievous tendency, without perhaps being themselves aware of it. They are endeavoring to convince England that we suffer more by the embargo than they do, and if they will but hold out awhile, we must abandon it. It is true the time will come when we must abandon it. But if this is before the repeal of the orders of council, we must abandon it only for a state of war. . . . If we have war with England, it will be solely produced by their manoeuvres.[68]

I am clear we ought . . . by a fair experiment know the power of this great weapon, the embargo. Therefore, to propositions to carry flour into the Chesapeake, the Delaware, the Hudson, and other *exporting* places, we should say boldly it is not wanted there for consumption, and the carrying it there is too suspicious to be permitted.[69]

The infractions of the embargo in Maine and Massachusetts are open. . . . The Tories of Boston openly threaten insurrection if their importation of flour is stopped. The next post will stop it.[70] I have requested General Dearborn to be on the alert and fly to the spot where any open and forcible opposition shall be commenced, and to crush it in embryo.[71]

This embargo law is certainly the most embarrassing one we have ever had to execute. I did not expect a crop of so sudden and rank growth of fraud and open opposition by force could have grown up in the United States. I am satisfied . . . that if the orders and decrees are not repealed, and a continuance of the embargo is preferred to war (which sentiment is universal here), Congress must legalize all *means* which may be necessary to obtain its *end*.[72]

Individual rights must yield to the social good

The sentiments expressed [by the Republicans of Boston] show that those who have concurred in them have judged with more candor the intentions of their government, and . . . such, I am persuaded, will be the disposition of the citizens of Massachusetts at large, whenever truth can reach them. Associated with her sister states in a common government, the fundamental principle of which is that the will of the majority is to prevail; sensible that, in the present difficulty, that will has been governed by no local interests or jealousies; that to save permanent rights, temporary sacrifices were necessary; that these have fallen as impartially on all as in a situation so peculiar they could be made to do, she will see in the existing measures a legitimate and honest exercise of the will and wisdom of the whole.[73]

The people approve, and elect Madison President

I have been highly gratified with the late general expressions of public sentiment in favor of a measure which alone could have saved us from immediate war and give time to call home eighty millions of property, twenty or thirty thousand seamen, and two thousand vessels. These are now nearly at home, and furnish a great capital, much of which will go into manufactures and seamen to man a fleet of privateers, whenever our citizens shall prefer war to a longer continuance of the embargo. Perhaps however the whale of the ocean may be tired of the solitude it has made on that element, and return to honest principles; and his brother robber on the land may see that, as to us, the grapes are sour. I think one war enough for the life of one man. . . . Still, if it becomes necessary we must meet it like men, old men indeed, but yet good for something.[74]

Mr. Madison is my successor [having received in 1808 more than two thirds of the electoral votes]. This insures to us a wise and honest administration.[75] In the electoral election Pennsylvania really spoke in a voice of thunder to the monarchists of our country, and while that state continues so firm with the solid mass of Republicanism to the south and west such efforts as we have lately seen in the anti-Republican portion of our country cannot ultimately affect our security. Our enemies may try their cajoleries with my successor. They will find him as immovable in his Republican principles as him whom they have honored with their peculiar enmity.[76]

Pressed by the belligerents to the very wall

The congressional campaign is just opening; three alternatives alone are to be chosen from: 1, embargo; 2, war; 3, submission and tribute. And, wonderful to tell, the last will not want advocates. The real question, however, will lie between the two first, on which there is considerable division. . . . On this occasion I think it is fair to leave to those who are to act on them the decisions they prefer, being to be myself but a spectator. I should not feel justified in directing measures which those who are to execute them would disapprove. Our situation is truly difficult. We have been pressed by the belligerents to the very wall, and all further retreat is impracticable.[77]

The idea of sending a special mission to France or England is not entertained at all here. After so little attention to us from the former, and so insulting an answer from Canning, such a mark of respect as an extraordinary mission would be a degradation against which all minds revolt here. . . . The course the Legislature means to pursue may be inferred from . . . a proposition before them for repealing the embargo in June [of 1809], and then resuming and maintaining by force our right of navigation. . . .

This last trial for peace is not thought desperate. If, as is expected, Bonaparte should be successful in Spain, however every virtuous and liberal sentiment revolts at it, it may induce both powers to be more accommodating with us. England will see here the only asylum for her commerce and manufactures, worth more to her than her orders of council. . . . Should a change in the aspect of affairs in Europe produce this disposition in both powers, our peace and prosperity may be revived and long continue. Otherwise we must again take the tented field, as we did in 1776 under more inauspicious circumstances. . . . If we can keep at peace eight years longer, our income, liberated from debt, will be adequate to any war, without new taxes or loans, and our position and increasing strength put us *hors d'insulte* from any nation.[78]

The Embargo superseded by non-intercourse

I thought Congress had taken their ground firmly for continuing their embargo till June, and then war. But a sudden and unaccountable revolution of opinion took place the last week, chiefly among the New England and New York members, and in a kind of panic they voted the 4th of March for removing the embargo, and by such a majority as gave all reason to believe they would not agree either to war or non-intercourse. This, too, was after we had become satisfied that the Essex Junto [the ultra-Federalist leaders of New England] had found their expectation desperate of inducing the people there to either separation or forcible opposition. The majority of Congress, however, has now rallied to the removing the embargo on the 4th of March, non-intercourse with *France* and *Great Britain*, trade everywhere else, and continuing war preparations.[79]

Our embargo has worked hard. It has in fact Federalized three of the New England states. Connecticut . . . was so before. We have substituted for it a non-intercourse with France and England and their dependencies and a trade to all other places. It is probable the belligerents will take our vessels under their edicts, in which case we shall probably declare war against them.[80] After using every effort which could prevent or delay our being entangled in the war of Europe, that seems now our only resource. . . . Fifty millions of exports, annually sacrificed, are the treble of what war would cost us; besides that, by war we should take something and lose less than at present. . . . But all these concerns I am now leaving to be settled by my friend Mr. Madison.

A prisoner released from his chains

Within a few days I retire to my family, my books and farms; and having gained the harbor myself, I shall look on my friends still buffeting the storm with anxiety indeed, but not with envy. Never did a prisoner released from his chains feel such relief as I shall on shaking off the shackles of power. Nature intended me for the tranquil pursuits of science, by rendering them my supreme delight. But the enormities of the times in which I have lived have forced me to take a part in resisting them, and to commit myself on the boisterous ocean of political passions. I thank God for the opportunity of retiring from them without censure, and carrying with me the most consoling proofs of public approbation. I leave everything in the hands of men so able to take care of them that if we are destined to meet misfortunes it will be because no human wisdom could avert them.[81]

It would have been a great consolation to have left the nation under the assurance of continued peace. Nothing has been spared to effect it; and at no other period of history would such efforts have failed to insure it. For neither belligerent . . . can say that we have in any instance departed from the most faithful neutrality; and certainly none will charge us with a want of forbearance. In the desire of peace, but in full confidence of safety from our unity, our position, and our resources, I shall retire into the bosom of my native state, endeared to me by every tie which can attach the human heart.[82]

To my neighbors of Albemarle

Returning to the scenes of my birth and early life, to the society of those with whom I was raised and who have been ever dear to me, I receive, fellow-citizens and neighbors, with inexpressible pleasure the cordial welcome you are so good as to give me. Long absent on duties which the history of a wonderful era made incumbent on those called to them, the pomp, the turmoil, the bustle and splendor of office have drawn but deeper sighs for the tranquil and irresponsible occupations of private life, for the enjoyment of an affectionate intercourse with you, my neighbors and friends, and the endearments of family love, which nature has given us all as the sweetener of every hour. For these I gladly lay down the distressing burden of power, and seek, with my fellow-citizens, repose and safety under the watchful cares, the labors and perplexities of younger and abler minds. . . .

The part which I have acted on the theatre of public life has been before them, and to their sentence I submit it; but the testimony of my native county, of the individuals who have known me in private life, to my conduct in its various duties and relations is the more grateful, as proceeding from eyewitnesses and observers, from triers of the vicinage. Of you, then, my neighbors, I may ask in the face of the world, 'Whose ox have I taken, or whom have I defrauded? Whom have I oppressed, or of whose hand have I received a bribe to blind mine eyes therewith?' On your verdict I rest with conscious security. Your wishes for my happiness are received with just sensibility, and I offer sincere prayers for your own welfare and prosperity.[83]

CHAPTER XV

Sage of Monticello

THE wave-worn mariner had at last made port. The squire of Monticello who forty years before had been caught up in the turmoil of the Revolution, and launched on 'the boisterous ocean of political passions,' now, at the age of sixty-six, returned to the tranquillity of private life and to those scientific and literary pursuits for which he believed Nature had designed him.

During his absences Monticello and his family had never been far from his thoughts. Now they became literally the center of his life. He was forever improving and embellishing his classic brick villa, that monument to his architectural taste and to his ingenuity. His estate, a little world in itself, provided him with all the occupation demanded by his still vigorous body and his enterprising spirit. He threw himself happily into the congenial tasks of restoring his neglected farmlands, directing his household manufactures, shops, and mills, and building terraced gardens along the mountainside. When the day's work was over he played games, and even ran races on the lawn, with his younger grandchildren, his daughter Martha's little girls and Francis Eppes, the motherless son of Maria. Except for visits in the neighborhood and journeys to his Bedford County estate of Poplar Forest (where he built an octagonal brick cottage), he did not leave his mountain during the remaining seventeen years of his life.

It was inevitable that Americans should now call him the 'Sage of Monticello.' President Madison and politicians throughout the Union wrote to him for advice; Robert Fulton and other inventors submitted their plans to him; educators, economists, scientists, and literary men asked for his opinions. No letter remained unanswered. He expressed his views on an amazing variety of subjects, and revealed a mind that was still fresh, inquiring, and untrammeled. Age and experience had only enlarged his progressive outlook and deepened his democratic faith. He welcomed innovations, whether scientific or social, which promised to improve the lot of mankind. He advised young legislators that the laws and institutions of preceding generations should be altered or repealed if they did not meet present needs; that each generation must be trusted to manage its own affairs in its own way, since the earth belonged to the living and not to the dead. Whatever the means and methods employed, in every generation the goal was eternally the same: the main objects of education, 'the sole objects of all legitimate government,' were always and eternally 'the freedom and happiness of man.'

Nothing pleased him more than the resumption of his old friendship with John Adams, brought about through the efforts of another Revolutionary patriot, Doctor Benjamin Rush of Philadelphia. In a correspondence that was to end only with their deaths, the two old friends out of their ripened wisdom exchanged views on everything under the sun: they compared the number of their progeny, argued amiably over methods of dealing with the 'pseudo-aristocracy' of wealth and birth, discoursed on Plato and religion, reviewed their comradeship during the Revolution, and (united again as in '76) prayed for the success of America's second war for independence.

After endeavoring for years to maintain neutral and national rights by measures of economic coercion, the United States in 1812 had to choose between war or abject submission to Britain. Jefferson had no doubt as to what the choice would be, and should be. The unrelenting aggressions of an England then ruled by reactionary Tories had forced him from his hobby, peace.

He followed the War of 1812 with keen interest, encouraged and sustained Madison, and roundly denounced the Anglo-Federalist extremists in New England, whose Hartford Convention of 1814 was regarded as preliminary to disunion. He never despaired of the unity of the Republic, or its ability to wage war successfully. He cheerfully accepted personal losses caused by the war, and when the British burned the Capitol at Washington and destroyed the Library of Congress, he turned over to the government his most cherished possession, his large and valuable library.

After the triumph of New Orleans and the Peace of Ghent, the Sage of Monticello advised his countrymen that the best interests of both nations required that wartime hatreds should be relegated to history and smothered in the living mind. Toward the recent enemy he advocated a policy as tolerant and as wise as that which in 1801 had restored political unity to his divided country. Jefferson looked forward hopefully to a change of spirit and of rulers in England which would permit, what he most ardently desired, future Anglo-American fraternity.

My farms, my garden, and my grandchildren

I am retired to Monticello, where, in the bosom of my family, and surrounded by my books, I enjoy a repose to which I have been long a stranger. My mornings are devoted to correspondence. From breakfast to dinner, I am in my shops, my garden, or on horseback among my farms; from dinner to dark, I give to society and recreation with my neighbors and friends; and from candle-light to early bedtime, I read. My health is perfect, and my strength considerably reinforced by the activity of the course I pursue; perhaps it is as great as usually falls to the lot of near sixty-seven years of age.

I talk of ploughs and harrows, of seeding and harvesting, with my neighbors, and of politics too, if they choose, with as little reserve as the rest of my fellow-citizens, and feel, at length, the blessing of being free to say and do what I please without being responsible for it to any mortal.[1]

No occupation is so delightful to me as the culture of the earth, and no culture comparable to that of the garden. Such a variety of subjects, some one always coming to perfection, the failure of one thing repaired by the success of another, and instead of one harvest a continued one through the year. Under a total want of demand except for our family table, I am still devoted to the garden. But though an old man, I am but a young gardener.[2]

Francis [Eppes, his grandson] has enjoyed constant and perfect health, and is as happy as the day is long. He has had little success as yet with either his traps or bow and arrows. He is now engaged in a literary contest with his cousin Virginia, both having begun to write together.[3] Your family of silkworms [my dear Cornelia] is reduced to a single individual. That is now spinning his broach. To encourage Virginia and Mary to take care of it, I tell them that as soon as they can get weddinggowns from this spinner they shall be married. I propose the same to you, that, in order to hasten its work, you may hasten home, for we all wish much to see you and to express in person, rather than by letter, the assurance of our affectionate love.   P.S. The girls desire me to add a postscript to inform you that Mrs. Higginbotham has just given them new dolls.[4]

I must desire you [Thomas Jefferson Randolph, then in Philadelphia] to send me nine feet of brass chain to hang the alabaster lamp ... and four dozen phials ... for holding garden seeds. ... I must pray you to put half a dozen pounds of scented hair powder into the same box. None is to be had here, and it is almost a necessary of life with me.[5]

Albemarle soil and neighbors; contour ploughing

This country ... is red and hilly, very like much of the country of Champagne and Burgundy, on the route of Sens, Vermanton, Vitteaux, Dijon, and along the Côte to Chagny, excellently adapted to wheat, maize, and clover; like all mountainous countries it is perfectly healthy. ... There is navigation for boats of six tons from Charlottesville to Richmond, the nearest tidewater and principal market for our produce. The country is what we call well inhabited, there being in our county, Albemarle, ... about twenty thousand inhabitants, or twenty-seven to a square mile, of whom, however, one half are people of color either slaves or free. The society is much better than is common in country situations; perhaps there is not a better *country* society in the United States. But do not imagine this a Parisian or an academical society. It consists of plain, honest, and rational neighbors, some of them well informed and men of reading, all superintending their farms, hospitable and friendly.[6]

The present delightful weather has drawn us all into our farms and gardens. We have had the most devastating rain which has ever fallen within my knowledge. . . . I have never seen the fields so much injured. Mr. Randolph's farm [Edgehill] is the only one which has not suffered. His horizontal furrows arrested the water at every step till it was absorbed or at least had deposited the soil it had taken up. Everybody in this neighborhood is adopting his method of ploughing.[7]

The plough is to the farmer what the wand is to the sorcerer. Its effect is really like sorcery. . . . We have discovered a new use for it equal in value almost to its services before known. . . . We now plough horizontally, following the curvatures of the hills and hollows. . . . In a farm horizontally and deeply ploughed scarcely an ounce of soil is now carried off from it. In point of beauty nothing can exceed that of the waving lines and rows winding along the face of the hills and valleys.[8]

I am not afraid of inventions: ploughs and submarines

The Agricultural Society of the Seine sent me one of Guillaume's famous ploughs, famous for taking but half the moving power of their best ploughs before used. They, at the same time, requested me to send them one of our best, with my mould-board to it. . . . I have made the plough and am greatly deceived if it is not found to give less resistance than theirs. In fact I think it is the finest plough which has ever been constructed in America.[9] It will be yet some time (perhaps a month) before my workmen will be free to make the plough I shall send you [Charles W. Peale]. You will be at perfect liberty to use the form of the mould-board, as all the world is, having never thought of monopolizing by patent any useful idea which happens to offer itself to me.[10]

Just esteem . . . attached itself to Dr. Franklin's science because he always endeavored to direct it to something useful in private life. The chemists have not been attentive enough to . . . domestic objects, to malting, for instance, brewing, making cider, to fermentation and distillation generally, to the making of bread, butter, cheese, soap, to the incubation of eggs, etc., [so as to] make the chemistry of these subjects intelligible to our good housewives.[11]

I am not afraid of new inventions or improvements, nor bigoted to the practices of our forefathers. It is that bigotry which keeps the Indians in a state of barbarism . . . and still keeps Connecticut where their ancestors were when they landed on these shores. . . . Where a new invention is supported by well known principles, and promises to be useful, it ought to be tried. . . . That the Tories should be against you [Robert Fulton] is in character.[12] Your steamboats . . . will be the source of . . . permanent blessing to your country. I hope your torpedoes will equally triumph over doubting friends and presumptuous enemies.[13] As we cannot meet the British with an equality of physical force, we must supply it by other devices . . . by subaqueous guns, torpedoes, or diving boats. . . . I confess I have more hopes of . . . the submarine boat. . . . No law of nature opposes it, and in that case nothing is to be despaired of by human invention.[14]

Imported sheep, and my household manufactures

I thank you [Madison] for your promised attention to my portion of the Merinos. . . . What shall we do with them? I have been so disgusted with the scandalous extortions lately practiced in the sale of these animals, and with the description of patriotism and praise to the sellers, . . . that I am disposed to consider as right whatever is the reverse of what they have done. . . . The few who can afford it should incur the risk and expense of all new improvements, and . . . I will throw out a first idea. . . . Give all the full-blooded males we can raise to the different counties of our state, one to each, as fast as we can furnish them. . . . Our whole state may thus . . . be filled in a very few years with this valuable race, and more satisfaction result to ourselves than money ever administered to the bosom of a shaver. There will be danger that what is here proposed, though but an act of ordinary duty, may be perverted into one of ostentation, but malice will always find bad motives for good actions. Shall we therefore never do good?[15]

My household manufactures are just getting into operation on the scale of a carding machine costing $60 only, which may be worked by a girl of twelve years old, a spinning machine, which may be made for $10, carrying six spindles of wool, to be worked by a girl also, another which can be made for $25, carrying 12 spindles for cotton, and a loom with a flying shuttle weaving its 20 yards a day. I need 2000 yards of linen, cotton, cotton and woolen yearly, to clothe my family, which this machinery, costing $150 only, and worked by two women and two girls, will more than furnish.

For fine goods there are numerous establishments at work in the large cities, and many more daily growing up; and of Merinos we have some thousands, and these multiplying fast. We consider a sheep for every person as sufficient for their woolen clothing. . . . In other articles we are equally advanced, so that nothing is more certain than that . . . we shall never again go to England for a shilling where we have gone for a dollar's worth.[16] Out of the evils of impressment and of the orders of council a great blessing for us will grow. I have not formerly been an advocate for great manufactories . . . but other considerations entering into the question have settled my doubts.[17]

I have indeed two great measures at heart

A part of my occupation, and by no means the least pleasing, is the direction of the studies of such young men as ask it. They place themselves in the neighboring village, and have the use of my library and counsel, and make a part of my society. . . . I endeavor to keep their attention fixed on the main objects of all science, the freedom and happiness of man. So that coming to bear a share in the councils and government of their country, they will keep ever in view the sole objects of all legitimate government.[18]

I have indeed two great measures at heart, without which no republic can maintain itself in strength. 1. That of general education, to enable every man to judge for himself what will secure or endanger his freedom. 2. To divide every county into hundreds, of such size that all the children of each will be within reach of a central school in it. But this division looks to many other fundamental provisions. Every hundred . . . should be a corporation to manage all its concerns . . . as the selectmen of the Eastern townships. . . . These little republics would be the main strength of the great one. We owe to them the vigor given to our Revolution in its commencement in the Eastern States, and by them the Eastern States were enabled to repeal the embargo in opposition to the Middle, Southern, and Western States, and their large and lubberly divisions into counties which can never be assembled. General orders are given out from a centre to the foreman of every hundred, as to the sergeants of an army, and the whole nation is thrown into energetic action, in the same direction in one instant and as one man, and becomes absolutely irresistible.[19]

Public libraries and an academical village

Nothing would do more extensive good at small expense than . . . a small circulating library in every county, to consist of a few well-chosen books to be lent to the people . . . such as would give them a general view of other history and particular view of that of their own country, a tolerable knowledge of geography, the elements of natural philosophy, of agriculture and mechanics. . . . My services in this way are freely at . . . command.[20]

No one more sincerely wishes the spread of information among mankind than I do, and none has greater confidence in its effect towards supporting free and good government. I am sincerely rejoiced, therefore, to find that so excellent a fund has been provided for this noble purpose in Tennessee. . . . I consider the common plan [for colleges] followed in this country, but not in others, of making one large and expensive building, as unfortunately erroneous. It is infinitely better to erect a small and separate lodge for each professorship, with only a hall below for his class and two chambers above for himself; joining these lodges by barracks for a certain portion of the students, opening into a covered way to give a dry communication between all the schools. The whole of these arranged around an open square of grass and trees would make it, what it should be in fact, an academical village. . . . Much observation and reflection on these institutions have long convinced me that the large and crowded buildings in which youths are pent up are equally unfriendly to health, to study, to manners, morals, and order.[21]

Our Negroes and Indians

No person living wishes more sincerely than I do to see a complete refutation of the doubts I have myself entertained and expressed on the grade of understanding allotted to [the Negro] by nature. . . . But whatever be their degree of talent it is no measure of their rights. Because Sir Isaac Newton was superior to others in understanding, he was not therefore lord of the person or property of others.[22] On the subject of slavery [my views] have long since been in the possession of the public, and time has only served to give them stronger root. The love of justice and the love of country plead equally the cause of these people, and it is a moral reproach to us that they should have pleaded it so long in vain. . . . Yet the hour of emancipation is advancing, in the march of time. It will come.[23]

The plan of civilizing the Indians is undoubtedly a great improvement on the ancient and totally ineffectual one of beginning with religious missionaries. Our experience has shown that this must be the last step of the process. The following is what has been successful: 1st, to raise cattle, etc., and thereby acquire a knowledge of the value of property; 2d, arithmetic, to calculate that value; 3d, writing, to keep accounts, and here they begin to enclose farms, and the men to labor, the women to spin and weave; 4th, to read *Aesop's Fables* and *Robinson Crusoe* are their first delight. The Creeks and Cherokees are advanced thus far, and the Cherokees are now instituting a regular government.[24]

Mathematics was ever my favorite study

I write . . . from a place [Poplar Forest] ninety miles from Monticello, near the New London of this state, which I visit three or four times a year, and stay from a fortnight to a month at a time. I have fixed myself comfortably, keep some books here, bring others occasionally, am in the solitude of a hermit, and quite at leisure to attend to my absent friends. . . . Having to conduct my grandson through his course of mathematics, I have resumed that study with great avidity. It was ever my favorite one. We have no theories there, no uncertainties remain on the mind; all is demonstration and satisfaction.[25] And thanks to the good foundation laid at college by my old master and friend Small, I am doing it with a delight and success beyond my expectation. . . . I have a pocket sextant of miraculous accuracy, considering its microscopic graduation. With this I have ascertained the latitude of Poplar Forest (say New London) by multiplied observations, and lately that of Willis Mountains.[26]

Friendship is like wine

My journey to [Poplar Forest] in a hard-going gig gave me great sufferings. . . . The loss of the power of taking exercise would be a sore affliction to me. . . . The sedentary character of my public occupations sapped a constitution naturally sound and vigorous, and draws it to an earlier close. But it will still last as long as I wish it. There is a fullness of time when men should go, and not occupy too long the ground to which others have a right to advance. We must continue while here to exchange occasionally our mutual good wishes. I find friendship to be like wine, raw when new, ripened with age, the true old man's milk and restorative cordial.[27]

I received with sensibility your observations on the discontinuance of friendly correspondence between Mr. Adams and myself, and the concern you [Doctor Benjamin Rush] take in its restoration. This discontinuance has not proceeded from me. . . . You know the perfect coincidence of principle and action in the early part of the Revolution . . . between Mr. Adams and myself. . . . And although he swerved, afterwards, towards the principles of the English constitution, our friendship did not abate on that account. . . . A little time and reflection effaced in my mind this temporary dissatisfaction [over Adams' 'midnight appointments']. . . . Two or three years after, having had the misfortune to lose a daughter between whom and Mrs. Adams there had been a considerable attachment, she made it the occasion of writing me a letter in which, with the tenderest expressions of concern at this event, she carefully avoided a single one of friendship towards myself, and even concluded it with the wishes 'of her who *once* took pleasure in subscribing herself your friend, Abigail Adams.' Unpromising as was the complexion of this letter, I determined to make an effort towards removing the cloud from between us. . . . I soon found . . . that conciliation was desperate. . . . I shall certainly not be wanting in anything on my part which may second your efforts.[28]

All my old affections revived for Honest John Adams

I recur . . . to the subject of your kind letters relating to Mr. Adams and myself, which a late occurrence has again presented to me. . . . Two of . . . my neighbors and friends . . . during the last summer [1811] ... fell into company with Mr. Adams, and by his invitation passed a day with him at Braintree. He spoke out to them everything which came uppermost, and as it occurred, to his mind. ... Among many other topics he adverted to the unprincipled licentiousness of the press against myself, adding, 'I always loved Jefferson, and still love him.'

This is enough for me. I only needed this knowledge to revive towards him all the affections of the most cordial moment of our lives. ... I knew him to be always an honest man, often a great one, but sometimes incorrect and precipitate in his judgments. ... I have ever done him justice myself, and defended him when assailed by others, with the single exception as to political opinions. But with a man possessing so many other estimable qualities, why should we be dissocialized by mere differences of opinion in politics, in religion, in philosophy, or anything else? His opinions are as honestly formed as my own. Our different views of the same subject are the result of a difference in our organization and experience. I never withdrew from the society of any man on this account, ... much less should I do it from one with whom I had gone through, with hand and heart, so many trying scenes.[29]

We rode through the storm with heart and hand

A letter from you [John Adams] calls up recollections very dear to my mind. It carries me back to the times when, beset with difficulties and dangers, we were fellow-laborers in the same cause, struggling for what is most valuable to man, his right of self-government. Laboring always at the same oar, with some wave ever ahead threatening to overwhelm us, and yet passing harmless under our bark, we knew not how we rode through the storm with heart and hand, and made a happy port. Still we did not expect to be without rubs and difficulties; and we have had them. First, the detention of the western posts, then the ... outlawing our commerce with France. ... In your day, French depredations; in mine, English, and the Berlin and Milan decrees; now, the English orders of council and the piracies they authorize. ... And so we have gone on, and so we shall go on, puzzled and prospering beyond example in the history of men.

And I do believe we shall continue to grow, to multiply and prosper until we exhibit an association powerful, wise, and happy beyond what has yet been seen by men. As for France and England, with all their pre-eminence in science the one is a den of robbers and the other of pirates. And if science produces no better fruits than tyranny, murder, rapine, and destitution of national morality, I would rather wish our country to be ignorant, honest, and estimable, as our neighboring savages are.

But whither is senile garrulity leading me? Into politics, of which I have taken final leave. I think little of them and say less. I have given up newspapers in exchange for Tacitus and Thucydides, for Newton and Euclid, and I find myself much the happier. Sometimes, indeed, I look back to former occurrences, in remembrance of our old friends and fellow-laborers who have fallen before us. Of the signers of the Declaration of Independence I see now living not more than half a dozen on your side of the Potomac, and on this side, myself alone. You and I have been wonderfully spared, and myself with remarkable health and a considerable activity of body and mind. I am on horseback three or four hours of every day; visit three or four times a year a possession I have ninety miles distant, performing the winter journey on horseback. I walk little, however, a single mile being too much for me, and I live in the midst of my grandchildren, one of whom has lately promoted me to be a great-grandfather.

I have heard with pleasure that you also retain good health, and a greater power of exercise in walking than I do. But I would rather have heard this from yourself, and that, writing a letter like mine, full of egotisms, and of details of your health, your habits, occupations and enjoyments, I should have the pleasure of knowing that in the race of life you do not keep, in its physical decline, the same distance ahead of me which you have done in political honors and achievements. No circumstances have lessened the interest I feel in these particulars respecting yourself; none have suspended for one moment my sincere esteem for you, and I now salute you with unchanged affection and respect.[30]

Ahead on the score of progeny

A kind note at the foot of Mr. Adams' letter ... reminds me of the duty of saluting you [Abigail Adams] with friendship and respect. . . . In no course of life have I been ever more closely pressed by business than in the present. Much of this proceeds from my own affairs, much from the calls of others; leaving little time for indulgence in my greatest of all amusements, reading. Dr. Franklin used to say that when he was young and had time to read he had not books; and now when he has become old and had books, he had no time. Perhaps it is that when habit has strengthened our sense of duties, they leave us no time for other things; but when young we neglect them and this gives us time for anything.

However, I will now take time to ask you how you do, how you have done? and to express the interest I take in whatever affects your happiness. . . . I have compared notes with Mr. Adams on the score of progeny and find I am ahead of him and think I am in a fair way to keep so. I have ten and one-half grandchildren, and two and three-fourths great-grandchildren, and these fractions will ere long become units.[31]

The true aristocracy

I agree with you [John Adams] that there is a natural aristocracy among men. The grounds of this are virtue and talents. Formerly, bodily powers gave place among the aristoi. But since the invention of gunpowder has armed the weak as well as the strong with missile death, bodily strength, like beauty, good humor, politeness, and other accomplishments, has become but an auxiliary ground of distinction. There is also an artificial aristocracy founded on wealth and birth, without either virtue or talents, for with these it would belong to the first class. The natural aristocracy I consider as the most precious gift of nature for the instruction, the trusts, and government of society. And indeed it would have been inconsistent in creation to have formed man for the social state and not to have provided virtue and wisdom enough to manage the concerns of the society. May we not even say that that form of government is the best which provides the most effectually for a pure selection of these natural aristoi into the offices of government? The artificial aristocracy is a mischievous ingredient in government, and provision should be made to prevent its ascendancy.

On the question what is the best provision, you and I differ; but we differ as rational friends. . . . You think it best to put the pseudo-aristoi into a separate chamber of legislation, where they may be hindered from doing mischief by their coordinate branches, and where, also, they may be a protection to wealth against the agrarian and plundering enterprises of the majority of the people. I think that to give them power in order to prevent them from doing mischief is arming them for it, and increasing instead of remedying the evil. . . . I think the best remedy is exactly that provided by all our constitutions, to leave to the citizens the free election and separation of the aristoi from the pseudo-aristoi, of the wheat from the chaff. . . .

It is probable that our difference of opinion may in some measure be produced by a difference of character in those among whom we live. . . . There seems to be [in Massachusetts and Connecticut] a traditionary reverence for certain families which has rendered the officers of the government nearly hereditary. . . . But although this . . . may in some degree be founded in real family merit, yet in a much higher degree it has proceeded from your strict alliance of Church and State. These families are canonized in the eyes of the people on common principles, 'You tickle me, and I will tickle you.'

In Virginia we have nothing of this. . . . Laws drawn by myself laid the axe to the root of pseudo-aristocracy. And had another which I had prepared been adopted·. . . our work would have been complete. It was a bill for the more general diffusion of learning. . . . Worth and genius would thus have been sought out from every condition of life, and completely prepared by education for defeating the competition of wealth and birth for public trusts. . . . I have great hope that some patriotic spirit will . . . call it up and make it the keystone of the arch of our government.[32]

Each generation should govern itself

The idea that institutions established for the use of the nation cannot be touched nor modified, even to make them answer their end, because of rights gratuitously supposed in those employed to manage them in trust for the public, may perhaps be a salutary provision against the abuses of a monarch, but is most absurd against the nation itself. Yet our lawyers and priests generally inculcate this doctrine, and suppose that preceding generations held the earth more freely than we do; had a right to impose laws on us, unalterable by ourselves, and that we, in like manner, can make laws and impose burdens on future generations which they will have no right to alter; in fine, that the earth belongs to the dead and not the living.[33]

The earth belongs to the living, not to the dead. The will and the power of man expire with his life, by nature's law. . . . Each generation has the usufruct of the earth during the period of its continuance. When it ceases to exist, the usufruct passes on to the succeeding generation, free and unencumbered. . . . The period of a generation, or the term of its life, is determined by the laws of mortality. . . . I turn, for instance, to Buffon's tables . . . and I find that of . . . the adults . . . living at one moment, a majority of whom act for the society, one half will be dead in eighteen years and eight months.[34] It is . . . found . . . convenient to suffer the laws of our predecessors to stand on our implied assent. . . . But this does not lessen the right . . . to repeal whenever a change of circumstances or of will calls for it. Habit alone confounds what is civil practice with natural right.[35]

Religion and morality: social good the test of virtue

I hold (without appeal to revelation) that when we take a view of the universe, in its parts, general or particular, it is impossible for the human mind not to perceive and feel a conviction of design, con-summate skill, and indefinite power in every atom of its composition. The movements of the heavenly bodies, so exactly held in their course by the balance of centrifugal and centripetal forces; the structure of our earth itself, with its distribution of lands, waters, and atmosphere; animal and vegetable bodies, examined in all their minutest particles; insects, mere atoms of life, yet as perfectly organized as man or mammoth; the mineral substances, their gen-eration and uses; it is impossible, I say, for the human mind not to believe that there is in all this design, cause, and effect up to an ultimate cause, a Fabricator of all things from matter and motion, their Preserver and Regulator.[36]

Reading, reflection, and time have convinced me that the inter-ests of society require the observation of those moral precepts only in which all religions agree (for all forbid us to murder, steal, plunder, or bear false witness), and that we should not intermeddle with the particular dogmas in which all religions differ, and which are totally unconnected with morality. In all of them we see good men, and as many in one as another. The varieties in the structure and action of the human mind as in those of the body are the work of our Creator, against which it cannot be a religious duty to erect the standard of uniformity.[37] It is a singular anxiety which some people have that we should all think alike. Would the world be more beautiful were all our faces alike? Were our tempers, our talents, our tastes, our forms, our wishes, aversions, and pursuits cast exactly in the same mould? If no varieties existed in the animal, vegetable, or mineral creation, but all move strictly uniform, catholic, and orthodox, what a world of physical and moral monotony would it be! [38]

Truth is certainly a branch of morality, and a very important one to society. But, presented as its foundation, it is as if a tree taken up by the roots had its stem reversed in the air, and one of its branches planted in the ground. Some have made the *love of God* the foundation of morality. This, too, is but a branch of our moral duties. . . . If we did a good act merely from the love of God . . . whence arises the morality of the atheist? . . . The *to kalon* of others . . . is not even a branch of morality. . . . Self-interest, or rather self-love, or *egoism*, has been more plausibly substituted as the basis of morality. But . . . indeed it is exactly its counterpart. . . . Good acts give us pleasure, but how happens it that they give us pleasure? Because nature hath implanted in our breasts a love of others, a sense of duty to them, a moral instinct, in short, which prompts us irresistibly to feel and to succor their distresses. . . . Nature has constituted *utility* to man the standard and test of virtue.[39]

The whimsies and jargon of Plato

I am just returned from one of my long absences, having been at my other home for five weeks past. Having more leisure there than here for reading, I amused myself with reading seriously Plato's *Republic*. I am wrong, however, in calling it amusement, for it was the heaviest task-work I ever went through. I had occasionally before taken up some of his other works, but scarcely ever had patience to go through a whole dialogue. While wading through the whimsies, the puerilities, and unintelligible jargon of this work, I laid it down often to ask myself how it could have been that the world should have so long consented to give reputation to such nonsense as this? . . .

In truth, he is one of the race of genuine sophists, who has escaped the oblivion of his brethren, first by the elegance of his diction, but chiefly by the adoption and incorporation of his whimsies into the body of artificial Christianity. His foggy mind is forever presenting the semblances of objects which, half seen through a mist, can be defined neither in form nor dimensions. Yet this, which should have consigned him to early oblivion, really procured him immortality of fame and reverence. The Christian priesthood, finding the doctrines of Christ levelled to every understanding, and too plain to need explanation, saw in the mysticism of Plato materials with which they might build up an artificial system which might, from its indistinctness, admit everlasting controversy, give employment for their order, and introduce it to profit, power, and pre-eminence. The doctrines which flowed from the lips of Jesus himself are within the comprehension of a child; but thousands of volumes have not yet explained the Platonisms engrafted on them; and for this obvious reason, that nonsense can never be explained. . . .

But why am I dosing you [John Adams] with these antediluvian topics? Because I am glad to have someone to whom they are familiar, and who will not receive them as if dropped from the moon. Our post-Revolutionary youth are born under happier stars than you and I were. They acquire all learning in their mother's womb, and bring it into the world ready made. . . . I hope our successors will turn their attention to the advantages of education. I mean of education on the broad scale, and not that of the petty *academies*, as they call themselves, . . . where one or two men possessing Latin and sometimes Greek, a knowledge of the globes, and the first six books of Euclid, imagine and communicate this as the sum of science.[40]

On the American language

The scanty foundation laid in at school has carried me through a life of much hasty writing, more indebted for style to reading and memory than to rules of grammar. I . . . appeal to usage as the arbiter of language; and justly consider that as giving law to grammar, and not grammar to usage. . . . Purists . . . would destroy all strength and beauty of style by subjecting it to a rigorous compliance with their rules. Fill up all the ellipses and syllepses of Tacitus, Sallust, Livy, etc., and the elegance and force of their sententious brevity are extinguished. . . . Wire-draw these expressions by filling up the whole syntax and sense, and they become dull paraphrases on rich sentiments.[41] To explain my meaning by an English example, I will quote the motto of one, I believe, of the regicides of Charles I [also the motto on Jefferson's seal ring], 'Rebellion *to* tyrants is obedience to God.' Correct its syntax, 'Rebellion *against* tyrants is obedience to God,' it has lost all the strength and beauty of the antithesis.[42]

I am no friend, therefore, to what is called *Purism* but a zealous one to the *Neology* which has introduced these two words without the authority of any dictionary. I consider the one as destroying the verve and beauty of language, while the other improves both and adds to its copiousness. . . . The Edinburgh Reviewers, the ablest critics of the age, set their faces against the introduction of new words into the English language; they are particularly apprehensive that the writers of the United States will adulterate it. Certainly so great growing a population, spread over such an extent of country, with such a variety of climates, of productions, of arts, must enlarge their language to make it answer its purpose of expressing all ideas, the new as well as the old. The new circumstances under which we are placed call for new words, new phrases, and for the transfer of old words to new objects. . . . The dread of innovation there . . . has I fear palsied the spirit of improvement. Here, where all is new, no innovation is feared which offers good. . . . And should the language of England continue stationary we shall probably enlarge our employment of it until its new character may separate it, in name as well as in power, from the mother-tongue.[43]

America has a hemisphere to itself

And behold! another example of man rising in his might and bursting the chains of his oppressor, and in the same hemisphere. Spanish America is all in revolt. The insurgents are triumphant in many of the states, and will be so in all. But there the danger is that the cruel arts of their oppressors have enchained their minds, have kept them in the ignorance of children, and as incapable of self-government as children.[44]

But in whatever governments they end they will be *American* governments, no longer to be involved in the never-ceasing broils of Europe. . . . America has a hemisphere to itself. It must have its separate system of interests, which must not be subordinated to those of Europe. The insulated state in which nature has placed the American continent should so far avail it that no spark of war kindled in the other quarters of the globe should be wafted across the wide oceans which separate us from them. And it will be so.[45]

What, in short, is the whole system of Europe towards America but an atrocious and insulting tyranny? One hemisphere of the earth, separated from the other by wide seas on both sides, having a different system of interests flowing from different climates, different soils, different productions, different modes of existence, and its own local relations and duties, is made subservient to all the petty interests of the other, to *their* laws, *their* regulations, *their* passions and wars.[46]

Peace is our principle and our interest

The hurricane which is now blasting the world, physical and moral, has prostrated all the mounds of reason as well as right.[47] In the eternal revolution of ages, the destinies have placed our portion of existence amidst such scenes of tumult and outrage as no other period within our knowledge had presented. Every government but one on the continent of Europe demolished, a conqueror roaming over the earth with havoc and destruction, a pirate spreading misery and ruin over the face of the ocean.[48] It would have been perfect Quixotism in us to have . . . undertaken the redress of all wrongs against a world avowedly rejecting all regard to right. We have, therefore, remained in peace, suffering frequent injuries but, on the whole, multiplying, improving, prospering beyond all example. . . . When these gladiators shall have worried each other into ruin or reason, instead of lying among the dead on the bloody arena we shall have acquired a growth and strength which will place us *hors d'insulte*. Peace then has been our principle, peace is our interest, and peace has saved to the world this only plant of free and rational government now existing in it.

If it can still be preserved we shall soon see the final extinction of our national debt, and liberation of our revenues for the defense and improvement of our country. These revenues will be levied entirely on the rich, [who now] alone use imported articles, and on these alone the whole taxes of the general government are levied. . . . Our revenues liberated . . . and its surplus applied to canals, roads, schools, etc., the farmer will see his government supported, his children educated, and the face of his country made a paradise by the contributions of the rich alone, without his being called on to spend a cent from his earnings. However, therefore, we may have been reproached for pursuing our Quaker system, time will affix the stamp of wisdom on it, and the happiness and prosperity of our citizens will attest its merit.[49]

The last hope of human liberty

Federalism, stripped as it now nearly is of its landed and laboring support, is monarchism and Anglicism, and whenever our own dissensions shall let these in upon us the last ray of free government closes on the horizon of the world. . . . The clouds which have appeared for some time to be gathering around us have given me anxiety lest an enemy always on the watch, always prompt and firm, and acting in well-disciplined phalanx, should find an opening to dissipate hopes with the loss of which I would wish that of life itself.[50] The situation of our country . . . is such as . . . will require the union of all its friends to resist its enemies within and without. If we schismatize on either men or measures, if we do not act in phalanx, as when we rescued it from the satellites of monarchism, I will not say our *party*, for the term is false and degrading, but our *nation* will be undone. For the Republicans are the *nation*. Their opponents are but a faction, weak in numbers, but powerful and profuse in the command of money, and backed by a nation powerful also and profuse in the use of the same means. . . . The last hope of human liberty in this world rests on us.[51]

Tory England forces the issue of war or submission

We are to have war, then? I believe so, and that it is necessary. Every hope from time, patience, and the love of peace is exhausted, and war or abject submission are the only alternative left us. I am forced from my hobby, peace.[52]

Never before has there been an instance of a nation's bearing so much as we have borne. Two items alone in our catalogue of wrongs will forever acquit us of being the aggressors: the impressment of our seamen, and the excluding us from the ocean. The first foundations of the social compact would be broken up were we definitively to refuse to its members the protection of their persons and property while in their lawful pursuits. ... We believe no more in Bonaparte's fighting merely for the liberty of the seas than in Great Britain's fighting for the liberties of mankind. ... We resist the enterprises of England first because they first come vitally home to us. And our feelings repel the logic of bearing the lash of George the Third for fear of that of Bonaparte at some future day. When the wrongs of France shall reach us with equal effect we shall resist them also. But one at a time is enough; and having offered a choice to the champions, England first takes up the gauntlet.

The English newspapers suppose me the personal enemy of their nation. I am not so. I am an enemy to its injuries, as I am to those of France. ... Had I been personally hostile to England, and biased in favor of either the character or views of her great antagonist, the affair of the *Chesapeake* put war into my hand. I had only to open it and let havoc loose. But ... now that a definitive adherence to her impressments and orders of council renders war no longer avoidable, my earnest prayer is that our government may enter into no compact of common cause with the other belligerent, but keep us free to make a separate peace whenever England will separately give us peace and future security.[53]

The War of 1812, a second war for independence

To make war on both would have been ridiculous. In order, therefore, to single out an enemy, we offered to both that if either would revoke its hostile decrees, and the other should refuse, we would interdict all intercourse whatever with that other; which would be war of course, as being an avowed departure from neutrality. France accepted the offer, and revoked her decrees as to us. ... It was not till England had taken one thousand of our ships, and impressed into her service more than six thousand of our citizens; till she had declared, by the proclamation of her Prince Regent, that she would not repeal her aggressive orders *as to us* until

Bonaparte should have repealed his *as to all nations*; till her minister, in formal conference with ours, declared that no proposition for protecting our seamen from being impressed, under color of taking their own, was practicable or admissible; that, the door to justice and to all amicable arrangement being closed, and negotiation become both desperate and dishonorable, we concluded that the war she had for years been waging against us might as well become a war on both sides.[54]

I have no fear of the award, and believe that this second weaning from British principles, British attachments, British manners and manufactures, will be salutary, and will form an epoch of a spirit of nationalism and of consequent prosperity which could never have resulted from a continued subordination to the interests and influence of England.[55]

The infamous intrigues of Great Britain to destroy our government [through John Henry and other secret agents sent among the New England Federalists], and with the Indians to tomahawk our women and children, prove that the cession of Canada, their fulcrum for these Machiavellian levers, must be a *sine qua non* at a treaty of peace.[56] 'Indemnification for the past and security for the future' should be painted on our banners. For 1000 ships taken and 6000 seamen impressed, give us Canada for indemnification, and the only security they can give us against their Henrys and the savages; and agree that the American flag shall protect the persons of those sailing under it, both parties exchanging engagements that neither will receive the seamen of the other on board their vessels.[57]

Land defeats and sea victories

Our thirty years of peace had taken off or superannuated all our Revolutionary officers of experience and grade; and our first draught in the lottery of untried characters had been most unfortunate. The delivery of the fort and army of Detroit by the traitor Hull; the disgrace at Queenstown, under Van Rensselaer; the massacre at Frenchtown under Winchester; and surrender of Boerstler in an open field to one third of his own numbers, were the inauspicious beginnings of the first year of our warfare.[58]

In every instance our men, militia as well as regulars, have acted with an intrepidity which would have honored veteran legions, and have proved that, had their officers understood their duty as well as those of our little navy, they would have shown themselves equally superior to our enemy who had dared to despise us.[59] I confess that three frigates taken by our gallant little navy do not balance in my mind three armies lost by the treachery, cowardice, or incapacity of those to whom they were intrusted. I see that our men are good, and only want generals.[60]

The Creator has not thought proper to mark those in the forehead who are of stuff to make good generals. We are first, therefore, to seek them blindfold, and then let them learn the trade at the expense of great losses. But our turn of success will come by-and-by. ... Our public ships, to be sure, have done wonders. They have saved our military reputation sacrificed on the shores of Canada; but in point of real injury and depredation on the enemy, our privateers without question have been most effectual.[61]

The tide turns

In our second campaign, although we have not done all to which our force was adequate, we have done much. We have taken possession of all Upper Canada except the single post of Kingston. . . . On the ocean, where our force consists only of a few frigates and smaller vessels, in six or seven engagements of vessel to vessel of equal force, or very nearly so, we have captured their vessel in every instance but one. . . . In a remarkable action on Lake Erie between about eight or ten vessels of a side, large and small from ships down to gunboats, the greater number of guns and men being on their side, we took their whole squadron, not a vessel or a man escaping. On this state of things our third campaign will open.[62]

We have taken their Upper Canada and shall add the Lower to it when the season will admit; and hope to remove them fully and finally from our continent. And what they will feel more, for they value their colonies only for the bales of cloth they take from them, we have established manufactures not only sufficient to supersede our demand from them but to rivalize them in foreign markets.[63] We have already probably a million of spindles engaged in spinning cotton and wool, which will clothe sufficiently our eight millions of people, and they are multiplying daily. . . . I have near 100 spindles in operation for clothing our own family.[64]

We have [proved] to those who have fleets that the English are
not invincible at sea, as Alexander [of Russia] has proved that
Bonaparte is not invincible by land. How much to be lamented
that the world cannot unite and destroy these two land and sea
monsters! [65]

The downfall of Bonaparte

Shall you [John Adams] and I last to see the course the sevenfold
wonders of the times will take? The Attila of the age dethroned, the
ruthless destroyer of ten millions of the human race, whose thirst
for blood appeared unquenchable, the great oppressor of the rights
and liberties of the world, shut up within the circle of a little island
of the Mediterranean, and dwindled to the condition of a humble
and degraded pensioner on the bounty of those he had most injured.
How miserably, how meanly, has he closed his inflated career!
What a sample of the bathos will his history present! He should
have perished on the swords of his enemies, under the walls of
Paris. . . .

But Bonaparte was a lion in the field only. In civil life a cold-
blooded, calculating, unprincipled usurper, without a virtue; no
statesman, knowing nothing of commerce, political economy, or
civil government, and supplying ignorance by bold presumption.
I had supposed him a great man until [he overthrew the French
Republic]. From that date, however, I set him down as a great
scoundrel only. . . .

I own that while I rejoice, for the good of mankind, in the deliverance of Europe from the havoc which would never have ceased
while Bonaparte should have lived in power, I see with anxiety the
tyrant of the ocean remaining in vigor, and even participating in
the merit of crushing his brother tyrant. . . . All the strong reasons,
indeed, place us on the side of peace; the interests of the Continent,
their friendly dispositions, and even the interests of England. Her
passions alone are opposed to it. Peace would seem now to be an
easy work, the causes of the war being removed. . . . And, war
ceasing, her impressment of our seamen ceases of course.[66]

England makes the war one of conquest

Although we neither expected nor wished any act of friendship
from Bonaparte, and always detested him as a tyrant, yet he gave

employment to much of the force of the nation who was our common enemy. So far, his downfall was illy timed for us; it gave to England an opportunity to turn full-handed on us.[67]

The war, undertaken on both sides to settle the questions of impressment and the orders of council, now that these are done away by events, is declared by Great Britain to have changed its object, and to have become a war of conquest, to be waged until she conquers from us our fisheries, the province of Maine, the Lakes, states and territories north of the Ohio, and the navigation of the Mississippi; in other words, till she reduces us to unconditional submission.[68]

No matter, we can beat her on our own soil, leaving the laws of the ocean to be settled by the maritime powers of Europe, who are equally oppressed and insulted by the usurpations of England on that element. Our particular and separate grievance is only the impressment of our citizens. We must sacrifice the last dollar and drop of blood to rid us of that badge of slavery; and it must rest with England alone to say whether it is worth eternal war, for eternal it must be if she holds to the wrong.[69]

We shall not flinch from enemies without or within

The orders of council had taken from us near one thousand vessels. Our list of captures from them is now one thousand three hundred, and, just become sensible that it is small and not large ships which gall them most, we shall probably add one thousand prizes a year to their past losses.... Each American impressed has already cost them ten thousand dollars, and every year will add five thousand dollars more to his price.... Had we adopted the other alternative of submission no mortal can tell what the cost would have been....

We shall indeed survive the conflict.... We shall retain our country, and rapid advances in the art of war will soon enable us to beat our enemy and probably drive him from the continent. We have men enough... but I wish I could see... a better train of finance. Their banking projects are like dosing dropsy with more water....

To me this state of things brings a sacrifice of all tranquillity and comfort through the residue of life. For although the debility of age disables me from the services and sufferings of the field, yet, by the

total annihilation in value of the produce which was to give me subsistence and independence, I shall be like Tantalus, up to the shoul-
ders in water yet dying with thirst. We can make indeed enough to
eat, drink, and clothe ourselves; but nothing for our salt, iron,
groceries, and taxes, which must be paid in money. For what can
we raise for the market? Wheat? we can only give it to our horses,
as we have been doing ever since harvest. Tobacco? it is not worth
the pipe it is smoked in. Some say whiskey; but all mankind must
become drunkards to consume it.

But although we feel, we shall not flinch. We must consider now,
as in the Revolutionary War, that although the evils of resistance
are great, those of submission would be greater. We must meet,
therefore, the former as the casualties of tempests and earthquakes,
and like them necessarily resulting from the constitution of the
world. . . .

Some apprehend danger from the defection of Massachusetts.
It is a disagreeable circumstance but not a dangerous one. If they
become neutral, we are sufficient for one enemy without them, and
in fact we get no aid from them now. If their administration determines to join the enemy, their force will be annihilated by equality
of division among themselves. . . . Everyone, too, must know that
we can at any moment make peace with England at the expense of
the navigation and fisheries of Massachusetts. But it will not come
to this. Their own people will put down these factionists.[70]

The nucleus of the Library of Congress

I learn from the newspapers that the vandalism of our enemy
has triumphed at Washington . . . by the destruction of the public
library with the noble edifice [the Capitol] in which it was deposited.
Of this transaction . . . the world will entertain but one sentiment.
. . . I presume it will be among the early objects of Congress to
recommence their collection. This will be difficult while the war
continues, and intercourse with Europe is attended with so much
risk.

I have been fifty years [collecting my library], and have spared
no pains, opportunity, or expense, to make it what it is. While residing in Paris I devoted every afternoon I was disengaged, for a
summer or two, in examining all the principal bookstores, turning

over every book with my own hand, and putting by everything which related to America, and indeed whatever was rare and valuable in every science. Besides this, I had standing orders during the whole time I was in Europe, on its principal bookmarts, particularly Amsterdam, Frankfort, Madrid, and London, for such works relating to America as could not be found in Paris.... During the same period, and after my return to America, I was led to procure, also, whatever related to the duties of those in the high concerns of the nation. So that the collection, which I suppose is of between nine and ten thousand volumes, while it includes what is chiefly valuable in science and literature generally, extends more particularly to whatever belongs to the American statesman....

It is long since I have been sensible it ought not to continue private property, and had provided that at my death Congress should have the refusal of it at their own price. But the loss they have now incurred makes the present the proper moment for their accommodation.... I ... tender ... it to the library committee of Congress.... Nearly the whole [of my books] are well bound, abundance of them elegantly, and of the choicest editions existing. They may be valued by persons named by themselves, and the payment made convenient to the public ... so as to spare the present calls of our country, and await its days of peace and prosperity. They may enter, nevertheless, into immediate use of it, as eighteen or twenty wagons would place it in Washington in a single trip of a fortnight.[71]

Victories on both land and sea

The affairs of war have taken the most favorable turn which was to be expected.... The third year has been a continued series of victories, to wit: of Brown and Scott at Chippewa; of the same at Niagara; of Gaines over Drummond at Fort Erie; that of Brown over Drummond at the same place; the capture of another fleet on Lake Champlain by M'Donough; the entire defeat of their army under Prevost, on the same day, by M'Comb; and recently their defeats at New Orleans by Jackson, Coffee, and Carroll, with a loss of four thousand men out of nine thousand and six hundred, with their two Generals, Pakenham and Gibbs, killed, and a third, Keane, wounded mortally, as is said.

This series of successes has been tarnished only by the conflagrations at Washington. . . . Still, in the end, the transaction has helped rather than hurt us, by arousing the general indignation of our country, and by marking to the world of Europe the vandalism and brutal character of the English government. . . .

And add further, that through the whole period of the war we have beaten them single-handed at sea, and so thoroughly established our superiority over them with equal force that they retire from that kind of contest, and never suffer their frigates to cruise singly. . . . The disclosure to the world of the fatal secret that they can be beaten at sea with an equal force, the evidence furnished by the military operations of the last year that experience is rearing us officers who, when our means shall be fully under way, will plant our standard on the walls of Quebec and Halifax, their recent and signal disaster at New Orleans, and the evaporation of their hopes from the [Anglo-Federalists'] Hartford Convention, will probably raise a clamor in the British nation which will force their ministry into peace.

The cement of Union is in our heart-blood

I say *force* them, because, willingly, they would never be at peace. . . . They found some hopes on the state of our finances. . . . But the foundations of credit still remain to us, and need but skill, which experience will soon produce, to marshal them into an order which may carry us through any length of war. But they have hoped more in their Hartford Convention. . . . They are playing the same game for disorganization here which they played [during the French Revolution]. . . . But they have very different materials to work on. The yeomanry of the United States are not the *canaille* of Paris. . . . The cement of this Union is in the heart-blood of every American. I do not believe there is on earth a government established on so immovable a basis. . . .

Have then no fears for us, my friend [Lafayette]. The grounds of these exist only in English newspapers. . . . Their military heroes, by land and sea, may sink our oyster boats, rob our hen roosts, burn our negro huts, and run off. But a campaign or two will relieve them from further trouble or expense in defending their American possessions.

Peace

February 26th [1815]. My letter had not yet been sealed when I received news of our peace. I am glad of it, and especially that we closed our war with the eclat of the action at New Orleans.[72]

The successes of New Orleans have established truths too important not to be valued: that . . . the militia are brave; that their deadly aim countervails the manoeuvering skill of their enemy; that we have officers of natural genius now starting forward from the mass; and that, putting together all our conflicts, we can beat the British by sea and by land with equal numbers. All this being now proved, I am glad of the pacification of Ghent, and shall still be more so if by a reasonable arrangement against impressment they will make it truly a treaty of peace.[73]

Future Anglo-American fraternity

If they adopt a course of friendship with us, the commerce of one hundred millions of people, which some now born will live to see here, will maintain them forever as a great unit of the European family. But if they go on checking, irritating, injuring and hostilizing us, they will force on us the motto *Carthago delenda est*. And some Scipio Americanus will leave to posterity the problem of conjecturing where stood once the ancient and splendid city of London! [74]

I hope in God she will change. There is not a nation on the globe with whom I have more earnestly wished a friendly intercourse on equal conditions. On no other would I hold out the hand of friendship to any.[75]

Were they once under a government which should treat us with justice and equity, I should myself feel with great strength the ties which bind us together, of origin, language, laws and manners; and I am persuaded the two peoples would become in future as it was with the ancient Greeks, among whom it was reproachful for Greek to be found fighting against Greek in a foreign army. . . . A purer government . . ., instead of endeavoring to make us their natural enemies, will see in us what we really are, their natural friends and brethren, and more interested in a fraternal connection with them than with any other nation on earth.[76]

No one feels more indignation than myself when reflecting on the insults and injuries of that country to this. But the interests of both require that these should be left to history, and in the meantime be smothered in the living mind. I have indeed little personal concern in it. Time is drawing her curtain on me. But I should make my bow with more satisfaction if I had more hope of seeing our countries shake hands together cordially.[77]

CHAPTER XVI

An American Heritage

FROM his mountaintop Thomas Jefferson surveyed America in the year 1816 and was content with what he saw. The country had come out of the war strong and united, and the election of James Monroe as successor to James Madison had ushered in a prosperous 'Era of Good Feeling.' Abroad, the long wars were over and Bonaparte, the hated dictator of Europe, 'the Attila of the age,' was finally and forever exiled. Pleased with the state of the world and sanguine as to the future, the Sage of Monticello said that he was then ready to make his final bow. Actually, however, he was filled with a zest for living; there were so many useful and pleasant things yet to do, so many 'diagrams and crotchets,' such as the invention of a hemp-break or the measuring of the high Peaks of Otter, which were visible from his Poplar Forest home.

As time went on, his semiannual visits to Poplar Forest, usually with one or two of his granddaughters, took on the nature of a retreat from the swarm of strangers that began to invade Monticello. There had come into existence a new generation of Americans who united with a reverence for the Founding Fathers a curiosity to see one of the few still living, and especially the author of the Declaration of Independence. In Jefferson's lifetime he had become a legend. Biographers besieged him for materials to write his life, artists were commissioned to paint him, and a lifemask was made for posterity. A few diehards of the older generation still regarded him as a radical 'rawhead and bloodybones,' but with the great mass of Americans he had already taken his place as democracy's 'Immortal Thomas Jefferson.'

Although the atmosphere had mellowed, the author of the Statute of Virginia for Religious Freedom was still annoyed by obscurantist clergymen who for years had tried to portray him as 'atheist, deist, or devil.' Jefferson considered his compilation of extracts from the New Testament, which he called the 'Philosophy of Jesus' (published after his death as the 'Jefferson Bible'), a document in proof that he was, and always had been, 'a *real Christian*.' Looking back to the days when he had struggled to remove legal shackles from men's minds and consciences, he rejoiced that America had become 'this blessed land of free enquiry and belief.' Yet he looked forward more often than he looked back, realizing that the struggle for the rights of man must eternally be fought, 'that laws and institutions must go hand in hand with the progress of the human mind.'

By 1816 he was well launched on his last great undertaking, the establishment in Virginia of that system of general education which he had first proposed in 1779. In spite of his advanced age, he resumed his 'crusade against ignorance' with the zeal of youth, drafted legislative bills, drew up plans of studies, and began the building of a 'Central College' near Charlottesville which in 1819 was adopted as the site of the University of Virginia. Not until six years later was the University ready to open its doors. Jefferson, its rector, and truly its father, planned the architecture of his 'academical village,' attended to every detail of planning and construction, and fought for legislative funds necessary to carry to completion 'this beautiful and hopeful institution *in ovo*,' which was to be based 'on the illimitable freedom of the human mind to explore and to expose every subject susceptible of its contemplation.'

Meanwhile he was hard hit by the Panic of 1819. His financial losses he bore with philosophic fortitude. More disturbing were the bitter debates in Congress over the request of Missouri to enter the Union as a slave state. Anti-slavery Northern members were unwilling to admit her as such, but in the end a compromise was arranged by which Missouri entered as a slave state, Maine as a free state, and slavery was prohibited in the remaining territory north of latitude thirty-six thirty. To Jefferson it at first seemed as if the Missouri question had sounded the knell of the Union. But his sanguine temperament soon reasserted itself, and he derived consolation from his belief that Americans not only had the means but the disposition always to settle their differences without resorting to civil war.

He deplored 'morbid passions' that tended to weaken the American Union, upon which rested more than ever before the hopes of all mankind. The reactionary powers of Europe, leagued together in the so-called Holy Alliance, were then stamping out liberalism in the Old World and threatening to crush the Spanish-American republics in the New. In the face of this threat he elaborated upon his idea, often expressed, that the Americas, North and South, should unite in 'an American system of policy totally independent of and unconnected with Europe.' In 1823 when England proposed a joint Anglo-American declaration against any attempt of the Holy Alliance to intervene in South America, Jefferson advised President Monroe (in a letter which influenced the subsequent Monroe Doctrine) that he would most cordially welcome English cooperation in maintaining the security of the New World.

From England, 'the land of our language, habits, and manners,' he imported professors for his University of Virginia. For this he was much criticized. But he was willing to improve American education, as American agriculture and manufactures had been improved, with 'borrowed skill.' Now in his eighties, he devoted all of his talents and energies to the University. He summoned his failing strength for a stubborn last-ditch fight to obtain funds in order that the buildings — unique in America for the beauty of their chastely classical architecture — might be worthy of the high order of education he aspired to offer the youth of his country. After the fight was won and the University opened, in March of 1825, he continued to watch over it with the tender concern of a father. In the last months of his life he was busy designing a clock for the Rotunda, planning an observatory, and laying out the grounds with groves, flowers, and an ingenious and beautiful serpentine wall.

His 'long and serene day of life,' now drawing to its close, was clouded by financial distress. With great mortification and anguish of mind he was compelled to ask the legislature for permission to sell by lottery enough of his property to satisfy his debts. The alternative, a forced sale at prevailing low prices, would not bring in enough to allow him to keep Monticello. His property at Poplar Forest had in part been sold. His anxiety was greatly lessened by the granting of his request; and the spontaneous offers of financial assistance that came from private citizens in North Carolina, New York, and several other states, contributed to the peace and felicity of his last days on the mountaintop.

Until he was forced to take to his bed late in June of 1826, he concealed from his family the rapid decline in his health and his own sense of his impending departure for that shore on which, as he wrote in his deathbed adieu to Martha Randolph, 'two seraphs,' his wife and his daughter Maria, were awaiting him. On June 24 he wrote his last letter. It was an appeal to his fellow Americans to renew with undiminished devotion their faith in the rights of man and the blessings of self-government. He died on July 4, 1826, the fiftieth anniversary of the Declaration of Independence.

On his simple tombstone at Monticello is inscribed the epitaph he himself wrote. It commemorates only three of his many services to his country and to mankind. The great democrat who had fought against every form of tyranny, political, religious, and intellectual, wished to be remembered as the author of the Declaration of Independence, of the Statute of Virginia for Religious Freedom, and father of the University of Virginia. Thus he epitomized a long and useful life, a gallant and persevering crusade for the freedom and happiness of man.

Post-war America

The British war has left us in debt, but that is a cheap price for the good it has done us. The establishment of the necessary manufactures among ourselves, the proof that our government is solid, can stand the shock of war, and is superior even to civil schism, are precious facts for us; and of these the strongest proofs were furnished. . . . But its best effect has been the complete suppression of party. . . .

Even Connecticut, as a state, and the last one expected to yield its steady habits (which were essentially bigoted in politics as well as religion), has chosen a Republican governor and Republican legislature. Massachusetts indeed still lags.[1] Her would-be dukes and lords . . . have been itching for coronets; her lawyers for robes of ermine, her priests for lawn sleeves and for a religious establishment ·which might give them wealth, power, and independence of personal merit. But her citizens, who were to supply with the sweat of their brow the treasures on which these drones were to riot, could never have seen anything to long for in the oppressions and pauperism of England. After the shackles of aristocracy of the bar and priesthood have been burst by Connecticut, we cannot doubt the return of Massachusetts to the bosom of the Republican family.[2]

Nor is the election of Monroe [in 1816] an inefficient circumstance in our felicities. Four and twenty years, which he will accomplish, of administration in Republican forms and principles will so consecrate them in the eyes of the people as to secure them against the danger of change. The evanition of party dissensions has harmonized intercourse and sweetened society beyond imagination. The war then has done us all this good, and the further one of assuring the world that although attached to peace from a sense of its blessings, we will meet war when it is made necessary.[3]

We are turning to public improvements. Schools, roads, and canals are everywhere either in operation or contemplation. The most gigantic undertaking yet proposed is that of New York, for drawing the waters of Lake Erie into the Hudson. . . . The expense will be great, but its effect incalculably powerful. . . . Internal navigation by steamboats is rapidly spreading through all our states, and that by sails and oars will ere long be looked back to as among the curiosities of antiquity.[4]

I steer my bark with Hope ahead and Fear astern

You [John Adams] ask if I would agree to live my seventy or rather seventy-three years over again? To which I say, yea. I think with you that it is a good world, on the whole; that it has been framed on a principle of benevolence, and more pleasure than pain dealt out to us. There are, indeed (who might say nay), gloomy and hypochondriac minds, inhabitants of diseased bodies, disgusted with the present and despairing of the future, always counting that the worst will happen because it may happen. To these I say, how much pain have cost us the evils which have never happened! My temperament is sanguine. I steer my bark with Hope in the head, leaving Fear astern. My hopes, indeed, sometimes fail; but not oftener than the forebodings of the gloomy.[5]

Putting to myself your question, would I agree to live my seventy-

three years over again forever? I hesitate to say. . . . From twenty-
five to sixty, I would say yes; and I might go further back, but not
come lower down. . . . There is a ripeness of time for death, regard-
ing others as well as ourselves, when it is reasonable we should drop
off and make room for another growth. When we have lived our
generation out, we should not wish to encroach on another. I enjoy
good health; I am happy in what is around me, yet I assure you I am
ripe for leaving all, this year, this day, this hour.[6]

Nothing proves more than this that the Being who presides over
the world is essentially benevolent. Stealing from us, one by one,
the faculties of enjoyment, searing our sensibilities, leading us, like
the horse in his mill, round and round the same beaten circle,

> To see what we have seen,
> To taste the tasted, and at each return
> Less tasteful; o'er our palates to decant
> Another vintage —

until satiated and fatigued with this leaden iteration, we ask our
own *congé*. I heard once a very old friend, who had troubled himself
with neither poets nor philosophers, say the same thing in plain
prose, that he was tired of pulling off his shoes and stockings at night
and putting them on again in the morning.

The wish to stay here is thus gradually extinguished; but not so
easily that of returning once in a while to see how things have gone
on. Perhaps, however, one of the elements of future felicity is to be a
constant and unimpassioned view of what is passing here. If so, this
may well supply the wish of occasional visits.

Meanwhile, good wines, science, and twilight walks

I promised you [President Monroe], when I should have received
and tried the wines I had ordered from France and Italy, to give you
a note of the kinds which I should think worthy of your procure-
ment. . . . They are the following: *Vin blanc liquoreux de M. Jourdan à
Tanis*. . . . *Vin de Ledarion* (in Languedoc), something of the port
character but higher flavored, more delicate, less rough. . . . *Vin de
Roussillon*. The best is that of Perpignan or Rives alte of the crop of
M. Durand. . . . There is still . . . the wine of Florence called
Montepulciano. . . . There is a particular very best crop . . . I have
imported . . . annually ten or twelve years. [8]

SAGE OF MONTICELLO
Portrait of Jefferson at seventy-eight, by Thomas Sully

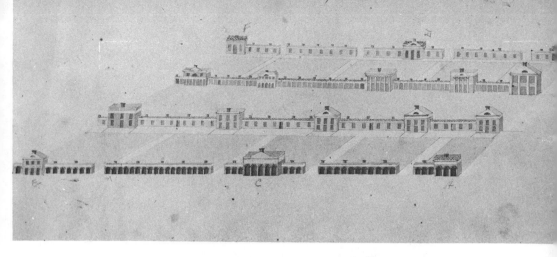

GENERAL PLAN FOR THE UNIVERSITY OF VIRGINIA
Drawn by Jefferson. The Rotunda was added later

THE LAWN OF THE UNIVERSITY OF VIRGINIA IN 1826
Engraving by Tanner

ELEVATION OF THE ROTUNDA. Drawn by Jefferson

THE ROTUNDA OF THE UNIVERSITY OF VIRGINIA

LIFE MASK OF JEFFERSON.   Done in 1825
when Jefferson was eighty-two, by John H. I. Browere

When lately measuring trigonometrically the height of the Peaks of Otter . . . my object was only to gratify a common curiosity as to the height of those mountains, which we deem our highest. . . . The ridge of mountains of which Monticello is one, is generally low; there is one in it, however, called Peter's Mountain, considerably higher than the general ridge. This being within a dozen miles of me, northeastwardly, I think in the spring of the year to measure it . . ., which may serve as another trial of the logarithmic theory.[9]

It might perhaps be possible to economize the steam of a common pot kept boiling on the kitchen fire until its accumulation should be sufficient to give a stroke, and although the strokes might not be rapid, there would be enough of them in the day to raise from an adjacent well the water necessary for daily use; to wash the linen, knead the bread, beat the hominy, churn the butter, turn the spit, and do all other household offices which require only a regular mechanical motion. . . .

A method of removing the difficulty of preparing hemp occurred to me. . . . To a person having a threshing machine, the addition of a hemp-break [constructed on my plan enables it to be] more perfectly beaten than I have ever seen done by hand. . . .I expect that a single horse will do the breaking and beating of ten men. Something of this kind has been so long wanted by the cultivators of hemp that . . . I shall probably describe it anonymously in the public papers, in order to forestall the prevention of its use by some interloping patentee.[10]

We all arrived here [at Poplar Forest] without accident. . . . The story of the neighborhood immediately was that I had brought a crowd of workmen to get ready my house in a hurry for Bonaparte. Were there such people only as the believers in this, patriotism would be a ridiculous passion.[11] Ellen and Cornelia are the severest students I have ever met with. They never leave their room but to come to meals. About twilight of the evening, we sally out with the owls and bats, and take our evening exercise on the terrace.[12]

All our inquiries end in four words: 'Be just and good'

The result of your [John Adams'] fifty or sixty years of religious reading, in the four words, 'Be just and good,' is that in which all our inquiries must end. . . . What all agree in, is probably right. What no two agree in, most probably wrong. One of our fan-coloring biographers, who paints small men as very great, inquired of me lately, with real affection too, whether he might consider as authentic the change in my religion much spoken of in some circles. . . . . My answer was, 'Say nothing of my religion. It is known to my God and myself alone. Its evidence before the world is to be sought in my life; if that has been *honest and dutiful* to society, the religion which has regulated it cannot be a bad one.' [13]

The priests indeed have heretofore thought proper to ascribe to me religious, or rather anti-religious, sentiments of their own fabric, but such as soothed their resentments against the Act of Virginia for Establishing Religious Freedom. They wished him to be thought atheist, deist, or devil who could advocate freedom from their religious dictations. . . . The imputations of irreligion having spent their force, they think an imputation of change might now be turned to account as a bolster for their duperies.[14]

The 'Jefferson Bible'

I . . . have made a wee-little book . . ., which I call the Philosophy of Jesus; it is a paradigma of his doctrines, made by cutting the texts out of the [New Testament] and arranging them on the pages of a blank book in a certain order of time or subject.[14a] The matter which is evidently his . . . is as easily distinguishable as diamonds in a dunghill. The result is an octavo of forty-six pages of pure and unsophisticated doctrines such as were professed and acted on by the *unlettered* Apostles, the Apostolic Fathers, and the Christians of the first century.[15]

A more beautiful or precious morsel of ethics I have never seen; it is a document in proof that *I* am a *real Christian*, that is to say, a disciple of the doctrines of Jesus, very different from the Platonists, who call *me* infidel and *themselves* Christians and preachers of the gospel, while they draw all their characteristic dogmas from what its author never said nor saw. . . . If I had time I would add to my little book the Greek, Latin, and French texts in columns side by side.[16] This shall be the work of the ensuing winter [of 1816–17]. . . . If a history of his life can be added, written with the same view of the subject, the world will . . . at length see the immortal merit of this first of human sages.[17]

Had the doctrines of Jesus been preached always as pure as they came from his lips, the whole civilized world would now have been Christian. I rejoice that in this blessed country of free enquiry and belief, which has surrendered its creed and conscience to neither kings nor priests, the genuine doctrine of one only God is reviving, and I trust that there is not a *young man* now living in the United States who will not die a Unitarian.[18] The population of my neighborhood is too slender, and is too much divided into other sects to maintain any one preacher well. I must therefore be contented to be a Unitarian by myself.[19]

In our Richmond there is much fanaticism, but chiefly among the women. They have their night meetings and praying parties, where, attended by their priests, and sometimes by a henpecked husband, they pour forth the effusions of their love to Jesus in terms as amatory and carnal as their modesty would permit them to use to a mere earthly lover. In our village of Charlottesville there is a good deal of religion, with a small spice only of fanaticism. We have four sects, but without either church or meeting house. The court house is the common temple, one Sunday in the month to each. Here Episcopalian and Presbyterian, Methodist and Baptist, meet together, join in hymning their Maker, listen with attention and devotion to each others' preachers, and all mix in society with perfect harmony.[20] I have subscribed to the building an Episcopal church, two hundred dollars; a Presbyterian, sixty dollars; and a Baptist, twenty-five dollars.[21]

The creed of a progressive

Only lay down true principles, and adhere to them inflexibly [he wrote in 1816, respecting a proposed revision of the constitution of Virginia]. Do not be frightened into their surrender by the alarms of the timid, or the croakings of wealth against the ascendancy of the people. . . . The true foundation of republican government is the equal right of every citizen, in his person and property, and in their management. Try by this, as a tally, every provision of our constitution, and see if it hangs directly on the will of the people. . . .

Some men look at constitutions with sanctimonious reverence, and deem them like the ark of the covenant, too sacred to be touched. They ascribe to the men of the preceding age a wisdom

more than human, and suppose what they did to be beyond amendment. I knew that age well; I belonged to it, and labored with it.
It deserved well of its country. It was very like the present, but
without the experience of the present; and forty years of experience
in government is worth a century of book-reading. . . . I am certainly not an advocate for frequent and untried changes in laws
and constitutions. . . . But I know also that laws and institutions
must go hand in hand with the progress of the human mind. As
that becomes more developed, more enlightened, as new discoveries
are made, new truths disclosed, and manners and opinions change
with the change of circumstances, institutions must advance also,
and keep pace with the times. We might as well require a man to
wear still the coat which fitted him when a boy, as civilized society
to remain ever under the regimen of their barbarous ancestors.[22]

Knowledge is power, safety, and happiness

I am now entirely absorbed in endeavors to effect the establishment of a general system of education in my native state, on the
triple basis: 1, of elementary schools which shall give to the children
of every citizen gratis competent instruction in reading, writing,
common arithmetic, and general geography. 2. Collegiate institutions for ancient and modern languages, for higher instruction in
arithmetic, geography, and history, placing for these purposes a
college within a day's ride of every inhabitant of the state, and adding a provision for the full education at the public expense of select
subjects from among the children of the poor, who shall have exhibited at the elementary schools the most prominent indications of
aptness of judgment and correct disposition. 3. A university in
which all the branches of science deemed useful at this day shall be
taught in their highest degree. . . . My hopes, however, are kept in
check by . . . our state legislature, the members of which do not
generally . . . perceive the important truths that knowledge is power,
that knowledge is safety, and that knowledge is happiness.

In the meantime, and in case of failure of the broader plan, we
are establishing [a Central College, of which Jefferson was rector,]
at the same situation near Charlottesville, the scale of which, of
necessity, will be much more moderate, as resting on private dona-

tions only. . . . If then we fail in doing all the good we wish, we will do at least all we can.[23]

We propose to lay off a square of about 700 or 800 feet, on the outside of which we shall arrange separate pavilions. . . . Between pavilion and pavilion a range of dormitories for the boys, one story high, giving to each a room. . . . The whole . . . to be united by a colonnade in front, of the height of the lower story of the pavilions, under which they may go dry from school to school. The colonnade will be of square brick pilasters (at first) with a Tuscan entablature. . . . These pavilions . . . shall be models of taste and good architecture, and of a variety of appearance, no two alike, so as to serve as specimens for the architectural lectures.[24]

Once again aided by Madison and Monroe

I do not entertain your [John Adams'] apprehensions for the happiness of our brother Madison in a state of retirement. Such a mind as his . . . can never know *ennui*. . . . For example, he and Monroe, the President, are now [May, 1817] here on the work of a collegiate institution . . ., of which they and myself are three of six visitors. This, if it succeeds, will raise up children for Mr. Madison to employ his attention through life. I say if it succeeds, for we have two very essential wants in our way, first, means to compass our views; and, second, men qualified to fulfill them. And these, you will agree, are essential wants indeed.[25]

Our Central College gives me more employment than I am equal to. The dilatoriness of the workmen gives me constant trouble. It has already brought into doubt the completion this year of the building begun, which obliges me to be with them every other day. I follow it up from a sense of the impression which will be made on the legislature by the prospect of its immediate operation. . . . I drew a plan of a college in its dormitories, such as the bill calls for, to demonstrate that it will not cost more than the sum allotted.[26]

My bantling of forty years' nursing

Would it promote the success of the institution most for me to be in or out of it? Out of it, I believe. . . . There are fanatics both in religion and politics, who, without knowing me personally, have long been taught to consider me as a rawhead and bloodybones, and ... we can afford to lose no votes.[27] Pray drop me a line [he wrote Joseph C. Cabell, state senator from his district] when any vote is passed which furnishes an indication of the success or failure of the general plan. I have only this single anxiety in this world. It is a bantling of forty years' birth and nursing, and if I can once see it on its legs I will sing with sincerity and pleasure my *nunc dimittas.*[28]

A system of general instruction, which shall reach every description of our citizens from the richest to the poorest, as it was the earliest, so will it be the latest of all the public concerns in which I shall permit myself to take an interest.[29] My bill ... is in fact and substance the plan I proposed ... forty years ago, but accommodated to the circumstances of this instead of that day.... Mine, after all, may be a Utopian dream, but being innocent, I have thought I might indulge in it till I go to the land of dreams, and sleep there with the dreamers of all past and future times.[30]

Making the dream a reality

The legislature [on February 21, 1818] passed an act establishing a university, endowing it for the present with an annuity of fifteen thousand dollars and directing commissioners to meet to recommend a site, a plan of buildings, ... etc. The commissioners [of whom Jefferson was chairman] by a vote of sixteen for the Central College, two for a second place and three for a third, adopted that for the site of the University. They approved by a unanimous vote the plan of building begun at that place and agreed on such a distribution of the sciences as it was thought might bring them all within the competence of ten professors; and no doubt is entertained of a confirmation by the legislature [this was given on January 25, 1819, and on March 29 of that year Jefferson was elected rector of the University of Virginia].

The plan of building is not to erect one single magnificent building to contain everybody and everything, but to make of it an academical village in which every professor should have his separate house [or 'pavilion'], containing his lecturing room with two, three, or four rooms for his own accommodation according as he may have a family or no family, with kitchen, garden, etc.; distinct

dormitories for the students, not more than two in a room; and
separate boarding houses for dieting them by private housekeepers.
We concluded to employ no professor who is not of the first order of
the science he professes, that when we can find such in our own
country we shall prefer them and when we cannot we will procure
them wherever else to be found.[31]

Our University, four miles distant, gives me frequent exercise,
and the oftener, as I direct its architecture. Its plan is unique, and
it is becoming an object of curiosity for the traveler.[32] Pavilion No.
X [is to be modeled on the] East Doric of the Theatre of Marcellus.
The columns to have no bases.... I have never seen an attic
pilaster with the measures of its parts minutely expressed except
that of the Temple of Nerva Trajan (Palladio, Book III, Plate 18)
That temple is overloaded with ornaments, and its pilaster frit-
tered away so minutely in its mouldings as to lose all effect. I have
simplified these mouldings to suit our plainer style, still, however,
retaining nearly their general outlines and proportions.[33] Seven of
the ten pavilions destined for the professors, and about thirty [one-
room] dormitories, will be completed [in 1820], and three other,
with six hotels for boarding, and seventy other dormitories, will be
completed the next year.... But means to bring these into place,
and to set the machine into motion, must come from the legislature.[34]

An uphill task

This institution of my native state, the hobby of my old age,
will be based on the illimitable freedom of the human mind to explore and to expose every subject susceptible of its contemplation.[35]
An opposition, in the meantime, has been got up.... The serious
enemies are the priests of the different religious sects.... Their
pulpits are now resounding with denunciations against the appointment of Doctor [Thomas] Cooper, whom they charge as a
monotheist in opposition to their tritheism.... But in despite of
their fulminations against endeavors to enlighten the general mind,
to improve the reason of the people and encourage them in the use
of it, the liberality of this state will support this institution, ... this
beautiful and hopeful institution *in ovo*.[36] I will not despair then of
the avail of [Dr. Cooper's] services in an establishment which I con-

template as the future bulwark of the human mind in this hemisphere.[37]

If our legislature does not heartily push our University, we must send our children for education to Kentucky or Cambridge. The latter will return them to us fanatics and Tories, the former will keep them to add to their population. . . . All the states but our own are sensible that knowledge is power . . . while we are sinking into the barbarism of our Indian aborigines.[38] Engage our friends to take in hand the whole subject . . . and promote in every order of men the degree of instruction proportioned to their condition and to their views in life.[39]

Hard times, and the fortitude of an Epicurean

The paper bubble is then burst [that is, the Panic of 1819]. . . . We were laboring under a dropsical fullness of circulating medium. Nearly all of it is now called in by the banks, who have the regulation of the safety-valves of our fortunes, and who condense and explode them at their will. . . . Unless our legislature have wisdom enough to effect a remedy by a gradual diminution only of the medium, there will be a general revolution of property in this state.[40] I explained . . . my project . . . and I now send its outline in writing ['A Plan for Reducing the Circulating Medium'].[41] My voice was raised against the establishment of banks in the beginning. But like that of Cassandra it was not listened to. I was set down as a madman by those who have since been victims to them. I little thought then how much I was to suffer by them myself, for I too am taken in by endorsements for a friend [Wilson Cary Nicholas] to the amount of twenty thousand dollars, for the payment of which I shall have to make sale of that much of my property.[42]

I . . . am an Epicurean. I consider the genuine (not the imputed) doctrines of Epicurus as containing everything rational in moral philosophy which Greece and Rome have left us. . . . Fortitude, you know, is one of his four cardinal virtues. That teaches us to meet and surmount difficulties; not to fly from them like cowards; and to fly, too, in vain, for they will meet and arrest us at every turn of our road.[43]

Daily routine at seventy-six

Like my friend [Doctor Benjamin Rush], I have lived temperately, eating little animal food. . . . I double, however, the Doctor's glass and a half of wine, and even treble it with a friend; but halve its effects by drinking the weak wines only. The ardent wines I cannot drink, nor do I use ardent spirits in any form. Malt liquors and cider are my table drinks. . . . I have been blest with organs of digestion which accept and concoct, without ever murmuring, whatever the palate chooses to consign to them, and I have not yet lost a tooth by age. I was a hard student until I entered on the business of life, . . . and now, retired, and at the age of seventy-six, I am again a hard student. Indeed, my fondness for reading and study revolts me from the drudgery of letter-writing. And a stiff wrist . . . makes writing both slow and painful. I am not so regular in my sleep . . ., devoting to it from five to eight hours, according as my company or the book I am reading interests me; and I never go to bed without an hour or half hour's previous reading of something moral whereon to ruminate in the intervals of sleep. But whether I retire to bed early or late, I rise with the sun.

I use spectacles at night, but not necessarily in the day, unless in reading small print. My hearing is distinct in particular conversation, but confused when several voices cross each other, which unfits me for the society of the table. I have been more fortunate than my friend in the article of health. So free from catarrhs that I have not had one (in the breast, I mean) on an average of eight or ten years through life. I ascribe this exemption partly to the habit of bathing my feet in cold water every morning for sixty years past. . . . Except on a late occasion of indisposition, I enjoy good health; too feeble, indeed, to walk much, but riding without fatigue six or eight miles a day, and sometimes thirty or forty. I may end these egotisms . . . by saying that my life has been so much like that of other people that I might say, with Horace, to everyone, *nomine mutato, narratur fabula de te.*[44]

My biography is in my letters

To [a] request of materials for writing my life . . . one answer indeed is obvious, that I am . . . unequal to such a task. Of the public transactions in which I have borne a part, I have kept no narrative with a view of history.[45] But ... my letters (all preserved) will ... command more conviction than anything I could have written after my retirement, no day having ever passed during that period without a letter to somebody, written too in the moment, and in the warmth and freshness of fact and feeling.[46] In these I have sometimes indulged myself in reflections on the things which have been passing. . . . From the voluminous mass, when I am dead, a selection may perhaps be made of a few which may have interest enough to bear a single reading.[47] The letters of a person, especially one whose business has been chiefly transacted by letters, form the only full and genuine journal of his life.[48]

I do not know how far you [Adams] may suffer, as I do, under the persecution of letters. . . . A curiosity was excited to count those received in a single year. . . . I found the number [for the year 1820] to be one thousand two hundred and sixty-seven, many of them requiring answers of elaborate research, and all to be answered with due attention and consideration. . . . Is this life? At best it is but the life of a mill-horse.[49]

A patriarch writes to Maria Cosway

'Over the length of silence I draw a curtain,' is an expression, my dear friend, of your cherished letter of April 7, 1819, of which it might seem I have need to avail myself; but not so really. . . . My wrist . . ., dislocated in Paris while I had the pleasure of being there with you, is, by the effect of years, now so stiffened that writing is become a most slow and painful operation. . . . But I have never lost sight of your letter, and give it now the first place among those of my transatlantic friends. . . . I rejoice in the first place that you are well. . . . And next that you have been so usefully and pleasingly occupied in preparing the minds of others to enjoy the blessings you have yourself derived from the same source, a cultivated mind. . . . I will talk about Monticello, then, and my own country, as is the wish expressed in your letter. My daughter Randolph, whom you knew in Paris a young girl, is now the mother of eleven living children, the grandmother of about half a dozen others, enjoys health and good spirits, and sees the worth of her husband attested by his being at present governor of the state in which we live. Among these I live like a patriarch of old.

Our friend Trumbull is well, and profitably and honorably employed by his country in commemorating with his pencil [for the
Capitol at Washington] some of its Revolutionary honors. . . . I
hear nothing . . . of Madame de Corny. Such is the present state of
our former coterie: dead, diseased, and dispersed. But 'tout ce qui
est differé n'est pas perdu,' says the French proverb, and the religion you so sincerely profess tells us we shall meet again; and we
have all so lived as to be assured it will be in happiness. Mine is the
next turn, and I shall meet it with good will, for after one's friends
are all gone before them, and our faculties leaving us, too, one by
one, why wish to linger in mere vegetation — as a solitary trunk in a
desolate field, from which all its former companions have disappeared? You have many good years remaining yet to be happy
yourself and to make those around you happy. May these, my dear
friend, be as many as yourself may wish, and all of them filled with
health and happiness, will be among the last and warmest wishes of
an unchangeable friend.[50]

I bid adieu to portraits and especially life masks

In May, 1800, I got [Gilbert Stuart] to draw my picture and . . .
paid him his price, one hundred dollars. . . . In 1805 he told me he
was not satisfied with it, and therefore begged me to sit again and he
drew another. . . . I soon after got him to sketch me in the medallion form, which he did on paper with crayons. . . . This I have; it
is a very fine thing, although very perishable.[51]

Mr. Sully, I fear, however, will consider . . . the employment of
his fine pencil as illy bestowed on an ottamy of 78. Voltaire, when
requested by a female friend to sit for his bust by the sculptor Pigalle, answered, 'J'ai soixante-seize ans; et M. Pigalle doit, dit-
on, venir modeler mon visage. Mais, Madame, il faudrait que
j'eusse un visage. . . .' I will conclude, however, with him, that
what remains is at [Sully's] service.[52]

I was taken in by Mr. Browere. He said his [life mask] operation
would be of about twenty minutes, and less unpleasant than Houdon's method. I submitted without enquiry. But it was a bold experiment on his part on the health of an octogenary worn down by
sickness as well as age. Successive coats of grout plastered on the
naked head and kept there an hour would have been a severe trial

of a young and hale man. He suffered the plaster also to get so dry that separation became difficult and even dangerous. He was obliged to use freely the mallet and chisel to break it into pieces and get off a piece at a time. These strokes of the mallet would have been sensible almost to a loggerhead. The family became alarmed and he confused till I was quite exhausted, and there became real danger that the ears would tear from the head sooner than from the plaster. I now bid adieu forever to busts and even portraits.[53]

The Missouri question: like a fire-bell in the night

This momentous question, like a fire-bell in the night, awakened and filled me with terror. I considered it at once as the knell of the Union. It is hushed, indeed, for the moment. But this is a reprieve only, not a final sentence. A geographical line [dividing free and slave territory] ... once conceived and held up to the angry passions of men will never be obliterated; and every new irritation will mark it deeper and deeper.... There is not a man on earth who would sacrifice more than I would to relieve us from this heavy reproach [of slavery], in any *practicable* way. The cession of that kind of property, for so it is misnamed, is a bagatelle which would not cost me a second thought if, in that way, a general emancipation and *expatriation* could be effected; and, gradually, and with due sacrifice, I think it might be. But as it is, we have the wolf by the ears, and we can neither hold him, nor safely let him go. Justice is in one scale, and self-preservation in the other.

Of one thing I am certain, that ... their diffusion over a greater surface would make them individually happier, and proportionally facilitate the accomplishment of their emancipation.... An abstinence, too, from this act of power, would remove the jealousy excited by the undertaking of Congress to regulate the condition ... of men composing a state. This is certainly the exclusive right of every state.... I regret that I am now to die in the belief that the useless sacrifice of themselves by the generation of 1776, to acquire self-government and happiness to their country, is to be thrown away by the unwise and unworthy passions of their sons, and that my only consolation is to be that I live not to weep over it. If they would but dispassionately weigh the blessings they will throw away, against an abstract principle more likely to be effected by union than by scission, they would pause before they would perpetrate this act of suicide on themselves, and of treason against the hopes of the world.[54]

There are means other than the cannon

The Missouri question is a mere party trick. The leaders of Federalism ... are taking advantage of the virtuous feelings of the people to effect a division of parties by a geographical line ...; but they are still putting their shoulder to the wrong wheel; they are wasting Jeremiads on the miseries of slavery as if we were advocates for it. Sincerity ... should ... unite their counsels with ours in devising some reasonable and practicable plan of getting rid of it.[55] Mr. Randolph [Jefferson's son-in-law] ... has had the courage to propose to our legislature a plan of general emancipation and deportation of our slaves. Although this is not ripe to be immediately acted on, it will ... force a serious attention to this object by our citizens.[56] The boisterous sea of liberty indeed is never without a wave, and that from Missouri ... we shall ride over ... as we have over all others.[57]

I rejoice ... that the State of Missouri is at length a member of our Union. Whether the question it excited is dead or only sleepeth, I do not know. ... I still believe that the western extension of our confederacy will ensure its duration, by overruling local factions which might shake a smaller association.[58] It is a fatal heresy to suppose that either our state governments are superior to the federal, or the federal to the states. ... Each party should prudently shrink from all approach to the line of demarcation, instead of rashly overleaping it, or throwing grapples ahead to haul to hereafter. But, finally, the peculiar happiness of our blessed system is, that in differences of opinion ... the appeal is to [the sovereign people] ... peaceably assembled by their representatives in convention. This is more rational than the *jus fortioris*, or the cannon's mouth, the *ultima et sola ratio regum.*[59]

America, and the Americas, united

We owe to all mankind the sacrifice of those morbid passions which would break our confederacy, the only anchor to which the hopes of the world are moored.[60] There are three epochs in history signalized by the total extinction of national morality. The first was of the successors of Alexander, not omitting himself; the next, the successors of the first Caesar; the third, our own age ... the conspiracy of Kings, the successors of Bonaparte, blasphemously calling themselves the Holy Alliance.[61] With respect to the European combinations against the rights of man, I join an honest Irishman of my neighborhood in his 4th of July toast, 'The Holy Alliance, to Hell with the whole of them.'[62]

Are we to surrender the pleasing hopes of seeing improvement in the moral and intellectual condition of man? The events [in Europe] cast a gloomy cloud over that hope. . . . Yet I will not believe our labors are lost. I shall not die without a hope that light and liberty are on steady advance. . . . And even should the cloud of barbarism and despotism again obscure the science and liberties of Europe, this country remains to preserve and restore light and liberty to them. In short, the flames kindled on the 4th of July, 1776, have spread over too much of the globe to be extinguished by the feeble engines of despotism; on the contrary, they will consume these engines and all who work them.[62a]

I hope [to see] a cordial fraternization among all the American nations, and . . . their coalescing in an American system of policy totally independent of and unconnected with that of Europe. The day is not distant when we may formally require a meridian of partition through the ocean which separates the two hemispheres, on the hither side of which no European gun shall ever be heard, nor an American on the other. . . . I hope no American patriot will ever lose sight of the essential policy of interdicting in the seas and territories of both Americas the ferocious and sanguinary contests of Europe. I wish to see this coalition begun. . . . I should rejoice to see the fleets of Brazil and the United States riding together as brethren of the same family, and pursuing the same object.[63]

Cooperation with England for New World security

The question presented by the letters you [President Monroe, who had asked for advice in 1823, when preparing what became the Monroe Doctrine] sent me is the most momentous which has ever been offered to my contemplation since that of Independence.

That made us a nation; this sets our compass and points the course which we are to steer through the ocean of time opening on us. And never could we embark on it under circumstances more auspicious. Our first and fundamental maxim should be, never to entangle ourselves in the broils of Europe. Our second, never to suffer Europe to intermeddle with cis-Atlantic affairs.... One nation, most of all, could disturb us in this pursuit; she now offers to lead, aid, and accompany us in it. By acceding to her proposition [England's proposal for a joint Anglo-American declaration against any attempt of the 'Holy Alliance' to crush the Spanish-American Revolution], we detach her from the bands, bring her mighty weight into the scale of free government, and emancipate a continent at one stroke.... Great Britain is the nation which can do us the most harm of any one, or all, on earth; and with her on our side we need not fear the whole world.

With her, then, we should most sedulously cherish a cordial friendship, and nothing would tend more to knit our affections than to be fighting once more, side by side, in the same cause. Not that I would purchase even her amity at the price of taking part in her wars. But the war in which the present proposition might engage us, should that be its consequence, is not her war, but ours. Its object is to introduce and establish the American system, of keeping out of our land all foreign powers, of never permitting those of Europe to intermeddle with the affairs of our nations. It is to maintain our own principle, not to depart from it. And if, to facilitate this, we can effect a division in the body of the European powers, and draw over to our side its most powerful member, surely we should do it.... With Great Britain withdrawn from their scale and shifted into that of our two continents, all Europe combined would not undertake such a war. For how would they propose to get at either enemy without superior fleets? [64]

The last act of usefulness I can render

I am very little able to walk, but ride freely without fatigue. No better proof than that on a late visit to the Natural Bridge I was six days successively on horseback from breakfast to sunset.[65] Crippled wrists and fingers make writing slow and laborious. But while writing to you [John Adams] I lose the sense of these things in the recollection of ancient times. . . . I forget for a while the hoary winter of age, when we can think of nothing but how to keep ourselves warm, and how to get rid of our heavy hours until the friendly hand of death shall rid us of all at once. Against this *tedium vitae*, however, I am fortunately mounted on a hobby, which, indeed, I should have better managed some thirty or forty years ago; but whose easy amble is still sufficient to give exercise and amusement to an octogenary rider.[66] The University will give employment to my remaining years, and quite enough for my senile faculties. It is the last act of usefulness I can render, and could I see it open I would not ask an hour more of life.[67]

A father's worry, pride, and hope

The time of opening our University is still as uncertain as ever. All the pavilions, boarding-houses, and dormitories are done. Nothing is now wanting but the central building [the Rotunda] for a library and other general purposes. For this we have no funds, and the last legislature refused all aid.[68] But the gloomiest of all prospects is in the desertion of the best friends of the institution, for desertion I must call it. . . . What object of our lives can we propose so important? What interest of our own which ought not to be postponed to this? Health, time, labor, on what in the single life which nature has given us, can these be better bestowed than on this immortal boon to our country? The exertions and the mortifications are temporary; the benefits eternal. If any member of our college of visitors could justifiably withdraw from this sacred duty it would be myself, who . . . have neither vigor of body nor mind left to keep the field; but I will die in the last ditch.[69]

We have proceeded from the beginning on the sound determination to finish the buildings before opening the institution, because once opened all its funds will be absorbed . . . and nothing remain ever to finish the buildings. . . . Patience and steady perserverance on our part will secure the blessed end. . . . Public opinion is advancing . . . and will force the institution on to consummation.[70] The great object of our aim from the beginning has been to make the establishment the most eminent in the United States, in order to draw to it the youth of every state, but especially of the South and West. We have proposed, therefore, to call to it characters of the first order of science from Europe, as well as our own country.... Had we built a barn for a college, and log huts for accommodations, should we ever have had the assurance to propose to a European professor of that character to come to it? [71] It will be a splendid establishment, would be thought so in Europe, and for the chastity of its architecture and classical taste leaves everything in America far behind it [72]

The opening of the University

Our legislature... liberated the revenue... and we propose to open it the beginning of [1825]. We require the intervening time for seeking out and engaging professors... some of them at least in ... Great Britain, the land of our language, habits, and manners.[73] In some departments of science we believe Europe to be in advance before us, and that it would advance ourselves were we to draw from thence instructors in these branches, and thus to improve our science as we have done our manufactures by borrowed skill. I have been much squibbed for this.[74] Would it have been either patriotism or fidelity in us to have sunk the youth of our state to a half-lettered grade of education by committing them to inferior instruction, ... and is this the way to advance the American character? We thought otherwise.[75]

The arrival of our professors from abroad has at length enabled us to get our University into operation.... We began on the 7th of March [1825].... Our [five] English professors give us perfect satisfaction.... Our professors of chemistry and moral philosophy are chosen from among our own fellow-citizens, as will be our professor of law.[76] The institution is at length happily advanced to completion, and has commenced under auspices as favorable as I could expect.[77] There are some novelties in it...., a professorship of the principles of government, ... of agriculture, ... and ... of Anglo-Saxon.[78]

The professors brought from [Great Britain] ... cannot fail to be one of the efficacious means of promoting that cordial good will which it is so much the interest of both nations to cherish.... For these two nations holding cordially together have nothing to fear

from the united world. They will be the models for regenerating
the condition of man, the sources from which representative government is to flow over the whole earth.[79]

Times and methods change but not the rights of man

At the age of eighty-two, with one foot in the grave and the other
uplifted to follow it, I do not permit myself to take part in any new
enterprises ... not even in the great one [of emancipating the
slaves] which has been through life that of my greatest anxieties.
The march of events has not been such as to render its completion
practicable within the limits of time allotted to me; and I leave its
accomplishment as the work of another generation. . . . The abolition of the evil is not impossible; it ought never therefore to be despaired of. Every plan should be adopted, every experiment tried,
which may do something towards the ultimate object.[80]

We have not yet so far perfected our constitutions as to venture to
make them unchangeable. . . . But can they be made unchangeable? ... I think not. The Creator has made the earth for the living, not the dead. Rights and powers can only belong to persons,
not to things. . . . A generation may bind itself as long as its majority continues in life; when that has disappeared, another majority is
in place ... and may change their laws and institutions to suit
themselves. Nothing then is unchangeable but the inherent and un-
alienable rights of man.[81]

Parties are ... censors of the conduct of each other, and useful
watchmen for the public. Men by their constitutions are naturally
divided into two parties: 1. Those who fear and distrust the people,
and wish to draw all powers from them into the hands of the higher
classes. 2. Those who identify themselves with the people, have
confidence in them, cherish and consider them as the most honest
and safe, although not the most wise, depository of the public interests. In every country these two parties exist, and in every one
where they are free to think, speak, and write, they will declare
themselves. Call them, therefore, ... Whigs and Tories, Republicans and Federalists, Aristocrats and Democrats, or by whatever
name you please, they are the same parties still, and pursue the
same object.[82]

The multiplication of public offices, increase of expense beyond income, growth and entailment of a public debt, are indications soliciting the employment of the pruning-knife. ... The great object of my fear is the federal judiciary. That body, like gravity, ever acting with noiseless foot and unalarming advance, gaining ground step by step, and holding what it gains, is engulfing insidiously the special governments into the jaws of that which feeds them.[83]

I see ... with the deepest affliction the rapid strides with which the federal branch of our government is advancing towards ... the consolidation in itself of all powers, foreign and domestic. ... And what is our resource for the preservation of the Constitution? ... Are we then *to stand to our arms* ...? No. That must be the last resource. ... If every infraction of a compact of so many parties is to be resisted at once, as a dissolution of it, none can ever be formed which would last one year. We must have patience and longer endurance, ... and separate from our companions only when the sole alternatives left are the dissolution of our union with them or submission to a government without limitation of powers. Between these two evils, when we must make a choice, there can be no hesitation.[84]

America's march of civilization

The delightful tour [taken by his granddaughter, Ellen Randolph Coolidge, in 1825] ... is almost exactly that which Mr. Madison and myself pursued in May and June, 1791. ... But from Saratoga till we got back to Northampton was then mostly desert. Now it is what thirty-four years of free and good government have made it. It shows how soon the labor of men would make a paradise of the whole earth were it not for misgovernment, and a diversion of all his energies from their proper object, the happiness of man, to the selfish interests of kings, nobles, and priests.[85]

Let a philosophic observer commence a journey from the savages of the Rocky Mountains eastwardly towards our seacoast. These he would observe in the earliest stage of association, living under no law but that of nature, subsisting and covering themselves with the flesh and skins of wild beasts. He would next find those on our frontiers in the pastoral state, raising domestic animals to supply the defects of hunting. Then succeed our own semi-barbarous citizens, the pioneers of the advance of civilization, and so in his progress he would meet the gradual shades of improving man until he would reach his, as yet, most improved state in our seaport towns. This, in fact, is equivalent to a survey, in time, of the progress of man from the infancy of creation to the present day. . . .

I have observed this march of civilization advancing from the seacoast, passing over us like a cloud of light, increasing our knowledge and improving our condition, insomuch as that we are at this time more advanced in civilization here than the seaports were when I was a boy. And where this progress will stop no one can say. Barbarism has, in the meantime, been receding before the steady step of amelioration; and will in time, I trust, disappear from the earth.[86]

With the University I am closing the last scenes of life

Withdrawn by age from all other public services and attentions to public things, I am closing the last scenes of life by fashioning and fostering an establishment for the instruction of those who are to come after us. I hope its influence on their virtue, freedom, fame, and happiness will be salutary and permanent.[87] Our University goes on well. . . . We studiously avoid too much government. We treat [the students] as men and gentlemen, under the guidance mainly of their own discretion. They so consider themselves, and make it their pride to acquire that character for their institution. . . . I am expecting . . . the clock for the Rotunda [an ingenious one, designed by Jefferson, with a bell which rang the hours automatically and yet permitted of being rung independently].[88] All here are well, except myself. . . . Going backwards and forwards on the rough roads to the University for five days successively has brought on me again a great deal of sufferance.[89]

I have been quite anxious to get a good drawing master in the military or landscape line for the University.[90] This [observatory, for which Jefferson drew plans and specifications] is proposed for the ordinary purposes of the astronomical professor and his school. . . . The mountain . . . was purchased with a view to a permanent . . . observatory, with an astronomer resident at it.[91] I have diligently examined all our grounds [selected a proper site, and planned botanical gardens, terraces, and groves]. Enclose the ground with a serpentine brick wall seven feet high. This would take about eighty thousand bricks, and cost eight hundred dollars. ... As to the seeds of plants ... I have ... a special resource, ... my good old friend Thouin, superintendent of the garden of plants at Paris. ... The trees I should propose would be exotics of distinguished usefulness. ... The Larch can be obtained from a tree at Monticello. ... The Marronnier and Cork Oak I can obtain from France.[92]

I verily believe that as high a degree of education can now be obtained here as in [England]. And a finer set of youths I never saw assembled for instruction. They committed some irregularities at first, until they learned the lawful length of their tether. ... A great proportion of them are severely devoted to study, and I fear not to say that ... they will exhibit their country in a degree of sound respectability it has never known, either in our days, or those of our forefathers. I cannot live to see it. My joy must only be that of anticipation.[93]

The closing scenes clouded by financial distress

Weakened in body by infirmities and in mind by age, now far gone in my eighty-third year, ... I am unable to give counsel in cases of difficulty. ... Yesterday the last of the year [1825] closed the sixty-first of my continued services to the public.[94]

My own debts had become considerable, but not beyond the effect of some lopping of property, which would have been little felt, when our friend [Wilson Cary] Nicholas gave me the *coup de grâce*. Ever since that I have been paying twelve hundred dollars a year interest on his debt, which, with my own, was ... making deep and rapid inroads on my capital. ... Had crops and prices for several years been such as to maintain a steady competition of substantial bidders at market, all would have been safe. But the long succession of years of stunted crops, of reduced prices, the general prostration of the farming business ... have ... glutted the land market. ... The practice occurred to me of selling on fair valuation and by way of lottery, often resorted to ... and still in constant usage in every state. ... If it is permitted in my case, my lands here alone, with the mills, etc., will pay everything and leave me Monticello and a farm free. If refused, I must sell everything here, per-

haps considerably in Bedford, move thither with my family, where I
have not even a log hut to put my head into. . . .

But why afflict you [Madison] with these details? Indeed, I cannot tell, unless pains are lessened by communication with a friend.
The friendship which has subsisted between us, now half a century,
and the harmony of our political principles and pursuits, have been
sources of constant happiness to me through that long period. And
if I remove beyond the reach of attentions to the University, or
beyond the bourne of life itself, as I soon must, it is a comfort to
leave that institution under your care. . . .

It has also been a great solace to me to believe that you are engaged in [writing a history] vindicating to posterity the course we
have pursued for preserving to them, in all their purity, the blessings
of self-government, which we had assisted too in acquiring for them.
If ever the earth has beheld a system of administration conducted
with a single and steadfast eye to the general interest and happiness
. . . it is that to which our lives have been devoted. To myself you
have been a pillar of support through life. Take care of me when
dead, and be assured that I shall leave with you my last affections.[95]

My beloved daughter and grandchildren

There are greater doubts than I had apprehended whether the
legislature will indulge me in my request [for a lottery]. . . . I see
in the failure of this hope a deadly blast of all peace of mind during
my remaining days. . . . I am overwhelmed at the prospect of the
situation in which I may leave my family. My dear and beloved
daughter, the cherished companion of my early life and nurse of my
age, and her children, rendered as dear to me as if my own from
having lived with them from their cradle, left in a comfortless situation, hold up to me nothing but future gloom, and I should not care
were life to end with the line I am writing were it not that . . . I
may yet be of some avail to the family. Their affectionate devotion
to me makes a willingness to endure life a duty as long as it can be of
any use to them. . . .

Perhaps however even in this case I may have no right to com-
plain, as these misfortunes have been held back for my last days
when few remain to me. I duly acknowledge that I have gone
through a long life with fewer circumstances of affliction than are the

lot of most men. Uninterrupted health, a competence for every reasonable want, usefulness to my fellow-citizens, a good portion of their esteem, no complaint against the world which has sufficiently honored me, and above all a family which has blessed me by their affection and never by their conduct given me a moment's pain; and should this my last request be granted I may yet close with a cloudless sun a long and serene day of life.[96]

A source of felicity never otherwise known

The single permission given me by the legislature of such a mode of sale as ensures a fair value for what I must sell will leave me still a competent provision.[97] I have received an application from persons in North Carolina desirous of manifesting their good will to me by contributions in money, if acceptable, and offering to dispose of a portion of tickets if the way of lottery is preferred. . . . It certainly is not for me to prescribe what shape my fellow-citizens shall manifest their kindness to me. The bounties from one's country, expressions of its approbation, are honors which it would be arrogance to refuse, especially where flowing from the *willing* only. The same approbation, however, expressed by promoting the success of the lottery would have the advantage of relieving the repugnance we justly feel against becoming a burden to our friends. . . .

The necessity which dictated this expedient cost me . . . unspeakable mortification. The turn it has taken, so much beyond what I could have expected, has countervailed all I suffered, and become a source of felicity which I should otherwise never have known.[98]

Serenity and love on the mountaintop

My dear Ellen [who was now Mrs. Joseph Coolidge of Boston], . . . our brandy, fish, tongues, and sounds are here, and highly approved. The piano forte is also in place, and Mrs. Carey *happening* here has exhibited to us its full powers, which are indeed great. Nobody slept the first night, nor is the tumult yet over on this the third day of its emplacement. . . . All here are well, and growing in their love to you, and none so much as the oldest.[99]

I address you the less frequently because I find it easier to write ten letters of business than one on the intangible affections of the mind. Were these to be indulged as calls for writing letters to express them, my love to you would engross the unremitting exercises of my pen.... Yesterday [June 4, 1826] closed a visit of six weeks from the younger members of [a neighboring family], during which their attractions had kept us full of the homagers to their beauty. According to appearances they had many nibbles and bites, but whether the hooks took firm hold of any particular subject or not is a secret not communicated to me.... Shall I say anything to you of my health? It is as good as I ever expect it to be. At present tolerable, but subject to occasional relapses of sufferance. I am just now out of one of these.... I commit my affections to Mr. Coolidge to my letter to him. Communicate those to Cornelia by a thousand kisses from me, and take to yourself those I impress on this paper for you.[100]

The Argonauts of 1776

My grandson, Thomas J. Randolph, the bearer of this letter, being on a visit to Boston, would think he had seen nothing were he to leave without seeing you [John Adams].... Like other young people he wishes to be able in the winter nights of old age to recount to those around him what he has heard and learnt of the heroic age preceding his birth, and which of the Argonauts individually he was in time to have seen.

It was the lot of our early years to witness nothing but the dull monotony of a colonial subservience; and of our riper years, to breast the labors and perils of working out of it. Theirs are the Halcyon calm succeeding the storm which our Argosy had so stoutly weathered. Gratify his ambition then by receiving his best bow, and my solicitude for your health.... Mine is but indifferent, but not so my friendship and respect for you.[101]

The fiftieth July 4th, a deathbed adieu, and my epitaph

The kind invitation I receive from... the citizens of the city of Washington to be present with them at their celebration on the fiftieth anniversary of American Independence, as one of the surviving signers of an instrument pregant with our own and the fate of the world, is most flattering to myself.... It adds sensibly to the sufferings of sickness to be deprived by it of a personal participation in the rejoicings of that day.... May it be to the world what I believe it will be (to some parts sooner, to others later, but finally to all), the signal of arousing men to burst the chains under which monkish ignorance and superstition had persuaded them to bind themselves, and to assume the blessings and security of self-government. That form which we have substituted restores the free right to the unbounded exercise of reason and freedom of opinion.

All eyes are opened, or opening, to the rights of man. The general spread of the light of science has already laid open to every view the palpable truth that the mass of mankind has not been born with saddles on their backs, nor a favored few booted and spurred, ready to ride them legitimately by the grace of God. These are grounds of hope for others. For ourselves, let the annual return of this day forever refresh our recollections of these rights, and an undiminished devotion to them.[102]

A Deathbed Adieu from Th. J. to M. R.

Life's visions are vanished, its dreams are no more;
Dear friends of my bosom, why bathed in tears?
I go to my fathers, I welcome the shore
Which crowns all my hopes or which buries my cares.
Then farewell, my dear, my lov'd daughter, adieu!
The last pang of life is in parting from you!
Two seraphs await me long shrouded in death;
I will bear them your love on my last parting breath.[103]

Could the dead feel any interest in monuments or other remembrances of them, . . . the following would be to my manes the most gratifying: on the grave a plain die or cube of three feet without any mouldings, surmounted by an obelisk of six feet height, each of a single stone; on the face of the obelisk the following inscription, and not a word more:

Here was buried
Thomas Jefferson,
Author of the Declaration of American Independence,
Of the Statute of Virginia for Religious Freedom,
And Father of the University of Virginia;

because by these as testimonials that I have lived I wish most to be remembered.[104]

NOTES AND SOURCES

My wife, Barbara Mayo, has been my collaborator, and to her my debt of gratitude is great indeed. I wish also to thank the librarians and archivists who have aided me, and particularly those of the Alderman Library of the University of Virginia.

The text of the book is Mr. Jefferson's; only the captions, material in brackets, and introductions are mine. Where it has seemed proper and necessary, I have modernized the spelling and punctuation, split up long paragraphs, and spelled out abbreviations. Pertinent unpublished writings, especially those bearing on Jefferson's private and non-political life, have been used. But the bulk of the material is from printed sources, which the reader can readily consult if he should wish to have the full text of any selection.

The sources are listed below, with key initials preceding those most frequently cited in the notes. Since the main source has been the twenty-volume edition of Jefferson's writings, I have thought it unnecessary to identify that by any key initials. It will be readily understood that a citation in the notes reading, for example, 'Dr. Thomas Cooper, Monticello, Feb. 10, 1814, 14:85,' means a letter of that date written to Cooper by Jefferson from Monticello, to be found in the Lipscomb and Bergh twenty-volume edition, volume 14, page 85. It might be noted that Jefferson's Autobiography, which covers his life only to March of 1790, was written at Monticello in 1821. His Anas, or notes, covering the years 1791 to 1806, with an introduction written in 1816, are practically a continuation of the Autobiography.

Sources, printed and manuscript

American Historical Review, volumes 12 (1906), 33 (1928).

Cabell, Nathaniel F., editor, *Early History of the University of Virginia, as contained in the letters of Thomas Jefferson and Joseph C. Cabell*. Richmond, 1856.

F   Ford, Paul Leicester, editor, *The Writings of Thomas Jefferson*. 10 volumes. New York, 1892–1899.

FB   Ford, Worthington Chauncey, editor, *Thomas Jefferson Correspondence. Printed from the originals in the collection of William K. Bixby*. Boston, 1916.

Ford, Worthington Chauncey, editor, Volume 2, *Journals of the Continental Congress, 1774–1789* (34 volumes, Washington, 1904–1937), Washington, 1905.

LC   Library of Congress, Jefferson Manuscripts collection.

Lipscomb, Andrew A., and Bergh, Albert Ellery, editors, *The Writings of Thomas Jefferson.* Library Edition. Issued under the auspices of the Thomas Jefferson Memorial Association. 20 volumes. Washington, 1903.

MHS   Massachusetts Historical Society, Jefferson Manuscripts collection.

New York Historical Society, Jefferson Manuscripts collection.

New York Public Library *Bulletin* No. 2. New York, 1898.

Pierson, Hamilton W., *Jefferson at Monticello. The Private Life of Thomas Jefferson. From entirely new materials.* (The papers and reminiscences of Jefferson's overseer, Edmund Bacon.) New York, 1862.

R   Randall, Henry S., *The Life of Thomas Jefferson.* 3 volumes. New York, 1858.

Randolph, Sarah N., *The Domestic Life of Thomas Jefferson. Compiled from Family Letters and Reminiscences by his great-granddaughter.* New York, 1871.

UV   University of Virginia, Alderman Library, Jefferson Manuscripts collection.

CHAPTER I

EDUCATION OF A VIRGINIAN

1. Autobiography, 1:1–4.
2. L. H. Girardin, Monticello, Jan. 15, 1815, 14:231–32.
3. Autobiography, 1:4.
4. John Saunderson, Monticello, Aug. 31, 1820, 1:165–70.
5. Thomas Jefferson Randolph, Washington, Nov. 24, 1808, 12:197–98.
6. William Wirt, Monticello, Aug. 5, 1815, 14:341.
7. William Wirt, Monticello, April 12, 1812, F9:343n.
8. Autobiography, 1:5–6.
9. John Page, Fairfield, Dec. 25, 1762, 4:1–5.
10. John Page, Shadwell, Jan. 20, 1763, 4:7–8.
11. John Page, Shadwell, July 15, 1763, 4:8–11.
12. William Fleming, Richmond, Sept. ?, 1763, F1:351–52.
13. John Page, Williamsburg, Oct. 7, 1763, 4:12.
14. William Fleming, Williamsburg, March 20, 1764, F1:357–58.
15. John Page, Williamsburg, Oct. 7, 1763, 4:12.
16. John Page, Devilsburg [i.e., Williamsburg], Jan. 23, 1764, 4:15–16.
17. John Page, Devilsburg [i.e., Williamsburg], April 9, 1764, 4:16.
18. John Page, Annapolis, May 25, 1766, *Bulletin* No. 2, NYPL, pp. 176–77.
19. Dr. Thomas Cooper, Monticello, Feb. 10, 1814, 14:85.
20. Herbert Croft, Monticello, Oct. 30, 1798, 18:363.
21. Essay on the Anglo-Saxon Language, 18:390, 386, 390–91.
22. Bernard Moore, about 1765, R1:53–56.
23. John Garland Jefferson, New York, June 11, 1790, F5:180–81.
24. Peter Carr, Paris, Aug. 19, 1785, 5:85–86.

25. Excerpts from MS. Account Books for 1768, and 1769, LC.
26. John Page, Charlottesville, Feb. 21, 1770, 4:18–21.

CHAPTER II

YOUNG SQUIRE OF MONTICELLO

1. James Ogilvie, Monticello, Feb. 20, 1771, 4:233.
2. Thomas Adams, Monticello, June 1, 1771, 4:235–36.
3. Robert Skipwith, Monticello, Aug. 3, 1771, 4:240.
4. Autobiography, 1:5.
5. MS. Account Book, 1772, MHS.
6. Autobiography, 1:76.
7. Excerpts from the Garden Book, R1:70–76.
8. MS. Account Book, 1773, LC.
9. Robert Skipwith, Monticello, Aug. 3, 1771, 4:237–39.
10. Dr. Joseph Priestley, Philadelphia, Jan. 27, 1800, 10:146–47.
11. Charles McPherson, Albemarle, in Va., Feb. 25, 1773, 4:22–23.
12. David Rittenhouse, Monticello, July 19, 1778, 4:42–43.
13. [Francis Alberti?], Williamsburg, June 8, 1778, 4:40–42.
14. Autobiography, 1:90–92.
15. Notes on Virginia, 2:211–13.
16. Notes on Virginia, 2:24–25.
17. Notes on Virginia, 2:30–31.
18. Notes on Virginia, 2:229–30.
19. Notes on Virginia, 2:225–28.
20. Notes on Virginia, 2:104–09.
21. Notes on Virginia, 2:115–16.
22. Notes on Virginia, 2:135–37.
23. Notes on Virginia, 2:61–95.
24. Inscribed in Jefferson's prayer book, R1:383.
25. James Monroe, Monticello, May 20, 1782, F3:60.
26. Elizabeth Thompson, Paris, Jan. 19, 1787, FB, p. 21.
27. François Jean, Chevalier de Chastellux, Ampthill, Nov. 26, 1782, F3:64–65.
28. Martha Jefferson, Annapolis, Nov. 28, 1783, 4:446–48.
29. Martha Jefferson, Annapolis, Dec. 22, 1783, R1:391–92.
30. François de Barbé-Marbois, Annapolis, Dec. 5, 1783, *Amer. Hist. Review*, 12:76–77.
31. Martha Jefferson, Aix en Provence, March 28, 1787, F4:374.

CHAPTER III

REVOLUTIONIST

1. Autobiography, 1:4–5.
2. François Soulés, Paris, Sept. 13, 1786, 17:133–34.

3. Dr. Benjamin Waterhouse, Monticello, March 3, 1818, 15:163–64.
4. Autobiography, 1:6–12.
5. A Summary View of the Rights of British America, 1:209–11.
6. Autobiography, 1:12–14.
7. Dr. William Small, ——, May 7, 1775, 4:26–27.
8. Autobiography, 1:14–16.
9. Declaration of Causes and Necessity of Taking up Arms, July 6, 1775, *Journals of the Continental Congress*, 2:153–57.
10. Francis Eppes, Philadelphia, July 4, 1775, 4:244.
11. John Randolph, Monticello, Aug. 25, 1775, 4:28–30.
12. John Randolph, Philadelphia, Nov. 29, 1775, 4:32–33.

CHAPTER IV

LIBERTY AND THE PURSUIT OF HAPPINESS

1. Autobiography, 1:17–26.
2. James Madison, Monticello, Aug. 30, 1823, 15:461.
3. Autobiography, 1:26–38.
4. Henry Lee, Monticello, May 8, 1825, 16:118–19.
5. James Madison, Monticello, Aug. 30, 1823, 15:461–63.
6. Robert Walsh, Monticello, Dec. 4, 1818, 18:169–70.
7. MS. Account Book, 1776, MHS.
8. Dr. James Mease, Monticello, Sept. 26, 1825, 16:123.
9. Ellen W. Coolidge, Monticello, Nov. 14, 1825, 18:348–50.
10. Notes on Virginia, 2:158–59.
11. James Madison, Monticello, Aug. 30, 1823, 15:463–64.

CHAPTER V

FIGHTING FOR MAN'S INALIENABLE RIGHTS

1. John Cartwright, Monticello, June 5, 1824, 16:44–45.
2. Autobiography, 1:53–59.
3. Notes on Virginia, 2:219–25.
4. Autobiography, 1:60–67.
5. A Bill for Establishing Religious Freedom, 1779, F2:237–39.
6. Autobiography, 1:70–71.
7. Notes on Virginia, 2:203–07.
8. George Wythe, Paris, Aug. 14, 1786, F4:268–69.
9. Notes on Virginia, 2:207–08, 160.
10. Autobiography, 1:71–73.
11. Dr. Richard Price, Paris, Aug. 7, 1785, 5:56–57.
12. M. de Meusnier, about June, 1786, 17:103.
13. Autobiography, 1:73–74.

14. Dr. Benjamin Franklin, Virginia, Aug. 13, 1777, 4:34–35.
15. James Madison, Paris, Dec. 16, 1786, 6:10–11.

CHAPTER VI

WAR GOVERNOR

1. Autobiography, 1:74–75.
2. Genl. George Washington, Richmond, June 11, 1780, F2:309.
3. Genl. George Washington, Richmond, Sept. 23, 1780, 4:107.
4. Genl. George Washington, Richmond, Oct. 22, 1780, 4:120–21.
5. Va. Delegates in Congress, Richmond, Oct. 27, 1780, F2:356–57.
6. Major-Genl. Horatio Gates, Richmond, Nov. 10, 1780, F2:361–62.
7. Brig.-Genl. George Rogers Clark, Richmond, Dec. 25, 1780, F2:383–90.
8. The President of Congress, Richmond, Jan. 10, 1781, F2:405–08.
9. [George Rogers Clark?], Richmond, Jan. 31, 1781, F2:441–42.
10. Genl. Horatio Gates, Richmond, Feb. 17, 1781, 4:161–62.
11. Major-Genl. Nathaniel Greene, Richmond, Feb. 10, 1781, 4:354.
12. Major-Genl. Baron Steuben, In Council, Feb. 24, 1781, 4:366.
13. Major-Genl. Marquis de Lafayette, Richmond, March 10, 1781, 4:383–84.
14. Colonel Vanmeter, Richmond, April 27, 1781, 4:417–18.
15. Genl. George Washington, Richmond, May 9, 1781, F3:32–33.
16. Chevalier de la Luzerne, Richmond, April 12, 1781, F3:8–10.
17. Genl. George Washington, Charlottesville, May 28, 1781, F3:41–43.
18. Memorandum relative to the invasion of Virginia, 17:17–18.
19. Notes on Virginia, F3:231–34.
20. Diary relative to the invasion of Virginia, 17:11–12.
21. Dr. William Gordon, Paris, July 16, 1788, F5:38–40.
22. Diary relative to the invasion of Virginia, 17:5–11.
23. Notes on Virginia, 2:240–41.
24. Autobiography, 1:77–80.
25. George Washington, Annapolis, Mar. 15, 1784, F3:420–21.
26. James Madison, Annapolis, Feb. 20, 1784, F3:403.
27. James Madison, Boston, July 1, 1784, 4:458.
28. Report of Government for the Western Territory [March 22, 1784], F3: 429–32.
29. James Madison, Annapolis, April 25, 1784, F3:470–71.
30. M. de Meusnier, Paris, [June 22, 1786], F4:181.
31. James Madison, Annapolis, Feb. 20, 1784, F3:406.
32. James Madison, Paris, Dec. 8, 1784, F4:17–18.
33. Autobiography, 1:89–90.

CHAPTER VII

AN AMERICAN IN PARIS

1. Charles Bellini, Paris, Sept. 30, 1785, 5:152–54.
2. Autobiography, 1:92–94.
3. [Rev. William Smith], Philadelphia, Feb. 19, 1791, 8:129–30.
4. Autobiography, 1:96.
5. Autobiography, F1:88–90.
6. John Page, Paris, May 4, 1786, 5:305–06.
7. C. W. F. Dumas, Paris, May 6, 1786, 5:310.
8. James Monroe, Paris, Nov. 11, 1784, F4:10–11.
9. James Monroe [Paris, Feb. 1785], F4:32–34.
10. Autobiography, 1:97–101.
11. Francis Eppes, Aug. 30, 1785, Randolph, *Dom. Life*, pp. 105–106.
12. Francis Eppes, Dec. 11, 1785, 19:20–21.
13. Mrs. John Bolling, Paris, July 23, 1787, F4:411–12.
14. Martha ('Patsy') Jefferson, Aix en Provence, March 28, 1787, F4:373.
15. Mrs. William Bingham, Paris, Feb. 7, 1787, 6:81–82.
16. John Bannister, Jr., Paris, Oct. 15, 1785, 5:186–88.
17. Mrs. John (Abigail) Adams, Paris, June 21 [1785], F4:60–61.
18. Mrs. John Adams, Paris, Sept. 25, 1785, F4:100–01.
19. Madame de Corny, Paris, June 30, 1787, 6:145.
20. Mrs. William Bingham, Paris, Feb. 7, 1787, 6:83.
21. Mrs. William S. Smith, Paris, Jan. 15, 1787, Randolph, *Dom. Life*. p. 78.
22. Mrs. Angelica Church, Paris, July 27, 1788, FB, p. 31.
23. Madame de Brehan, Paris, March 14, 1789, 7:307–08.
24. George Washington, Paris, Aug. 14, 1787, 6:275.
25. Francis Hopkinson, Paris, Jan. 3, 1786, 5:239.
26. François J. de Chastellux [undated, but presumably written while in Paris], 18:414; and, for the essay, 18:415–51.
27. Rev. James Madison, Paris, July 19, 1788, 7:73–76.
28. Charles Thomson, Paris, Nov. 11, 1784, F4:14.
29. Joseph Jones, Paris, June 19, 1785, 5:23.
30. John Jay, Paris, Aug. 30, 1785, 5:105–06.
31. Dr. Joseph Willard, Paris, March 24, 1789, 7:328–29.
32. Francis Hopkinson, Paris, Dec. 23, 1786, 6:21.
33. Comte de Buffon, Paris, Oct. 3, 1787, 6:325–27.
34. William Drayton, Paris, May 6, 1786, 5:311–12.
35. Ralph Izard, Paris, Aug. 1, 1787, 6:209.
36. Rev. James Madison, Fontainebleau, Oct. 28, 1785, 19:20.
37. George Wythe, Paris, Sept. 16, 1787, 6:297.
38. James Madison, Paris, Jan. 30, 1787, 6:72–73.
39. Baron de Geismar, Paris, Nov. 20 [1788], 19:71.
40. Dr. Edward Bancroft, Paris, Feb. 26, 1786, 5:285–86.
41. Autobiography, 1:68–69.

CHAPTER VIII

MY HEAD AND MY HEART

1. Mrs. Maria Cosway, Paris, Oct. 12, 1786, 5:430–48.
2. Mrs. Maria Cosway, Paris, Oct. 13, 1786, 5:448–49.
3. James Madison, Paris, Jan. 30, 1787, 6:70–71.
4. Comtesse de Tessé, Nismes, March 20, 1787, 6:102–06.
5. Martha Jefferson, ——, May 21, 1787, F4:388–89.
6. Marquis de Lafayette, Nice, April 11, 1787, 6:106–09.
7. Rev. James Madison, Fontainebleau, Oct. 28, 1785, F7:35–36.
8. George Wythe, Paris, Aug. 13, 1786, F4:268–69.
9. George Washington, Paris, Nov. 14, 1786, 6:4
10. William Carmichael, Paris, Dec. 26, 1786, 6:30
11. Col. Edward Carrington, Paris, Jan. 16, 1787, 6:57–58.
12. James Madison, Paris, Jan. 30, 1787, 6:65.
13. Col. William S. Smith, Paris, Nov. 13, 1787, 6:372–73.
14. James Madison, Paris, Dec. 20, 1787, 6:392.
15. Francis Hopkinson, Paris, March 13, 1789, 7:300–02.
16. Edward Rutledge, Paris, July 18, 1788, 7:81.
17. Dr. Richard Price, Paris, Jan. 8, 1789, 7:253–54.
18. Autobiography, 1:139–60.
19. Baron de Geismar, Paris, Sept. 6, 1785, 5:128–29.
20. Dr. George Gilmer, Paris, Aug. 11, 1787, 6:265.
21. Autobiography, 1:160–61.

CHAPTER IX

WASHINGTON'S SECRETARY OF STATE

1. Autobiography, 1:160–64.
2. Thomas Mann Randolph, New York, March 28, 1790, 8:7–8.
3. Marquis de Lafayette, New York, April 2, 1790, 8:11–13.
4. The Anas, 1:270–71.
5. William Short, Monticello, Jan. 8, 1825, 16:94.
6. Martin Van Buren, Monticello, June 29, 1824, 16:60, 59, 60.
7. The Anas, 1:357.
8. The Anas, 1:271–78.
9. Dr. Walter Jones, Monticello, Jan. 2, 1814, 14:48–51.
10. The Anas, 1:278–79.
11. Dr. Benjamin Rush, Jan. 16, 1811, 13:4.
12. The Anas, 1:279.
13. Opinion against the constitutionality of a National Bank, Feb. 15, **1791**, 3:146–52.
14. Col. George Mason, Philadelphia, Feb. 4, 1791, 8:124–25.

15. James Monroe, Philadelphia, July 10, 1791, 8:208–09.
16. Edward Rutledge, Philadelphia, Aug. 25, 1791, 8:233.
17. William Short, Philadelphia, March 18, 1792, 8:317.
18. Thomas Mann Randolph, Philadelphia, April 19, 1792, F5:509–10.
19. Francis Eppes, Philadelphia, April 14, 1792, F5:507.
20. Col. George Mason, Philadelphia, Feb. 4, 1791, 8:123–24.
21. Edward Rutledge, New York, July 4, 1790, 8:60–61.
22. William Carmichael, New York, Aug. 2, 1790, 8:70–73.
23. William Short, New York, Aug. 10, 1790, 8:79–82.
24. Gouverneur Morris, New York, Aug. 12, 1790, 8:84–85.
25. George Hammond (the British Minister), Phila., Dec. 15, 1793, 9:271–72.
26. Charles Carroll of Carrollton, Philadelphia, April 15, 1791, 8:177–78.
27. Gouverneur Morris, Philadelphia, March 10, 1792, 8:312.
28. Messrs. Carmichael and Short, Philadelphia, Nov. 3, 1792, 8:425–26.
29. Messrs. Carmichael and Short, Philadelphia, June 30, 1793, 9:159–60.
30. William Short, Philadelphia, July 28, 1791, 8:219–20.
31. Report on the privileges and restrictions on the commerce of the United States in foreign countries, Dec. 16, 1793, 3:275–76.
32. President Washington, Philadelphia, May 23, 1792, 8:341–47.

CHAPTER X

THE THORNY PATH OF NEUTRALITY

1. Thomas Mann Randolph, Bennington, Vt., June 5, 1791, 8:204–05.
2. Martha Jefferson Randolph, Lake Champlain, May 31, 1791, F5:337.
3. Major Peter Charles L'Enfant, Phila., April 10, 1791, 8:162.
4. Opinion on proceedings to be had under the Residence Act, Nov. 29, 1790, 3:83–84.
5. Major Peter Charles L'Enfant, Phila., April 10, 1791, 8:163.
6. President Washington, Philadelphia, April 10, 1791, 8:166.
7. Daniel Carroll, Philadelphia, Feb. 1, 1793, 9:18.
8. Benjamin Vaughan, New York, June 27, 1790, 8:50.
9. Eli Whitney, Germantown, Nov. 16, 1793, F6:448.
10. Plan for establishing uniformity in the Coinage, Weights, and Measures of the United States. Communicated to the House of Representatives, July 13, 1790, 3:33, 49.
11. President Washington, Philadelphia, May 1, 1791, 8:190–91.
12. A list of services, about 1800, 1:258–59.
13. Martha Jefferson Randolph, Philadelphia, Dec. 1, 1790, R2:14.
14. Martha Jefferson Randolph, Philadelphia, July 24, 1791, MS., MHS.
15. Martha Jefferson Randolph, Philadelphia, Dec. 23, 1790, R2:15.
16. Maria Jefferson, Philadelphia, April 24, 1791, R2:18–19.
17. Martha Jefferson Randolph, Philadelphia, Jan. 15, 1792, F5:422.
18. Maria Jefferson, Philadelphia, March 31, 1791, R2:17–18.

19. Martha Jefferson Randolph, Philadelphia, March 22, 1792, F5:488.
20. Martha Jefferson Randolph, Philadelphia, Dec. 31, 1792, 18:191–92.
21. Martha Jefferson Randolph, Philadelphia, Jan. 14, 1793, R2:191.
22. Martha Jefferson Randolph, Philadelphia, July 7, 1793, R2:191–92.
23. Martha Jefferson Randolph, Philadelphia, June 10, 1793, R2:191.
24. Martha Jefferson Randolph, Philadelphia, March 22, 1792, F5:487–88.
25. Francis Eppes, Philadelphia, April 14, 1792, F5:506–07.
26. Edmund Randolph, Monticello, Sept. 17, 1792, 8:411.
27. President Washington, Monticello, Sept. 9, 1792, 8:396–408.
28. The Anas, 1:315–19.
29. Thomas Paine, Philadelphia, June 19, 1792, F6:87–88.
30. Sir John Sinclair, Philadelphia, Aug. 24, 1791, 8:231.
31. Edward Rutledge, Philadelphia, Aug. 25, 1791, 8:234.
32. ——, Philadelphia, March 18, 1793, 9:45.
33. Gouverneur Morris, Philadelphia, March 12, 1793, 9:36–37.
34. William Short, Philadelphia, Jan. 3, 1793, 9:9–10.
35. James Monroe, Philadelphia, May 5, 1793, 9:75–77.
36. Dr. Walter Jones, Monticello, March 5, 1810, 12:371.
37. James Madison, Philadelphia, May 13, 1793, 9:88–89.
38. Thomas Pinckney, Philadelphia, May 7, 1793, 9:79–81.
39. James Madison, Philadelphia, May 19, 1793, 9:96–97.
40. Thomas Mann Randolph, Philadelphia, June 24, 1793, F6:318.
41. James Madison, ——, July 7, 1793, F6:338–39.
42. Gouverneur Morris, Philadelphia, Aug. 16, 1793, 9:180–208.
43. James Madison, Philadelphia, Aug. 25, 1793, 9:211.
44. James Madison, Philadelphia, Sept. 1, 1793, 9:212–13.
45. Thomas Pinckney, Philadelphia, Sept. 7, 1793, 9:223–24.
46. Mrs. Angelica Church, Germantown, Nov. 27, 1793, F6:455–56.
47. President Washington, Philadelphia, Dec. 31, 1793, 9:278–79.
48. James Madison, Philadelphia, June 9, 1793, 9:118–19.

CHAPTER XI

THE STRUGGLE FOR DEMOCRACY

1. John Adams, Monticello, April 25, 1794, F6:505.
2. Edmund Randolph, Monticello, Feb. 3, 1794, 9:280.
3. Mann Page, Monticello, Aug. 30, 1795, 9:306.
4. William B. Giles, Monticello, April 27, 1795, 9:305.
5. Tench Coxe, Monticello, May 1, 1794, 9:284–85.
6. N. and J. Van Staphorst and Hubbard, Monticello, Feb. 28, 1790, F5:145.
7. George Washington, Monticello, May 14, 1794, 9:287.
8. Jonathan Williams, Monticello, July 3, 1796, 9:347.
9. John Taylor, Monticello, Dec. 29, 1794, 18:199.
10. John Taylor, Philadelphia, June 4, 1798, 18:206.

11. William B. Giles, Monticello, March 19, 1796, 9:328.
12. C. F. C. de Volney, Monticello, Jan. 8, 1797, 9:363–64.
13. M. Démeunier, Monticello, April 29, 1795, F7:14.
14. James Madison, Monticello, Dec. 28, 1794, 9:293–97.
15. James Monroe, ——, March 2, 1796, F7:58–59.
16. Edward Rutledge, Monticello, Nov. 30, 1795, 9:314.
17. James Monroe, Monticello, July 10, 1796, 9:348–49.
18. Philip Mazzei, Monticello, April 24, 1796, 9:335–36.
19. Notes on Professor C. D. Ebeling's letter of July 30, 1795, F7:48.
20. Edward Rutledge, Monticello, Dec. 27, 1796, 9:352–53.
21. C. F. C. de Volney, Monticello, Jan. 8, 1797, 9:363.
22. James Madison, Monticello, Jan. 1, 1797, 9:357–58.
23. Dr. Benjamin Rush, Monticello, Jan. 22, 1797, 9:374.
24. Elbridge Gerry, Philadelphia, May 13, 1797, 9:381.
25. James Madison, Monticello, Jan. 22, 1797, 9:367–68.
26. James Madison, Monticello, Jan. 22, 1797, 9:368.
27. French Strother, Philadelphia, June 8, 1797, 9:396.
28. Horatio Gates, Philadelphia, May 30, 1797, 9:392.
29. Elbridge Gerry, May 13, 1797, 9:383–85.
30. Elbridge Gerry, Philadelphia, June 21, 1797, 9:405–06.
31. Edward Rutledge, Philadelphia, June 24, 1797, 9:411.
32. Martha Jefferson Randolph, Philadelphia, Feb. 8, 1798, R2:405.
33. Martha Jefferson Randolph, Philadelphia, June 8, 1797, R2:358.
34. Martha Jefferson Randolph, Philadelphia, May 17, 1798, R2:407.
35. Martha Jefferson Randolph, Philadelphia, Feb. 11, 1800, R2:535.
36. Dr. Benjamin Rush, Monticello, Jan. 22, 1797, 9:374.
37. Col. John Stuart, Monticello, Nov. 10, 1796, 9:350.
38. Col. Benjamin Hawkins, Philadelphia, March 14, 1800, 10:161.
39. Robert R. Livingston, Philadelphia, Feb. 28, 1799, 10:117–18.
40. George Wythe, Philadelphia, Feb. 28, 1800, F7:427.
41. Preface to A Manual of Parliamentary Practice, 2:333–34.
42. Col. Aaron Burr, Philadelphia, June 17, 1797, 9:403–04.
43. Col. Arthur Campbell, Monticello, Sept. 1, 1797, 9:419–21.
44. James Madison, Philadelphia, April 6, 1798, 10:24–26.
45. James Madison, Philadelphia, April 26, 1798, 10:33.
46. James Madison, Philadelphia, May 3, 1798, 10:33–34.
47. James Madison, Philadelphia, April 26, 1798, 10:31.
48. James Madison, Philadelphia, May 31, 1798, 10:41–42.
49. James Lewis, Jr., Philadelphia, May 9, 1798, 10:37.
50. James Madison, Philadelphia, April 26, 1798, 10:33, 31–32.
51. James Lewis, Jr., Philadelphia, May 9, 1798, 10:37.
52. Samuel Smith, Monticello, Aug. 22, 1798, 10:57.
53. James Madison, Philadelphia, June 7, 1798, F7:266–67.
54. John Taylor, Philadelphia, June 1, 1798, 10:44–47.
55. Stephens Thompson Mason, Monticello, Oct. 11, 1798, 10:61–62.

56. James Madison, Monticello, Nov. 17, 1798, 10:62–63.
57. Archibald Stuart, Philadelphia, Feb. 13, 1799, 10:103–04.
58. Edmund Pendleton, Philadelphia, Jan. 29, 1799, 10:87–88, 87.
59. Archibald Stuart, Philadelphia, Feb. 13, 1799, 10:103–04.
60. James Madison, Philadelphia, Feb. 5, 1799, 10:96.
61. Edmund Pendleton, Feb. 19, 1799, 10:114.
62. James Madison, Philadelphia, Feb. 19, 1799, 10:112.
63. General Thaddeus Kosciusko, Philadelphia, Feb. 21, 1799, 10:115–16.
64. James Madison, Philadelphia, March 4, 1800, 10:157–59.
65. Philip Norborne Nicholas, Philadelphia, April 7, 1800, F7:440.
66. Uriah McGregory, Monticello, Aug. 13, 1800, 10:171–72.
67. James Monroe, Eppington, May 26, 1800, F7:447–48.
68. Dr. Benjamin Rush, Monticello, Sept. 23, 1800, 10:174–75.
69. Elbridge Gerry, Philadelphia, Jan. 26, 1799, 10:76–79.
70. Spencer Roane, Poplar Forest, Sept. 6, 1819, 15:212.
71. Dr. Benjamin Rush, Monticello, Jan. 16, 1811, 13:5–6.
72. James Madison, Washington, Dec. 19, 1800, 10:184–85.
73. John Breckinridge, Washington, Dec. 18, 1800, 10:183.
74. Thomas Mann Randolph, Washington, Jan. 9, 1801, 18:230.
75. Tench Coxe, Washington, Feb. 11, 1801, 10:198.
76. James Monroe, Washington, Feb. 15, 1801, 10:201–02.
77. The Anas, 1:440.
78. The Anas, Dec. 31, 1803, 1:442.
79. The Anas, April 15, 1806, 1:451–52.
80. Thomas Mann Randolph, Washington, Feb. 19, 1801, F7:497.
81. Thomas Lomax, Washington, Feb. 25, 1801, 10:211.
82. Governor Thomas McKean, Washington, March 9, 1801, 10:221.
83. John Dickinson, Washington, March 6, 1801, 10:217–18.

CHAPTER XII

PHILOSOPHER-PRESIDENT

1. Inaugural address, March 4, 1801, 3:318–22.
2. Dr. Benjamin Rush, Washington, March 24, 1801, 10:241.
3. John Page, Washington, March 22, 1801, 10:234.
4. James Monroe, Washington, March 7, 1801, 10:220.
5. Dr. Benjamin Rush, Washington, March 24, 1801, 10:242–43.
6. Henry Knox, Washington, March 27, 1801, 10:247.
7. Dr. Benjamin Rush, Monticello, Jan. 16, 1811, 13:7.
8. Henry Knox, Washington, March 27, 1801, 10:247.
9. Dr. Joseph Priestley, Washington, March 21, 1801, 10:228–29.
10. Mrs. John Adams, Washington, July 22, 1804, 11:43–44.
11. Mrs. John Adams, Monticello, Sept. 11, 1804, 11:50–51.
12. Dr. Walter Jones, Washington, March 31, 1801, 10:255–56.

13. Nathaniel Macon, Washington, May 14, 1801, 10:261.
14. Thomas Mann Randolph, Washington, May 14, 1801, 18:242.
15. Circular to Heads of the Departments, Washington, Nov. 6, 1801, F8:100–01.
16. John Langdon, Washington, May 23, 1801, 19:126.
17. Joel Barlow, Washington, May 3, 1802, 10:321.
18. Levi Lincoln, Monticello, Aug. 26, 1801, 10:274–76.
19. Du Pont de Nemours, Washington, Jan. 18, 1802, F8:126–27n.
20. Elias Shipman and others, Washington, July 12, 1801, 10:271–72.
21. Du Pont de Nemours, Washington, Jan. 18, 1802, F8:127n.
22. Albert Gallatin, Washington, Dec. 12, 1803, 10:437–39.
23. John Dickinson, Washington, Dec. 19, 1801, 10:301–02.
24. Dr. Benjamin Rush, Washington, Dec. 20, 1801, 10:303–04.
25. Albert Gallatin, Washington, April 1, 1802, 10:306–08.
26. Genl. Thaddeus Kosciusko, Washington, April 2, 1802, 10:309–10.
27. Joel Barlow, Washington, May 3, 1802, 10:319–22.
28. Gideon Granger, Washington, May 3, 1801, 10:259–60.
29. Levi Lincoln, Monticello, Aug. 26, 1801, 10:275–76.
30. Moses Robinson, Washington, March 23, 1801, 10:237.
31. Dr. Benjamin Rush, Washington, April 21, 1803, 10:379–85.
32. C. F. C. de Volney, Washington, Feb. 8, 1805, 11:63–67.
33. Gov. William Henry Harrison, Washington, Feb. 27, 1803, 10:368.
34. C. F. C. de Volney, Washington, Feb. 8, 1805, 11:67–69.
35. Charles Willson Peale, Washington, Nov. 17, 1804, MS., LC.
36. James Bowdoin, Washington, July 10, 1806, 11:118–19.
37. Abraham Baldwin, Washington, April 14, 1802, 19:128–29.
38. Rules of Etiquette [Nov. ? 1803], F8:276–77.
39. James Monroe, Washington, Jan. 8, 1804, F8:290–92.
40. Martha Jefferson Randolph, Washington, Oct. 7, 1804, 18:246.
41. Maria Jefferson Eppes, Washington, Oct. 26, 1801, R2:675.
42. Analysis of Expenditures, March 4, 1801–March 4, 1802, R3:21–22.
43. Pierson, *Jefferson at Monticello*, pp. 45–49.
44. Message of Dec. 8, 1801, 3:327–30.
45. James Monroe, Washington, Nov. 24, 1801, 10:296.
46. Message of Dec. 15, 1802, 3:344–45.
47. Robert R. Livingston, Washington, Oct. 10, 1802, 10:336.
48. Levi Lincoln, Washington, Oct. 25, 1802, 10:339.
49. Dr. Thomas Cooper, Washington, Nov. 29, 1802, F8:178.
50. John Dickinson, Washington, Dec. 19, 1801, 10:301.
51. Dr. Joseph Priestley, Washington, June 19, 1802, 10:324–25.

CHAPTER XIII

LOUISIANA PURCHASE

1. Robert R. Livingston, Washington, April 18, 1802, 10:311–16.
2. Du Pont de Nemours, Washington, April 25, 1802, 10:317–18.

3. William Dunbar, Washington, March 3, 1803, 19:131–32.
4. James Monroe, Washington, Jan. 13, 1803, 10:343–44.
5. Dr. Hugh Williamson, Washington, April 30, 1803, 10:385–86.
6. Gov. W. C. C. Claiborne, Washington, May 24, 1803, 10:391.
7. Sir John Sinclair, Washington, June 30, 1803, 10:397.
8. Horatio Gates, Washington, July 11, 1803, 10:402.
9. John Dickinson, Monticello, Aug. 9, 1803, F8:261.
10. John Breckinridge, Monticello, Aug. 12, 1803, 10:408–09.
11. Second inaugural address, March 4, 1805, 3:377–78.
12. Horatio Gates, Washington, July 11, 1803, 10:402–03.
13. James Monroe, Washington, Jan. 8, 1804, F8:291–92.
14. John Breckinridge, Monticello, Aug. 12, 1803, 10:410–11.
15. Henry Dearborn, Monticello, Aug. 23, 1803, 19:134–35.
16. Wilson Cary Nicholas, Monticello, Sept. 7, 1803, 10:420.
17. Levi Lincoln, Monticello, Aug. 30, 1803, 10:417.
18. Dr. Joseph Priestley, Washington, Jan. 29, 1804, 10:447.
19. Robert R. Livingston, Washington, Nov. 4, 1803, 10:425.
20. Du Pont de Nemours, Washington, Nov. 1, 1803, 10:422–23.
21. Message of Oct. 17, 1803, F8:269.
22. Maria Jefferson Eppes, Washington, March 3, 1804, R3:98.
23. Martha Jefferson Randolph, Washington, March 8, 1804, MS., MHS.
24. John W. Eppes, Washington, March 15, 1804, R3:98–99.
25. John Page, Washington, June 25, 1804, 11:30–31.
26. Timothy Bloodworth, Washington, Jan. 29, 1804, 10:444–45.
27. William Short, Washington, Jan. 23, 1804, *Amer. Hist. Rev.*, 33:834.
28. Second inaugural address, March 4, 1805, 3:378–80.
29. Elbridge Gerry, Washington, March 3, 1804, 11:16.
30. Philip Mazzei, Washington, July 18, 1804, 11:40.
31. John Taylor, Washington, Jan. 6, 1805, 11:56–57.
32. C. F. C. de Volney, Washington, Feb. 8, 1805, 11:68.
33. Second inaugural address, March 4, 1805, 3:380–81.
34. George Clinton, Washington, Dec. 31, 1803, 10:440.

CHAPTER XIV

PEACE IS MY PASSION

1. Second inaugural address, March 4, 1805, 3:383.
2. Message, Dec. 3, 1805, 3:387–88.
3. James Madison, Monticello, Aug. 7, 1805, 11:84.
4. James Madison, Monticello, Aug. 25, 1805, 11:85–86.
5. Albert Gallatin [Washington], Oct. 23, 1805, F8:382.
6. The Anas, Nov. 12, 1805, F1:308.
7. Message, Dec. 3, 1805, 3:386–87.
8. Message, Jan. 17, 1806, 3:407–08.

9. James Monroe, Washington, May 4, 1806, 11:110–11.
10. James Bowdoin, Washington, July 10, 1806, 11:120–21.
11. ——, Washington, March 25, 1807, 11:172–73.
12. James Bowdoin, Washington, April 2, 1807, 11:184–85.
13. Message, Jan. 22, 1807, 3:428–35.
14. Charles Clay, Washington, Jan. 11, 1807, 11:133.
15. James Bowdoin, Washington, April 2, 1807, 11:186.
16. Marquis de Lafayette, Washington, May 26, 1807, F9:65–66.
17. James Bowdoin, Washington, April 2, 1807, 11:186.
18. William B. Giles, Monticello, April 20, 1807, 11:187–91.
19. Genl. James Wilkinson, Monticello, Sept. 20, 1807, 11:375.
20. William Thomson, Monticello, Sept. 26, 1807, F9: 143–44.
21. Isaac Weaver, Jr., Washington, June 7, 1807, 11:220–21.
22. Marquis de Lafayette, Washington, May 26, 1807, F9:66.
23. James Madison, Monticello, May 5, 1807, 11:202–03.
24. Message, Dec. 3, 1805, 3:389–90.
25. Barnabas Bidwell, Washington, July 5, 1806, 11:116.
26. Chandler Price, Washington, Feb. 28, 1807, 11:160.
27. Comte Diodati, Washington, March 29, 1807, 11:181–82.
28. Message, Oct. 27, 1807, 3:452.
29. Message, Dec. 2, 1806, 3:422–23.
30. Message, Dec. 2, 1806, 3:420–21.
31. Dr. Caspar Wistar, Washington, Dec. 19, 1807, 11:403–04.
32. Dr. Caspar Wistar, Washington, March 20, 1808, 12:15–16.
33. M. Silvestre, Washington, May 29, 1807, 11:212.
34. A. Thouin, Washington, April 29, 1808, FB, p. 163.
35. Memoranda to Edmund Bacon, 1806–07, Pierson, *Jefferson at Monticello*, pp. 51, 59, 63–64, 39.
36. Anne Cary Randolph, Washington, June 7, 1807, MS., MHS.
37. Martha Jefferson Randolph, Washington, Oct. 18, 1808, MS., MHS.
38. Martha Jefferson Randolph, Washington, Oct. 12, 1807, MS., MHS.
39. Cornelia Jefferson Randolph, Washington, April 3, 1808, R3:633.
40. Cornelia Jefferson Randolph, Washington, Dec. 26, 1808, R3:633.
41. Dr. Benjamin Rush, Washington, Jan. 3, 1808, 11:412–13.
42. Thomas Jefferson Randolph, Washington, Nov. 24, 1808, 12:198–201.
43. Marquis de Lafayette, Washington, May 26, 1807, F9:67.
44. Isaac Weaver, Jr., Washington, June 7, 1807, 11:219–20.
45. Comte Diodati, Washington, March 29, 1807, 11:182.
46. William Short [Washington], May 19, 1807, F9:50–51.
47. Charles Clay, Washington, Jan. 11, 1807, 11:132.
48. Comte Diodati, Washington, March 29, 1807, 11:182.
49. Martha Jefferson Randolph, Washington, Jan. 5, 1808, MS., MHS.
50. Martha Jefferson Randolph, Washington, Feb. 6, 1808, MS., MHS.
51. Martha Jefferson Randolph, Washington, Feb. 27, 1809, MS., MHS.
52. Message, Oct. 27, 1807, 3:445–46.

53. Du Pont de Nemours, Washington, July 14, 1807, 11:274–75.
54. John Page, Washington, July 17, 1807, 11:287.
55. William Duane, Washington, July 20, 1807, 11:291.
56. Col. John Taylor, Washington, Aug. 1, 1807, 11:304–05.
57. Thomas Paine, Monticello, Sept. 6, 1807, 11:362–63.
58. Thomas Leiper, Monticello, Aug. 21, 1807, F9:130.
59. James Maury, Washington, Nov. 21, 1807, 11:397.
60. Thomas Mann Randolph, Washington, Nov. 30, 1807, **MS., MHS.**
61. Genl. John Mason [Dec.], 1807, 11:402.
62. Message, March 17, 1808, F9:185.
63. John Taylor, Washington, Jan. 6, 1808, 11:414.
64. Levi Lincoln, Washington, March 23, 1808, 12:21.
65. James Bowdoin, Monticello, May 29, 1808, 12:69.
66. Caesar A. Rodney, Washington, April 24, 1808, 12:36.
67. William Lyman, Washington, April 30, 1808, 12:42.
68. Dr. Thomas Leib, Washington, June 23, 1808, 12:77.
69. Albert Gallatin, Washington, May 6, 1808, 12:52–53.
70. Henry Dearborn, Monticello, Aug. 9, 1808, 12:119.
71. Jacob Crowninshield, Monticello, Aug. 9, 1808, 12:121.
72. Albert Gallatin, Monticello, Aug. 11, 1808, 12:122.
73. Dr. William Eustis, Washington, Jan. 14, 1809, 12:228–29.
74. Gov. John Langdon, Monticello, Aug. 2, 1808, 16:309–10.
75. Baron Alexander von Humboldt, Washington, March 6, 1809, 12:264.
76. Dr. Elijah Griffith, Monticello, May 28, 1809, 12:285–86.
77. Levi Lincoln, Washington, Nov. 13, 1808, 12:195.
78. James Monroe, Washington, Jan. 28, 1809, F9:242–44.
79. Thomas Mann Randolph, Washington, Feb. 7, 1809, 12:248.
80. William Short, Washington, March 8, 1809, 12:265.
81. Du Pont de Nemours, Washington, March 2, 1809, 12:259–60.
82. General Assembly of Virginia, Washington, Feb. 16, 1809, 16:334.
83. Inhabitants of Albemarle County, Monticello, April 3, 1809, 12:269–**70.**

CHAPTER XV

SAGE OF MONTICELLO

1. Thaddeus Kosciusko, Monticello, Feb. 26, 1810, 12:369.
2. Charles W. Peale, Poplar Forest, Aug. 20, 1811, 13:79.
3. John W. Eppes, Monticello, Dec. 8, 1809, R3:319.
4. Cornelia Jefferson Randolph, Monticello, June 3, 1811, R3:634.
5. Thomas Jefferson Randolph, Monticello, May 6, 1809, MS., MHS.
6. Jean Baptiste Say, Monticello, March 2, 1815, 14:260–62.
7. William A. Burwell, Monticello, Feb. 25, 1810, FB, pp. 193–94.
8. Charles W. Peale, Monticello, April 17, 1813, 18:278.
9. Robert Fulton, Monticello, April 16, 1810, 19:173.

10. Charles W. Peale, Monticello, June 13, 1815, 18:288.
11. Dr. Thomas Cooper, Monticello, July 10, 1812, 13:176–77.
12. Robert Fulton, Monticello, March 17, 1810, 12:380–81.
13. Robert Fulton, Monticello, March 8, 1813, 19:188.
14. Robert Fulton, Monticello, July 21, 1813, 19:192–93.
15. James Madison, Monticello, May 13, 1810, 12:389–91.
16. Thaddeus Kosciusko, Monticello, June 28, 1812, 13:170–71.
17. John Melish, Monticello, Jan. 13, 1813, 13:207–08.
18. Thaddeus Kosciusko, Monticello, Feb. 26, 1810, 12:369–70.
19. Gov. John Tyler, Monticello, May 26, 1810, 12:393–94.
20. John Wyche, Monticello, May 19, 1809, 12:282–83.
21. Hugh L. White and others, Monticello, May 6, 1810, 12:387–88.
22. Henri Gregoire, Washington, Feb. 25, 1809, 12:255.
23. Edward Coles, Monticello, Aug. 25, 1814, F9:477–78.
24. James Jay, Monticello, April 7, 1809, 12:270–71.
25. Dr. Benjamin Rush, Poplar Forest, Aug. 17, 1811, 13:74–75.
26. Rev. James Madison, Monticello, Dec. 29, 1811, 19:183–84.
27. Dr. Benjamin Rush, Poplar Forest, Aug. 17, 1811, 13:76–77.
28. Dr. Benjamin Rush, Monticello, Jan. 16, 1811, 13:2–9.
29. Dr. Benjamin Rush, Poplar Forest, Dec. 5, 1811, 13:115–16.
30. John Adams, Monticello, Jan. 21, 1812, 13:123–25.
31. Mrs. John Adams, Monticello, Aug. 22, 1813, 19:193–94.
32. John Adams, Monticello, Oct. 28, 1813, 13: 396–401.
33. Gov. William Plumer, Monticello, July 21, 1816, 15:46–47.
34. John W. Eppes, Monticello, June 24, 1813, 13:270–71.
35. Thomas Earle, Monticello, Sept. 24, 1823, 15:470–71.
36. John Adams, Monticello, April 11, 1823, 15:426–27.
37. James Fishback, Monticello, Sept. 27, 1809, 12:315.
38. Charles Thomson, Monticello, Jan. 29, 1817, F10:76.
39. Thomas Law, Poplar Forest, June 13, 1814, 14:139–43.
40. John Adams, Monticello, July 5, 1814, 14:147–51.
41. John Waldo, Monticello, Aug. 16, 1813, 13:339–40.
42. Edward Everett, Monticello, Feb. 24, 1823, 15:415.
43. John Waldo, Monticello, Aug. 16, 1813, 13:340–46.
44. Thaddeus Kosciusko, Monticello, April 13, 1811, 13:43.
45. Alexander von Humboldt, Monticello, Dec. 6, 1813, 14:22–23.
46. Clement Caine, Monticello, Sept. 16, 1811, 13:90.
47. Caesar A. Rodney, Monticello, Feb. 10, 1810, 12:357.
48. Dr. Walter Jones, Monticello, March 5, 1810, 12:372.
49. Thaddeus Kosciusko, Monticello, April 13, 1811, 13:41–42.'
50. William Duane, Monticello, July 25, 1811, 13:66–67.
51. William Duane, Monticello, March 28, 1811, 13:28–29.
52. Charles Pinckney, Monticello, Feb. 2, 1812, 18:271–72.
53. James Maury, Monticello, April 25, 1812, 13:145–48.
54. Madame de Staël-Holstein, ——, May 24, 1813, 13:241, 238–39.

55. William Duane, Monticello, April 20, 1812, MS., LC.

56. Thaddeus Kosciusko, Monticello, June 28, 1812, 13:172.

57. Robert Wright, Monticello, Aug. 8, 1812, 13: 184–85.

58. Marquis de Lafayette, Monticello, Feb. 14, 1815, 14:248–49.

59. Thaddeus Kosciusko, Monticello, Nov. 30, 1813, 19:202.

60. William Duane, Monticello, April 4, 1813, 13:230–31.

61. Genl. Theodorus Bailey, Monticello, Feb. 6, 1813, 13:216–17.

62. Philip Mazzei, Monticello, Dec. 29, 1813, F9:441–42.

63. Madame de Tessé, ——, Dec. 8, 1813, F9:440.

64. Philip Mazzei, Monticello, Dec. 29, 1813, F9:442.

65. Dr. Samuel Brown, Monticello, July 14, 1813, 13:312.

66. John Adams, Monticello, July 5, 1814, 14:145–46.

67. William H. Crawford, Monticello, Feb. 11, 1815, 14:240.

68. James Madison, Monticello, Oct. 15, 1814, 14:202.

69. William H. Crawford, Monticello, Feb. 11, 1815, 14:240–41.

70. William Short, Monticello, Nov. 28, 1814, 14:213–18.

71. Samuel H. Smith, Monticello, Sept. 21, 1814, 14:190–93.

72. Marquis de Lafayette, Monticello, Feb. 14, 1815, 14:248–55.

73. Henry Dearborn, Monticello, March 17, 1815, 14:287–89.

74. Francis C. Gray, Monticello, March 4, 1815, 14:270–71.

75. Caesar A. Rodney, Monticello, March 16, 1815, 14:285–86.

76. John Adams, Poplar Forest, Nov. 25, 1816, 15:85–86.

77. James Maury, Monticello, June 15, 1815, 14:315.

CHAPTER XVI

AN AMERICAN HERITAGE

1. Marquis de Lafayette, Monticello, May 14, 1817, 15:115–16.

2. Samuel Adams Wells, Monticello, June 23, 1819, F10:133n.

3. Marquis de Lafayette, Monticello, May 14, 1817, 15:115–16.

4. Alexander von Humboldt, Monticello, June 13, 1817, 15:128.

5. John Adams, Monticello, April 8, 1816, 14:467.

6. John Adams, Monticello, Aug. 1, 1816, 15:56–58.

7. Mrs. John Adams, Monticello, Jan. 11, 1817, 15:95–97.

8. James Monroe, Monticello, April 8, 1817, 19:244–45.

9. Captain A. Partridge, Monticello, Jan. 2, 1816, 19:377–79.

10. George Fleming, Monticello, Dec. 29, 1815, 14:366–69.

11. Martha Jefferson Randolph, Poplar Forest, Aug. 31, 1815, MS., MHS.

12. Martha Jefferson Randolph, Poplar Forest, Aug. 31, 1817, MS., MHS.

13. John Adams, Monticello, Jan. 11, 1817, 15:97–100.

14. Mrs. Samuel H. Smith, Monticello, Aug. 6, 1816, 15:60–61.

14a. Charles Thomson, Monticello, Jan. 9, 1816, F10:5.

15. John Adams, Monticello, Oct. 13, 1813, 13:390.

16. Charles Thomson, Monticello, Jan. 9, 1816, F10:5–6.

17. F. A. Van Der Kemp, Poplar Forest, April 25, 1816, 15:2–3.
18. Dr. Benjamin Waterhouse, Monticello, June 26, 1822, 15:383–85.
19. Dr. Benjamin Waterhouse, Monticello, Jan. 8, 1825, F10:336.
20. Dr. Thomas Cooper, Monticello, Nov. 2, 1822, 15:404.
21. MS. Account Book, March 8, 1824, NYHS.
22. Samuel Kercheval, Monticello, July 12, 1816, 15:32–43.
23. George Ticknor, Poplar Forest, Nov. 25, 1817, F10:95–96.
24. Dr. William Thornton, May 9, 1817, facsimile, 17:396.
25. John Adams, Monticello, May 5, 1817, 15:110.
26. Joseph C. Cabell, Monticello, Oct. 24, 1817, 19:251–52, 250.
27. Joseph C. Cabell, Monticello, Feb. 26, 1818, N. F. Cabell, ed., *Early Hist. Univ. of Va.*, p. 128.
28. Joseph C. Cabell, Poplar Forest, Dec. 18, 1817, *ibid.*, p. 88.
29. Joseph C. Cabell, Monticello, Jan. 14, 1818, F10:102.
30. J. Correa de Serra, Poplar Forest, Nov. 25, 1817, 15:155–57.
31. Nathaniel Bowditch, Monticello, Oct. 26, 1818, 19:264–65.
32. John Adams, Monticello, Aug. 15, 1820, 15:269.
33. Specifications for Pavilion X, MS., UV.
34. William Short, Monticello, April 13, 1820, 15:245.
35. A. C. V. C. Destutt de Tracy, Monticello, Dec. 26, 1820, F10:174.
36. William Short, Monticello, April 13, 1820, 15:245–47.
37. Dr. Thomas Cooper, Monticello, Aug. 14, 1820, 15:269.
38. Joseph C. Cabell, Monticello, Jan. 22, 1820, F10:154–55.
39. Joseph C. Cabell, Poplar Forest, Nov. 28, 1820, 15:289–93.
40. John Adams, Monticello, Nov. 7, 1819, 15:224–25.
41. William C. Rives, Monticello, Nov. 28, 1819, 15:229.
42. Thomas Leiper, ——, May 31, 1823, F10:254.
43. William Short, Monticello, Oct. 31, 1819, 15:219–22.
44. Dr. Vine Utley, Monticello, March 21, 1819, 15:187–88.
45. Horatio G. Spafford, Monticello, May 11, 1819, 15:189.
46. Judge William Johnson, Monticello, March 4, 1823, 15:420–21.
47. Francis A. Van Der Kemp, Monticello, Jan. 11, 1825, F10:337.
48. Robert Walsh, Monticello, April 5, 1823, MS, UV.
49. John Adams, Monticello, June 27, 1822, 15:386–87.
50. Mrs. Maria Cosway, Monticello, Dec. 27, 1820, 18:308–10.
51. Henry Dearborn, Monticello, July 5, 1819, 19:271.
52. Jared Mansfield, Monticello, Feb. 13, 1821, 15:313–14.
53. James Madison, Monticello, Oct. 18, 1825, 19:287.
54. John Holmes, Monticello, April 22, 1820, 15:249–50.
55. Charles Pinckney, Monticello, Sept. 30, 1820, 15:280.
56. David Baillie Warden, Monticello, Dec. 26, 1820, F10:173.
57. Marquis de Lafayette, Monticello, Dec. 26, 1820, 15:300–01.
58. Henry Dearborn, Monticello, Aug. 17, 1821, 15:329–30.
59. Spencer Roane, Monticello, June 27, 1821, 15:328–29.
60. Sanuel H. Smith, Monticello, April 12, 1821, F10:191.
61. Autobiography, 1:152.

62. Thomas Leiper, Monticello, April 3, 1824, F10:298–99.

62a. John Adams, Monticello, Sept. 12, 1821, 15:333–34.

63. William Short, Monticello, Aug. 4, 1820, 15:262–63.

64. James Monroe, Monticello, Oct. 24, 1823, 15:477–80.

65. [William Short], Monticello, Nov. 24, 1821, 18:315.

66. John Adams, Monticello, Oct. 12, 1823, 15:474.

67. Spencer Roane, Monticello, March 9, 1821, 15:326.

68. Dr. Thomas Cooper, Monticello, Nov. 2, 1822, 15:406.

69. Joseph C. Cabell, Monticello, Jan. 31, 1821, 15:311–12.

70. Genl. James Breckinridge, Monticello, April 9, 1822, 15:363–65.

71. Joseph C. Cabell, Monticello, Dec. 28, 1822, Cabell, ed., *Early Hist. Univ. Va.*, p. 260.

72. [William Short], Monticello, Nov. 24, 1821, 18:315.

73. Richard Rush, Monticello, April 26, 1824, 16:31–32.

74. John Adams, Monticello, Jan. 8, 1825, 16:90.

75. Edward Everett, Monticello, July 21, 1825, 19:284.

76. Joseph Coolidge, Jr., Monticello, April 12, 1825, 18:337–38.

77. Edward Livingston, Monticello, March 25, 1825, 16:115.

78. John Cartwright, Monticello, June 5, 1824, 16:51.

79. Hon. J. E. Denison, M.P., Monticello, Nov. 9, 1825, 16:130.

80. Miss Frances Wright, Monticello, Aug. 7, 1825, 16:119–20.

81. John Cartwright, Monticello, June 5, 1824, 16:47–48.

82. Henry Lee, Monticello, Aug. 10, 1824, 16:73–74.

83. Spencer Roane, Monticello, March 9, 1821, 15:325–26.

84. William B. Giles, Monticello, Dec. 26, 1825, 16:146–48.

85. Ellen W. Coolidge, Monticello, Aug. 27, 1825, 18:341.

86. William Ludlow, Monticello, Sept. 6, 1824, 16:74–75.

87. Augustus B. Woodward, Monticello, April 3, 1825, 16:117.

88. Ellen W. Coolidge, Monticello, Aug. 27, 1825, 18:341–42.

89. Joseph Coolidge, Jr., Monticello, Oct. 13 [1825], 18:345 46.

90. James Madison, Monticello, Jan. 2, 1826, F10:360.

91. MS specifications, UV.

92. Dr. John P. Emmet, Monticello, April 7, 1826, 16:165–67.

93. William B. Giles, Monticello, Dec. 26, 1825, 16:150–51.

94. William F. Gordon, Monticello, Jan. 1, 1826, F10:358–59.

95. James Madison, Monticello, Feb. 17, 1826, F10:376–78.

96. Thomas Jefferson Randolph, Monticello, Feb. 8, 1826, F10:374–75.

97. James Monroe, Monticello, Feb. 22, 1826, F10:379.

98. Thomas Ritchie, Monticello, March 13, 1826, F10:382n.

99. Ellen W. Coolidge, Monticello, March 19, 1826, 18:352–53.

100. Ellen W. Coolidge, Monticello, June 5, 1826, F10:387–90.

101. John Adams, Monticello, March 25, 1826, 16:159–60.

102. Roger C. Weightman, Monticello, June 24, 1826, 16:181–82.

103. Deathbed adieu to Martha Jefferson Randolph, Randolph, *Dom. Life*, p. 429.

104. Epitaph, facsimile, 1:262.

INDEX

Abbaye de Panthemont, convent attended by Jefferson's daughters, 118, 143, 179
'Academical village,' 292; and see University of Virginia
Adams, John (2d President of the U.S.), bill of attainder against him in British Parliament, 53; on committee to prepare Declaration of Independence, 59, 60, 62; critical observations on Declaration as drafted by Jefferson, 61, 70; urged immediate adoption of resolution of independence, 62; supported the Declaration in Congress, 71; associated with Jefferson and Franklin in negotiating treaties, 110, 111, 114; appointed minister to London, 114-16; his view of the Constitution, 162, 163; elected President, 192; defeated for re-election, 194; speech to Congress deemed a national affront by France, 204; nominates a minister to the French Republic, 209; declaration of loyalty to Jefferson, 213; his midnight appointments condemned, 224, 225, 294; reconciled with Jefferson through Dr. Rush, 286, 294, 295; letters from Jefferson, 295, 297, 301, 319, 321; letters from Jefferson on the downfall of Bonaparte, 308; — on the persecution of letters, 330; — on his ability to ride horseback without fatigue, 336; 199, 200, 214, 216
Adams, Mrs. Abigail, wife of the preceding, letter to, 120; her attachment to Jefferson's daughter Maria, 294; 118, 296
Aenead mentioned, 272
Aesop, fables of, cited, 39; read with delight by the Indians, 293
Agricultural Society of the Seine (France), sends Jefferson a Guillaume plough, 289
Agriculture, Jefferson's interest in, 22-24, 34, 194, 283, 285, 287-89; his tobacco crops, 26; profits from, in 1801-02, 236; other crops and their rotation, 195; live stock, 23, 237, 270; Merino sheep, 290, 291; gardens and orchards, 27, 28, 270, 271; importation of European plants, 23, 125, 178, 271; mould-board of least resistance, 195, 196, 270, 289; contour ploughing, 289; on French farmers, 143, 144; domestic animals of Europe and America, 38; for encouragement of agriculture, with commerce its handmaid,

223; a professor of, at University of Virginia, 337; general prostration of farming, and effect on Jefferson, 341. See Gardening
Albemarle County, 1, 3, 27, 284, 288
Alexander I of Russia cited, 334
Alien and Sedition Acts, passed by the Federalists, 193; considered by Jefferson an experiment on the American mind, 208; their victims released from imprisonment or indictment by Jefferson, 219, 220, 225, 226; 239
Alliances: informal talk of an Anglo-American alliance, in 1790, 168; no 'entangling alliances,' 223; provisional alliance with Great Britain contemplated in 1802, 241, 243; in 1805, 257, 261
Ambler, Jacquelin, married to Rebecca Burwell, 14
America, genius of, 24, 25, 40; character of people, 118; science in, 124; progress and prosperity of, 135, 238, 258; beyond example in the history of man, 295, 296; language of, 302; has a hemisphere to itself, 303; despite injuries of belligerents, 303, 315; an asylum for the oppressed, 220, 225, 230; an experiment in freedom and self-government, 238; last hope of human liberty, 304; march of civilization in, during Jefferson's lifetime, 339, 340
American Philosophical Society, Jefferson president of, 193; account for, of his plough, 195; writes account of the *Megalonyx* for, 202; bones of animals collected by Lewis and Clark expedition given to, 270
American Revolution, causes of, 44, 46, 47 73, 74; preliminaries in Virginia, 47, 53; Lexington and Concord, 53, 54; Bunker Hill, 56, 57; reluctance to separate, 57, 58; debate over independence, 61-63; over the Declaration, 64; the Declaration as written and as approved, 64-69; the Revolution as a social movement, 75; social revolution in Virginia, 75 *ff*; British invasion of, 96-105; Yorktown, 94, 106; influence upon French Revolution, 146, 149; its permanence, in some degree, dependent on success of French Revolution, 166, 175, 184; influence of,

to see navies of Brazil and U.S. in coalition, 334. *See also* Monroe Doctrine

South Sea Bubble in England cited, 165

Spain, and navigation of Mississippi, 153, 166, 167; retrocedes to France the port of New Orleans and the province of Louisiana, 241; reopens Mississippi to commerce, 247; asked to sell the Floridas, 261, 262

Spanish America, *see* South America

Spectacles, used by Jefferson only on small print, 329

Sports, recreation essential, 18; walking best form of exercise, 18; a bold and skillful horseman, 23; his Virginia thoroughbreds, 23; horse-racing, 2, 7, 19; fishing, 176; fox-hunting, 2, 7; 'Game of the Goose,' for Jefferson's grandchildren, 202; foot races, as old man, with grandchildren, 285; twilight walks at Poplar Forest, 321

Spotswood, Mrs. Dorothea Dandridge, 8

Stamp Act, Resolutions of 1765 against the, 9; its repeal, 16; Federalist Stamp Act criticized by Jefferson, 208; 44

States (American), happy compromise of interests of, in Constitution, 145; assumption of debts of, 158, 160; rights of reserved by Constitution, 163, 164; threatened by Hamilton's 'corrupt squadron,' 173; usurped by Alien and Sedition Acts, 208; and Missouri question, 332; powers of, and those of federal government, 333; disputes of, with federal government, should be peaceably settled, 333; encroachments on, of federal government, 339; separation of, justified only when sole alternative is submission to a federal government of unlimited powers, 139

Statute of Virginia for Religious Freedom, 76, 86, 316, 318, 322, 345

Steam, its use in driving mechanisms suggested by Jefferson, 321

Steam engines adaptable for houses to pump water, suggested by Jefferson, 202, 203

Sterne, Laurence, British author, 29

Steuben, Major Gen. Frederick William Augustus Henry Ferdinand, Baron von, in the Revolution, 100

Stevens, Gen. Edward, 96

'Strongest government on earth,' Jefferson's opinion of American, 222

Stuart, Gilbert, paints Jefferson's portrait, 331

Style in writing, Jefferson's debt to reading and memory, 301

Submarine boat, mentioned by Jefferson in letter to Robert Fulton, 290

Suffrage, its extension advocated, 89, 90

Sully, Thomas, American portrait painter, 331

Summary View of the Rights of British America, A, by Jefferson, 45, 51, 60

Supreme Court of U.S., *see* Judiciary

Syntax, Jefferson no friend of *Purism,* but zealous for *Neology,* 302

Tacitus mentioned, 296, 302

Taliaferro, Jenny, 13

Talleyrand-Perigord, Charles Maurice de, in the X, Y, Z affair, 193, 205; assures respectful treatment of an American representative, 209

Tantalus cited, 310

Tarleton, Col. Banastre, raid on Charlottesville, 94, 103; occupies Jefferson's house without injuring it, 104

Taxes, odious excise, 172; excise tax on whiskey, 192, 197; Federalist war taxes, 193, 208; suppression of all internal taxes, 229, 230, 239, 252; economy substituted for, 239; none needed for Louisiana Purchase, 253; would divert revenue from imposts to public works, 269; taxes levied solely on imports, and thus on the rich alone, 304

Temple of Nerva Trajan, the model for a pavilion of the University of Virginia, 327

Terrapiniad, satire on Jefferson, mentioned, 272

Tessé, Comtesse de, letter from Jefferson, 142

Texas, claimed as part of Louisiana Purchase, 248, 257, 262

Theatre of Marcellus, the model for a pavilion of the University of Virginia, 327

Theatre, Jefferson's love of, 2, 3; in Williamsburg, 3, 19; in Petersburg, 12; in Paris, 112, 122

Themistocles and the battle of Salamis cited, 150

Third term, of President, 255, 274

Thompson, John, the hatter, his story told by Franklin to Jefferson, 60, 71

Thompson, student at William and Mary, 15

Thornton, Dr. William, his plan for the capitol at Washington, 177

'Thoughts on English Prosody,' essay by Jefferson on poetry, opposing Dr. Johnson, 123

Thouin, André, of the National Garden at Paris, sends seeds to Jefferson, 271, 341

Thucydides mentioned, 296

Ticonderoga, captured by the Americans, 59

Tidewater plantations, 2

Torture as penalty for non-uniformity, 82